INVENTING THE ADDICT

INVENTING THE ADDICT

Drugs, Race, and Sexuality in Nineteenth-Century British and American Literature

Susan Zieger

University of Massachusetts Press
AMHERST

Printed in the United States of America

LC 2008031442
ISBN 978-1-55849-680-4 (paper); 679-8 (library cloth)

Designed by Dennis Anderson
Set in Janson Text
Printed and bound by The Maple-Vail Book Manufacturing Group

Library of Congress Cataloging-in-Publication Data

Zieger, Susan Marjorie.
Inventing the addict : drugs, race, and sexuality in nineteenth-century British and American literature / Susan Zieger.
p. cm.
Includes bibliographical references and index.
ISBN 978-1-55849-680-4 (pbk. : alk. paper) —
ISBN 978-1-55849-679-8 (library cloth : alk. paper)
1. American literature—19th century—History and criticism.
2. English literature—19th century—History and criticism.
3. Addicts in literature. 4. Drug abuse in literature.
5. Alcoholism in literature. 6. Addicts—History. 7. Drug abuse—History
I. Title.
PS217.A32Z54 2008
820.9'3561—dc22
2008031442

British Library Cataloguing in Publication data are available.

In memory of Nancy Zieger,
and to Herman Zieger
and Nathan Boyd

CONTENTS

ACKNOWLEDGMENTS

MANY PEOPLE and institutions have enabled me—in the best sense of the word—to complete this book, and I am grateful to them all. They brought out the best in the project; the flaws are all my own.

Generous grants and fellowships from the ACLS Fellowship Program and the Huntington Library provided the time and money to conduct the research for this book. Additionally, two Regents' Faculty Development Awards from the University of California, Riverside, and a number of Academic Senate Research Awards funded trips for research and conference presentations. At UC Berkeley, a Townsend Center for the Humanities Fellowship, Mellon Fellowship, Vice Chancellor Research Fund Award, Humanities Research Grant, and Phi Beta Kappa Fellowship helped launch this project in its formative stages.

Staff at several research institutions were most helpful: the British Library, the Wellcome Library for the History and Understanding of Medicine, the Royal Society of Medicine, UCLA's Michael Sadleir Collection, and UC Riverside's Eaton Collection. Two librarians whose tireless efforts to locate a copy of Maria Weed's 1895 novel, *A Voice in the Wilderness*, deserve special thanks: Janet Moores and Maria Mendoza at UC Riverside's Interlibrary Loan. I am also indebted to Steve Gertz, formerly of William Dailey Rare Books in Los Angeles, for introducing me to E. P. Roe's *Without a Home*.

Catherine Gallagher, Tom Laqueur, and Sharon Marcus at UC Berkeley have remained supportive mentors to whom I am grateful. Ian Duncan continues to give generous intellectual and professional advice. Priya Joshi, Celeste Langan, and David Lloyd influenced the project at its origins. Tina Choi, Genevieve Guenther, Rachel Teukolsky, Karen Tongson, and others offered an intellectually rich environment for developing this project. The Nineteenth Century and Beyond British Cultural Studies

Working Group, then and now, has been a productive environment for testing my ideas, as was the Social History of Medicine Working Group (the "Med Heads") under the leadership of Lara Friedenfelds, a vibrant interlocutor and friend.

This project benefited greatly from the year I spent earning an MSc. under the direction of the late Roy Porter at the London Centre for the History of Science, Medicine, and Technology. From this period, I owe thanks to Hasok Chang, John Heard, and Louise Jarvis, as well as to the Science in the Nineteenth-Century Periodical Project Research Team, particularly Gowan Dawson.

At UC Riverside, I am fortunate to enjoy an environment of intellectual support and friendship that every beginning scholar should have. Joe Childers has been a tireless mentor and friend. Parts of the manuscript have benefitted from the advice of my colleagues, including Andrea Denny-Brown, Jennifer Doyle, Tiffany López, Vorris Nunley, Michelle Raheja, and Jim Tobias. Steve and Rise Axelrod, Emory Elliott, George Haggerty, Katherine Kinney, Toby Miller, Parama Roy, and Traise Yamamoto also have provided helpful support and mentorship. My quarter at the Center for Ideas and Society, thinking through addiction with Bill Bracken, Chrissy Crockett, Gary Watson, and Deborah Willis, helped me shape the introduction. A Mellon workshop on histories and theories of slavery brought my work into dialogue with that of Jayna Brown, John Kim, and others.

Colleagues from the Dickens Universe at UC Santa Cruz have formed a hospitable intellectual home: John Jordan, James Buzard, Jonathan Grossman, Priti Joshi, Helena Michie, Catherine Robson, Rebecca Stern, Robyn Warhol, and many others. Colleagues in the profession have quite selflessly given their time mentoring me, reading the project, and otherwise engaging me intellectually and professionally: Virginia Berridge, Regenia Gagnier, Denise Gigante, Pamela Gilbert, Barry Milligan, and Otto Santa Ana. Anonymous readers and referees have also helped improve the project immeasurably.

I would like to thank the University of Massachusetts Press, particularly my acquiring editor, Clark Dougan, for taking on the project and ushering it through the publication process with what seems like amazing speed. Carol Betsch, Martin Schneider, and Mary Bellino have produced the book with efficiency, care in detail, and responsiveness to all the questions and concerns of a first-time author.

For those looking for a self-confession of addiction, here it is: copious quantities of coffee fueled the writing and revising of this book over the years. Many people labored making it, but I would particularly like to thank the staff of The Coffee Table in Eagle Rock and Peet's, Zephyr, and Zeli in Pasadena. Friends and family continue to sustain and cheer me with their enthusiasm, especially Sarah Bruck, Kristina Chambers, Emily Davis, Genevieve Guenther, Lois Jones, Sabrina Leon, Myck Schwetz, Chantal Sulkow, Rochelle Thielen, Aman Thind, Carletta Woods, Jennifer Wulff, and Barbara Zieger.

My mother, Nancy Zieger, passed away while this book was being copyedited. Her love and self-sacrifice throughout my life prepared me to undertake a long, challenging project, and I wish she could have lived to see its fruition. My father, Herman Zieger, first showed me the pleasure of intellectual inquiry, and remains my steadfast supporter. My partner, Nathan Boyd, offered helpful dialogue about this project; he never tires of sharing all of my challenges. I learn from his love every day.

A portion of chapter 2 was published as "Pioneering Inner Space: Drug Autobiography and Manifest Destiny," *PMLA* 122:5 (October 2007): 1531–47. Reprinted by permission of the copyright owner, The Modern Language Association of America.

A portion of chapter 3 was published as "Impostors of Freedom: Southern White Manhood and Hypodermic Morphine in E. P. Roe's *Without a Home*," *American Literature* 80 (September 2008): 527–54. Copyright © 2008 by Duke University Press; reproduced with permission.

A portion of chapter 5 was published as " 'How far am I responsible?': Women and Morphinomania in Late Nineteenth-Century Britain," *Victorian Studies* 48:1 (Autumn 2005): 59–81. Copyright © 2005 by the Trustees of Indiana University; reproduced with permission.

INVENTING THE ADDICT

INTRODUCTION

Addiction and History

Addiction . . . explains both too much and too little;
but we seemingly cannot do without it.

Marc Redfield and Janet Farrell Brodie, *High Anxieties: Cultural Studies in Addiction*

Two CURIOUSLY related stories tell of the power and the weakness of the will in modern Anglo-American culture. The first comes from the biography of George Harley (1829–1896), a Scottish researcher in physiology who orbited such luminaries in the development of modern medical science as François Magendie, Claude Bernard, Rudolf Virchow, and Justus von Liebig. During his illustrious career, Harley discovers several functions and diseases of the liver, finds an antidote for strychnine, and builds a better microscope. One day, overworked, sleepless, and suffering from agonizing eyestrain induced by his relentless research, Harley begins taking morphia. Two months pass, during which Harley becomes addicted, joining the ranks of late Victorian medical men who developed dependencies on the drug. A concerned fellow physician suggests gradually tapering off, but Harley only replies, "Man, if I made up my mind to cut off my own arm, I would do it; and with the morphia bottle within my reach, I shall lie here until Nature gives me sleep, or until I change my mind. My resolve, however, I will *not* break." The story concludes by reaffirming Victorian faith in the possibility of self-mastery: "From the first hour I left off morphia I never again returned to it, so my sceptical medical friend was forced to become a reluctant convert to 'the power of resolve.' "[1] Harley's steadfastness performs the triumph of the will described by John Reed: "The modern Christian Englishman stood at the pinnacle of progress because he represented the highest development of will."[2] The story performs one popular nineteenth-century response to addiction, echoes of which can still be heard in the twenty-first century: addiction may be a disease, but it is one that can be overcome by the sufferer's will, conceived of primarily as the power of mind over matter. Each overcoming represents the progress of a civilization upon which God and nature smile.

Yet Harley's narrative is more complicated than its moral implies, especially since it tacitly engages a lurid piece of lore often repeated in nineteenth-century medical, temperance, and mainstream discourses. The story circulated in many forms, but it goes more or less like this:

> A few years ago . . . a tippler was put into the almshouse in Massachusetts. Within a few days he devised numerous expedients to procure rum, but failed. At length, however, he hit upon one which was successful. He went into the wood-yard of the establishment, and placing one hand upon a block and with an axe in the other, he struck it off at a single blow. With the stump raised and streaming he ran into the house, and cried, "Get some rum, get some rum, my hand is off." In the confusion and bustle of the occasion a bowl of rum was brought, into which he plunged the bleeding member of his body, then raised the bowl to his mouth, drinking freely, and exclaimed, "I am satisfied."[3]

On the one hand—so to speak—this fable neatly performs its temperance function, producing in its audience a profound horror of the apparently purposeful, radical self-subtraction that drunkards were thought to undergo as they consistently destroyed family, home, livelihood, minds, and bodies.[4] In this context, the drunkard's self-mutilation negates social progress itself, by eliminating that symbolic engine of human labor and self-advancement, the hand. Harley's exertion of his will to withstand morphine's allure echoes the determined self-assertion motivating his physiological research and discovery; it recapitulates the progressive history it makes. By contrast, the nameless drunkard's auto-amputation forms the spectacle of a crippling self-inversion that snarls such teleological history. Harley's boast that he would be up to cutting off his own arm was meant to indicate an inspiring strength of will, but the drunkard who actually performs the deed demonstrates a horrifying lack of willpower in the face of his addiction. After the shock of the drunkard's gruesome story subsides, a fascinated curiosity remains: how does an individual become someone who would go to such extremes for something as inconsequential as a drink? In other words, why does one become an alcoholic or an addict?[5]

This question seems to invite a biographical, often autobiographical, narrative of a certain kind of seduction, one that follows this basic narrative formula: a protagonist is searching for relief from trauma or pain, questing after euphoria, or seeking something that everyday life does not provide; he or she is enchanted into a habit; falls into a relentless oscillation between bliss and despair; experiences the misery of abject compulsion; and ends at a crossroads: either spurn the fatal substance and embrace recovery, or die. The voracious mass cultural demand to rehearse versions of this basic plot, with its formulaic, implacable rigidity, might represent a way of managing the curiously recursive loop at the heart of the common definition of *addiction*: "the compulsion and need to use a drug as a result of having used it in the past."[6] That is to say, this definition posits a past, before the addiction began its time-destroying repetitions, but the precise moment of this past—of the beginning of the addiction—is always on the horizon, never fully specifiable. Personal narrative, whether it inventories life experiences or excavates psychological ground, thus becomes the principal discursive mode of addiction in a failed but irresistible bid to identify its origin.

The Victorian social commentator Sarah Ellis noted this conundrum in her argument for sympathy toward the drunkard: "Of twenty persons seated at the same table, and regaling themselves with the same wine, it is more than probable that the fatal drop at which intemperance begins, would not be in the same glass with any two among them. Who then shall decide this momentous question? for it is momentous, since eternal condemnation depends upon it."[7] The questions that addiction begs—"How did it start?" "When did it all begin?" and, bathetically, "How did it come to this?"—are questions that generate narrative. Ellis's preoccupation with the drunkard's damnation has survived even the massive cultural shift to secularism, in which his suffering is characterized as the abjection of hell on earth. But the stories these questions produce ultimately always fail to answer satisfactorily the real question for which they substitute: "Why do people become addicts?" Social science offers explanations that often seem distant from the lived experience of addiction; autobiographical and twelve-step testimonials supply this deficiency but are nonetheless limited by their individual scope and genre-bound predictability.

In this book, I change that question and pursue the meaning of addiction differently, primarily considering it neither as a set of events in the lives of individuals nor as a medico-scientific phenomenon to be weighed and measured but rather as an idea that has changed throughout its cultural and literary history. What if the "past" that inheres in addiction were collective, historical? Considered together, what do the common tropes and themes of addiction narratives have to tell us about the concept's function in public culture? Pursuing such questions permits us to think about how cultural forces invented the figure of the addict, rather than dwelling on how individuals acquired their addictions. In the present popular culture, dominated by twelve-step philosophy and its outgrowth, the recovery movement, all addiction narratives are "owned" by their recovering narrators, and their public utterances primarily signify evidence of the appropriate moral transformation undergone by their tellers.[8] By contrast, I contend that we all have a stake in narratives of and about addiction, because they have important things to tell us about changing conceptualizations of Anglo-American selfhood, freedom, and identity. Rather than asking why individuals become addicts, I want to know why addiction becomes us.

I answer this question in part by reexamining the history of addiction, which, some general contours notwithstanding, is a rather shapeless scholarly field. There are many addiction memoirs, biographies of famous addicts, histories of substances—but no comprehensive cultural history of compulsive, habitual dependencies on those substances. As Eve Kosofsky Sedgwick facetiously glosses this ill-defined history, "Once upon a time, the story goes, back in the old country, some people sometimes took opium."[9] But these were not "addicts." Nor were those who could not control their appetites for drink. These were primarily sinners, cousins of Rabelaisian gluttons; they had yet to join the ranks of the habituated, the substance-dependent, the psychologically compelled, and the physiologically coerced.[10] Instead, they first became enchanted with marvelous substances from exotic locales: spices, sugar, tobacco, chocolate, coffee, tea, rum. Imperial commerce in the period from 1500 to 1800 laid the groundwork for a "psychoactive revolution," in which the masses "acquired progressively more, and more potent, means of altering their ordinary waking consciousness"; but it was not until the nineteenth and twentieth centuries that "their successors changed their minds and restricted or prohibited many—but not all—drugs," including alcohol.[11]

This happened unevenly, at different times, for different substances, and among different groups of people. For example, in spite of Thomas De Quincey's description in *Confessions of an English Opium-Eater* (1821) of what would later be readily identifiable as addiction, opium's "luxurious" use made it the offbeat hobby of dilettantes.[12] A significant strain of addiction history has focused on De Quincey, Coleridge, and other late Romantic and Victorian writers, valorizing their experiences as ones given in "a universal language" that disguises their social privilege and cultural authority as literary geniuses.[13] More recent scholarship has focused attention on how, from the 1820s onward, the temperance movement, which advocated moderate use of alcohol, and the teetotal movement, which promoted total abstinence, both configured the immoral lack of personal moderation known as "intemperance" as a social problem activating questions of gender, race, and sexuality.[14] Yet the elite and populist strands of the history of addiction tend to remain separate, especially since the temperance movement, with its extremist renunciations, seems the very antithesis of the philosophical and aesthetic delights of "high" culture.[15] This book relates the two phenomena while also drawing on the medical history of addiction, which formed in some measure under temperance pressure but primarily as the result of professional physicians' overenthusiastic prescription of hypodermic morphine.[16] By the 1880s, former temperance activists who had become physicians substituted the frequent phrase "habitual drunkenness" with the more scientific-sounding term *inebriety*; they founded medical societies, held conferences, published their proceedings, and agitated for legislation to incarcerate inebriates.[17] Through their efforts, *inebriety* became an umbrella term, conceptually uniting the compulsion to consume alcohol and drugs such as morphine, chloral hydrate, opium, ether, and cocaine, as variations on a single disease or disorder.[18] Though it has been continually resurrected, this medical, materialist model was relatively short-lived at the time: by the First World War, the term *addiction*, with its paradoxical hybrid meaning of a "disease of the will," emerged from casual use to command consensus and overtake *inebriety*.[19] In both Britain and the United States, this shift led to addiction's closer alignment with criminality, its location in underground urban subcultures, and an increasing emphasis on the control of drug supplies.[20]

This book tells the story of how "addiction" emerged at this point. It offers a loose narrative linking imperial consumption, intemperance, the disease of inebriety, and the disease of the will, bringing some unity to a heretofore fragmented historical field. Because it is about the century between 1820 and 1920, it focuses on the substances around which the concept of addiction began to be articulated: alcohol, opium, morphine, and a few others. Since readers more familiar with recent discourses of addiction are likely to recognize themes and tropes, I occasionally indicate the relevance of nineteenth-century formations of addiction for its subsequent history.[21] Entirely new, however, is the critical lens that brings into focus addiction's configurations of race, gender, sexuality, and class. We are used to the notion that addiction is a democratic disease, capable of striking anyone, anywhere; yet as my research reveals, even this seemingly egalitarian idea engages and deploys hidden social power.

Addiction and Politics

Although I have already begun to suggest some of the differences separating "intoxication," "habitual drunkenness," "intemperance," "inebriety," "habit," "dependency," and "addiction," for the clarity and convenience that synthetic history demands, I sometimes speak of them collectively as *addiction*. This term has been superseded in some quarters by "dependence," "substance abuse," and other monikers, but *addiction* captures the condition's central feature, the extreme ambivalence of self-enslavement. In Latin usage, an addict was a slave or bondsman, someone "formally made over or bound (to another)," oftentimes to pay a debt.[22] The concept of self-enslavement also animated the Western ethical tradition descending from Paul, who, including drunkards among those who would not inherit God's kingdom, stated, "'All things are lawful for me,' but not all things are helpful. 'All things are lawful for me,' but I will not be enslaved by anything."[23] By this logic, Christians are distinguished from Jews, Muslims, and others in being exempt from restrictions on food and drink; but in exchange for this liberty, they must enforce their freedom upon themselves, and avoid becoming "enslaved." In the early modern period, this power relation became an aspect of individual psychology, as the reflexive quality of "self-addiction" accrued to the term. Gradually, a sense of compulsion replaced the connotation of straightforward devotion to a practice or substance. In the seventeenth and eighteenth centuries, U.S. writers used terms like *love* to describe a person's relationship to drink; by the end of the eighteenth century, they were more often "overwhelmed" or "overpowered" by it.[24] The English essayist Charles Lamb described the agony of addiction as a form of slavery forceful enough to stop time: "a submission to bondage, the springs of the will gone down like a broken clock, the sin and the suffering co-instantaneous, or the latter forerunning the former, remorse preceding action—all this represented in one point of time."[25] The term's current connotation, lying somewhere between illness and moral failing, compresses these conceptual and emotional histories. The metaphor of self-enslavement, which appears incessantly in the nineteenth century, still offers a vivid idea of the excruciating, totalizing, and profoundly ironic experience of addictive self-damage. But even more importantly, it implants a social and legal relationship of extreme domination—slavery—within the individual's own psychology.

The self-enslavement of addiction was insidious: it crept into a life via everyday habits, only gradually transforming a self-mastered man into an abject "slave." But the nineteenth-century history of habit was already structured by expectations of self-control and self-domination that made it increasingly amenable to concepts of addiction. Early and mid-nineteenth-century writers such as William Wordsworth strongly believed in each individual's ability to inculcate "habits of mind," familiar modes of perception and thought. For example, having famously defined poetry as "the spontaneous overflow of powerful feelings," in the preface to *Lyrical Ballads* (1800), Wordsworth also associated it with automated mental habit: "such habits of mind will be produced, that, by obeying blindly and mechanically the impulses of those habits, we shall describe objects, and utter sentiments, of such a nature . . . that the understanding of the Reader must necessarily be in some degree enlightened, and his affections strengthened and purified."[26] Wordsworth illustrates a process of mental discipline that will, paradoxically, produce the spontaneity and dynamism of poetic self-transcendence.

Versions of this idea became the conventional wisdom of the early and mid-nineteenth century: the individual's will set his mental habits; after this initial act of volition, the will could be withdrawn and the habit would continue. David Lloyd and Paul Thomas see this process of self-cultivation, particularly its dimension of aesthetic judgment, as the development of "an ethical disposition that is most clearly elaborated within the concept of culture" and, in turn, as the cornerstone of citizenship within the liberal state.[27] Habit is here a critical instrument in the liberal subject's self-formation as a stable but flexible conduit for culture. Indeed, in the same capacity habit was also crucial to discourses of self-improvement, perfectibility, and social mobility, as in Samuel Smiles's enormously popular *Self-Help* (1859). William B. Carpenter, perhaps the most widely read nineteenth-century physiologist, had described the very growth of the human organism as an oscillation between volitional and habitual forces.[28] Far from neutral descriptions of mental behavior, these concepts of habit were highly normative. As William James wrote, "Habit is . . . the enormous fly-wheel of society, its most precious conservative agent."[29] By commanding their wills to train their habits, middle-class Victorians pursued their bourgeois prerogatives of accumulating wealth, preserving health, and promoting their best selves.

But these loose ideas of habit contained an ambivalence that, in the latter half of the century, began to tilt in the other direction. It was not merely that a lax will, having allowed bad habits to take hold, would lead to a flawed character. Rather, under the pressure of materialist and evolutionary theories, the compulsive qualities of habit seemed increasingly beyond the individual's control: "Many feared that if the human psyche was biologically compelled to repeat mental experiences, and thus to trap the individual in predictable and inflexible patterns of behavior, this compulsion constrained possibilities for change and challenged conceptions of free will."[30] In *The Descent of Man* (1871), Charles Darwin declared that man "will through long habit acquire . . . perfect self-command"; but he also thought it probable "that the habit of self-command may, like other habits, be inherited. Thus at last man comes to feel, through acquired and perhaps inherited habit, that it is best for him to obey his more persistent impulses."[31] Habit had come to seem less the guarantor of spontaneity, aesthetic judgment, and self-culture, and more the sign of natural, inborn compulsions, alienated from the will. In his famous conclusion to *The Renaissance* (1873), Walter Pater articulated an ideal of spontaneous, intense individual experience in which habit featured as the failure to convert experience into meaning.[32] The story of the emergence of addiction is closely linked to this story of the transformation of habit, all the way from its earlier associations with spontaneity, learning, and mental mobility to its more modern connotations of artificiality, inflexibility, and ruts. Habit was the primary context for habituation in the nineteenth century; as Dolores Peters writes, "There was no explicit or widely accepted basis for defining the nature of [drug] habituation beyond its component element of mere habit."[33] Though habit is an attractive concept for thinking about the relationship between acts and identities, it is the very background of disappointed agency from which addiction emerges, not some value-free or discrete alternative for unthinking addiction.[34] Whether as self-enslavement or self-liberation, habit conjures a region of the self that withdraws from and controls the individual's activities, for ill or for good.

As I have been hinting, these were not objective or politically neutral ideas; they were shaped within and across specific cultural landscapes. Because addiction formed in conjunction with bourgeois self-making, commercial imperialism, metropolitan consumerism, reform movements, a widening public sphere, and modernizing medicine, it makes sense to study it where those conditions developed most intensively, in this case Britain and the United States. From the perspective of metropolitan Britain, the idea of intoxication connotes a desire to experience the colonies, with their exotic enchantments, by consuming their products—in the paradigmatic example of De Quincey, opium. Intoxication thus coalesces within a broad metaphor of mental travel or transport, a trip. But such instances of intoxication have a way of seducing subjects into dangerous habits and dependencies, from which they do not always return; for example, in Tennyson's famous poem, Ulysses' sailors want only "In the hollow Lotos-land to live and lie reclined."[35] Intoxication can thus transform into addiction, which—once discovered and named—encompasses the horror of realizing that one's identity as a modern person, on the cusp of the future, results from a habituated dependence upon the primitive colony, which metamorphoses from a place of seduction to the locus of death. In the United States, the intoxicated delight of mid-nineteenth-century imperialism is typically figured as the westward mobility of the self across a supposedly vacant continental interior, where it can manifest individual freedom as destiny; addiction demarcates the moments in which that abstract self-making experiences its own embodiment as exile.

When I began this project, I followed the conventional historicist assumption that U.S. and British cultures of addiction were too distinctive to be discussed together without distortion. I realized, however, that those differences are best explained in relation to each other, because the overarching connections between their two histories of addiction are so similar: the British antislavery movement of the 1790s influenced the temperance movement in both nations; in both places, the temperance movement had close ties to abolition; the medical establishment shared disciplinary knowledge through strong professional connections; and the novels that engaged and developed representations of addicted subjectivity were popular on both sides of the Atlantic.[36] Indeed, Amanda Claybaugh's persuasive demonstration of the close relationship between Anglo-American social reform movements and print culture takes abolition and temperance as its two foremost examples.[37] Although they have significantly different inflections, British and U.S. cultural histories of addiction both form around a mobile concept of colonial seduction leading inexorably to a debilitating imperial dependency and compulsion.

Aside from these pragmatic concerns, a more theoretical *and* political reason motivates my transatlantic framing of addiction: because the central nineteenth-century metaphor of addiction, self-enslavement, activates an entire network of meanings involving chattel slavery, race, and modernity, illuminating them requires a critical tool that does not preserve cultural nationalism, in which ideologies of cultural and ethnic purity can lurk. For example, critiquing addiction from the standpoint of the inviolability of a "drinking culture" would reinscribe the very modes of power that rituals of drinking and addictions more broadly deploy. More to the point, because the history of chattel slavery is bound up with the history of addiction, studying them together engages the project, articulated by Paul Gilroy, of making chattel slavery and colonialism "part of the ethical and intellectual heritage of the West as a whole."[38] Such a critique helps us rethink "such central categories of the Enlightenment project as the idea of universality, the fixity of meaning, the coherence of the subject, and, of course, the foundational ethnocentrism in which these have all tended to be anchored."[39] Addiction, with its incoherent subjects, chronic repetitions, wretched stupidity, and debilitating intransigence, presents its own distinct burr in the side of rational Enlightenment modernity and progress. But there is a hidden history in which the genealogical strands of addiction and slavery tie together, forming a critique of democratic freedom, liberal subjectivity, and self-making as personified, in the nineteenth century, by white, middle-class men. Because they were the same people who, as the majority of addicts, seemed to squander their liberty, they appear in addiction discourses as ironic impersonators of Enlightenment knowledge and freedom.

This cultural formation differs between Britain and the United States, but analyzing its settings together helps demonstrate the argument of this book: addiction began as an exceptional story of white, masculine, middle-class self-making gone awry, ironically confronting its own embodiment as a mode of compulsion rather than freedom, habituation rather than spontaneity, dependency rather than autonomy, and disease rather than health.[40] Toward the end of the century, these signs of addicted compulsion merged with signs of femininity, queerness, and biological racialization, encroaching on the normative liberal subject and investing him with uncontrollable, deviant desire, disease, and racial defect. Narratives of individuals who become addicts thus rehearse a story of a subject's fall from freedom into addiction, in which the external social world mires him, paradoxically, in the newly estranged materiality of his own body. This broad conceptualization of addiction entails a vision of freedom as sobriety or an amalgam of self-reliance, moderation, self-control, and autonomy; it is an essentially private experience that only the individual can attain for himself. Even when assisted by temperance and teetotal societies, physicians, or sympathetic others, the addicted individual must paradoxically reassert her own defective will in order to liberate herself. This configuration makes addiction a profoundly private phenomenon, isolated from its social contexts. Describing the widespread reform language of metaphorical "bondage" and "enslavement" to various social ills, Russ Castronovo writes that its "willingness to emblematize the private, corporeal self constitutes a retrograde rhetorical strategy in which the language used to describe states of unfreedom becomes dehistoricized and narrowed to the confines of the self."[41] This model of freedom, which is contingent on biological purity, is internationalized with the expansion of U.S. imperialism across the globe at the end of the nineteenth century. This new form of imperialism marks the point at which the history of addiction really becomes the history of drug control, which had been attempted only partially and fitfully in the nineteenth century.[42] Of course, these parameters by no means exhaust Atlantic or European formations of addiction, but perhaps the breadth and suggestiveness of this book will open the field to new scholarship relating addiction to modernity in different transnational, imperial, and postcolonial contexts.[43]

Addiction and Metaphor

Some might object that, far from treating the cultural and literary history of addiction too broadly, I am unduly narrowing a concept that has far wider application. But one of the abiding features of the discourse of addiction—and one of the pitfalls of analyzing such a concept—is the very observation that virtually everything is potentially addictive. Sedgwick noted that the figure of the exercise addict—someone paradoxically addicted to healthy behavior and the substance of his or her own body—bankrupted the concept; afterwards, "any substance, any behavior, even any affect may be pathologized as addictive."[44] William S. Burroughs, writing in 1959, made a similar point about the term's promiscuity: "We speak of addiction to candy, coffee, tobacco, warm weather, television, detective stories, crossword puzzles. . . . So misapplied the term loses any useful precision of meaning."[45] But this objection is at least as old as the medical identification of addiction itself. In the text often cited as the concept's medical origin, *Die Morphiumsucht* (1877; English trans. *Morbid Craving for Morphia*, 1878), Edward Levinstein warned that morphine cravings could not be taken as symptoms of derangement: "We should otherwise, by following this mode of judging mental conditions, soon be compelled to pronounce as insane every person subject to some hobby."[46] Other voices joined the chorus of ambivalence about addiction's seemingly limitless potential. At an 1885 meeting of the British Society for the Study and Cure of Inebriety, the surgeon Carsten Holthouse argued that inebriety was a sin rather than a disease. "Why call the condition produced by alcohol a disease, while analogous conditions which result from opium-eating, tobacco chewing, and smoking are only called habits? Again, wherein does this craving and weakened or lost will-power differ from that which is induced by indulgence in any other inveterate habit, as sensuality or gambling?"[47]

Holthouse's queries exposed the unevenness of the shift from moral to medical perspectives, but it also indexed a suspicion of the concept's expansion via analogy and metaphor. Other commentators merely replicated a confusion that has never really been dispelled; for example, the Earl of Shaftesbury, arguing for a bill to incarcerate habitual drunkards in 1879, stumbled in categorizing the condition: habitual drunkenness "was now to be treated, in a great measure, as a disease, or something akin to disease. It was, perhaps, difficult to discover at all times which it was, but that in many persons it was a vice was beyond all dispute. . . . Disease was, perhaps, too strong a term to be applied to all cases, but no other could be found. In some it was called morbid appetite, craving, a tendency against which it was difficult to contend, and so on."[48] Almost as soon as the technical-sounding "inebriety" had replaced the more shameful "habitual drunkard" in medical and legal parlance, it was itself replaced by "addiction," which resigned medical optimism in favor of the strange metaphorical indication, "disease of the will."[49] "Disease" thus counts as a metaphor for addiction, not because of its failure to describe a biological reality, but because it formed a discursive bridge from earlier nineteenth-century temperance discourses to early-twentieth-century models of criminality and eugenics.[50] Well over a century since the objection was first voiced, the metaphorical proliferation of "addiction," along with its observation by critics, continues unabated. Accordingly, the ontological status of addiction—is it a sin, vice, disease, illness, habit, compulsion, or choice?—is still in question. This perpetual rehearsal suggests that metaphor has been a durable cultural mechanism by which addiction has assumed its various forms within Anglo-American culture. Addiction's immense explanatory power derives precisely from its defiance of categorization:

having colonized a rich terrain of habits, hobbies, practices, pursuits, commitments, loves, acts of ingestion, behavioral tics, idiosyncrasies, and the rest of the multifarious world of description by which humans designate their pleasurable everyday actions, it now verges on a prosaic concept of simple attachment.

At the same time that addiction snowballs toward banality, however, it still describes a very real, intensively horrible mode of life for millions of people who suffer from it. It is in a similar context, of defending the lived reality of diseases such as tuberculosis and cancer, that Susan Sontag, in *Illness as Metaphor* (1978), attacked the gratuitous violence of "giv[ing] a disease a meaning": "Any important disease whose causality is murky, and for which treatment is ineffectual, tends to be awash in significance. First, the subjects of deepest dread (corruption, decay, anomie, weakness) are identified with the disease. The disease itself becomes a metaphor. Then, in the name of the disease (that is, using the metaphor), that horror is imposed on other things."[51] Sontag's argument bears pointedly on addiction, on the methodology of this book, and on the cultural studies of medicine more generally. Compared to addiction, even such culturally freighted diseases as tuberculosis and cancer strike us as "less metaphorical" and "more real," but Sontag's own logic exposes such comparisons as lapses in her argument: a disease cannot *become* metaphorical, because it already is a metaphor for varieties of disorder and horror characterizing the borders between individual and social bodies. This book shows how addiction and its metaphors imposed horror on "other things"—the consumption of print media; citizenship status; sexual desire; racial, gender, and sexual difference—to name a few. Helen Keane finds that through such characteristic displacements of addiction discourse, "certain ways of being are categorised as unnatural, disordered and self-destructive, while others are constituted as natural, healthy and self-enhancing, and these ways of being are regarded as expressions of a totalised self or identity."[52]

Just as disease is inherently metaphorical, so too is it innately political, though its politics tend to appear in inverse proportion to its medico-scientific articulation. The burgeoning of medical, psychological, and sociological expertise on a revitalized taxonomy of addictions in the 1980s helped to depoliticize not just addiction but also all of the multifarious areas of life into which it penetrated, which came to seem mildly compulsive and diseased.[53] Uncovering the nineteenth-century metaphors that organized thinking about addiction helps to reveal some of the politics that silently underlie it now. Some of those metaphors resonated more than others: I devote two chapters to the metaphor of self-enslavement because it engaged the related reform politics of temperance and abolition, generating more cultural and literary meaning, than did, for example, the moribund metaphor of demonic possession.[54] Both metaphors are ubiquitous in nineteenth-century comment on addiction, but the metaphorical comparison of addicts to slaves raised a host of politically charged questions about identity and freedom that remain relevant, whereas laments about "the Fiend alcohol" or the "evil spirit" of hypodermic morphine did not.

Addiction and Fiction

By using measures of meaning such as metaphors, dramatic irony, and novelistic form, I can show how their successive iterations moved the concept of addiction through history, changing it along the way. Focusing on the metaphors of addiction exposes their procedure of annexing conceptual territory. Because metaphors circulate among medical, journalistic, legal, and fictional texts, they help us connect the various institutional, regional, and national settings in which addiction was formulated. Yet because metaphors can be imaginatively limited, I discuss novels about addicts and addiction, which furnish extended meditations on how addiction relates the self to its environment. This is the classic remit of the novel, which arguably reached the apogee of psychological expression—not to mention its famously loosest, baggiest form—in the nineteenth century. In the realm of fiction, authors could reimagine addicted subjectivity and agency in ways that both replicated and changed how the broader culture viewed addiction. Yet as we will see, addicts tend to make bad nineteenth-century protagonists, mainly because they could rarely manage the requisite moral transformation that typically moves narratives from conflict to resolution. Where such protagonists could transform themselves through recovery, the narratives often seemed inauthentic because they replicated the propaganda of temperance. Drunkards and addicts thus tended to occupy the margins of nineteenth-century novels, often as spectacles of moral self-limitation: one thinks of Stephen Blackpool's nameless wife in Charles Dickens's *Hard Times* (1854) or the sodden Mr. Dolls in his *Our Mutual Friend* (1865). When they move closer to the narrative center, their habituations and dependencies tend not to define their identities, playing only a minor role in the narrative action. The tippling of Sidney Carton in Dickens's *A Tale of Two Cities* (1859) is contiguous with his gormandizing, merely one element of his larger misanthropy; in Elizabeth Gaskell's *Mary Barton* (1848), John Barton's opium habit is another one of his working-class difficulties; it contributes to his actions without directing them. In pursuing meatier literary depictions of addicts, I have largely eschewed canonical texts such as these.

Rather, I have found significant literary treatments of addiction in slightly disguised form in nineteenth-century novels that have an oblique relationship to realism: Harriet Beecher Stowe's abolitionist novel *Uncle Tom's Cabin* (1852), where the infamous Simon Legree embodies a potent critique of "intemperate" slave mastery; Robert Louis Stevenson's "shilling shocker," *The Strange Case of Dr. Jekyll and Mr. Hyde* (1886), where Jekyll's increasingly uncontrolled use of his potion expresses a putatively universal self-division; and Bram Stoker's supernatural novel *Dracula* (1897), where the compulsive, habitual drinking of blood functions as an analogy for modern, addicted subjectivity. I have also unearthed a small but fascinating archive of novels, stories, and autobiographies devoted to excavating addicted subjectivity, which I put into counterpoint with these more famous texts: Fitz Hugh Ludlow's *The Hasheesh Eater* (1857) and D. F. MacMartin's *Thirty Years in Hell* (1921), which I discuss in chapter 1; E. P. Roe's *Without a Home* (1881), the subject of chapter 3; Richard Pryce's *An Evil Spirit* (1887), the focus of chapter 4; *Queer Lady Judas* (1905) by "Rita," discussed in chapters 4 and 5; and Florence Marryat's *The Blood of the Vampire* (1897), analyzed with *Dracula* in chapter 6. I hope to elicit readerly interest in these undeservedly forgotten texts as captivating social documents of addiction.

My focus on fiction has another methodological function: it serves as a corrective to the reigning popular discursive mode of addiction, oral and written autobiographical narrative. While overtly invested in empiricism, this discourse nevertheless also coerces the personal narratives that constitute it into following the same narrative formula.[55] By contrast, this book is not the history of individuals; nor does it rely on the progressive history of Enlightenment modernity; rather, it strives to fulfill an attitude of ethical opposition to that project that Foucault has described as countermodernity.[56] In this practice, novels and metaphors are better tools to document cultural logics than they typically are in traditionally "objective" historical accounts. Their efficacy is especially relevant to this topic: the intense demand for true stories about addiction—the most effective of which will necessarily be recognizable within a cultural logic that remains entirely unstated—means that fictional narratives must both satisfy and transform those expectations. At any given historical moment, they show what addiction is, what else it might be, and what it might have been. For this reason, five chapters deal with fiction; one, about drug autobiographies, reads them against the grain of their real-life reference, more in line with recent cultural turns in autobiography and life-writing studies.[57] To begin to delimit this vast horizon, I borrow a phrase to describe addiction that Ian Baucom has applied to Atlantic discourse more generally: "an unsettled and unsettling way of inhabiting and experiencing the modern."[58] If, as Roland Barthes has evocatively suggested, "Sugar is a time, a category of the world," then so are coffee, chocolate, alcohol, opium, morphine, and all other addictive substances—not because they have the pharmacological effect of altering subjective perceptions of time but because they mark time through repetition, disconnecting their users from the flow of history.[59]

Of course, fiction itself unfolds in its own time and space, beyond history proper, and reading it was described, throughout the nineteenth century, as an addictive practice. One reviewer enacted a concept of addiction in the assertion that sensation novels had been "called into existence to supply the cravings of a diseased appetite, and contribut[ed] themselves to foster the disease, and to stimulate the want which they supply," going on to compare this sickness to that of "the dram-drinker."[60] I discuss this formation in conjunction with a generalized print culture in chapter 1 and with respect to fiction in passing throughout this book, but it appears most pointedly in chapter 4, where reading about addicts and addiction emerges as a substitute for experiencing it oneself. This compulsive acquisition of a simulacrum of addicted knowledge is a response to a central double bind of addiction: in order to really know about addiction, one must experience it oneself, but this experience also prevents the subject from possessing legitimate knowledge, since the addiction destroys the perspective that makes the knowledge meaningful. Only recovered addicts, therefore, are permitted to speak with authority about their experiences. Reading about addiction thus becomes a very attractive alternative, not least because it permits a vicarious flirtation with physical danger, self-dissolution, and death without any of the risk. As the author of a book about addiction, I obviously cannot avoid participating in this practice to a certain degree; but my interlocking critiques offer a different kind of historical knowledge of addiction, a value that I hope makes the reading of it both pleasurable and productive.

Overview

By relating nineteenth-century fiction about addiction to its cultural contexts, I avoid the well-trodden paths of studying writers who drank excessively or took drugs or describing the aesthetics of intoxication and addiction.[61] Conversely, though I draw on them for source material, I avoid replicating social histories of drug use that focus narrowly on particular communities or drugs.[62] My reliance on metaphors and novels does not divorce my conclusions from a putatively objective reality: showing that something is "socially constructed" is not the same as claiming that it is illusory. Addiction is therefore both a contingent social idea and a lived reality, neither a mass nor a personal delusion. That is why, though I draw on their insights, I have generally avoided both Marxist and psychoanalytic paradigms of addiction: each exposes addiction as merely a form of false consciousness.[63] Like other cultural studies of medicine, science, and technology, my method destabilizes those disciplines' implicit claims to produce knowledge free from cultural bias.[64] My objective is not to dispute the reality of biochemical phenomena like tolerance and withdrawal, but rather, by illustrating their nineteenth-century histories, to show that they could not be observed or theorized apart from their social contexts. For this reason, too, the book is not organized around individual drugs and their properties. Historically, the medical interpretation has attempted to motivate social sympathy for addicts on the grounds that they suffer from a disease; while I too sympathize with addicts, I develop that impulse into a broader critique of various configurations of cultural power that draw on class, race, gender, and sexuality, ones written as if on a palimpsest, beneath the visible shorthand of "disease." At the end of this introduction, I will revisit an early popular articulation of the disease argument in order to demonstrate the paradigmatic tradeoffs involved in its cultural politics. Finally, just as this book is not a conventional history, it is also not written from "that forbidden focus, the user's point of view."[65] Indeed, one of this book's tasks is to illuminate the historical underpinnings of present ideological investments in both the prohibitive concept of drugs, in which addiction is a ubiquitous, looming bogeyman, and the permissive concept of intoxicated resistance or transcendence, in which addiction does not exist or does not matter.[66] Broadly speaking, these two familiar positions have endured since the early nineteenth century in part because each forms in the blind spot of the other.

Just as addiction was not discovered at a particular moment in history, it will also not be cured in a single stroke but rather will gradually lose its cultural significance. Thus the mode of history required to trace the concept's orbit cannot be the progressive teleology that the addict's characteristic repetitions and intransigence resist. Rather, to do justice to its subject, a history of addiction needs to be more like a genealogy: in Foucault's words, "it must record the singularity of events outside of any monotonous finality; it must seek them in the most unpromising places, in what we tend to feel is without history—in sentiments, love, conscience, instincts; it must be sensitive to their recurrence, not in order to trace the gradual curve of their evolution, but to isolate the different scenes where they have engaged in different roles."[67] In other words, rather than considering addiction either as the same problem in all time periods, or as a superior alternative to the archaic concepts of sin and vice, or as a concept configuring the identity of "the addict" as an objective designation, this book instead identifies the moments when addiction and the addict became newly visible through changes in the narratives and metaphors used in describing them. In a genealogical context, the times and spaces of addiction are not solely the boundaries of individual bodies, psychologies, and lifetimes interacting with external substances, whether to demonstrate their absolute victimization or to reaffirm their mastery. If, as Fernand Braudel characterized his method, "we have been brought to the breaking-down of history into successive levels . . . or again, to the breaking-down of man into a succession of characters," then this book breaks down the new human character of the addict.[68]

The character of the addict thus reappears onstage, as if in different costume, as addiction becomes newly visible throughout history. The first section of this book, "Travel, Exile, and Self-Enslavement," shows how those metaphors work together to produce an addict ethically ensnared within a new world of consumption. Chapter 1 describes how, through metaphors of travel and exile, the opium-eating scholar metamorphoses into the "pioneer of inner space" and then into the dispossessed, addicted hobo. For De Quincey, author of *Confessions of an English Opium-Eater* (1821), the intoxicating consumption of opium and print blended Orientalist delight with imperial mastery. European enchantment with the exotic trifle that becomes powerful enough to make its consumer its devotee had impelled fifteenth-century Europeans to augment their trade with India to pursue pepper; it moved Parisian men, after the Turkish ambassador's introduction of coffee to France in 1669, to drink the new import while wearing Arab costumes and reclining on floor cushions rather than chairs; and it would send Victorian botanical adventurers such as Richard Spruce down the Amazon Basin to collect quinine bark and dabble with *ayahuasca*, the "telepathic" vine ritually ingested by Amazonian peoples.[69] These desires to consume, embody, perform, and above all to know the larger world can be described as a particularly corporeal and performative mode of Orientalism, and they provide a context for De Quincey's intoxication by laudanum, or opium dissolved in alcohol, which—as other critics have noted—was also a metaphor for his delirious incorporation of print culture. Because this insatiable consumption threatened to overwhelm his ability to produce original material, De Quincey revised the concept of Romantic genius, shifting its locus to the otherworldly, esoteric knowledge of the scholar, dilettante, and mental tourist of altered states. Because reading and opium-eating were techniques of bringing the exotic home, the curious appearance of the Malay at the door of Dove Cottage can be read as a hallucination in which the random contents of print culture become manifest. De Quincey's narrator's efforts to master print culture were inseparable from his desires to embody imperial, and thus explicitly racial, mastery.

The drug autobiography emerged as a genre in the United States primarily through imitations of De Quincey's *Confessions*. Texts such as Fitz Hugh Ludlow's *Hasheesh Eater* (1857) adapted the association between drug-taking and imperial knowledge to suit the westward expansion of the United States and its accompanying ideology of manifest destiny. Under the influence of hashish, Ludlow explored his inner psychic space as if it were the U.S. frontier. In the historical and narrative time before the abjection and degradation of addiction, there is the transcendent wonder of intoxication, the mobility and self-expansion that feels like freedom. This dimension of intoxication emphasizes mental thrill rather than torpor; it is "the action or power of exhilarating or highly exciting the mind; elation or excitement beyond the bounds of sobriety."[70] Because the real boundaries of this exhilarating travel are the self, the "American De Quincey" can dispense with print culture and merely delight in his own sensations of continental mastery. As nineteenth-century Romantic models of intoxicated dreaming gave way to early-twentieth-century theories of addiction, drug autobiographies such as D. F. MacMartin's *Thirty Years in Hell* (1921) readapted the genre, representing the disappointments of manifest destiny as addicted exile. While drug autobiographies accrued countercultural authority, appearing to signify the irrational underside of Enlightenment modernity, their fantasies of esoteric exploration derived from broader cultural ideals of imperial power and knowledge. Chapter 1 thus explains two crossings: how intoxication becomes addiction, and how the drug autobiography begins as a British form of imperial mastery before shifting to a continental U.S. one.

In chapter 2, I show how the metaphor of intemperance as self-enslavement creates two paradigmatic figures, the sodden, vicious slave master and the drunken slave. As a result of the consumer revolution of the eighteenth century, a new commodity culture "suffused with lust and greed" increasingly stimulated the appetites of metropolitan subjects for goods.[71] Critiques of this rampant consumption created new ethical demands that one restrain one's desires and consume goods moderately or selectively.[72] These demands were politicized: to the British antislavery movement of the 1790s, the international temperance movement that grew out of it, and the U.S. abolitionist movement, the newly popular concept of "intemperance" signified metropolitan consumers' reckless, compulsive complicity with chattel slavery. Because sugar was so irresistible, fashion textiles so desirable, and rum so pleasurable, enfeebled metropolitan consumers continued to demand them in spite of their morally tainted origins; in an ironic twist, many became known as "slaves" to the bottle, their plight often eclipsing that of the chattel slaves whose labor they were addictively consuming. As Britain and the U.S. continued trading slaves, using sugar, and imbibing rum, their apparent inability to morally reform themselves seemed ever more acute, and began to be described as its own metaphorical form of slavery. In the words of U.S. preacher James Dana, only "Christian freedom" could deliver traders and consumers "from the slavery of vicious passions."[73] Those who perpetuated chattel slavery by trading in and owning slaves ironically "enslaved" themselves to profit.

At the same time that the slave trade and slave mastery were being represented as a sort of moral illness, a loose collection of writers and orators, themselves typically part of the antislavery movement, began to borrow the "slavery" metaphor to describe actual habitual drunkenness. Advocates of moderation, abstainers from spirits, and those who limited their intake to medicinal stimulants were the loose beginnings of the temperance and teetotal movements. The common enemy of antislavery and temperance was a slave trade steeped in liquor: rum was instrumental in purchasing and capturing slaves, coercing sailors to become slavers, keeping slaves docile, and blunting the sensitivities of overseers.[74] In chapter 2, I discuss the awkwardly intertwined politics motivated by the "slavery" metaphor, especially in the United States, where temperance organizations were segregated. I trace the political ascendancy of abolition over temperance through the metaphor's inversion from "the slavery of drink" to the "intemperance of chattel slavery," using it to re-read a classic text in which the two movements intersect, Harriet Beecher Stowe's *Uncle Tom's Cabin* (1852). Simon Legree, the iconic drunken slave master, and Prue, the degraded, intemperate slave, together form a raced paradigm with a long legacy in the cultural history of addiction.

Chapter 3 shows how the slave master becomes the "opium slave" when, as the nation attempts to forget its slave-owning past, white southerners figuratively fail to become modern industrial workers. This ambivalence about chattel slavery informed the awkward transition from the self-enslavement metaphor to the metaphor of illness. The first U.S. novel about hypodermic morphine addiction, E. P. Roe's *Without a Home* (1881), aptly combines aspects of the temperance movement with aspects of the more modern conceptualization of addiction. Temperance fiction typically had run like a bildungsroman in reverse, since it featured a promising young man about to make his mark on the world and marry his sweetheart, who, "enslaving" himself to drink, lost his middle-class advantages, good reputation, prospects for further prosperity, romantic attachment and other kinship relations, self-respect, spiritual well-being, health, sanity, and, often, life itself.[75] Such stories made "intemperance" and "habitual drunkenness" bywords for the systematic depletion of white, middle-class, masculine subjective dynamism; the "slavery of drink" metaphor ironically recast white men as figuratively black, disempowered, static, and emasculated.

When drug habituation became a noted phenomenon beginning in the 1860s, the slavery metaphor expanded to include opium and morphine. The temperance plot was updated to include the idea that addiction might be a nervous illness affecting white professional men. In an early British example, the eponymous protagonist of Coke Richardson's *Horace Saltoun* (1861) confesses that his family has "a morbid propensity to drink anything, no matter what, provided it intoxicates us. . . . We don't drink for *drinkee*, as the black man says, but for *drunkee*. It's no outbreak of convivial cheer, but a mad, animal instinct for solitary excess."[76] Medical writings replicated this distinction between morbid white illness and simplistic black conviviality: according to one southern physician, "We can see some reason why the colored man is not as susceptible to the habit as the white. He has not the same delicate nervous organization, and does not demand the form of stimulant conveyed in opium."[77] The same racist ideology governed comparisons between Chinese and white opium addiction. "I do not now refer to the miserable and grovelling Chinese, who are fed on [opium] almost from the cradle," the anonymous writer of the essay "A Morphine Habit Overcome" declared, "but to the ordinary cases of educated and intellectual men in this country and in Europe. . . . [G]iven a man of cultivated mind, high moral sentiment, and a keen sense of intellectual enjoyment, blended with strong imaginative powers, and just in proportion as he is so endowed will the difficulty be greater in weaning himself from it."[78] Like a delicate hothouse orchid, similarly "cultivated" or civilized white nerves and brains have trouble enforcing their subjects' wills.

Given the thoroughgoing nature of nineteenth-century racism, we might expect whites to be represented as people above addiction, unquestionably their own masters, but quite the opposite is true. For example, in *Doctor Judas* (1895), William Rosser Cobbe attributed greater willpower to racially marked opium habitués: "Dark races, as the African and Asiatic, are not so easily affected by the pipe as the white peoples. While it is impossible for one of the latter to leave off smoking, once the habit is formed, it is by no means uncommon for members of the former class to quit of their own volition."[79] Because addiction unfolds as an ironic narrative of self-loss, it requires subjects who have much to lose—socially, financially, and psychologically; in the racist imagination of the nineteenth century, this meant white men and, increasingly, women. As Hickman painstakingly demonstrates, Cobbe's reasoning is racist, essentializing opium *use* as a naturalized feature of being dark and brutish, while simultaneously construing the horrible compulsions of *addiction* as an affliction of fragile white nerves.[80] At the same time, although such writings construed addiction as a disease or illness, they also continued to blame sufferers for "enslaving" themselves; hence, white, masculine addicts were represented as secretly ill "slaves" who could only hope to pass as breadwinners, husbands, and fathers. Chapter 3 shows how addicted white men, unable to fulfill their social roles as the engines of modern progress, became impostors of freedom.

The second half of the book, "Disease, Desire, and Defect," delves into the social causes and consequences of the incomplete medicalization of addiction. "Inebriety," "morphinomania," "cocainism," and a variety of other medico-scientific labels formed a loose taxonomy that conceptualized the phenomenon as an illness, a condition, a disease, a symptom of degeneration, even a racial defect. With these developments in the period from 1860 to 1900, the white, middle-class masculinity of the habitual drunkard or intemperate began to fragment, and addiction began to organize new configurations of gender, sexuality, and race. In earlier temperance narratives, women and girls had been the disappointed fiancées, victimized wives, and agonized mothers of drunkards, but toward the end of the nineteenth century, they also become secret drunkards and addicts themselves. This is because the first cohort of medically recognized "addicts"—those whose growing habituations required higher dosages, who then suffered when they could not obtain them—were often upper- and middle-class women whose doctors had inadvertently habituated them to hypodermic morphine for pain relief. When physicians realized that the drugs they were administering had created their own regime of demand within patients' bodies, they began to articulate the modern symptoms of tolerance and withdrawal.[81] In order to rebuild a tarnished reputation, they began to control the use of the syringe more tightly; many also published a petition forswearing the administration of alcohol. By generating a medical consensus about the norms of habituation and the rules for preventing or ameliorating it, they began to reconfigure their patients' habits as diseases.

Addiction thus first appeared as a dangerously individualized form of self-medication because it was beyond the control of physicians; it harked back to the previous era of aristocratic medicine, in which doctors were merely servants who treated symptoms.[82] More significantly, these founding moments of medical knowledge could not be separated from a cultural fear of, and fascination with, women's sexual appetites and imagined potential for deception. A discursive contest ensued between a mostly male medical profession trying to save face and its female patients, whose shocking habits made them convenient scapegoats. As a result, addiction remained stuck in an ominous twilight between immorality and disease: women's imagined potential for maintaining a deceptive veneer of propriety while nurturing an inwardly vicious depravity lent itself well to the idea that addiction was a moral failing; meanwhile, physicians managed to represent it as a pathological illness only they could remedy. Addiction thus acquired a certain mixture of self-abjection and illness that in the nineteenth century was the traditional province of white middle-class femininity.

In *Desire and Domestic Fiction*, Nancy Armstrong demonstrated that self-discipline was central to domestic femininity as the emergent icon of modern subjectivity in the late eighteenth century.[83] But by the mid-nineteenth century, women's self-discipline had metamorphosed into self-denial, which was "represented as a spontaneous and essentially static surrender of the will to external authority."[84] This surrender created a double bind whereby women's power of self-control was understood essentially as submission to social forces beyond themselves; according to James Eli Adams, who uses John Stuart Mill's *The Subjection of Women* (1869) as his starting point, this cultural logic becomes the reason why women could not be perceived as autonomous. In the context of addiction, women's folly typically presented itself as submission to, and dependency upon, the wrong external force. As I demonstrate in chapter 4, this is precisely what had happened when the scandals of upper-class women's iatrogenic morphinomania and alcoholism broke. These phenomena fit neatly with the assumption that women's autonomy was really submission. But the debacles also represented the end of the expectation that women could reasonably influence men to be abstemious. Temperance discourse had constantly exhorted women to exert a benign, sober influence over their husbands, male relations, acquaintances, and guests, particularly by making the sober home a pleasant place that could compete with the pub for men's leisure hours. By the 1870s, women—thought to be increasingly intoxicated by their own meaningless consumer experiences of fashion and urban manners as well as alcohol or morphine—seemed unequal to their social duty to keep men sober.

Although women had been seen as a force for sobriety, the enormous specter of men's drunkenness suggests that their efficacy had been actually quite illusory. Men could always escape from the domestic sphere to take their pleasure in the smoking room or at the pub, club, or university—exclusively masculine homosocial spaces. In these ways, addiction began to coalesce through the gendered segregation of private pleasure for women and social or public pleasure for men. This distinction speaks to the broader emergence of addiction as a perversion of Enlightenment reason and as a withdrawal from the classical public sphere into abnormal, unproductive, over-embodied solitude. Indeed, in Jürgen Habermas's account of its eighteenth-century formation, the public sphere owes its existence in part to a psychoactive substance originally consumed by men together in public that is only "addictive" in a narrow, biochemical sense, since it is now otherwise ubiquitously associated with alertness, productivity, industry, and reason: coffee.[85] Women's addictions thus developed completely apart from such a public sphere and in apparent opposition to it; while men's dependencies unfolded within it, normally in the *pub*, short for "public house," as a perversion of rational, homosocial community.

This public/private segregation leads to two gendered models of social relations in which addiction appears to mediate queer desire. Because the prescription of alcohol and morphine made women's addictions private, women's clandestine dosage of each other begins to resemble same-sex desire; their subjective pleasures deviate from the moral and domestic management of men to intensively physiological mutual self-gratification. Because men's addictions are more often enacted in public, in the company of other men, they have a longer and more visible history of coinciding with the appearance of homoerotic desire. In chapter 5, I analyze the way in which representations of queer desire, for men and women, are scarcely distinguishable from representations of addicted desire in popular fiction written between 1880 and 1920. The centerpiece of my analysis is Robert Louis Stevenson's *The Strange Case of Dr. Jekyll and Mr. Hyde* (1886), which has recently generated queer readings of the desire and identification between the two parts of its protagonist. I demonstrate that because the cultural signs of addiction and queerness are so similar, all of the textual evidence used to support the reading of Jekyll as a closeted gay man also supports a reading of him as an addict. Far from eliding a representation of gay desire—indeed, the commensurability of addiction and queerness in my survey of popular texts opens a new archive to queer interpretation—this chapter refines our historical pictures of both queer sexuality and addiction and their relationship to desire, identity, habit, and compulsion. Conversely, I show how addiction represented a queering of gendered norms that was nevertheless distinct from same-sex desire. In spite of this critical difference, medical discourse and popular literature used identical representational strategies to marginalize queer people and addicts.

The sixth and final significant development in the nineteenth-century cultural history of addiction is the concept's shift from disease and deviant desire to racial defect under the pressure of the discourses of degeneration and eugenics. Beginning in the 1890s, both medical and mainstream discourses began to represent inebriates and other addicts as social parasites, unproductively sapping life from the social body. Here, the racial politics implicit in the discourses on chattel slavery become explicit and begin to reverse: whereas earlier, the characteristic addict had been a white man harboring an inner, secret "slave" to the bottle, those racial signs of inner division now rise to the surface, becoming visible in a physiognomic register of degeneration and biological defect. This racial shift also indexes an imperial ambivalence: the addict as racially marked social parasite typically appears as a colonial figure feeding off of the white metropole, but it also has the power to expose the metropole's potentially debilitating, habituated dependency on its colonies. I read these related developments through two fin-de-siècle vampire narratives, Bram Stoker's *Dracula* (1897) and Florence Marryat's *The Blood of the Vampire* (1897). As a compulsive, degenerate, pathological habit, vampirism functioned as a metaphor for the ambivalent racialization of addiction and its imperial discontents.

As a metaphor for addiction, vampirism reveals the addict's apparent desire for and flirtation with death. Gradually, indirectly, the inexorable force of habitual compulsions seemed to drag addicts to the grave, where they could embrace the death they had been nurturing inside them. As an anonymous former chloroform addict put it in the mid-1880s, "I loved the valley of the shadow of death. I knew there was danger that some night I should pass over the line, into a sleep from which there would be no waking, but death had no terrors for me. Nay, to bring all my faculties, and powers, and ambitions into the sweet oblivion of transient death was the one pleasure for which I cared to live."[86] This description speaks to the mixture of seduction and pleasure with which death appeared to beckon addicts: being high was like being dead, the pleasure lay both in touching the void and returning, in dipping in and out of life. This fascination held a transgressive allure: in Foucault's terms, because power administrates life, "death is power's limit, the moment that escapes it; death becomes the most secret aspect of existence, the most 'private.' "[87] By choosing her substance over and over again, in preference for all else that "life" appears to offer, the addict appears to be incipiently or already dead. Within the larger eugenic imagination, however, this incipient death appears as the racial defect that dooms addicts to extinction, and that threatens the greater life of the race. Stoker's concept of the vampires as "un-dead" thus signifies the addict's racial status as paradoxically already dead.

These vampire fictions bring the cultural history of addiction to the brink of a twentieth century about to recategorize addicts as habitual criminals and racial defectives, denizens of a shadowy, parasitic underworld. In the afterword, I parse the political ramifications of the vampire's or addict's "un-death" using Giorgio Agamben's concept of "bare life," or life that "*may be killed and yet not sacrificed.*"[88] Those who appear as "bare life" seem to inhabit their biology beyond the political sanction of the classical social contract, in which only the sovereign was empowered to take life.[89] Since their existence threatens the national social body, they must not be excluded, they must be exterminated outright. The vampire narratives enact such eugenic and genocidal conclusions in ways that anticipate the twentieth-century history of addiction.[90] In the first two decades of the twentieth century, addiction becomes a matter for international control of populations and of drug supplies. As U.S. drug policies begin to reach around the globe, the scale and scope of biopolitics expand to contain the world threat addiction now seems to pose.

"Remorse": A Case History of Addiction

I mentioned earlier that this introduction would conclude with a story involving an early articulation of the disease model of addiction. On 24 August 1891, *The Daily Telegraph* printed a letter from someone identified only as "Remorse." This person had written to plead for help with his or her drinking problem; the appeal provoked a flurry of letters in response, which the *Telegraph* printed over the next two months under the newly anachronistic heading "The Slavery of Drink." Remorse's letter, which I reprint in its entirety, offers us a point of entry into the enormous body of similar stories that form the history of addiction:

> Sir—Now that the opinion gains ground that intemperance is a disease, may I acquaint you with my own sad experience? I myself at times take more than is good for me, but while doing so I can never rest. I walk on and on, miles and miles, up one street, down another. . . . If anyone I know meets me and speaks kindly to me then I can cry and I am better; but if, as is usually the case, my friends are angry and disgusted, on I must go, even although it is torture for me to place my foot on the ground. . . . When I am busy I am all right, but when I have nothing to do or anyone acts unkindly to me, I seem to fly to the anodyne of drink. Yet I am so much better in every way without it, and I hate it. I once went to a physician and told him my case, asking him if he could do anything for me. He said I was very honest—most people who were slaves to the passion said they did not drink to excess—but that it was just like a lunatic afflicted with some paroxysm of madness; that in the case of drunkenness one's friends were so disgusted with the form the lunacy takes that they were unkind, when, on the contrary, the poor drunkard required the greatest kindness and plenty of excitement. I know he was right. I could understand it better if I liked what I took. If this will be the means of my learning what to take

> or do, how thankful I shall be that I have written to you. I enclose my name and address, not for publication.
>
> REMORSE.[91]

If the details of Remorse's story are sad, they are also entirely unremarkable—no severed hands, secret habits, illicit desires, or biological monstrosities here. What arrests us immediately, however, is the way that medical authority licenses the narrative: "*Now* that the opinion gains ground that intemperance is a disease," Remorse can begin to unfold his or her personal experience.[92] If intemperance was a disease, the basis of its sufferers' appeals for sympathy were now personal and emotional symptoms, rather than physiological ones. Yet Remorse's friends still displayed scorn for an affliction they must have deemed volitional and shameful. If the condition was really like "slavery," as the title over the letter suggested, then how could the afflicted free themselves? If it was properly considered a version of "lunacy," then how could the insane bring themselves to reason?

Perhaps because such questions opened the problem to various interpretations, Remorse's plea had an electrifying effect, generating waves of letters in response. The *Telegraph* was deluged with an outpouring of personal narratives, as people attempted to substantiate or witness the new norm:

> I have read with a great deal of interest the letter written to your paper to-day, and signed "Remorse," relative to drink being a disease. I am suffering from even a worse state of things, and I can assuredly put my seal to everything which "Remorse" states.
>
> The sad but open confession of "Remorse" has touched me to the quick. I am myself determined to adopt the only remedy, namely, to give up drink altogether. I have been for along time "drifting," and have gone through exactly the same sad experience.
>
> Perhaps you will allow one who has graduated in that most efficient tippling school, the City, to offer a word of advice to those interested in the question of drink and its effects, now being discussed in your columns. I too, can speak as one having the authority of "experience."
>
> Will you allow a reclaimed drunkard the liberty of occupying a small space in your valuable columns?[93]

Such testimonials show that the metaphor of "disease," though it helped consolidate medical authority, also inspired the reading public to seize a new kind of discursive and authorial power in the public sphere. Ordinary people now seemed to have permission to narrate their stories of personal compulsion in public without shame, and yet many of them—not least "Remorse"—chose to remain anonymous. Although they seemed to be taking control of their problems, many claimed to feel powerless. And although habitual drunkenness was now being described as a disease, it was still discussed as a moral problem of self-control. Every aspect of addiction seemed to be mired in paradox.

Thus, despite the enthusiasm and volume of the response, the shift from silence to public discussion was not simple or even. Of the dozens of letters published over the next two months—a small segment of the hundreds the *Telegraph* received—many failed to enter into the new mode of public, anonymous intimacy and witness, offering advice that instead seemed both rational and obtuse: "My antidote is cycling—a bicycle for the more adventurous and a tricycle for others," wrote "Cyclist," who assured readers that the remedy "will afford untold pleasures." "Pour into a wine-glass a little Worcester sauce, a few drops of vinegar, and add some pepper; then break in a raw egg, taking care not to injure the yolk . . . and drink in one mouthful. It is very bracing, and I have known several cases where it has stifled the craving for drink," wrote "Prairie Oyster." Emigration occurred to someone signed A. Dauglish: "I would suggest that a colony should be formed in the North-West of Canada, where the selling of drink is prohibited. . . . The colony should be placed under the charge of a competent man, with a certain amount of power, and conducted parties should be formed and taken there."[94] The breadth of the suggestions—inebriate homes for the poor, stronger licensing laws, longer open hours for libraries and museums—recalls the liberal faith that social problems could be addressed through the welfare state. Arthur Conan Doyle wrote to suggest that "if we were to absolutely drop all foreign policy and all domestic legislation for ten years, and were to devote that time entirely to devising methods for stamping out this monstrous evil, those ten years would seem to our descendants to have been the most noble and profitable of the national life."[95] Of course, no state government ever attempted this strategy, but it seems likely that even such exclusive attention would not have solved the problem.

As the subsequent decades have made clear, addiction could not be eradicated, either from national or individual physical bodies; nor could it be separated from other social ills. Statements such as Doyle's index both the nineteenth-century faith in modern progress and—from a countermodern perspective—a determined blindness to the notion that addiction might have some connection to imperial foreign policy and domestic legislation, that it might take shape, not as the antithesis, but precisely as a contiguity of Enlightenment reason, liberal subjectivity, and bourgeois self-making. Indeed, the very pursuit of modern freedom and—in the United States, "happiness"—construes those ideal states as ones often indistinguishable from the habitual self-gratifications of addiction. Addiction explains too much because it describes both the normal and the deviant; it explains too little because the interlocking cultural forces of race, sexuality, gender, and class that help set those values too seldom get interrogated. Addiction could not be eliminated merely by detoxifying every member of the body politic, even if such a feat could be achieved. Rather, it could become something new and different if interpretive pressure were placed on the discursive conditions of its possibility. How did these conditions first come together in a way that made addiction a startling new idea?

I

TRAVEL, EXILE, AND SELF-ENSLAVEMENT

1

PIONEERS OF INNER SPACE

Drug Autobiography and Manifest Destiny

The reader, the thinker, the person who waits, the *flâneur*, are types of illuminati—just as much as the opium eater, the dreamer, the ecstatic. And more profane. Not to mention that most terrible drug—ourselves—which we take in solitude.

Walter Benjamin, "Surrealism," 1929

For the intellectual teenager, Poughkeepsie in the 1840s held few diversions. How else to explain an adolescent Fitz Hugh Ludlow haunting his friend Anderson the apothecary's shop, where rows of bottles offered "an aromatic invitation to scientific musing"—and also to personal experimentation?[1] Yet having sampled chloroform, ether, opium, and the handful of other largely unregulated exhilarants then available to medical professionals by the tender age of 17, Ludlow comically describes his plunder of the supplies with a telling imperial allusion: "I ceased experimenting, and sat down like a pharmaceutical Alexander, with no more drugworlds to conquer" (*HE* 17). Just at that moment, of course, Anderson reveals his latest acquisition, an East Indian plant used to treat lockjaw; Ludlow takes ten grains, initiating the artificially stimulated mental conquests of the minor nineteenth-century U.S. author-to-be of *The Hasheesh Eater* (1857).

Ludlow's autobiography and other books like it illuminate how the hallucinatory "inner space" of white male subjectivity engaged the imperial tropes of travel, exploration, and conquest that governed nineteenth-century conceptualizations of geographical space.[2] As the first U.S. autobiography of drugged experience, *The Hasheesh Eater* not only appropriated the genre established by Thomas De Quincey's *Confessions of an English*

Opium-Eater (1821) but adapted its British imperial model too.[3] Indeed, Ludlow's relationship to hashish transforms De Quincey's opium-tinted Orientalism into a version of Myra Jehlen's concept of "American incarnation," in which an individual could "know and possess the entire world, to penetrate to outermost limits because they are at the same time innermost."[4] This rhetorical trope, so characteristic of drug autobiography, helped define a particular kind of masculine subjectivity in terms that might otherwise seem contradictory: bold imperial vigor and obscure spiritual introspection. But in this emergent genre, the intermingled discourses of intoxicated and addicted travel abstracted white masculine power from its real racial and economic coordinates. For example, of his hashish visions in Damascus, the travel writer Bayard Taylor wrote, "My journey was that of a conqueror—not of a conqueror who subdues his race, either by love or by will, for I forgot that Man existed—but one victorious over the grandest as well as the subtlest forces of nature. The spirits of Light, Color, Odor, Sound and Motion were my slaves; and having these, I was master of the universe."[5] Because such a fantasy exhausts itself within the subject's own psychic space, it appears to renounce the real social power to which it owes its structuring language in favor of imaginary or fictional dominance. Similarly, although *The Hasheesh Eater* is usually considered an esoteric, politically unengaged memoir by an obscure writer, it and its emergent genre engage the relationships linking subjectivity, imperialism, and embodied and geographical space now at the forefront of U.S. literary and cultural studies.[6]

In Britain since the mid-eighteenth century, opium and hashish had been bywords for a particularly acute, sensory version of what Gayatri Spivak has termed "worlding": ingesting them and thereby bypassing print media altogether, the white subject could imaginatively create, enter, and roam Orientalized realms closed to the uninitiated.[7] This was an imperial encounter intensely physiological but also epistemic, since the drug-induced illusion of travel produced illusory knowledge. Jacques Derrida has likened the simulacral quality of this "knowledge" to that poisonous form generated by the *pharmakon* itself: drugs generate "a pleasure taken in an experience without truth."[8] Yet the social opprobrium reserved for such artificially induced knowledge has rarely coincided with a critique of the illusory, fanciful knowledge promoted through the pervasive Orientalism of drug discourses. Indeed, De Quincey's *Confessions*, with its narrator's opium-fueled, nightmare flights through Asian, Indian, and Egyptian landscapes, has become exemplary of the abiding racist psychopathology within rational metropolitan modernity itself.[9] In this critical model, the intoxication of laudanum, or opium dissolved in alcohol, cures the narrator's desire for travel to the exotic East but also installs a poisonous addiction that imprisons his English self from within.[10]

By contrast, Ludlow lingers in fascination with the psychic transcendence of spatial limits, which he adapts to serve the different cultural requirements of a westward-looking, nascent U.S. empire. Nineteenth- and early twentieth-century U.S. drug autobiographers and writers such as Ludlow, Walter Colton, Bayard Taylor, John Harrison Hughes, and D. F. MacMartin adapted De Quinceyan tropes of exotic mental voyaging to an underlying rhetoric of U.S. individualism and manifest destiny.[11] From within Anderson's Poughkeepsie shop, Ludlow mentally sallies forth on hashish travels through "boundless" space, a journey that would engage all of the tropes of the frontier experience, particularly the solipsistic notion that he will ultimately find himself within the vacant and magically expanding territory of the continent. Projecting the deep subjectivity of inner space onto the vast and seemingly unpopulated continent, the drugged dreamer appears oblivious of the imperial power giving shape to his fancies.

Amy Kaplan has identified a central paradox within U.S. exceptionalism in its ideal of "boundless expansion" that nevertheless discloses "an anxiety about the anarchic potential of imperial distension."[12] Kaplan's model of empire and anarchy mirrors the development, during the same late nineteenth- and early twentieth-century period, from a Romantic-influenced model of *intoxication*, understood as unlimited psychic expansion, to the more modern concept of drug *addiction* as the mire of self-dissolution and abject imprisonment or exile. Reconstruction and the frontier's closing coincide with the emergence, within medical and mainstream culture, of a model of addiction that rewrites intoxicated freedom as compulsion. While these are not evenly paced, much less causally related developments, the archive of primary texts certainly maps both the pioneering of inner space and the wandering-in-exile of addiction onto reconfigured continental and national space. Together, these models evoke a self keen to use chemical assistance to rove the continent and the world, yet anxious about falling under the influence of the Others it might meet there. Under the spell of hallucinogens, the psychic adventurer insulates himself from any actual "contact zone" or possibilities for transculturation of the sort described by Mary Louise Pratt.[13] The resulting texts display their own vexed and self-conscious relationship to the very concept of mapping inherent in both the drug experience, which is thought to chart a uniquely subjective trip, and the notion of genre itself, which gives form to the writer's otherwise inchoate, inimitable experience.

In these drug autobiographies, intoxication operates as a metaphor for mediated knowledge, constructing a preserve of white masculine authority that is rarely read in conjunction with more populist discourses of addicted compulsion. As a result, the drug experiences of writers such as De Quincey, S. T. Coleridge, and Walter Benjamin are typically discussed in terms of philosophy and aesthetics, receiving the elite mark of what the editors of a recent volume label "high culture," unlike raced and gendered subjects' experiences of addicted abjection, which typically occupy debased forms of popular culture.[14] This chapter describes the genre of drug autobiography, then traces three significant thematics within it: print consumption's status as the subject's addictive, deliriously sickly incorporation of a British imperial archive in the writings of De Quincey and William Blair; the mirroring of intoxicated self-expansion in U.S. continental settlement in Ludlow's *Hasheesh Eater* and *The Heart of the Continent* (1870); and the genre's postmodern turn in MacMartin's parody of manifest destiny as addicted exile. Throughout, we will see how the autobiographers' intoxication paradoxically proclaims universal mastery from a countercultural standpoint. Ultimately, although the extensive literature of drug-induced hallucination may superficially appear to be a counterculture of Enlightenment modernity, it actually neatly reinscribes its gendered and racial antinomies.

Tracing the transatlantic vectors of De Quincey's influence by recovering and interpreting the writings of his U.S. followers presents a different critical narrative than literary scholars have typically described. Alina Clej, for example, plots his formative influence on the "Club des Hachischins"—Charles Baudelaire, Théophile Gautier, Alexandre Dumas, Honoré de Balzac, and others—as well as on Continental modernists such as Benjamin.[15] In general, critical attempts to depict De Quincey's influence in his historical moment have only recently begun to displace him from an orbit around the Romantic luminaries Wordsworth and Coleridge.[16] Drug historians and literary critics have noticed the function of the *Confessions*, for a surprisingly long time, as evidence in medical writings as well as a totem for drug subcultures, but few have explored the book's relevance to the history of addiction.[17] The critical strategies of this chapter achieve three important objectives at the outset of this book: first, tracing the shift from intoxication as travel to addiction as exile helps distinguish different kinds of drugged experience—pleasure, fascination, incorporation, habit, disorientation, euphoria, compulsion, isolation. Second, charting these experiences in relation to two different modes of imperialism gives readers different points of entry into the century from 1821 (De Quincey) to 1921 (MacMartin) covered in this book. Finally, comparing the transatlantic sites of drug autobiographies illuminates the social power underwriting what has come to seem a countercultural or marginal political position.

Drug Autobiography and the Rhetoric of Canonical Minority

Drug autobiography differs from teetotal and temperance confessions and fiction, on the one hand, and from sensational narratives of drug use influenced by medical case studies, on the other. As we will see in chapters 2 and 3, temperance fiction characteristically adhered to a narrative formula that traced the writer's descent from bourgeois promise to destitution, followed by either recovery and moral transformation or abjection and death. By contrast, drug autobiography self-consciously flaunts its more elite, literary origins, deriving authority from the drugged self's experiences that is not primarily didactic or regulatory but scholarly and aestheticized. The famously stylized, erudite texture of De Quincey's *Confessions* can be differentiated, for example, from its slightly later imitation, the temperance-tinged *Advice to Opium Eaters* (1823), which more straightforwardly attempts to dissuade its readers from trying or continuing opium use.[18] De Quincey's authority is generated by the play between his firsthand experience of opium and his credentials as a philosopher who has read much and deeply; but these constantly threaten to undo each other, leaving the reader unsure of any value apart from the excessive, periphrastic, intoxicating prose. Following this model, the drug autobiographical form is only dubiously productive, a trait that accordingly shapes its content, the dalliance with the fantastic and idiosyncratic. *The Confessions* inaugurates the genre by both modeling and theorizing acts of reading as intoxicatingly anti-utilitarian. Margaret Russett has theorized this effect as a peculiar but powerful form of cultural capital sustaining De Quincey's professional critical authority in a position of "canonical minority."[19] In her view, De Quincey has always been received as a "minor" Romantic because he valorizes the addictive consumption of print culture as "the intoxicating boundlessness [that inheres] in the experience of reading," drawing a self-portrait "of the artist as a young parasite, feeding on delirious texts," rather than just writing his own memoir based on a purer or more original experience.[20] His prose itself models this consumption, indeed, conjures the autobiographical illusion of subjectivity not as unique personhood but as the very capacity to reproduce ideas from other texts or, better still, images originating in an artificial substance. Following this pattern, drug autobiographies use copious allusion and direct address to the reader, bending the conventional referential frame of autobiography in order either to imply their narrators' inauthenticity or to grapple ambivalently with their self-conscious status as textual effects originating in experience that has already been mediated.

Drug autobiography came into being within the search for originality in the post-Enlightenment period, indexing the tension between consuming and producing print culture. Just as De Quincey crafted his canonical minority in relation to Wordsworth's poems and their imagined source in simple or common experiences, so nineteenth- and early twentieth-century drug autobiographies obsessively reference De Quincey, for the often conflicting purposes of establishing their own literary pedigree and claiming the superior authority of their authors' drug experiences. Ludlow, in spite of emphasizing hashish rather than opium, feared "being hailed satirically as Coleridge *le petit*, or De Quincey in the second edition" (*HE* 215).[21] The anonymous author of *Opium-Eating: An Autobiographical Sketch by An Habituate* (1876) begins by warning his reader "that "in the perusal of the succeeding pages, he will not find the incomparable music of De Quincey's prose, or the easy-flowing and harmonious graces of his inimitable style."[22] Often these anxieties emerge as aggression: "The world at large has accepted [De Quincey's] utterances as the pronouncement of one who spoke with authority . . . it may not therefore regard with favor any attempt to break in pieces this idol of general worship."[23] At the same moment that these texts help form the genre, they invoke and disavow its putative origin in De Quincey's *Confessions*, reproducing and intensifying the effect of canonical minority, which shades into countercultural authority.

Thus Ludlow praises his forebear's psychic trailblazing: just as all poets must follow Homer, "so must every man hereafter, who opens the mysteries of that great soul within him, speak, so far as he can, down the channels through which Thomas De Quincey has spoken, nor out of vain perversity refuse to use a passage which the one grand pioneer has made free to all" (*HE* 9). Yet Ludlow's homage unconsciously expresses the paradox of following someone else's trail to reach a place that, given the context of mind-altered activity, can only be a uniquely individual psychic destination. What if, deep in the supposedly unique landscape of his mind's eye, Ludlow discovers his self to be merely a reproduction of De Quincey's? Distinguishing oneself from De Quincey was a problem for every nineteenth-century drug autobiographer, but the same problem inhered in the idealism underwriting the individualist model of self-discovery through popular narratives and fantasies of British imperial adventure and continental manifest destiny.[24] The resulting genre was peculiarly self-conflicted: each individual's psychic realm was supposedly unique, yet writers used similar substances to arrive there, employed identical imperial tropes to describe it, and exhibited similar hysterical reactions to the prospect of being read as "a minor De Quincey."[25] More recent drug autobiographies dispense with obsessive De Quincey references even as their narrators locate the authority of their memoirs in their supposedly scholarly investigations of the esoteric counter-tradition associated with their drug connoisseurship.

Addicted to the Archive: De Quincey, Blair, and Print Culture

The figure of the "addicted" student was embedded in English culture when De Quincey took it up, fashioning his opium-eating as the eight-year-long accompaniment to his anchoritic scholarship: "And what am I doing amongst the mountains? Taking opium. Yes, but what else? Why, reader . . . For some years previous, I have been chiefly studying German metaphysics, in the writings of Kant, Fichte, Schelling, &c."[26] Indeed, De Quincey's narratorial persona as a scholar conditions his authority on opium, which was otherwise a working-class commodity.[27] The association of scholarly reading with compulsive pleasure was a very old one: Richard Burton's *Anatomy of Melancholy* (1621) had characterized the masculine scholar's appetite for reading and writing in terms of "addiction" in the early modern sense of *devotion*: "The like pleasure there is in all other studies, to such as are truly addicted to them . . . the like sweetness, which as Circe's cup bewitcheth a student, he cannot leave off, as well may witness those many laborious hours, days and nights, spent in the voluminous treatises written by them; the same content."[28] Burton's allusion figures the scholar as Ulysses, the original imperial adventurer of Western culture, melancholically "addicted" to reading and writing because of the sensual mastery it bestows. More recently, Alexander Crichton's *Inquiry into the Nature and Origin of Mental Derangement* (1798), in a chapter on "Genius, and Its Diseases," had warned against the disorders "men of study" risked by indulging in "dangerous habits of intense study," most notably "indirect debility of the brain" and body as well as "a sense of languor, anxiety, dejection of mind, peevishness, spasmodic affections, and all the consequences of a debilitated fibre, and disordered state of nerves. . . ."[29]

Joseph Sheridan LeFanu would build a plot around the figure of the addicted scholar in "Green Tea" (1869): the vicar, Mr. Jennings, at work on a treatise about paganism, drinks green tea to help him write, and promptly becomes habituated, hallucinating a malevolent monkey. Jennings says, "I believe that every one who sets about writing in earnest does his work, as a friend of mine phrased it, *on* something—tea, or coffee, or tobacco." He continues, "I suppose there is a material waste that must be hourly supplied in such occupations, or that we should grow too abstracted, and the mind, as it were, pass out of the body, unless it were reminded often of the connexion by actual sensation."[30] Hesselius, who is treating Jennings, later notes that the "inner eye which Mr. Jennings had inadvertently opened" with green tea is the same one opened "in delirium tremens."[31] In the nineteenth century, delirium tremens, with its terrifying hallucinations and tremors, was frequently represented as the dramatic culmination of alcoholism in insanity and death. Brenda Hammack, reading LeFanu's story in the context of "the chemical intellectual," notes that "even orthodox pharmacologists and psychologists of the day were publishing articles in mainstream journals that posed similar prognoses for those who indulged in 'mentally abusive lifestyles.' "[32] This is an emphatically masculine discourse: with no supporting context of scholarship, women's habitual excessive reading was characterized by the unproductive and uncritical consumption of novels.[33] The common theme of this genealogical thread is that the excessive consumption of print through reading, though it affords the intoxicating sensation of mastering an empire of knowledge, can also become a compulsion, generating the false knowledge of hallucination. Although Jennings speculates that green tea, tobacco, and coffee remind the scholar that his mind and body are connected, his habituation has precisely the opposite effect: having consumed too much tea and print, his mind wanders into a hallucinatory zone, leading his health to fail. To this tradition De Quincey and his followers added the substances opium, hashish, and morphine as metaphors for the mental travel associated with consuming books.

If, as Margaret Russett has asserted, addiction for De Quincey "is first a condition of reading and only secondarily a physiological fact; it begins when readers identify themselves with figures in books," then we can reread the racist hallucinations of the *Confessions* as a fear of consuming too much print culture.[34] Consider the episode of the Malay arriving at De Quincey's narrator's Lake District cottage, to whom he quotes the *Iliad* in order to preserve his scholarly reputation before his servants and neighbors, confident that "the Malay had no means of betraying the secret" (*CEOE* 57). The comedy of this episode springs from the Malay's abrupt and random appearance: "One day a Malay knocked at my door. What business a Malay could have to transact among English mountains, I cannot conjecture" (*CEOE* 55). Materializing as if out of a book, the Malay already seems a textual figure; as the comedy of his embodied racial difference develops, especially through the comparison to the "exquisite fairness" of De Quincey's mountain maid, the scene plays upon familiar literary tropes of the foreigner as either a fearsome "tiger-cat" or an obsequious, "slavish" lackey inclined to "worship" the narrator (*CEOE* 56–57). This ambivalence signals the way in which the Malay's uninvited appearance performs the revenge of too much reading and opium eating. Although consuming both the media technology of print and opium induces delightful visions of the mysterious East or other mythic worlds, losing control of that consumption means that visions arrive unbidden. After all, the Malay "fastened afterwards upon my dreams, and brought other Malays with him worse than himself, that ran 'a-muck' at me, and led me into a world of troubles" (*CEOE* 58). In the nineteenth century, "running amuck" referred specifically to a Malaysian cultural practice that seemed to Europeans to place opium at the heart of savagery; under its influence, the vengeful Malay, "who is a prey to this double paroxysm of opium and frenzy, snatches up a sharp weapon, dashes forth furiously, shouting 'Kill! Kill!' and strikes everyone who crosses his path."[35] This spectacularly violent erethism suggests the subjective chaos of the addicted reader. Reading, like taking opium, implants images and ideas that can return spectrally at any moment, generating still other images and ideas, so that the mind loses all control of its own thoughts, descending into violent confusion.

De Quincey develops the association of the reader's psychic chaos with racialized revenge toward the end of the *Confessions* when he reports being "every night, through his means, transported into Asiatic scenes" (*CEOE* 72). When the narrator imagines the Malay's homicidal urges toward him, he links dying to a kind of transposition away from his English home and into an Orientalized textuality. This chaotic confusion of texts piles scene on top of scene: "I ran into pagodas: and was fixed, for centuries, at the summit, or in secret rooms; I was the idol; I was the priest; I was worshipped; I was sacrificed. I fled from the wrath of Brama. . . . Vishnu hated me: Seeva laid wait for me. I came suddenly upon Isis and Osiris" (*CEOE* 74). These rapid disjunctions replicate those of copious, diverse reading, particularly with that foremost emblem of early nineteenth-century print culture, the periodical, which compressed diverse locales and topics within its pages. When the narrator gives the Malay a large piece of opium, he swallows it whole and departs, vanishing back into the imaginary world of opium and print. The narrator's concern that he may have killed his visitor of course performs his racist desire to eliminate "the other"; it also figuratively asserts his command over a vast, multifarious body of print that otherwise threatens to engulf him.

This totality of print has an imperial character, and we can usefully adapt Thomas Richards's concept of the "imperial archive" to describe it. According to Richards, the imperial archive emerges when a Romantic fantasy of total knowledge becomes a Victorian mandate to control the flow of imperial information. De Quincey's writings appear in the crux of this shift, perhaps best exemplified in *Suspiria de Profundis* (1845), in which a youthful De Quincey gullibly believes a bookseller's offhand joke that the history of British navigation he has ordered will run to hundreds of volumes. "Now, when I considered with myself what a huge thing the sea was, and that so many thousands of captains, commodores, admirals, were eternally running up and down it . . . I began to fear that such a work tended to infinity"[36] To represent infinity, De Quincey chooses the chronicles of Britain's nearly global imperial presence. The anecdote demonstrates that the individual reader's terror at confronting the totality of print is also a problem of incorporating knowledge of the empire. Nigel Leask posits a similar formation when he writes that De Quincey's text exemplifies the desire for a "literature of power" that will stand as "evidence for a legitimation of one's destiny as an imperial power."[37] Hence the need to be an "English" opium eater is not merely to be distinct from Turks and Malays; it also means to be in control of the chaotic images and illusions produced when opium and print are recklessly consumed.

Revisiting De Quincey's *Confessions* in a review of Ludlow's *Hasheesh Eater* and Mordecai Cooke's *The Seven Sisters of Sleep* in 1862, D. W. Cheever sounded a similar note: "The quickened locomotion and facilitated intercourse of the present day bring us weekly to the doors of the Eastern nations; increased familiarity is producing its natural effects in the imitation of Oriental habits . . . books of personal experience are written by enlightened Christians on these pagan delights [of narcotics]; and, finally, the over-wearied brains, as well as the corrupt hearts, of this busy world of competition demand them."[38] Cheever describes the world-weariness of the common reader of periodicals and books who cannot help but consume Westerners' drug autobiographies and thereby develop a craving for Eastern narcotics. Later in the century, the ideal of the reader who could master both the information contained within print culture and his drug habit would be realized in a popular literary figure for whom the consumption of drugs signifies his countercultural masculinity, erudition, and British imperial command: Sir Arthur Conan Doyle's Sherlock Holmes. Although Holmes is routinely referred to as an addict, the craving for "mental exaltation" that his much-noted cocaine habit satisfies is really a late installment of the genealogy of the intoxication of knowledge I have been tracing here.[39]

The English immigrant William Blair's brief memoir "An Opium-Eater in America," published in 1842 in the U.S. *Knickerbocker Magazine*, was the first important imitation of De Quincey's *Confessions*.[40] Through his compulsive reading, Blair performs "the scholar's tragedy" identified by Friedrich Kittler in the delirious, overwhelming "intoxication" with the dominant discourse network of 1800, print.[41] The English scholar's malaise is particularly tragic because his imaginative "worlding" is always haunted by the geopolitical reality of the British Empire. Echoing De Quincey, Blair's text speaks to its readers from the site of an imperial unconscious undone by its own excessive vision of total knowledge. It dispenses with nightmares of racial invasion but retains the fascination with and fear of the imperial archive that produces scholarly subjectivity.

Mimicking De Quincey, Blair narrates his literary and classical precocity, the abrupt termination of his education, and his career as a struggling man of letters and habitual opium-eater. He begins his narrative by describing his childhood acquisition of a fateful, self-destructive habit: "a decided and absorbing passion for reading" that grew "to be a confirmed habit of mind" by which he "devoured all books of whatever description . . . with an indiscriminating appetite" ("OEA" 47). Addicted, he gorges himself on classical texts and opium, cramming himself with the corpus of Western literary civilization: "the whole of Cicero, Tacitus, the Corpus Poetarum (Latinorum), Boëthius, Scriptores Historiae Augustinae, Homer, Corpus Graecarum Tragedarium, great part of Plato, and a large mass of philological works" ("OEA" 51). Evacuating the space of subjectivity accreted through individual experience, Blair refills it with the archive itself, attempting to model global mastery. In the context of scholarship, excessive consumption characterizes masculinity because the act of incorporation bestows power, however fantasmatic. The analogue of this textual consumption, obsessive opium-eating, gives him a nearly omniscient power to conjure imaginatively the world itself: taken at the theater, opium reveals to him a "lost globe . . . worlds which had been destroyed to make way for our pigmy earth" ("OEA" 50). With this trope, his ravenous opium eating/reading forms the nineteenth-century history of that late twentieth-century phenomenon, the "media addict" who "craves to *become* the medium itself."[42] Alina Clej has historicized this position of the English man of letters as an affliction "by a surfeit of knowledge—a post-Enlightenment syndrome aggravated by the rapid proliferation of journals and books."[43] This excess of knowledge—which, like an addictive drug, is always both too much and not enough for its consumer—is the information that constitutes imperial power.

Opium merely bestows the illusion of archival mastery; it more frequently appears in the narratives of De Quincey and Blair as the catalyst for a loss of self within a sea of print. If the scholar can master the archive, he can rule the world; if he cannot, he becomes the archive's instrument, processing information himself. Josephine McDonagh has described De Quincey's scholarly ambition as "the colonizing impulse, the desire to cover the vast globe" that, obeying the logic of addiction, exacts compensation in the "loss of a coherent self."[44] This is precisely what happens to Blair: one night, high on opium and reading an obscure confession of a Russian fratricide to a French priest, he dreams himself into the vivid fictional scene: "I dozed while reading it; and immediately I was present in the prison-cell of the Fratricide; I saw his ghastly and death-dewed features, his despairing yet defying look, the gloomy and impenetrable dungeon . . . but there I lost my identity" ("OEA" 52). As a medium that accompanies and is analogous to print, opium therefore performs the scholar's imperial extension, expansion, and dissolution. Blair's immersion in the metropolitan archive and attendant loss of self spurs his emigration to New York, where he (mistakenly) expects to find less literary competition and to reassert himself as an author. This episode in Blair's narrative illustrates the necessarily transatlantic formation of the genre from De Quincey's text. Anticipating the city to be an outpost "where the ground was comparatively unoccupied" by native writers, Blair is disappointed to find no literary or journalistic work anywhere ("OEA" 56). Alone, penniless, and alienated in a strange city, Blair accepts a commission to write the story of his life as opium-eater in two volumes. Finding this work nauseatingly impossible, he draws his failed narrative to a close, biding time in Brooklyn and scraping together the fare for passage home. Blair miscalculates the value of his cultural capital in a former colony that now has its own literary market. To succeed, he must write original material about his own experiences, but this, ironically, only proves that he has imitated De Quincey. As an opium eater "in America," he becomes mere generic grist.

Blair and his narrative thus exist in the space between two empires. In the British one, the self is lost in the archive through a process of media immersion akin to, and accelerated by, opium addiction. By contrast, the imperial nature of authorship in antebellum America has been described as the cultural articulation of freedom understood as continental expansion.[45] Whereas British drug autobiography is linked to the textual consumption of an archive of imperial information and global control, in the United States the vastness of the archive is replaced by the immensity of the continent itself, in which the drugged individual must lose and then find himself. It would take an U.S.-identified author to enlist the drugged imagination in the service of a new imperial authorship and expansion.

Ludlow's Oriental West and Boundless Space

No writer did more to develop the De Quinceyan model of hallucinogenic travel within the contexts of American individualism and manifest destiny than Fitz Hugh Ludlow. Whereas De Quincey trumpets of opium that "happiness might now be bought for a penny," Ludlow reframes that delight touristically: "For the humble sum of six cents I might purchase an excursion ticket all over the earth" (*CEOE* 39; *HE* 50). Whereas De Quincey and Blair fretted about consuming print culture that constituted the imperial archive, Ludlow invented a solution by using hashish to valorize the mere simulation or fantasy of embodying total knowledge. Inspired by the success of Taylor's Orientalist rendering of hashish in *Putnam's Monthly Magazine*, Ludlow tapped his teenage hashish experimentation for an article, "The Apocalypse of Hasheesh"; the success of the longer memoir to come propelled him into a New York Bohemian circle that also included Walt Whitman and Adalı Isaacs Menken and that worshipped Edgar Allan Poe.[46]

At first glance, *The Hasheesh Eater* appears larded with stock Orientalist images: under the drug's influence, the narrator dances with houris, quaffs sherbet, and visits elaborately decorated temples. Often this imagery is exaggerated to outright absurdity: "I pelted with figs the rare exotic birds, whose gold and crimson wings went flashing from branch to branch, or wheedled them to me with Arabic phrases of endearment" (*HE* 35). As with De Quincey's *Confessions*, which emphasizes rapid mental travel between different locales, *The Hasheesh Eater* in swift succession transports its narrator, ensconced in his "marvelous inner world," from "the moonlit lagoons of Venice" to "the topmost icy pinnacle" of the Alps and "some unexplored tropical forest" (*HE* 21). "I may writhe in Etna and burn unquenchably in Gehenna, but almost never, in the course of the same delirium, shall Etna or Gehenna witness my torture a second time" (*HE* 37). In Ludlow's model, there is no rereading or study; the repetition associated with true incorporation or learning is transcended by the narrator's personal mobility. The torture of extreme physical sensation becomes endurable and even, as a singular experience, pleasurable because it is temporary and artificial. By replicating the range and discontinuity of periodical writing, such juxtapositions perform a De Quinceyan mastery of print culture, but they differ by dispensing with De Quinceyan nightmares in which the archive returns as uninvited hallucination. Instead of disorientation and terror, the narrator experiences contented mastery because, having distended his identity to the point of vacancy, there is nothing in particular against which he must define himself.

Using this strategy, Ludlow frequently conjures unidentifiable locations that are simply foreign: "Before me rose the buildings of a grand square, in some city whose name, whose nation I could not even imagine, so utterly foreign did it appear to any thing in the world of modern days" (*HE* 95). The location is simply elsewhere in space and time; the experience is alluring because it offers a sense of commanding "other" places and times without the cumbersome task of digesting information such as place names and historical periods. Within this representational scheme, hallucinogenic experience offered a pretense of imperial dominance of the archive by replacing archival information with generalized, idiosyncratic imperial fantasy. Devoid of any specific qualities, scholarly masculinity is preserved as a formal gesture of self-extension. Baudelaire critiqued this phenomenon in *Les Paradises Artificiels* (1860) when he mocked the typical hashish-eater's self-centered imperial appetite: "These museums crowded with beautiful forms and startling colors—these libraries that hold the works of Science and the dreams of the Muse . . . all of these marvels have been made *for me*, *for me*, *for me!* Humanity has labored, has been martyred and immolated, for me!—to serve as fodder, as *pabulum*, for my insatiable appetite for emotion, knowledge, and beauty!"[47] In Baudelaire's critique, the hashish eater narcissistically appropriates and thereby debases the accumulated achievements of Western civilization, precisely as happens in Ludlow's fantasy. Indeed, one imagines Baudelaire had Ludlow in mind, especially when he describes "the luminous abyss" in which the hashish eater "admires his Narcissan face."[48]

Ludlow's reduction of Oriental travel to the experience of a nonspecific foreignness reveals an intriguing reconceptualization of mapping and remapping as performative, imitative acts that, leading nowhere in particular, take on the character of rituals. He begins with the complaint that whereas "Eastern narrative" typically ranges far and wide, pushing the imagination "into unknown regions of imagery," Occidental narratives are "heavy with the reek and damp of ordinary life" (*HE* 11). Ludlow claims to have discovered the singular reason for this massive cultural difference between East and West; furthermore, he discovered it not through the Enlightenment method of deduction but by replicating the experience of Eastern writers' imaginative travel himself—by ingesting hashish. As Ludlow's map, hashish does not lead to the Orient but rather to an unknowable realm from which Oriental travelers borrowed their narratives' content. By imagining hashish as the magic supplement upon which narratives and cultures are built, Ludlow implies that the Orient was once as boring as the Occident before it discovered the drug's transportive properties. Ludlow's Orientalism thus differs profoundly from De Quincey's because it does not reimagine the East as a monolithic, exotic realm to be mapped, incorporated, and known by ingesting a substance. Rather, Ludlow imagines visiting the same places that Eastern writers have already seen and documented; his is a performative model of travel as imitated experience. As Sadie Plant writes, "He wasn't seeing the East in his dreams, but he was sharing its experience of the drug."[49]

Ludlow's experiences are less vexed by racial specters than De Quincey's, since he did not need to incorporate or consume the Orient in order to master it, only inheriting its empires as gifts magically given. Describing the ideology in which the frontier could endlessly supply the metropolitan areas of the East Coast, Richard Slotkin notes the magical plenitude ascribed to agricultural market yields; the repeating movement westward of the frontier's margin seemed to work like a magic trick, repeatedly generating wealth.[50] Ludlow's performative Orientalism operates with a similar reliance on the magic effects of hashish, which give him seemingly inexhaustible psychic dividends. This emphasis on magic abundance also organizes Ludlow's vision of Orientalized western landscapes in *The Heart of the Continent*: "It was as if some great agricultural nation had suddenly been driven out of its ancient possessions, or stricken quickly asleep by magic in the deep green groves along the river-bank."[51] Who will inherit these sleepers' vacant holdings? Analyzing similar imagery, Slotkin writes that "the oriental association suggests . . . resorts of fabulous leisure, the final reward of a race of heroes who have risen from drudgery to the status of aristocratic consumers or enjoyers of nature's and mankind's 'final goods.'"[52] In other words, U.S. writers could Orientalize western landscapes without forfeiting the valuable concept of "virgin territory" because the association evoked an incipient U.S. empire.[53] This incipience helps explain the disparity between De Quincey's British disgust for Asian antiquity and Ludlow's fondness for it. Retooling Barrell's infection model, Barry Milligan contends that De Quincey's prose discovers that East and West were never separate to begin with—the terror is that the English self had been invaded and compromised from the start.[54] Yet Ludlow is the precise opposite: "We sang the primal simplicity of Asia, the cradle of the nations, the grand expectancy of the younger continents, looking eastward to their mysterious mother for the gift of races still treasured in her womb" (*HE* 45). In Ludlow's hashish view, the Orient will give the United States its great empire in a process of natural reproduction. Therefore Ludlow's hallucinogenic version of manifest destiny relies not on the virgin landscape characteristic of manifest destiny discourse but on one birthed from classical and Eastern ancient empires.[55]

Ludlow continues to transform De Quincey's Orientalism from imperial nightmare to blessing, most interestingly by developing the abstract or formal features of empire: rather than an Oriental destination, he relishes describing hashish-induced imaginative flight and the experience of immensity itself. This trope unfolds when his perception expands; his view "stretched endlessly away," impressing him with "the sublimity of distance" (*HE* 21). This altered state becomes limitless, "a horizonless sea," and then expands again, to gesture at multiple infinitudes: "Through all the infinitudes around me I looked out, and met no boundaries of space" (*HE* 34). Such a figuration would appear to destroy the conditions of experience's intelligibility, yet Ludlow presses on to describe universal mastery: "Now I was transferred to the deck of this infinite ship; her name was whispered in my ear, 'The Ship of the Universe,' and the helm was put in my hand. With unutterable symphonies we floated out upon the boundless space, and on the distant bows there broke in music the waves of resplendent ether" (*HE* 141). Ludlow's narrator is no longer merely moving through space but rather moves space itself as he steers an apparently mobile universe. The question of where the universe might go becomes irrelevant; the ship never needs to land because the true delight is in the infinite recession of space. This recessive gesture echoes Slotkin's description of the magically receding but—in the mid-nineteenth century—apparently neverending frontier.

If we read Ludlow's mind-expanding experience in this context, we can make sense of its paradoxes: only in the context of manifest destiny does white masculinity find its own apparently boundless subjective depth in direct proportion to the subject's immense journey westward. At the same moment, Ludlow's helmsmanship transforms De Quincey's fear of British navigation chronicles. Whereas for De Quincey opium enabled the consumption of the imperial archive through reading, for Ludlow hashish simply bypasses this consumption, allowing its eater to experience the sensation of total exploration, rather than to command mere knowledge of it. In the context of the individual fulfillment at the core of manifest destiny, the experience of total mastery is more significant than its reality; the archival mastery can be simulated because its knowledge has no communal value.[56] What appears to be a detached, cosmic roaming through the universe can be historically grounded in a familiar U.S. ideology. De Quincey's concept of empire, like his concept of print culture, radiates from a metropolitan center, drawing the periphery in as he draws the Malay into his home and mind; for Ludlow, by contrast, mental expansion suggests dominance not through incorporation but through the apparently infinite travel of self-expansion.

The same individualist logic underlies the representation of continental space in Ludlow's *The Heart of the Continent*, in which he consistently valorizes his own spiritual experience of the landscape over its empirical measurement or literal mapping. Having practiced conveying limitlessness in *The Hasheesh Eater*, in this new undertaking Ludlow felt equipped to describe the sublime immensities of the U.S. landscape. In 1863, the height of the Civil War, Ludlow and the painter Albert Bierstadt set out, encountering what Slotkin describes as an "internal frontier . . . bracketed by the former Frontiers of the Mississippi and California."[57] The party traveled by rail to the end of the line, then headed for Atchison in Kansas Territory, passing through Nebraska, Colorado, Wyoming, and Utah before the trip's San Francisco conclusion. Yet Ludlow's text continually gestures toward destroying spatial markers, boundaries, and borders, opening up new territory in which to insert himself: "The traveler behold[s] such stretches of grass running to the horizon, everywhere level like the sea," he gushes (*HC* 12). Once out on the Plains, Ludlow writes, "for a while we were accompanied by picket fences; but these, in despair at the idea of limiting immensity, soon gave way to rails, and by the time we reached Lancaster,—a station merely, not a town,—ten miles out of Atchison, the rails themselves had succumbed, and we were running through an unbroken waste" (*HC* 11–12). "After the darkness came on, and we rolled away from Seneca into its darkness, I began to realize that we were not going to stop anywhere for the night. It was a strange sensation, this; like being in an armchair, and sentenced not to get out of it from the Missouri to California" (*HC* 13). Here the armchair functions as the residue of the British model, with its association of domestic confinement and metropolitan insulation with imperial archival consumption. Detached from the coordinates of home and city, however, the armchair also becomes Ludlow's new model of personal spatial transcendence.

With this emphasis on the individual experience of limitlessness, Ludlow combines a polemic against empirical mapping. Describing a mirage, he writes, "Our best dreams of beauty are generally of that sort, belonging to the soul, and not to the intellect. We hated to have this vision disturbed by Gradgrind measurements of space" (*HC* 110). The sublimity of western vastness echoes the metaphysical sense of endless space Ludlow had experienced via hashish. Perhaps that is why *The Heart of the Continent* consistently suppressed its instrumentality to actual imperial mapping—even though Ludlow and Bierstadt were conducting surveys at the request of the Smithsonian Institute, recently founded in 1846.[58] Ludlow himself took copious notes on soil, fossils, and plants that never appeared in his letters east, first published in *The Golden Era* and the *New York Evening Post* in 1863 and 1864 and later collected in *The Heart of the Continent*. Although the continent was supposed to function quite literally as the common ground of U.S. identity, Ludlow emphasized it as a private mental experience. It is no wonder that he repeated the lore that "many people go insane crossing to California overland."[59] Just as hashish dreaming ran the risk of conjuring madness, so too did hallucinogenic manifest destiny unfold as a bid for psychic transcendence that risked self-dissolution.

What does it mean that manifest destiny takes place within a hallucinatory dimension? By interiorizing this ideology, Ludlow appears to offer a quaint, fanciful alternative to the utilitarian, "Gradgrind" realities and materialities of westward expansion. Turning hemispheric expansion inward creates a vast psychic realm of aesthetic delight and a corresponding disavowal of worldly interests: the hashish dreamer is interested only in finding and contemplating himself, apparently an endless, Whitmanesque project. The vastness of both the imperial archive and continental geography are imaginatively reconstituted as the hashish eater's psychic terrain. But because imperial tropes govern these voyages of self-discovery, they become the model for the exploration of one's own deep subjectivity and the basis of one's ethical self-relation. Non-hallucinated imperialism then appears as the expression of one's deepest desires to know oneself or to manifest one's destiny, and it is revealed as a natural progression of individual freedom. At midcentury, hallucinogenic manifest destiny appears to perform a desultory, unique bidding that signifies as free "roaming"—a U.S. continental inflection of Romantic "roving"—while really being driven westward by the dictates of imperial ideology.

Not all of Ludlow's writings celebrate the visionary possibilities of altered mental states. Afflicted by illness and opium habituation through most of his life, Ludlow also wrote about addiction, most notably in the superior temperance novel *The Household Angel*, serialized in *Harper's Bazaar* in 1868, and the essay "What Shall They Do to Be Saved?"[60] *The Hasheesh Eater*, which had made his reputation, and *The Heart of the Continent*, which revived it, linked hallucinogenic travel to a distinctively nineteenth-century, white, bourgeois, masculine project of self-making. But the ebullience of a hallucinated imperial self would yield, in Ludlow's later writings as well as in later imitations of De Quincey's *Confessions*, a self distended and attenuated by addiction. This later phase of drug autobiography represents the underside of manifest destiny, no longer self-expansion but self-reduction or exile, a fresh perspective that permits a critique of U.S. continental expansion.

Thirty Years in Hell: From Intoxication to Addiction

In the period between Ludlow's Romantic hashish visions and Colonel Daniel Frederick MacMartin's morphine memoir/travelogue *Thirty Years in Hell* (1921), the phenomenon of drug addiction became a topic of medical, legal, and popular discourses, merging pathological and then criminal models with the older concept of vice. One of the shapers of this concept was Harry Hubbel Kane, who made a name for himself as an expert on addiction with texts such as *The Hypodermic Injection of Morphia* (1880); E. P. Roe consulted him in his research for the novel *Without a*

Home, which we will investigate in chapter 3. Kane also wrote "A Hashish House in New York," setting the Orientalized scene with a synesthetic hallucination of an organ playing the odors of flowers, "clear and sharp, intense and less intense, sweet, less sweet, and again still sweeter, heavy and light, fast and slow, deep and narcotic, the odors all in perfect harmony, rose and fell, and swept by me, to be succeeded by others."[61] Kane helped detach Ludlow's Oriental reveries from the context of manifest destiny and instead insert them into the faddish genre of stories and sketches depicting urban opium dens where the fashionable middle-class could go slumming: on entering, the narrator finds himself in a "dark vestibule . . . the boundary line separating the cold, dreary streets and the ordinary world from a scene of Oriental magnificence."[62] The craze for opium den stories, sketches, and images had struck Britain and the United States beginning in the 1870s; at first they appealed to the bourgeois urban tourist's curiosity about quaint foreign customs, but eventually they conjured the "dens" as spaces of interracial sexual transgression, deviance, and criminality. Gustave Doré and Blanchard Jerrold's *London: A Pilgrimage* (1868), Charles Dickens's unfinished novel *The Mystery of Edwin Drood* (1871), Sir Arthur Conan Doyle's Sherlock Holmes stories such as "The Man with the Twisted Lip" (1891), and Frank Norris's "The Third Circle" (1897) all represented white English or U.S. citizens decaying into degraded, opium-induced stupors.[63] In the afterword I discuss opium den fiction in the context of white racial degeneration, but it merits a mention here in order to explain how the exotic, Orientalized imagery of Ludlow and Kane ceased operating as a signifier of quaint intoxication and took on the more sinister connotations of underworld vice. The anonymous author of "A Modern Opium Eater" (1914) succinctly illustrated this shift from intoxication as dreamy pursuit to addiction as criminal pathology: "There are no visions of Orientalized beauty, no loving women, sweetly-perfumed, no luxurious air castles filled with jewels, gold and sensuous luxury," he wrote under the nom de plume "No. 6606," ostensibly from a penitentiary.[64]

A reaction to the Harrison Anti-Narcotic Act of 1914, which regulated the sale and nonmedical use of drugs such as morphine, the urban junkie subculture developed a new model of white lower- and working-class outlaw masculinity.[65] During the same period, the tramp subcultures that had sprung up along the railways after the Civil War had produced the cultural icon of the hobo, as a virile, "belated frontiersman"; as Todd DePastino notes, by World War I this figure "had become a staple of the new mass media and urban popular culture."[66] MacMartin's autobiography, which covers a period from 1890 to 1920, blends these subcultural backgrounds, telling the stories of his ramblings by boxcar around the continental United States and, by steamer, around the world; the theme of almost every encounter is his thralldom to hypodermic morphine, which parodically deflates and reframes his cosmopolitanism as hellish wanderings.[67] Rather than the hashish-tinged, sublimely transcendent soarings of Ludlow's texts, MacMartin describes the U.S. heartland ironically as a "new Utopia," a series of "boom cities" that represent the seedy underside of spreading capital investment, attracting "stranded humanity, scum and offscourings and human birds of passage in every stage of shipwrecked penury."[68] The alcoholic saturation of this closing frontier landscape has been well documented; less well known, however, is its status as a series of "dope colonies": MacMartin, searching for an eye-opener one morning, takes his first shot from a "bum confrere" and quickly becomes initiated into the narcotic subculture beneath the scrim of alcoholic mayhem.

Hypodermic morphine, which became widely available in the 1860s and 1870s, as well as its older cousin opium, were minor parts of demimonde and transient experience throughout the late nineteenth and early twentieth centuries, as other hobo autobiographies such as Jack Black's and Boxcar Bertha's confirm.[69] Its use as outlaw pathology is central to MacMartin's revision of Ludlow's intoxicated western reveries. MacMartin insists on his right to self-destructive experience in a way that directly contravenes the ideology of individual and national self-realization associated with frontier expansion: "Possibly while I was not free from the weaknesses of the flesh, I may have been above the temptations of the spirit. In this I must have been working out my own manifest destiny" (*TYH* 37). By appropriating the term in the context of morphine addiction, MacMartin proposes an alternative narrative of the self's emergence into a western space that is not sublime but already littered—at the very scene of its "settlement"—with the human detritus accompanying capital flows. MacMartin's Oklahoman landscape therefore cradles not the freedom of self-making but the criminality of lawlessness: "The hills, the uplands, the dense forests, the streams and the thickets and the underbrush invited these fugitives and held them under cover secure from federal or other molestation" (*TYH* 27). *Thirty Years in Hell* both reflects and engages the cultural shift from viewing addiction solely as a disease to considering it as a blend of disease and criminality; it transforms the pixilated delights of manifest destiny and self-making into self-enslavement and annihilation.

Hypodermic technology is crucial to the shift from Ludlow's model of intoxication and its metaphoric scheme of mobility and expansion to MacMartin's model of addiction as compulsive travel. The crux of this shift is the nearly instantaneous effect of morphine that the needle permits. Hypodermic needles were deemed far superior to ingestion or epidermal absorption, the other methods of administering drugs, because of their speed and efficiency.[70] In MacMartin's autobiography, hypodermic speed becomes the governing metaphor for the railways' accelerating continental penetration: he brags to his readers that he can shoot up "while the train rambled as high as seventy miles an hour, without the snapping of a needle or the puncture of a blood vessel" (*TYH* 115–16). The analogy between hypodermic drug use and rail travel was well developed in U.S. culture: the slang phrase "hot shot," which would come to denote a lethal dose of heroin, also referred to a fast-moving freight train. For MacMartin, hypodermic morphine, like the trains he rides on, "slays" or "annihilates" distance; just as morphine unites his body in a single euphoric sensation, so do trains unite the far-flung boom towns of the continent. The user's movement through the landscape at the high speed of modern life indexes both the rate of capital investment in a closing frontier and the accelerations of addiction. MacMartin's text updates and inverts another of De Quincey's hallmarks, his nostalgia for horse-driven coach travel in his famous essay "The English Mail Coach." In that essay, De Quincey lauded the "glory of motion" created in the sublime communication between horse and man, and lost with the advent of the railway. Whereas De Quincey's laudanum-inspired dreams of the coach swiftly spreading the news of "Waterloo and Recovered Christendom!" satisfied the longing for a triumphant, unified English imperial past, MacMartin's boasting of riding rails while shooting up enacts a profound disconnection, between himself and the landscape, and between the different points on the journey (*CEOE* 229). In this novel formation, journeys to new places are described primarily in terms of managing drug supplies until every stop begins to seem the same. MacMartin becomes the human analogue of the global commodity morphine, circulating around the world almost unconsciously.

Whereas a Romantic sensibility would connect such mobility with the consciousness of freedom, MacMartin significantly revises that idea by characterizing it as addicted slavery: Through "the *fiend intemperance*, I was for the period of upwards of thirty years a bounden slave to this flattering poison. . . . I was addicted to it not only in the U.S.A., but the mandragora had me body and soul as a citizen of the world in cosmopolitan ventures from the Land of the Midnight Sun in the North, to the mangrove swamps of the Solomon Islands in the South, from the Occident to the Orient" (*TYH* 12–13). Here MacMartin describes his wanderings as enslavement—a metaphor common throughout the nineteenth century in the temperance and teetotal literature that the passage at first parodies. We will see much more of this metaphor in the next two chapters. The intoxicated model of mobile freedom associated with Ludlow's version of manifest destiny can now only be posited ironically, as the white, male subjects that typically embodied U.S. freedom become racialized as slaves. Such a critique becomes possible when those subjects are increasingly dispossessed by the economic upheavals of the Gilded Age, disenchanted by the closure of the frontier, and criminalized for formerly lawful drug habits. Celeste Langan has posited the Romantic vagrant, rather than Marx's proletarian, as the true hallucinatory double of capital: "He is endless mobility and the endless circulation of capital; identity shorn of property."[71] MacMartin's addict doubles the vagrant's dispossession, since his drug-induced mental wandering destroys his capacity to put down roots in land or property, banishing him before he ever travels. Because his habit converts all of his ill-gotten worldly possessions into dope, which he must continuously consume to maintain his person, MacMartin's narrator remains—in spite of his supposed social privilege—unpropertied.

Within this idiom of addicted vagrancy, MacMartin extends the slavery metaphor and its critique to include the land run in Oklahoma. Throughout the nineteenth century, land ownership had been central to the conceptualization of U.S. identity and freedom; the 1889 land run in the Oklahoma Territory epitomized this ideal and its attendant anxiety about the closing of the frontier. Lacking any provision for government, in the years after this frenzy of "settlement" Oklahoma was dominated by gangs, prostitution, gambling, and bootlegging—spawning a legend of Wild West freedom as reckless license. The "hell" of MacMartin's title is both the personal torment of morphine addiction and alcoholism and the colloquial reference to a seemingly infernal landscape.[72] In evoking the seediness of an Oklahoma City dancehall, MacMartin significantly revises this legend: "The carbon dioxide created by fetid breaths sodden with cheap hootch, and the copious perspiration that rolled from these dancers, seemed like the foggy fumes that issue from a slave-ship's between-decks. . . . The dissoluteness and the abandon of these festivities were such that it put the promised land in a class by itself" (*TYH* 24). The slave ship, a sign of the international mobility of capital, ironically describes newly "settled" land, and rewrites dancehall delights as suffering. Investment might pause in the boomtown of Oklahoma City, but addictive consumption dissipates any property and contentment it might otherwise amass there.

For MacMartin, the heart of the United States is only an illusory "Promised Land," since its people remain slaves; their supposed exercise of freedom in the land run is, instead, a sickening compulsion. MacMartin infuses the longstanding metaphors of "slavery" and the addict's life as a kind of "middle passage" with a far wider criticism than they tended to produce in the nineteenth century. At the core of his critique is an analogy between agricultural exhaustion and the addict's worn-out body: just as land "denuded of its essential fertility" requires artificial fertilization, so do the addict's hardened tissues create "a lust of the nerves that prompts . . . increased dosage" (*TYH* 48). MacMartin maps the "promised land" of the United States onto a self-depleting, morphine-addicted body. The giddy intoxication of manifest destiny, of the frontier experience, and of the fabled land run are all converted into modes of unfreedom, exile, and self-annihilation. This betrayal of promised enchantment also structures addiction, which typically begins with a desire for transcendence and ends in abjection. While maintaining the genre's characteristic mapping of the drugged self against the landscape of the United States, *Thirty Years in Hell* also tends to reverse its political valence, bringing into relief a critique of manifest destiny, especially its function as, in Eve Kosofsky Sedgwick's trenchant phrase, "the propaganda of free will."[73]

Vibrant formal innovations help perform MacMartin's critique of manifest destiny, reshaping the genre's contours, complicating white masculine authority, and inspiring the later, more recognizably postmodern writings of Beats such as William S. Burroughs, Jack Kerouac, and Allen Ginsberg. For although *Thirty Years in Hell* presents itself as a confessional drug autobiography narrated by a distinctive, authentic voice, on closer inspection it is really an extended pastiche of unattributed quotations from the *Confessions*, Robert Louis Stevenson's *The Strange Case of Dr. Jekyll and Mr. Hyde*, Shakespeare's *The Tempest*, and myriad popular and classical texts; "MacMartin" inhabits only the interstices. Since his authority on hypodermic morphine derives from everywhere and nowhere,

MacMartin transforms the genre's anxiety over De Quincey's influence into more playful assertions of his superior authority to De Quincey, who he punningly disparages as "the dope" even as he steals his words. This literary expropriation both fulfills and mocks the conventional wisdom that addicts were incapable of telling the truth. Alternately challenging and meeting this expectation, MacMartin plays exuberantly with his reader as he trades his predecessors' aspirations of archival and imperial command into out-and-out literary theft: "In this volume I have assembled some chapters on narcotic indoctrination, and others which deal with the grotesque and terrible, blended with the farcical, the ludicrous and the emotional. . . . The asbestos is rolled up, and before you is Col. D. F. Mac Martin, who will, without the constraint of conventionality, serve the good gravy himself" (*TYH* 13). As such a compendium, *Thirty Years in Hell* functions as a metaphor for print culture itself, the combination of sources, voices, and authorities that defy a single experience. Dispensing with De Quincey's and Blair's efforts to consume and embody the archive, MacMartin's stolen patchwork text cheerfully breaks it apart and mislabels the pieces. This fragmentation mirrors the disintegration of frontier and other imperial notions of authentic visionary experience: MacMartin's title parodies narratives of imperial exploration such as Henry Bevan's *Thirty Years in India* (1839) or Richard Parkinson's *Thirty Years in the South Seas* (1907). Rather than attempting to read and digest such imperial chronicles, MacMartin ransacks them; his lack of real literary property mirrors his financial dispossession. The result is a constant invocation and deflation of white masculine authority on morphine.

Because the genealogy I have been tracing was amazingly generative, influencing writers for decades to come, it is worthwhile to sketch its range. A parallel path, traced by John W. Crowley, leads to the alcoholic masculinity of modernism seen in texts such as Jack London's *John Barleycorn* (1913) and Ernest Hemingway's *The Sun Also Rises* (1926).[74] But Ludlow's wanderings more clearly prefigure the Beat movement, which crafted its countercultural authority by rejecting mainstream pharmaceutical and alcoholic self-anesthetization in favor of a more ecstatic, mobile experience of U.S. space mediated by marijuana, heroin, Benzedrine, and hallucinogens. Jack Kerouac's *On the Road* (1957) engages Ludlow's fantasies of North American travel as self-expansion, substituting marijuana and alcohol for hashish. *On the Road*, *Junky* (1953), and *The Dharma Bums* (1958) also appropriated MacMartin's hobo aesthetic to critique the suburban legacy of manifest destiny. Indeed, MacMartin's text is a hitherto unacknowledged antecedent of Burroughs's dystopian visions of addiction as both the signature of a transient Romantic underworld and as the brainwashed abjection associated with mainstream U.S. consumption. Burroughs admired Black's iconic hobo autobiography, *You Can't Win*, which recounts opium smoking in "hop joints" and casual morphine use. From texts such as Black's and MacMartin's, Burroughs borrowed the hobo idiom, transforming its iconic outlaw names (Morphine Annie, Salt Chunk Mary, the Smiler) into the criminal identities of pulp fiction in *Junky*—"Pantopon Rose," "Louie the Bellhop," and "the Beagle"—and then into the more fantastic embodiments of "Willy the Disk" and "Bradley the Buyer" in *Naked Lunch* (1959). In *Naked Lunch*, Burroughs also translates the insider lingo of hoboes ("mulligan," "hot shot," "yegg") into an amalgam of underworld and fictitious slang ("junk," "mark," "Latah") and formalizes their episodic narratives into his cut-up technique. Burroughs uses these stylistic elements to extend MacMartin's critical revision of manifest destiny: "America is not a young land: it is old and dirty and evil before the settlers, before the Indians. The evil is there waiting."[75]

Yet these aspects of the Beat movement relied on the same imperialist gestures it seemed to repudiate. For example, Burroughs's critique of manifest destiny often undercuts itself, since addiction is both lamented as its ruthless culmination and valorized as an illuminating critical perspective. In his work, the drug autobiographer's vexed embodiment of print culture's imperial archive is succeeded by his grotesque embodiment of the "junk virus," which, as Timothy Melley has insightfully shown, operates as a metaphor for mass media thought-control; and yet also lends subcultural authority.[76] In this way, Burroughs replicates the canonical minority of his forebears, De Quincey, Blair, Ludlow, and MacMartin. Ginsberg and Burroughs also restaged Victorian botanical imperialism by traveling to Colombia to sample the indigenous hallucinogen *ayuahuasca*, a series of trips documented in *The Yage Letters* (1963). De Quincey and Blair attempted to incorporate print culture via opium; Ludlow, the continent itself through hashish. The Beat aesthetic similarly attempted to bypass institutional and mediated modes of knowing, striving instead for mystical enlightenment or gnosis. For Ginsberg and others, hallucinogenic drugs stripped away the conditioning of Western media, touching their human cores—an achievement expressed in terms from Eastern mysticism such as *satori*.[77]

Ludlow had figured the vastness of the United States as psychological, imperial inheritance from the Orient, accessible via hashish; similarly, the

Beats thought marijuana and hallucinogens opened the door to their own inner space, where the fruits of Eastern mysticism beckoned. Aldous Huxley, writing in Los Angeles in the 1950s, made the metaphor of hallucinogenic enlightenment as westward travel central to his definition of "man": "A man consists of . . . an Old World of personal consciousness and, beyond a dividing sea, a series of New Worlds—the not too distant Virginias and Carolinas of the personal subconscious and the vegetative soul; the Far West of the collective unconscious, with its flora of symbols, its tribes of aboriginal archetypes; and, across another, vaster ocean, at the antipodes of everyday consciousness, the world of Visionary Experience."[78] Even the more scientific literature on LSD that validated the psychedelic movement, such as Sidney Cohen's *The Beyond Within* (1964), couched its argument in the tropes of continental penetration: "The brain is an almost unspoiled wilderness; its exploration and charting have just begun."[79] Hallucinogens were deployed much as hashish had been by Ludlow a century earlier: by promising access to a limitless psychic reservoir, they also helped construct it. Books like *The Private Sea* (William Braden; 1968), *The Frontiers of Consciousness* (ed. John White; 1974), and *The Beyond Within* indicated that this space had become the interior shadow of colonized territory. The very concept of "inner space" echoed rather than inverted the imperialism underpinning Cold War "outer space" exploration of the period. In the countercultural discourse of the 1960s, the same paradoxical fantasy of transcending the self by exploring its deep subjectivity was also significantly embedded in masculine fantasies of omniscience, mobility, and other worldly—and continental—incursion. More recently, cyberpunk fiction by William Gibson and others has crafted masculine countercultural authority using the same Romantic logic of media dependency in which "an ecstatic mind" is, in the words of Alan Liu, "caught in an endless loop between transgressive transcendence and corrective legitimation"; only the drugs have been updated to synthetic and futuristic ones.[80]

Thus, in spite of MacMartin's representation of addicted exile, the critical potential of the genre of drug autobiography has been limited. Because the apparent knowledge of freedom that drugs furnish their consumers tends to be solipsistic and abstracted from intersubjective and material contexts, it merely echoes the cultural capital of "straight" or Enlightenment knowledge in a countercultural key. The insight from Benjamin that forms the epigraph to this chapter links yet another traditional figure of masculine canonical minority, the *flâneur*, to the camouflage that drugs provide for solipsism. Indeed, because it is idealized as intensely idiosyncratic, esoteric, and incommunicable, hallucinogenic knowledge ultimately gestures mainly to the social power of its subjects. Hence the longstanding critique that drug intoxication represents, in Baudelaire's words, "a false joy, a false light" merely perpetuates a faulty distinction between Enlightenment and countercultural knowledge.[81] Imaginary experiences—whether mediated by print or hallucinogens—have real social effects, just as unique, hallucinated fantasies are socially formed and, indeed, often recognizably banal. Drug autobiographies remind us that imperialism was continually imagined, reimagined, and hallucinated; and, conversely, that it governed the realms of visionary insight that were conventionally assumed to transcend worldly interests.

2

"MANKIND HAS BEEN DRUNK"

Race and Addiction in *Uncle Tom's Cabin*

Yes, in this nation there is a "middle passage" of slavery and darkness
and chains and disease and death. But it is a middle passage,
not from Africa to America, but from time to eternity,
and not of slaves whom death will release from suffering,
but of those whose sufferings at death do but just begin.
Could all the sighs of these captives be wafted on one breeze,
it would be loud as thunder. Could all their tears be assembled,
they would be like the sea.

Lyman Beecher, *Six Sermons on the Nature, Occasions, Signs, Evils and Remedy of Intemperance* (1827)

Mankind has been drunk.

Frederick Douglass, October 20, 1845, Cork, Ireland

The "Slavery" of Drink

Within the context of the cultural history of addiction, "slavery" furnished a powerful metaphor expressing the body's compulsive, habitual consumption of illicit substances. Nineteenth-century writers routinely invoked the "slavery of drink" and "slaves to the bottle," casting drunkards as the abject devotees of alcohol, here represented as master. The metaphor expressed the irony whereby the article that had once served the intentions and desires of its user became all-powerful, compelling that user, now its servant.[1] In so doing, the metaphor also distinguished a nascent form of addiction—known variously as intemperance, vice, and habit—from unrelated instances of intoxication. The literary stylings of De Quincey's and Ludlow's sublime opium and hashish hallucinations largely insulated them from the dire urgency of this separate discourse, which was shaped by popular rather than elite writers and orators and which was focused on alcohol, the most widespread and scariest social specter of addiction in the nineteenth century. The temperance novelist Catherine Sinclair captured the imprisoning repetitions of "enslaved" compulsion: "Oh what depth of degradation exists to which a man may not be reduced who is the slave of intoxication! Sinning and repenting—repenting and sinning again!"[2] If, as Michael Warner has claimed, "The temperance movement *invented* addiction," then it did so through an ongoing comparison to chattel slavery.[3]

This comparison staked national life and identity on a concept of sobriety and personal self-management as liberation. To draw attention to the "slavery of drink" in Britain, temperance and teetotal writers ironically invoked William Cowper's *The Task* (1785), with its confident claim that "Slaves cannot breathe in England; if their lungs / Receive our air, that moment they are free, / They touch our country and their shackles fall."[4] They also challenged the truth of the chorus of the unofficial national anthem, "Rule, Britannia!": "Rule, Britannia! Britannia, rule the waves! / Britons never, never, never will be slaves!"[5] In the United States, future president Abraham Lincoln claimed that the freedom temperance would bring to the nation would represent greater liberation than the American Revolution. In the temperance revolution, "we shall find a stronger bondage broken; a viler slavery, manumitted; a greater tyrant deposed. In it, more of want supplied, more disease healed, more sorrow assuaged."[6] Liberation from the "slavery of drink" articulated the highest ideals of modern political freedom and liberal subjectivity. But the metaphor was continually haunted by its vehicle, the ongoing existence of chattel slavery.

More so than any other nineteenth-century metaphor of addiction, self-enslavement organized and mobilized politics in a way that polarized addiction by race. Normally, the advocates of temperance and the advocates of abolition could count on one another for support. Activists and men of letters such as Anthony Benezet and Benjamin Rush in the United States and Joseph Sturge, R. T. Cadbury, and J. S. Buckingham in Britain wrote and spoke against both the slave trade and intemperance.[7] The two movements were intimately related: they were progressive, idealistic, rational, and patriotic. Both decried the "slavery"—actual chattel slavery and the metaphorical "slavery" of drink—that compromised national ideals. Lyman Beecher hoped that "ardent spirits" would one day be banned "by a correct and efficient public sentiment; such as has turned slavery out of half our land, and will yet expel it from the world."[8] Temperance and abolitionist writers considered the liquor trade and the proslavery faction to be their united antagonists; as another writer put it in *The Colored American*: "The reasons are obvious. The same principles that sustain the system of slavery will apply, equally well, to the justification of rum-selling."[9] The shared feature apparent to such writers throughout the nineteenth century was a callous disregard for human suffering: just as slaveholders and slave traders ignored the humanity of their slaves, so liquor vendors appeared not to care that they created and perpetuated drunkards' miseries. It may seem curious now, but the force of this simple analogy cannot be overestimated. In the 1840s, the link between temperance and abolition was so self-evident that the founding pledge of the Rochester Colored Total Abstinence Association resolved "that intemperance and slavery are the allied foes of the African race" and "that we will not cease to promote the great cause of temperance, as long as a son or daughter of Africa is in bondage."[10] Within northern antebellum reform politics, both white and African American, antislavery and temperance were articulated together as two linked visions of freedom.

But the metaphor of the "slavery of drink" inevitably disclosed racial and social hierarchies, since it operated primarily in the context of drunkards who were nominally free. Heman Humphrey, a white Massachusetts clergyman, could count on his audience not to blink when he claimed that the "slavery of drink" was a worse evil than chattel slavery: "acquitted at the bar of conscience," the chattel slave "can lie down in his cabin and be at rest," while the drunkard's conscience accuses him "of selling his own flesh and blood for nothing, to the most cruel master—of *buying*, and when his money is gone *begging* the privilege of being a slave."[11] The language of Beecher's quotation, the first of this chapter's epigraphs, similarly suggests that the self-generated problems of drunkards were worse than the atrocities of chattel slavery. British teetotal campaigners such as Benjamin Parsons also claimed that drunkenness was the worse scourge of the two: "Talk of the West Indian slavery, or the Russian slavery! the slavery of strong drink is the most debasing and most destructive of all. To this unnatural appetite everything is sacrificed," argued the *Teetotal Times* in 1846.[12]

I have found only one nineteenth-century writer, the British legal theorist James Fitzjames Stephen, who objected vociferously to the metaphor, in an 1891 essay arguing against the restriction of opium in India: "What sort of comparison can be rationally drawn between the case of black slaves dealt with as brutes and denied the first essential gifts of human beings, and persons whose faults, be they what they may, are the results of their own intemperance?"[13] The historian W. J. Rorabaugh concurs: "That men in the 1830s emphasized abstinence over abolition seems grotesque today. We find the equation of a liquor store with a slave market absurd."[14] Part of this absurdity derives from the subsequent history of the temperance movement, especially the enactment and repeal of Prohibition in the United States, as an outmoded, failed ideology; perhaps part of it also stems from the seeming ridiculousness of the idea of self-enslavement. As David Brion Davis reminds us, there was a lot of metaphorical "slavery" going on in the mid-nineteenth century in both the United States and Britain: "When radical American reformers later contended that the wage system was slavery, that conventional marriage was slavery, and that submission to any government using coercion was slavery, their rhetoric surely diluted the charge that Negro slavery in the South was a system of exceptional and intolerable oppression."[15] Douglass himself was more politc and circumspect when he made the same point at the time: "I do not wish for a moment to detract from the horror with which the evil of intemperance is contemplated—not at all. . . . But I am here to say that I think the term slavery is sometimes abused by identifying it with that which it is not."[16] As obnoxious as temperance activism against the "slavery of drink" may seem when compared with movements to abolish slavery and to secure workers' or women's rights, it merits attention because it reveals the intertwined and frequently vexed racial politics of temperance and abolition and plays a profound and overlooked role in the history of addiction.

Like his white counterparts Humphrey and Parsons, the African-American abolitionist, businessman, and Underground Railroad operative William Whipper had to choose his words carefully when he argued before the Colored Temperance Society of Philadelphia in 1834 that intemperance was worse than slavery: "Probably to no people on earth would this language be more objectionable to the present audience; yet I firmly believe it to be strictly true."[17] According to Whipper, although chattel slavery heaped "obsequious degradation, multiplied injuries and tyrannical barbarity" upon its victims, intemperance was "a greater tyrant" because "it despises the prejudices of caste . . . of nation or continent; but disdaining all local attachments, it claims for its domain the map of the universe" ("SWW" 120). Whipper's speech challenged his northern black audience to indulge in political universalism at a time when its most urgent commitment was abolition. Characterizing drunkenness as a social ill that transcended racial difference, Whipper shifted the African (-American) activism of the Negro Conventions to the broader aims of the American Moral Reform Society in 1835.[18] Temperance, along with education and economy, would be the key to the moral regeneration of blacks and whites alike. The short, embattled life of the AMRS has led scholars of African(-American) reform politics to claim that Whipper's temperance universalism "actually limited blacks to a white agenda."[19] The political deprioritization of abolition to a more generalized moral reform can be clearly seen in the metaphoricity of the "slavery of drink," which applied to whites more than it ever did to either free or enslaved African Americans. The "slavery of drink," though ostensibly uniting abolition and temperance to fight a universal foe, actually disclosed a political realm of competing aims and segregated temperance societies.[20] Most obviously, free black temperance found itself attempting to appease the racist order: "If [temperance] be left to the whites, we shall be as widely separated in morals as complexion; and then our elevation is scarcely to be hoped for. To succeed and be respected, we must be superior in morals, before the balance of power will allow us to be admitted as their equals" ("SWW" 126).[21] By the 1850s, white and black reformers had moved away from this position and toward the direct demand for immediate abolition, a shift that necessarily subordinated temperance and muted the metaphorical deployment of intemperance as "slavery." At bottom, temperance activism against the "slavery of drink" was revealed to be an irony of whiteness, since whites were the only ones "begging the privilege of being a slave."[22] As a cultural metaphor, the "slavery of drink" produced intemperance as a white phenomenon, embedding the racially charged politics of chattel slavery within the history of addiction.

Temperance fiction reproduced the claim that the slavery of drink was more horrible than chattel slavery. Lamenting his intemperate sufferings, the eponymous hero of J. K. Cornyn's novel *Dick Wilson* (1853) claims, "Often as I have seen the slave dragging out his weary life, have I wished that I had been born a slave!"[23] Supporting this argument was the idea that chattel slaves could follow the gospel and receive God's grace and salvation, whereas slaves of drink bartered away their souls.[24] Often temperance fiction and sermons pursued a strategy of graphic representation to support the claim that, as Humphrey put it, "intemperance in the United States is worse than . . . that traffic [in slaves], all dripping with gore, which it makes every muscle shudder to think of" (*PI* 8). In the prose of T. S. Arthur's endlessly reprinted and theatrically adapted novel *Ten Nights in a Bar Room* (1854), to portray the horror of intemperance, characters' faces are "trampled down, until all was a level surface," and eyes are "fairly gouged out, and broken up. . . . [L]ast night, his eye was lying on his cheek. I pushed it back with my own hand!"[25] Humphrey's sermon, which has been described as the first temperance tract to be published in the United States, begins by conjuring the spectacle of the "poor African captive," instructing his audience sympathetically to "trace his bloody footsteps to the ship," but it reserves its most wretched description for the "slave of drink":

> Then look again: at the self-immolated victim of intemperance—hobbling—ulcerated—bloated—cadaverous—fleshless;—every nerve and muscle and sensitive organ of his body, quivering in the deadly grasp of some merciless disease, occasioned by swallowing the fiery element. Hear him cry out under the hand of his tormentors. Follow him, too, through the middle passage from health and freedom and happiness, to all the woes of habitual intoxication; and thence through scenes of the most grinding and crushing bondage that ever disgraced and tortured humanity, to his final rotting place, and tell me which of these slaves suffers most. Ah, give me, you say, the chains and stripes and toil and perpetual servitude of a West-India plantation, rather than the woe, the wounds, and the diseases of the dram-shop. (*PI* 18–19)

In this passage, intemperance reduces the body of its victim more spectacularly and invasively than does the damage inflicted through chattel slavery. Humphrey's underlying implication is that the slave's capacity for toil and servitude—his injured but functional body—is preferable to the slave of drink's body, which can barely sustain life. Whereas chattel slaves can both work and rest, "slaves of drink" can do neither; underwriting this differential in degrees of self-alienation was the "conception of the individual as essentially the proprietor of his own person or capacities."[26] If in the political economy, chattel slaves do not count as subjects because they figure instead as undifferentiated flesh, drunkards are represented as constantly losing their skin, flesh, and viscera, and yet remaining ghoulishly individual, since intemperance "not only blisters the skin, but scorches the vitals"; it "boils away his blood," and finally reduces him to a "panting skeleton" (*PI* 14,16). This gory subtraction implicitly naturalizes the chained, whipped, and toiling black bodies of chattel slavery in order to stage, as an ironic spectacle, the dissolution of white middle-class physical plenitude and the liberal, possessive individualism that serves as a condition for it. The emplotment of this thematic is the central preoccupation of temperance fiction, which I explore at length in chapter 3; for now, I simply emphasize that this spectacle of white, typically masculine depletion works via dramatic irony, because the person most entitled to realize modern freedom is the person who sentences himself to the worst form of "slavery."

Accordingly, the least ironic version of the "slavery of drink" is that site where the metaphor vanishes: among chattel slaves themselves. Here, intemperance signifies no squandered freedom or inverted social order but rather reflects and intensifies the overwhelming suffering and abjection of slavery. Furthermore, its metaphoricity dissolves into the factual argument, frequently made by abolitionists, that both the trade in alcohol and the intemperance it bred were literally instrumental to the conduct of the slave trade and the maintenance of order on plantations. The figure of the drunken slave, a popular comic staple since the late eighteenth century, has the effect of exposing the implicit whiteness of the metaphorical "slave of drink"; in doing so, it calls into question the entire ideal of self-government, both of men and of nations, at the core of temperance ideology and the history of addiction.

Around midcentury, when abolition began to surpass temperance as the most important issue in reform politics, the metaphor began to turn inside out. A moment in Frederick Douglass's speech to a temperance rally organized by Irish temperance celebrity Father Mathew, which forms this chapter's second epigraph, succinctly deploys the inverted metaphor to indict the civilization that produced and nurtured slavery: "Mankind has been drunk." This new metaphor accordingly transfers pride of place to the abolitionist message over temperance aims. Within this configuration, white participation in chattel slavery is represented as cruel, unnatural over-enjoyment in the commodity of the chattel slave, signified by the master's habitual drunkenness. Here, the "slavery of drink" metaphor inverts, and "intemperance" becomes the metaphor for slave mastery. The "intemperance of slave mastery" is figured often in nineteenth-century literature, in the figure of the vicious, drunken, violent master or overseer who inflicts his own intemperance on the bodies of the chattel slaves under his care. Two figures come to dominate the racial history of addiction: the master, whose drunkenness signifies his vicious enjoyment of violence toward chattel, and the drunken slave, whose condition signifies the intense suffering and misery of all chattel slaves. These two figures dominate a text that has become central to the U.S. cultural history of chattel slavery, Harriet Beecher Stowe's novel *Uncle Tom's Cabin* (1852). Reading this novel anew through the context of the "intemperance of slavery" and the "slavery of drink" reveals the racial contours of addiction, which would remain in place long afterwards.

The relationship of addiction to chattel slavery in Stowe's novel is worth examining not merely because it illuminates their largely unacknowledged relationship within U.S. cultural history but also because it engaged longstanding, indeed, still relevant, philosophical questions about the relationship of affect and sentiment to epistemology and social change. In *Slavery, Philosophy, and American Literature*, Maurice S. Lee has laid the groundwork for thinking about the philosophical challenges Stowe's sentimental fiction poses. Although Stowe's novel famously claims that "feeling right" is the means to reforming chattel slavery, Lee demonstrates that the novel also paradoxically suggests otherwise.[27] I read this interpretive problem in *Uncle Tom's Cabin* as an index of the difficulty of theorizing intemperance, which characteristically prevents people from both experiencing and recognizing the "right" feeling within themselves. These difficulties in turn generate the specter of an intemperance—both as proto-addiction and as a metaphor for chattel slavery—that is intransigent and unreformable. In the 1850s, the related questions of whether or not drunkards could reform themselves and whether or not slave masters could see the errors of their ways were both indexes of the possible failure of Enlightenment ideals that would come to characterize modernity as the historical repetition of error. Pursuing this critical strategy, I follow Paul Gilroy by tracing the intertwined history of addiction and chattel slavery through the Black Atlantic as a locus of a "counterculture of modernity."[28] Likewise, I suggest that addiction—rather than the elite model of intoxication associated with Thomas De Quincey and Fitz Hugh Ludlow, described in chapter 1—operates as a material negation of Enlightenment perfectibility. Before we can get to Stowe's novel, however, we must first return to a large swath of history of which alcohol—particularly, rum—is the protagonist: the Atlantic slave trade and the "sentimental market" of consumption to which it gave rise.

"The Moral Market": Alcohol and the Slave Trade's Primal Scene

Before they became addicts, people first became mass consumers. For the British, this happened during the consumer revolution of the eighteenth century mentioned in the introduction.[29] The wider availability of trivial commodities such as tea, sugar, and luxury textiles prompted critics of the newly widespread hedonistic consumption to urge restraint in terms that anticipated addiction.[30] For example, in his "Letter to a Friend, Concerning Tea," John Wesley wrote that the seductions of tea "have too much Hold on the Hearts of them that use it. That (to use a Scriptural Phrase) they are *under the Power* of this Trifle."[31] Jonas Hanway also railed against the excessive drinking of sweetened tea, which was causing English society to destroy itself: "If we do not become more moderate in our consumption of [sugar] and indeed of many other articles, we shall find ourselves grown poor, and the cause of the decline of our wealth will be very difficult to account for in any other way than that we have *devoured* it."[32] Such critiques were motivated in part by an ideal of self-reliance and an attendant disparagement of dependence on inanimate objects and substances. British self-fashioning required the consumption of colonial goods, but only insofar as they did not diminish mastery, dilute identity, or deplete imperial wealth.

These ideals of personal freedom—autonomy, self-restraint, moderation, accumulation, sensibility—became inextricably intertwined with the radical politics of the antislavery movement in the 1780s and 1790s. By demanding that ordinary Britons give up using sugar, tea, and rum, antislavery activists hoped that slave labor would become unprofitable to planters; to this end, they contended that continued consumption implicated drinkers of sugared tea or rum in the barbaric violence of the trade. The British consumer's ethical well-being became contingent on his or her fulfillment of a moral obligation to the slaves laboring at the other end of the commodity exchange. Philip Gould calls this influence of sentiment upon enlightened commerce the "moral market" (*BT* 25). From the antislavery point of view, Europeans' unrestrained self-indulgence in the slave trade threatened to degrade their characters; as William Wilberforce put it in 1807, slavery produced "a most pernicious effect, both on [the] morals, habits, and manners" of the nations that conducted it.[33] According to Timothy Morton, sugar functioned as a metonym for the blood of slaves who were tortured to harvest it; it was the substance that morally degraded both its laborer and consumer.[34] In this discourse, sugar became more than usually seductive; its sweetness dulled the moral faculties, making its eaters impervious to moral claims. Asking why chattel slavery persisted, one antislavery activist wrote, "That we may have sugar in sweetened tea, that debilitates us—Rum to make punch, to intoxicate us—And indigo to dye out cloths" (quoted in *BT*, 30). The inclusion of indigo on this list shows that the early addictive imaginary was not constrained by ingestion but could include other items perceived to be frivolous or luxurious, such as the fripperies of fashion. One of the most eloquent antislavery spokespeople was Samuel Taylor Coleridge, whose "Lecture on the Slave Trade," given—interestingly—at a Bristol coffee house in 1795, put a fine point on the virtues of quitting the consumption of commodities that were not merely trivial but themselves harmful: "If one tenth part only of you [who] profess yourselves Christians, were to leave off not all the West India Commodities but only Sugar and Rum—the one useless and the other pernicious—all this Misery might be avoided."[35]

Typically, Coleridge figures in accounts of the history of addiction only because of his own opium habit, but his antislavery rhetoric was part of a much broader intellectual and political shift within the history of addiction. His statements, and similar statements by others, conjure some of the primary aspects of addiction discourse: rendering the substances themselves useless or harmful, they make their consumption irrational and immoral; sugar and rum become the loci of irresistible but meaningless desire, invested with the power to compel their users through habit. The problem was no longer simply the complaints of Hanway and Wesley, that consumers were eroding their own capacity for self-rule, but rather that, by blunting their physical sensibilities through habit, they were losing their moral sensitivity as human beings. Sugar, tea, and rum become distinctive substances in the history of addiction not for any of their own pharmacological effects but because they formed the crux of a new public discussion about the morality of imperial consumption. As formerly desirable luxury goods that metamorphosed into mass, pernicious, habit-forming substances, they became ironic double-agents of empire.

Antislavery discourse sentimentalized not just consumption but participation in the slave trade, too. Influential abolitionist writers such as the Rev. James Ramsay argued that the trade in humans degraded the habits and manners of white colonists themselves (*BT* 25). Such writers used the metaphor of slavery to describe the barbaric avarice with which traders pursued mammon; James Dana referred to it as the "slavery of vicious passions."[36] Commercial trade was supposed to be the participants' tool, but it took hold of their baser natures until it claimed the upper hand, until they became the instruments of their own viciousness. In *American Slavery as It Is* (1839), Theodore Dwight Weld used the vocabulary of appetite and desire at the core of addiction to explain that chattel slave mastery was not simply motivated by greed: "Though the love of money is strong, yet appetite and lust, pride, anger and revenge, the love of power and honor, are each an overmatch for it. . . . Look at the hourly lavish outlays of money to procure a momentary gratification for those passions and appetites."[37] Weld's language construed slave trading and mastery themselves as paradoxical forms of self-enslavement resembling addiction. Trade was likened to a compulsive habit. In some antislavery texts, this was true for both European and African trading partners. Describing African authorities' strategic turn from supplying slaves through the legal fiction of criminal punishment toward outright war and kidnapping, Thomas Clarkson wrote:

> When men once consent to be unjust, they lose, at the same instant with their virtue, a considerable portion of that sense of shame, which, till then, had been a successful protector against the follies of vice. From that awful period, almost every expectation is forlorn: the heart is left unguarded: its great protector is no more: the vices therefore, which so long encompassed it in vain, obtain an easy victory: in crowds they pour into the defenseless avenues, and take possession of the soul: there is nothing now too vile for them to meditate, too impious to perform. Such was the situation of the despotic sovereigns of Africa.[38]

Striking here is how closely Clarkson's language anticipates the terms and philosophy that the temperance movement would soon use to describe the drunkard. According to this logic, a single moment of folly opens the floodgates to pernicious habituation to vice; once shame is gone, the drinker has no internal bar to continuous drinking and, ultimately, self-destruction. In the same way, once African elites permit themselves to sell their people, slave-trading becomes a vice for them, too. This passage is embedded in a longstanding Western ethical framework about the hardening effects of unrepented sins; at the same time, the cultural moment it helps to define is a foundational one for the modern history of addiction, since it engenders the narrative of spiritual defenselessness and the multiplication of incurable vice.

A more popular version of the slave trade's origin literalized this figure of addiction, contending that African elites were "seduced" or "persuaded" by alcohol to permit European traders to kidnap their subjects. As every U.S. elementary school student learns, New England rum, along with African slaves and West Indian sugar, formed the triangular trade that organized the Atlantic world throughout the eighteenth and early nineteenth centuries. Benezet, arguing against both liquor and the slave trade as "potent enemies" of the United States, wrote that the African leadership had been "bewitched" by liquor into selling their people into slavery.[39] Clarkson himself elsewhere noted that "the Europeans . . . intoxicated the African princes with their foreign draughts."[40] John Newton, a slave ship captain turned abolitionist, attested that "strong liquor being an article much in demand, so that, without it, scarcely a single slave can be purchased, it is always at hand."[41] The historian Charles Ambler views this temperance claim of habituation skeptically while at the same time confirming the centrality of alcohol to the slave trade.[42] Significantly, demand for rum gave rise to European traders' impression of an African susceptibility to drink. "Excessive Brandy-Drinking seems the innate Vice of all *Negroes*," wrote trader William Bosman around 1700, but those living along the coast of present-day Nigeria "really . . . exceed all others that I have ever Conversed with. They consume in this all they can come at."[43] At the same time, this supposed predisposition was implanted and nourished by eager European slave traders, as Ignatius Sancho suggests when he refers to "the horrid cruelty and treachery of the petty kings—encouraged by their Christian customers—who carry them strong liquors—to enflame their national madness."[44] All of these writings make alcohol instrumental to the trade, but they tend either to depict innocent African leaders being seduced, thereby romanticizing them as noble savages, as Gould notes, or to essentialize their receptivity to alcohol as a predisposition or innate madness (*BT* 28). Abolitionists and temperance activists, keen to stop the slave and liquor trades on the grounds that they were immoral, leaned toward the former view: in their version of the primal scene of chattel slavery, Africans are lured into decadent European commerce by the evil magic of alcohol.

Historians walk this line carefully. Eric Williams writes, "It was profitable to spread a taste for liquor on the coast. The Negro dealers were plied with it, were induced to drink till they lost their reason, and then the bargain was struck."[45] According to Gould, rum therefore "functions as both the corrupt medium of exchange as well as the trope for a form of trade based on the intoxication of one's senses" (*BT* 30).[46] At stake is the politically charged and painful problem of assessing African responsibility for the trade, a challenge Anne Bailey has recently taken up.[47] Such assessments risk complicity with the historical invocation of African responsibility for the trade by those seeking to diminish white responsibility for slavery. For our purposes, this problem intersects, quite crucially, with another vexed question: where does one locate responsibility in narratives of intoxication and addiction?

Then as now, "intoxication" has often been interpreted metaphorically, to denote the magically attractive qualities of any commodity; that is how Quobna Ottobah Cugoano saw it as early as 1787, when he claimed that "the artful Europeans have so deceived [African slave traders], that they are bought by their inventions of merchandize"—that is, "gaudy cloaths" and "gewgaws."[48] Indeed, the conflation of alcohol with "baubles" figures prominently in the history of British and French colonial trade with Native Americans. In 1744, Governor George Thomas of Pennsylvania wrote, "Our Traders in defiance of the law carry Spirituous Liquors amongst [Indians], and take Advantage of their inordinate Appetite for it to Cheat them of their Skins, and their Wampum, which is their Money, and often to Debauch their Wives into the Bargain."[49] But early nineteenth-century abolitionists and temperance activists, more keen on eradicating liquor than on critiquing exploitative trade, interpreted "intoxication" literally to mean rum. "One of [intemperance's] earliest achievements," said William Whipper, "was to secure the 'slave trade' by inducing the native Africans to sell their brethren while under its influence, and by that artifice it was effected" ("SWW" 124). Such statements constructed alcohol as the ultimate commodity fetish, so utterly valueless and poisonous that it would only be purchased under the influence of a demented reverie that, in circular fashion, it itself induces in primitive, susceptible people. For the trade to carry on over centuries, the temporary intoxication had to be repeated, forming a habit or addiction.

An important raced distinction emerges here: for the Europeans, the slave trade was what we might regard as a metaphorical addiction insofar as their greed wore down their better moral nature into the grooves of a malicious habit. Within the counterpart sphere of consumption, this habit could be cured discursively, through a shock tactic Morton has described, with respect to drinking tea sweetened with sugar produced by the forced labor of slaves, as "blood sugar": "The flows of blood, rum, and tea are all pooled in the same place, generating revulsion (and revolution)."[50] Using this rhetorical strategy, antislavery reformers attempted to convince their generally female readers to stop sweetening their tea. In this discourse, sugar is a luxury food that can be taken or refused. By contrast, Africans and Native Americans are thought to lack the cognitive capacity to distinguish value and to reason. Insofar as they are "addicted," it is because their simpler natures are more open and susceptible to influence, namely the literal intoxication that attends the consumption of alcohol, which becomes a special category of commodity that they cannot take or decline, forming an addiction that cannot be cured through discursive appeals. Therefore, insofar as alcohol prevents white traders and consumers from participating in the sentimental market because of the drunken lack of feeling and blunted cognition it induces, they are approximating raced subjects already victimized by vicious commerce. Within this cultural logic, a nascent discourse of addiction centered on alcohol glimmers into being as something distinct from wider, sensory intoxication by the new world of goods. But this raced disparity and convergence will carry over to the cultural narrative's next phase, the space of slave labor on the plantation.

Cruel Habits: Intemperance and Plantation Slavery

Within the abolitionist-temperance critique, the intemperance of the slave trade did not end when the transaction was completed but rather extended to the overall conduct of chattel slavery, particularly plantation management. The figure of the drunken planter appears as early as 1791, in Rush's *Enquiry into the Effects of Spiritous Liquors*, as the textbook example of alcohol-induced dropsy: "This disorder begins first in the lower limbs, and gradually extends itself throughout the whole body. I have been told that the merchants in Charleston, South Carolina, never trust the planters when spirits have produced the first symptom of this disorder upon them. It is very natural to suppose that industry and virtue have become extinct in that man, whose legs and feet are swelled, from the use of spirituous liquors."[51] Rush establishes the paradigm of the planter physically and morally debilitated by excessive drinking. Well after the official end of the slave trade in 1807, the generations that fought chattel slavery in the United States continued to maintain that slavery blunted moral sense and human affect—a belief shared by, among others, Harriet Beecher Stowe, Lydia Maria Child, Harriet Jacobs, and Ralph Waldo Emerson.[52] The critique coalesced in the figure of the master or overseer in thrall to an excessive appetite, of which his own enslavement to drink was a sign. In the abolitionist imaginary, the planter class had long been depicted as habituated to luxury and inactivity, since it lived off the stolen labor of its slaves: "While the slave worked, the planter 'lolled under the shade of the piazza, drinking, smoking, talking, sleeping,' or else he squandered a year's profits on racing, gambling, or the luxuries of city life."[53]

Such enfeebling activities were linked to another well-known vice of elite southern white men, their supposed sexual profligacy, which was thought to ruin their reproductive abilities.[54] "Drinking accompanied gaming, horse racing, dueling, and the pursuit of young black women," observes Rorabaugh.[55] But this emphasis on luxury also encompassed a coarse taste for brutality among plantation overseers and those masters of smaller farming operations who acted as their own overseers. Donald Yacovone notes that, to abolitionists, "slaveholders seemed drunk with power, and all of society anesthetized by proslavery arguments."[56] And these were not merely punchy metaphors: the specter of the drunken overseer, which gathered critical mass in slave narratives and testimony after 1830, helped signal a shift from the temperance politics of the "slavery of drink" engaged by Beecher, Humphrey, and Whipper to the politics of the "intemperance of slavery," in which abolitionism became the more imperative social issue to address.

The drunken overseer is a common figure in Frederick Douglass's autobiographies, steeped in the irony that the master could not master himself. For example, in *My Bondage and My Freedom*, Mr. Plummer is characterized by liquor, insanity, and violence toward slaves: "This overseer—a Mr. Plummer—was a man like most of his class, little better than a human brute; and, in addition to his general profligacy and repulsive coarseness, the creature was a miserable drunkard. . . . In a fit of drunken madness, he committed the outrage which brought the young woman in question down to my old master's for protection."[57] Douglass's language reverses the polarities of chattel slavery: the slave is no longer the "human brute," a category now reserved for the masters and overseers. Drunken violence is represented as a form of insanity, but this temporary mental state is nevertheless merely an extension of Plummer's normal "coarseness."

The drunken, abusive slave master also appears in slave narratives such as Francis Fedric's *Life and Sufferings of Francis Fedric* (1859) and *Slave Life in Virginia and Kentucky* (1863) and William Craft's *Running a Thousand Miles for Freedom* (1860).[58] In Fedric's *Slave Life*, the drunken young master often loiters in the kitchen; as the eponymous narrator relates, "[I] soon began to wish that I was a field-hand, for day by day he was drunk and hanging about. . . . I began to have a terrible life of it."[59] As in the other narratives, violence coincided with the master's intoxication: "He would cut at me, or when drunk would make me stand with my hands down, and strike me in the face and ribs, and threaten, if I got out of his way, to shoot me with his revolver, which he always carried with him."[60] In Craft's narrative, the drunken slave dealer Hoskens purchases the beautiful, chaste Antoinette for his sexual convenience, but after she throws herself out a window rather than endure his intoxicated embrace, "he drank more than ever, and in a short time died, raving mad with delirium tremens."[61] Another evil owner, Slator, gets drunk while transporting his newly purchased chattel, children he had cheated out of their master's inheritance—"like most tipsy men, [he] thought he was all right; and as he had with him some of the ruined family's best brandy and wine, such as he had not been accustomed to, and being a thirsty soul, he drank till the reins fell from his fingers."[62] When the coach crashes, the slaves handcuff him and make their escape. In this little tale of poetic justice, the master's drunkenness is the sign not just of his viciousness but also of his incompetence; it is the plot point that permits the literal transfer of chains from slaves to master. Ethically evacuated by their fatal decisions to collude with slavery, Plummer and his ilk demonstrate that drunkenness is merely a symptom of the larger dependency on chattel slavery.

In abolitionist writing, the master's brutish drunkenness often appears as the sign of a perverse overindulgence in the trade or, put differently, of over-consumption of his chattel slaves. In the *Narrative of the Life of Moses Grandy* (1843), the link between the master's physical economy of drink and the slave trade is rendered in a single succinct sentence: "The master, Bill Grandy, whose slave I was born, was a hard-drinking man: he sold away many slaves."[63] The speed of the master's dissolution, via drink, into incapacity and debt accelerated the pace at which the trade severed families and disrupted slaves' lives. Fitz Hugh Ludlow, who, as author of *The Hasheesh Eater* (1857) promoted the lofty, spiritual intoxications of hashish, did not hesitate to portray slave masters' monstrous appetites, as if they were feeding directly off their slaves. In "If Massa Put Guns into Our Han's," his remarkable essay mocking the Confederacy's threat to arm slaves against the North, Ludlow relates an account of "Mossa Cutter," who inherited a South Carolina plantation; the proceeds of its sale "rapidly disappeared at horse-races, poker-parties, cock-fights, and rum-shops. If Mossa Cutter speculated, he was always unsuccessful, because he was always hotheaded and always drunk." Cutter runs through his money and sells away the wife and child of one of his slaves, Sol: "Four doors away Mossa Cutter could be seen between the flaunting red curtains of a bar-room window, drinking Sol's heart's blood at sixpence the tumblerful."[64] Ludlow demonstrates the inequities of chattel slavery by showing how its proceeds finance nothing but dissipation; it converts Sol's noble love for his family into drunken slave-master's poison.

In his discussion of slavery as parasitism, Orlando Patterson notes: "When the conceptual framework of parasitism is used . . . the dominator, in the process of dominating and making another individual dependent, also makes himself (the dominator) dependent. . . . [T]he slaveholder fed on the slave to gain the very direct satisfactions of power over another, honor enhancement, and authority."[65] The trope of liquor-drinking as blood-drinking activates the antislavery discourse warning against the bloody teacup even as it engages a certain progressive ambivalence, the odd mixture of outrage at plantation violence and fears of racial contamination. In chapter 6, we will see how this ambivalence develops in Florence Marryat's novel *The Blood of the Vampire* (1897), in which a West Indian heiress discovers that her vampiric identity results from both her planter father's sadism and her mulatto mother's black blood. Ludlow's account is more straightforward: he accentuates the ethical deficit of intemperate slavery by recalling how, when Mossa Cutter returns home one night "with *mania a potu*," demanding a decanter of brandy from his teenage quadroon servant, the slave protests: " 'Oh, don't, *dear* Mossa! you surely kill you'self!' Upon this, his master, damning him for a 'saucy, disobedient nigger,' drew his bowie-knife and inflicted on him a frightful wound across the abdomen, from which he died the next day."[66] The ironies in this anecdote all derive from Cutter's lack of self-care, signified by his pathological drunkenness. Having eroded his own moral nature, he becomes a danger to others. The fatal violence against the slave is an extension of the violence Cutter routinely inflicts on himself—and from which the slave had tried to save him.

Here, habituation to alcohol is not merely a technology that enables the violence of chattel slavery to take place; it is also a sign of the slave master's profound neglect of himself. Douglass demonstrates this generalized neglect through the overseer who is perhaps the cruelest of them all, Mr. Sevier, who abuses himself through tobacco rather than alcohol: "Nature, or his cruel habits, had given to his face an expression of unusual savageness, even for a slave-driver. Tobacco and rage had worn his teeth short, and nearly every sentence that escaped their compressed grating, was commenced or concluded with some outburst of profanity."[67] Here, the unnatural habits of "tobacco and rage" deform Sevier's body, grinding his teeth down as he metaphorically consumes himself in a kind of continuously savage self-cannibalism. The temperance movement also vilified tobacco use; tobacco was occasionally substituted for alcohol as a euphemistic gesture of discretion in discussions of habitual drunkenness.[68] But the sign of the slaver's generalized viciousness was far more frequently drunkenness. Weld had depicted slave masters and drivers corrupted by their own exercise of power in what would become the language of addiction: "The more absolute the power, the stronger the desire for it; and the more it is desired, the more its exercise is enjoyed."[69] This was the intemperate enjoyment of self-destruction turned upon others and transformed into cruel atrocity. Unlike Humphrey's earlier half-dead "panting skeletons," these drunkards generated a violent rage that eroded their own bodies and souls, attacking those within their power. They formed the antithesis of Benjamin Franklin's ideal of the well-regulated, disciplined, examined self, a state Franklin insisted was best achieved through the virtue of temperance: "Eat not to Dullness / Drink not to Elevation."[70]

Just as, via alcohol, vicious traders were thought to have infected African kings with their moral callousness, so too did drunken masters seem to communicate their own lack of self-care to their slaves. In general, slaves did not usually indulge in drunkenness. Indeed, Eugene Genovese documents their great sobriety in spite of the easy availability of alcohol; he attributes it to the effect of preaching and strong community ties.[71] Furthermore, both Genovese and Herd recount planters' fear of slaves' drunkenness as a possible fomenter of rebellion and accordingly attempted to restrict the sale of liquor to slaves as well as slaves' access to grogshops.[72] And obviously excessive slave drunkenness would have curtailed plantation efficiency.[73] And yet inducing drunkenness and nausea among slaves also appears to have been a technique of keeping them distracted and docile. In his *Narrative*, Douglass describes how drunkenness was systematically encouraged in order to forestall rebellion by quelling slaves' desire for freedom. During the holidays, Douglass reports, most of the slaves "engaged in such sports and merriments as playing ball, wrestling, running foot-races, fiddling, dancing and drinking whisky; and this latter mode of spending the time was by far the most agreeable to the feelings of our masters. . . . It was deemed a disgrace not to get drunk at Christmas."[74] Harriet Jacobs notes the collection of rum by the slave performers of the Johnkannaus, who "carry the rum home in jugs, to have a carousal."[75] Here drinking is supposedly one of many fun activities designed to give slaves relief from their everyday labor. But as Douglass reveals, the masters' objectives are far more sinister:

> The slaveholders not only like to see the slave drink of his own accord, but will adopt various plans to make him drunk. One plan is, to make bets on their slaves, as to who can drink the most whisky without getting drunk; and in this way they succeed in getting whole multitudes to drink to excess. Thus, when the slave asks for virtuous freedom, the cunning slaveholder, knowing his ignorance, cheats him with a dose of vicious dissipation, artfully labeled with the name of liberty. The most of us used to drink it down, and the result was just what might be supposed: many of us were led to think that there was little to choose between liberty and slavery. We felt, and very properly too, that we had almost as well be slaves to man as to rum.[76]

Here Douglass employs the slavery metaphor of drink to reflect on the nature of freedom. By passing extreme drunkenness off as the pleasures of freedom, slave masters suggest to slaves that freedom is not "virtuous" but vicious, not worth desiring or designing for. The nausea and self-disgust following such competitive drinking is "almost" as bad as the violence and suffering of chattel slavery itself. This confirms and complicates Saidiya Hartman's insight that "the instrumental recreations of plantation management document the investment in and obsession with 'black enjoyment' and the significance of these orchestrated amusements as part of a larger effort to dissimulate the extreme violence of the institution and disavow the pain of captivity."[77] Although Hartman does not mention it specifically, drunkenness and its concomitant nausea may be the perfect example of the ambivalence with which the slaves' "pleasure was ensnared in a web of domination, accumulation, abjection, resignation, and possibility."[78] Since masters attempted to stage slaves' nausea as the outcome of their drunken frivolity, this sickness certainly counts as a form of intimate, institutional violence.

By midcentury, the focus on the plantation context allowed the trader and the "primal scene" of the African elites' "seduction" by alcohol to drop out of abolitionist-temperance arguments. However, it was submerged and restaged in the abolitionist imaginary of everyday plantation life. These scenes of masters' drunken violence and slaves' drunken degradation accentuated the racial polarities of intemperate slavery, so that habitual drunkenness came to signify an original white ethical deficit that, communicated to chattel slaves, represents their miring in a degraded system from which they cannot free themselves. This racial polarity is significant for the history of addiction, because it positions the phenomenon as white self-destruction and black lack of agency to resist white racist violence; these racial valuations would continue to shape narratives of addiction long after the moral and ethical model of intemperance gave way to the medical model of disease. In this context, we should return to a text that has been a byword for the abolitionist movement's intervention in the larger U.S. cultural landscape, Stowe's *Uncle Tom's Cabin*. As a novel, it develops the racial logic of addiction I have been describing by unfolding a narrative sequence of causes and effects, in an attempt to explain the relationship between chattel slavery and intemperance.

"Whipping and abuse are like laudanum": *Uncle Tom's Cabin* and Addiction to Slavery

As Lyman Beecher's daughter, Harriet Beecher Stowe and her work exemplified the uneven historical shift from the "slavery of drink" metaphor that privileged temperance over abolition to the "intemperance of slavery" metaphor that placed abolition first. Temperance ideals surrounded and helped define the abolitionism central to both *Uncle Tom's Cabin* and her second novel, *Dred: A Tale of the Great Dismal Swamp* (1857), and she returned to temperance again, making it a theme in her late novels, *My Wife and I* (1871) and *We and Our Neighbors* (1875).[79]

Intemperance and drug habituation plagued Stowe's own family. Her son Fred struggled with habitual drunkenness from his school years at Andover until he disappeared in San Francisco in 1871; her daughter Georgiana contracted a morphine dependency from medical treatment in her teenage years, from which she suffered until her death in her forties.[80] Stowe herself was an acute theorizer of intemperance, particularly because of her religious skepticism. As Karen Halttunen has pointed out, she was well aware of the double bind whereby Calvinists were expected to assert their depraved moral nature to effect their own conversion.[81] The metaphor Stowe chooses to express this paradox is telling:

> The case seems to me exactly as if I had been brought into the world with such a thirst for ardent spirits that there was just a possibility, but no hope that I should resist, and then my eternal happiness made to depend on my being temperate. Sometimes when I try to confess my sins I feel that I am more to be pitied than blamed, for I have never known the time when I have not had a temptation within me so strong that it was certain that I should not overcome it. This thought shocks me, but it comes with such force, and so appealingly, to all my consciousness, that it stifles all sense of sin.[82]

I quote this passage at some length to demonstrate two salient features of Stowe's reasoning. First, she is keenly aware of the intractability common to both a generalized fallenness and the specific condition of intemperance—a compulsion so similar that intemperance becomes *the* exemplary sin. Second, however, Stowe opens up the radical possibility that since temptations such as drinking simply cannot be resisted, intemperance must be understood as something other than sin. This dilemma about intemperance—whether it was a vice or more akin to a condition—was pressing because the answer would inform the solution. Since, within the reformist imaginary, the potential for intemperance to be cured bore directly on the potential for chattel slavery to be reformed, the question of the habitual drunkard's status was crucial to the imagined future of slavery.

Because the place of slavery in U.S. history remains contentious, the intersections of affect, agency, epistemology, and ethics within it continue to be vexed. To be sure, a similar ambivalence still pervades thinking about addiction, which is viewed as an ethical deficiency, an epistemic limit, and both. These ambivalences can become productive when brought together: we can use them to complicate an otherwise superficial view of a character that has been described as Stowe's "archvillain" and "arguably the most infamous figure in nineteenth-century literature," Simon Legree.[83] As a vicious drunkard and cruel slave master, Legree is the apotheosis of Douglass's Mr. Plummer and Ludlow's Mossa Cutter; but his drinking is also complexly related to the habits of the more sympathetic characters, St. Clare, Cassy, and Prue. Within the extended environment of the novel, Stowe elaborates and transforms the figure of the drunken slave master found in Douglass's and Ludlow's sketches, where it signifies mere evil. The novel's ambivalence about the causes and nature of habitual drunkenness is keyed to its self-imposed challenge of suggesting precisely whether and how white participation in chattel slavery can be reformed. Focusing on intemperance and drawing Legree into relationship with St. Clare and Prue represents a shift of focus within the valuable critical conversation on the novel's racial and gender politics, led by Halttunnen, Hortense Spillers, Robyn Wiegman, Karen Sánchez-Eppler, Lauren Berlant, Christina Zwarg, and others.[84] Discussions of the novel's uneasy combination of abolitionism and feminism tend to portray Legree as an icon of white patriarchy, a monstrous locus of unfeeling that elicited and politicized readers' outraged sentimental response. But Legree performs more specific cultural work. Linking the affective hardening associated with intemperance to chattel slave mastery, Legree symbolizes an ironic deflation of white masculinity into dependency and debility. His spectacular habitual drunkenness refracts the more genteel tippling of St. Clare. Yet Legree's most significant pairing is with Prue, the novel's other habitual drunkard, an old slave woman who drinks herself to death in St. Clare's cellar. The two characters perform the division of race and gender within the history of addiction: on the one hand, the loss of white masculine subjective plenitude through complicity with an immoral market; on the other hand, the human disfigurement that results from bearing the force of the institutional violence of chattel slavery. This raced division effectively reframes the question of whether intemperance is a vice or a condition, suspending it between different racial models.

At first glance, Stowe seems to offer Legree as another iconic example of the intemperate slave master who, lacking the ability to treat himself humanely, turns that inward violence and erosion outward, upon his slaves—most obviously by his spectacular beating of Tom, but more insidiously by his distribution of brandy to slaves throughout the plantation. Like the despicable trader Haley, who takes Tom as payment for Mr. Shelby's debt, Legree is initially characterized by his use of brandy: on the journey back from purchasing Tom and Emmeline, he "occasionally pull[ed] away at a flask of spirit, which he kept in his pocket"; by the time they reach the plantation, "he had been drinking to that degree that he was inclining to be very gracious."[85] When in this humor, Legree would call Sambo and Quimbo, his overseers, to his room, "and, after warming them up with whiskey, amuse himself by setting them to singing, dancing or fighting, as the humor took him" (*UTC* 325); after midnight one night, Cassy hears them "in a state of furious intoxication, . . . singing, whooping, upsetting chairs, and making all manner of ludicrous and horrid grimaces at each other" (*UTC* 325). Legree also uses brandy to manage his sexual coercion of Cassy and Emmeline: Emmeline reveals that "he wanted to make me drink some of his hateful brandy" (*UTC* 326). Whiskey greases both of the hunts for Cassy and Emmeline; Legree promises "a glass of spirits to every one" of his own slaves (*UTC* 352); on the second day, when a "hard-favored set" of overseers and slaves from neighboring plantations as well as "Legree's associates at the tavern-bar" come to join the hunt, "Legree was serving brandy, profusely, round among them, as also among the negroes . . . for it was an object to make every service of this kind, among the negroes, as much of a holiday as possible" (*UTC* 355–56). Here Stowe links the exceptional status of the slave-hunt-as-holiday to Douglass's description of drunken holidays as the plantation manager's way of controlling the slaves. Alcohol keeps the slaves divided from each other, willing to hunt each other, and competing with each other for status. This stratagem helps maintain the plantation system, proving Haley's earlier contention that "them stupid [slaves], as doesn't care whar they go, and shifless, drunken ones, as don't care for nothin', they'll stick by" (*UTC* 86). By contrast to the bibulous slaves, the sober Tom favors his Bible over Legree's liquid bribes, incurring his wrath: "You might have been better off than Sambo, or Quimbo either, and had easy times . . . ye might have had liberty to lord it round . . . and yet might have had, now and then, a good warming of whiskey punch" (*UTC* 339). Stowe's use of the word "liberty" is far from accidental; here we encounter the temperance-abolitionist rhetoric that drunkenness is no freedom at all. Whiskey and brandy saturate the social relations at Legree's plantation to such a degree that Tom's abstinence forces a crisis. But Tom's sobriety does not subvert the established order; it merely elicits a more direct expression of the institutional violence latent within chattel slaves' intemperance.

Yet Stowe offers a more complex and at times contradictory analysis of Legree's habitual drinking: at first, the novel claims that he is not a habitual drunkard, but by the book's end, Legree is dying of delirium tremens, the conventionally understood demise of habitual drunkards. The novel devotes so much attention to Legree's drinking that its pages fairly reek of brandy; for this reason, perhaps, Stowe feels obliged to offer a somewhat counterintuitive clarification: "Legree was not an habitual drunkard. His coarse, strong nature craved, and could endure, a continual stimulation, that would have utterly wrecked and crazed a finer one. But a deep, underlying spirit of cautiousness prevented his often yielding to appetite in such measure as to lose control of himself" (*UTC* 327). By the 1850s, "habitual drunkard" was becoming a technical category, to be distinguished from ordinary, willed, sinful drunkenness. This passage suggests that since his drinking is a moral choice, Legree naturally and viciously chooses sin.

In keeping with this formulation of Legree as villain, Stowe waxes poetic on the topic of brandy as the antithesis of human appreciation of God's creation:

> O, with what freshness, what solemnity and beauty, is each new day born; as if to say to insensate man, "Behold! Thou hast one more chance! *Strive* for immortal glory!" There is no speech or language where this voice is not heard; but the bold, bad man heard it not. He woke with an oath and a curse. What to him was the gold and purple, the daily miracle of morning! What to him the sanctity of that star which the Son of God has hallowed as his own em-

> blem? Brute-like, he saw without perceiving; and, stumbling forward, poured out a tumbler of brandy, and drank half of it. (*UTC* 327)

In this passage, Legree is merely a "bold, bad man" who refuses to be redeemed; the sign of this is the brandy that obliterates his perception of the new day and the attendant ability to glorify God. Consider how much this description resembles William Whipper's depiction, not of the slaveholder but of the exemplary slave: "His mind, that was formed to soar into infinite space, and there admire and explore the beauties of creation, and the splendor of worlds—scarcely moves beyond the measure of his chains" ("SWW" 122). Legree has become like the paradigmatic cognitively limited slave; if brandy is his chain, he cannot see beyond it to the aesthetic and spiritual realm that would dignify his humanity. Here the novel suggests that Legree is already suited to be a slave owner because he is coarse and insensitive. Departing from the long-rooted antislavery argument that the immoral market gradually eroded its participants' ethical relations, passages such as these seem to contend that the business of chattel slavery simply attracts those who are already intemperate and imbruted. Stowe hews to this idea as she recites her polemic in *The Key to Uncle Tom's Cabin* (1853): "To the half-maniac drunkard, to the man notorious for hardness and cruelty, to the man sunk entirely below public opinion, to the bitter infidel and blasphemer, the law confides this power [to own slaves], just as freely as to the most honorable and religious man on earth."[86] The comment plays up the novel's argument that chattel slavery must end, not because every slaveholding situation is de facto barbaric but because not all masters are as sober and benevolent as the Shelbys. Insofar as Legree's drunkenness is a vice, then, the novel asks readers to compare him to Mr. Shelby and St. Clare, the more benign and relatively more sober masters. In this vein, the intemperance of slavery is not a thoroughgoing condition; it is unevenly distributed. But this is not Stowe's final word, either on Legree's intemperance or on the intemperance of slave mastery in general.

Indeed, the novel equivocates, since Legree later develops the very disease from which Stowe had exempted him. Because of Cassy's pretense of haunting his house and because of his remorse over failing to imitate his mother's piety, Legree loses the caution that the narrator had earlier cited as the reason he did not give way to appetite:

> After this, Legree became a harder drinker than ever before. He no longer drank cautiously, prudently, but imprudently and recklessly. There were re-

> ports around the country, soon after, that he was sick and dying. Excess had brought on that frightful disease that seems to throw the lurid shadows of a coming retribution back into the present life. None could bear the horrors of that sick room, when he raved and screamed, and spoke of sights which almost stopped the blood of those who heard him, and, at his dying bed, stood a stern, white, inexorable figure, saying, "Come! come! come!" (*UTC* 367)

In this passage, Legree loses the two things that had kept him from being categorized as a habitual drunkard: his strong endurance and his caution. Stowe's depiction could be drawn directly from temperance fiction, which frequently described the transformation of "excess" to "disease," framing the latter as divine retribution for prior lax habits. Temperance and other novelists routinely described the hallucinatory throes of delirium tremens as the sign of a drunkard paying for past sins in an agonizing death; for example, in *Great Expectations*, Charles Dickens has Arthur Havisham die of the condition as recompense for his misdeeds toward his sister, a form of poetic justice similar to Stowe's.[87] In the specific narrative economy of *Uncle Tom's Cabin*, Legree's development of habitual drunkenness and delirium tremens coincides with his "haunting" by Cassy, who doubles the ghostly visitations of Legree's mother. As Nicholas Warner and Mattingly have pointed out separately, Legree's drunken behavior fits a common temperance trope of masculine rebellion against maternal domestic authority.[88] But given the novel's polemic, his "frightful disease" also stands as an inexpiable sin, a ghost that cannot be exorcised—in other words, the slave owner's bad conscience. The absence of sympathy that had characterized Legree, embodying his role as the book's villain to the hilt, returns as a chaotic, terrorized subjectivity.

Stowe's vacillation can now be understood as a double reframing: just as Legree's drinking metamorphoses from a set of immoral decisions to a sickness, so too does chattel slave mastery transform from a simple act of willed villainy to a condition. This and similar scenes are crucial to comprehending the whiteness of addiction, because they name intemperance as an affliction at the same moment that they inscribe its suffering as the retribution for participation in the immoral commercial project of chattel slavery. If intemperance becomes synonymous with the gradual and insidious erosion of ethics caused by chattel slave mastery, then the novel's argument about abolition changes. Slavery must end—not because some masters are crueler and more vicious than others but because all masters are potentially cruel and vicious. Intemperance is positioned as an incipience of whiteness, particularly of masculine whiteness.

Stowe develops the idea that intemperance is a condition, rather than a mere vice, most intensively in the figure of St. Clare, who operates most obviously as a genteel contrast to Legree but who tellingly shares his intemperance. When Stowe begins to pursue this alternative conceptualization of intemperance as chattel slave mastery, a more modern, recognizable language of addiction begins to appear, most obviously around the figure of St. Clare and his household. Spillers's quip that " 'Simon Legree' is 'really' 'Augustine St. Clare' with his drawers down" is a more capacious insight than a simple comparison between "polite" sexual attention and the rape of slaves by masters.[89] The two men also define the gamut from careless tippling to pathological intemperance as well as the difference between St. Clare's laissez-faire attitude to his slaves and Legree's violent control. Tom criticizes St. Clare's drinking habits by citing a well-known temperance slogan from Proverbs: " 'O, my dear young Mas'r! I'm 'fraid it will be *loss of all—all—*body and soul. The good Book says, 'it biteth like a serpent and stingeth like an adder!' my dear Mas'r!' " (*UTC* 178).[90] Tom's accompanying observation, that " 'Mas'r isn't good to *himself*" (*UTC* 178) also functions more generally, to indict St. Clare's skepticism, which is generated by his self-division over his complicity in chattel slavery. Hence St. Clare's drinking operates as a symptom of his paralytic inability to reconcile his political sympathies with his actions.

Stowe further demonstrates St. Clare's paralysis in the following exchange with Miss Ophelia. This passage uses the language of Christian temperance, with its cycles of "temptation," "repentance," and "resolution," to invoke the banality of all sinful behavior in rational beings:

> "Of course, you defend it,—you all do,—all you Southerners. What do you have slaves for, if you don't?"
>
> "Are you such a sweet innocent as to suppose nobody in this world ever does what they don't think is right? Don't you, or didn't you ever, do anything that you did not think quite right?"
>
> "If I do, I repent of it, I hope," said Miss Ophelia, rattling her needles with energy.
>
> "So do I," said St. Clare, peeling his orange; "I'm repenting of it all the time."
>
> "What do you keep on doing it for?"
>
> "Didn't you ever keep on doing wrong, after you'd repented, my good cousin?"
>
> "Well, only when I've been very much tempted," said Miss Ophelia.
>
> "Well, I'm very much tempted," said St. Clare; "that's just my difficulty."

> "But I always resolve I won't, and I try to break off."
>
> "Well, I have been resolving I won't, off and on, these ten years," said St. Clare; "but I haven't, some how, got clear. Have you got clear of all your sins, cousin?" (*UTC* 192)

This Christian language of temperance was also the vernacular of addiction, conjuring an ongoing fall followed by declarations of reform that never work—a problem that, over time, calls into question the good intentions expressed. By hitching her abolitionist polemic to this trope of everyday, banal sin, Stowe implicitly positions the white masters' participation in chattel slavery as its own form of chronic intemperance. The insidiousness of intemperance and chattel slavery as lived conditions emerges here, in the bourgeois drawing room, more so than in Legree's frenzied bouts of drinking, violence, and terror. Legree's dysfunctional plantation and delirium tremens are spectacular, but St. Clare's disordered household, lax habits, and secret tippling are no less corrosive. Each man's drunkenness is a sign of his lack of self-care, which in turn jeopardizes those for whom they are responsible. Stowe's double-edged strategy is designed both to remind abolitionists that they are not without sin and to prick the consciences of slave-owning readers.

Intriguingly, the novel's most vivid articulation of the analogy between intemperance and chattel slave mastery occurs in another discussion between St. Clare and Ophelia, this one about how to encourage chattel slaves to be ethical subjects. This challenging project occupies the subplot of Miss Ophelia's moral education of Topsy, and occurs in St. Clare's musings on her refractory behavior: "In many cases, it is a gradual hardening process on both sides,—the owner growing more and more cruel, as the servant more and more callous. Whipping and abuse are like laudanum[:] you have to double the dose as the sensibilities decline. I saw this very early when I became an owner; and I resolved never to begin, because I did not know when I should stop,—and I resolved, at least, to protect my own moral nature" (*UTC* 214). Using the language and philosophy of temperance, St. Clare explains the effects of slavery as a habitual practice. But within the analogy lurks a surprise: readers of the second sentence would at first assume that the slave is like the laudanum-drinker—dull and insensitive because over stimulated. Yet St. Clare applies the analogy to himself as a slave *owner*: constantly whipping his slaves would make him, as well as them, addicted and coarse. Whipping, the iconic and nauseating spectacle of slavery, is an addictive practice that once begun, demands constant indulgence and escalation. Furthermore, it is the most visible sign of the master's enjoyment of his slaves as commodities. And according to the logic of addiction, it operates ironically because it begins as an expression and enforcement of the master's will but quickly gets the upper hand, becoming the masterful, compelling force. The passage embodies the slippery ground of addiction: as the addicted subject undergoes his ethical diminishment, his capacity for empirical discernment also declines, rendering him unaware of the ethical despoliation. Intemperance prevents its subject from discerning whether or not he is, to parse Stowe's phrase, "feeling right."

But in St. Clare's analysis, the whipped slave is important only as a prop in the drama of ethical and epistemic degeneration playing out within the master. The injunction to metaphorical temperance and moral self-protection is thus not a concern for the slave's welfare or ethical state, in spite of the original context of the conversation, Topsy's potential regeneration. That is why, in this conversation, St. Clare's moral nature displaces Topsy's as the site of crisis. In the process of making intemperance serve as an analogy for chattel slave mastery, Stowe also makes it—like the "slavery of drink" analogy before it—a white subjective dilemma.

Stowe's abolitionist novel helps build a model of intemperance as a white condition rather than simple willed villainy in order to open up the narrative and the political possibilities for white moral self-reformation. This move mobilizes the techniques of psychological realism surrounding St. Clare, techniques by which Stowe also attempts to deepen the characterization of Legree. Between them, Stowe manages to create intemperance as an effect of chattel slave mastery. But once again, the novel complicates its own paradigm: by introducing a "slave of drink" who is also a chattel slave, Stowe depicts yet another model of addiction to trouble the white, masculine embodiment of the first.

Prue and the Limits of Temperance Ethics

The novel's representation of habitual drunkenness as a problem of whiteness is complicated by the character Prue, the slave who is also a habitual drunkard. On the one hand—and in keeping with the "whiteness" of addiction—Prue's intemperance is presented as the consequence of her mistress Marie's intemperate behavior and hypochondria. As with Legree and St. Clare, Marie's intemperate slave mastery is presented in the idiom of addiction: " 'Well, at any rate,' said Marie, as she reclined herself on a lounge, 'I'm thankful I'm born where slavery exists; and I believe it's right,—indeed, I feel it must be; and, at any rate, *I'm sure I couldn't get along without it*' " (*UTC* 160, emphasis added). With this phrase, Stowe signals Marie's addiction *to slave mastery*—a debilitating dependency-within-a-dependency that has eroded her ability to feel or think independently. In true liberal fashion, Marie's lack of self-care only becomes a problem when it affects others—when her self-centeredness and hypochondria cause harm to Prue and to her baby. Prue tells Tom she was a breeder slave in Kentucky until she came to St. Clare's, where she had a baby she could keep. In an extension of the trope of white infection and decadence spreading to blacks, Marie becomes ill, infecting Prue and the baby; she then refuses to buy milk for it, wishes it dead, and forces Prue to keep it in a garret, where "it cried itself to death, one night. It did, and I tuck' to drinkin', to keep its crying out of my ears!" (*UTC* 189). Whereas Legree's intemperance is figured as frightened guilt and St. Clare's as philosophical nihilism, Prue's attempts to drown the memory of her child figure as both an expression and extension of Marie's domination—and as a gesture against it: drinking causes its own problems, but it also muffles the painful sounds of woe. In this way, Prue's habitual drunkenness begins to escape the status of transmitted white illness.

Yet how is one to understand the phenomenon of "self-enslavement" to drink with respect to someone who never was her own master? Of chattel slaves, Achille Mbembe writes, "As an instrument of labor, the slave has a price. As a property, he or she has a value. His or her labor is needed and used. The slave is therefore kept alive but in a *state of injury*, in a phantom-like world of horrors and intense cruelty and profanity."[91] Prue's habitual drunkenness corresponds to this injured condition: habitual drunkards, like slaves, are alive but damaged; their apparently self-destructive physical processes obscure the true causes of their injuries. Both the baby and Prue appear to commit a kind of suicide—the baby "cried itself to death," Prue drinks herself to death—but, because these are responses to extreme domination, they do not count as expressive, rational acts. When Prue speaks, it is to resist an insistent demand, made by both St. Clare and Tom, that she muster the strength to abstain from drink and re-establish an appropriate ethical relation so that she may be saved: "Mas'r says I shall go to torment, and I tell him I've got thar now!" (*UTC* 189). Prue counters the Christian imperative of self-management by speaking from the coordinates of the lived experience of chattel slavery, in which ethical agency appears to be evacuated; in this negative space, time collapses and the afterlife exists in the present. Habitual drunkenness becomes the trope of this series of double binds.

The challenge of interpreting Prue's habitual drunkenness, then, falls to readers, who must judge it, ultimately, as either the weight of domination or the expression of her volition. If habitual drunkenness expresses the extreme domination of chattel slavery, then it might not describe a self-relation at all, but merely the effects of Marie's actions and St. Clare's paralysis. The danger of this interpretation is that Prue might become the tragic version of the Sambo figure, whose characteristic drunkenness merely amplifies his cognitive and psychological simplicity. Readers of the day might have related this simplicity to various court cases in which slaves bought alcohol and died in drunken accidents: judges ruled that since "slaves would naturally drink alcohol if it were offered to them," the white vendors were responsible for paying their owners for the destruction of their property.[92] As Elaine Frantz Parsons notes, such judgments presumed that slaves lack the ordinary volition of whites; offering them alcohol was the legal equivalent of forcing it on them.[93] On the one hand, Prue's story is more complexly motivated; on the other, her statement that she merely "tuck' to drinkin' " tends to collude with the psychological effacement effected by the Sambo figure and the legal judgments. Unlike temperance narratives about free whites, Prue's story contains no dramatic moment of consent to temptation in which the protagonist discards his ethical relation to wallow in drink. Such moments typically conjure the psychological turmoil of deep subjectivity, for example in the representative temperance text *Minnie Hermon, or, The Curse of Rum* (1857): "None knew the mad whirl of Howard's thoughts, or saw the dark vision passing before him. . . . [A]n old and dangerous custom was hanging over him, and he knew not which way to turn or what to do."[94] The same generic convention cannot apply to Prue, because the unrelenting narrative negations characteristic of temperance fiction—the logic whereby drink causes the disappearance of the promising young white man's financial prospects, the disintegration of his family, the loss of his health and capacity to labor, and ultimately, his death—are reversed for her. Her personal history of forced sexual labor that substituted breeding for familial reproduction and, later, the foreclosure of any possibility of family occasioned by the death of the child, cause Prue to drink. Intemperance loses its irony because it becomes a logical response to the suffering of enslavement. Unlike the drama of white intemperance that plays out between the white individual's better and worse natures, here, black intemperance instead becomes the sign of institutional imposition of prolonged suffering upon the chattel slave.

How then to respond to the perverse moment of apparently volitional, ethical self-fashioning Stowe assigns to Prue: "I did [drink],—and I will drink! I will, if I do go to torment for it!" (*UTC* 189). This singular moment of self-determination suggests that Prue chooses drunkenness over sobriety, a proposition that necessarily excludes the possibility that drunkenness expresses her domination. And yet the volition appears only to declare self-annihilation. This figuration precisely inverts that of Legree: whereas Legree willfully drinks until, at the very end, his choices have ironically turned into a disease beyond his control, Prue's intemperance could be interpreted as being determined by the domination of her enslavement until the final moment, when she discursively begins to will it. In another significant irony, whereas Legree's choice to drink made him a simplistic villain, the chattel's fullest expression of will and subjective plenitude articulates the drive to intemperance and death. Suicide by intemperance only represents resistance to slavery's domination insofar as it prevents the master's ultimate enactment of it through homicide, a possibility the novel stages in Legree's murder of Tom, but rules out for Prue.

Readers therefore seem to be caught between two interpretive models of Prue's intemperance: in the first, it is the massive force of chattel slavery focused on a single point and speaking through it, such that Prue merely ventriloquizes an irresistible, compulsive "drink." In this model, history transcends and rules the subject, who becomes its monument. Prue's death in St. Clare's cellar is therefore also her conversion into a memorial to the pain of chattel slavery, here signified by the ruinous fatality of intemperance. Hence Philip Fisher constructs Prue's timelessness by relating her to the ruins that appear in sentimental narratives, figures "that cannot be repaired, nor can they be erased or forgotten."[95] In this model, Prue's experience would be the fictional analogue of the felt pain of chattel slavery Hartman and others have described as "the history that hurts." Prue's death beneath the surface of the household signifies the inability to repair the ethical damage seeping from the white intemperance above: the historical force of chattel slavery exempts her from ethical possibility. As a theory of chattel slavery, this model has the defects of ethically excluding the enslaved, conceding chattel slavery's inevitability, and imagining the enslaved body as lying inertly beyond the essentially white history that reaches down to inscribe it.

The second model is little better, since regarding the will to self-annihilation as an ethical moment could be seen as assimilating the chattel slave to a free white model of subjective transcendence, thereby minimizing the scenario of extreme domination. Taking this position requires readers to align themselves with Miss Ophelia's characteristically myopic chastisement: " 'You are very wicked and very foolish . . . to steal your master's money *to make yourself a brute with*" (*UTC* 186, emphasis added). Any assent to such a characterization of Prue's drinking would require the reader to overlook the novel's polemic against the institution of extreme domination in which she already functions precisely as a brute meant only to labor and breed. The expectation that chattel slaves should inhabit free norms of personal conduct is precisely what affronts many readers about the figure of Tom, whose Christian piety and forbearance appear uncomfortably to collude with his domination, making his character seem at best bogus and at worst racist.[96]

But Prue could also be viewed as exposing and deconstructing these subjective models, since her speech appears both to enact and to refuse any agency she might have, inhabiting an ethical space simultaneously imagined to be foreclosed. The convergence of the two metaphors, the intemperance of chattel slavery and the self-enslavement of drink, produces a subject who inverts the characteristic self-squander of the originally free drunkard. This convergence actually offers us a way out of our interpretive impasse. That is, once the implicit freedom of action is deconstructed, addiction, like the actions of chattel slaves, can no longer be judged as either the effect of external domination, or a failed attempt to simulate the norms of free conduct. Prue destroys the principal nineteenth-century fiction of addiction that the metaphor of self-enslavement obscures: intemperance may not be a zone of self-destruction into which the free subject wanders through incompetence or miscalculation, but rather a mode of life that—while far from ideal—relieves the pressure of other, already unbearable, coerced conditions of embodiment and subjectivation.

Addiction and Countermodernity

The two models of intemperance imagined in Stowe's novel, slave and free, bring together the most tyrannous character, Legree, and the most abject character, Prue. Their deaths by habitual drunkenness signify their participation in the extremes of chattel slavery as perpetrator and victim. But Legree dying of delirium tremens is the more ironic figure, since he has systematically exchanged his subjective plenitude—which is, in the unconscious racist order, his white birthright—for brutishness. By having Legree transform from a vicious brute to a dying addict, Stowe covertly uses the metaphor of slavery's intemperance to make Legree a more complex figure. This gesture tempers a depiction of white responsibility for chattel slavery's atrocities by positioning it not merely as an enormous sin but also as a habit, a form of insanity, and a disease—all of the conceptual rubrics used to define intemperance and, later, addiction by removing it from the realm of pure agency.

Stowe deploys a similar equivocal representational strategy in her characterization of Tom Gordon, the drunken slave owner villain of *Dred*. Against his sister's dying wishes, Tom continues to treat her slaves badly; when reminded of her request, he attempts to drown his guilt: he "rang violently for a hot brandy-toddy, and a fresh case of cigars. The devil's last, best artifice to rivet the fetters of his captives is the opportunity which these stimulants give them to command insanity at will."[97] Here Stowe uses the "slavery of drink" metaphor to suggest that Gordon's intemperance is both willed and unwilled: he appears to command his own mental condition—but only by bringing about insanity, and only at the behest of the devil. Stowe even has Gordon's uncle, a bibulous old planter, explain that Gordon's "ugliness is nothing but because he is drunk."[98] In a moment of transparent alignment with the omniscient narrator, Stowe has the elder Gordon suggest that temperance societies could help young southern men to drink more moderately, which would make them less apt to violate their slaves. In a neater and more efficient characterization than that of Legree, Stowe positions excessive drunkenness as the cause of the moral ugliness of violent chattel slave mastery. Abolitionism required such a discourse of intemperance to explain white participation in chattel slavery because the alternative, imagining the enormity of chattel slavery as a massive complex of acts freely chosen in every instance, implies a staggering level of malevolence that threatens to implode the very concept of the human.

In the postbellum period, intemperance came to be conceptualized more as a disease, though its status as ethical defect also abided. Its association with the immoral market of the slave trade and with plantation cruelty diminished, creating room for sympathetic drunkard characters, such as Bolton, the erudite, avuncular editor of Stowe's *My Wife and I*: "In short, the use of stimulant to the brain-power brings on a disease, in whose paroxysms a man is no more his own master than in the ravings of fever, a disease that few have the knowledge to understand, and for whose manifestations the world has no pity.”[99] The idea that habitual drunkenness was a disease rather than vicious immorality opened new fictional opportunities for its portrayal. As I demonstrate in the next chapter, however, even though the complicity of drunkenness with chattel slavery would recede in the postbellum period, its coordinates of white masculinity would remain as traces of the national shame of intemperate mastery. On the other hand, abolitionism had no problem imagining the intemperance of the enslaved subject as a monument to the injuries of chattel slavery. Prue’s monstrosity, written in scars on her back so numerous that, according to Dinah, “she can’t never get a dress together over it,” are authored by her masters and make her suffering visible in a way that her intemperance does not (*UTC* 187). Her drunkenness, then, comes to locate its origins in the violence inflicted by her masters, not in her own lack of self-care or willed misuse of the body. The intemperance of chattel slaves is none at all, since readers are invited to see in Prue’s scars the signs of a slave master’s addiction to whipping and abuse. In the subsequent history of addiction, African-American addiction is often represented similarly, as undifferentiated from the legacy of slavery: it rarely attains the level of individualized ethical abstraction and irony that narratives of white addiction do.

As the most prominent abolitionist and one of the temperance movement’s more effective spokespeople, Frederick Douglass also derived the political calculus of the “slavery of drink” and the “intemperance of slavery.” Indeed, perhaps more than any other nineteenth-century thinker, he linked intemperance to chattel slavery and used the metaphor to critique Enlightenment modernity. Douglass’s address to a rally organized by the Irish temperance activist and popular saint Father Mathew makes this critique and forms the fuller context of this chapter’s second epigraph: “I believe . . . that if we could but make the world sober, we would have no slavery. *Mankind has been drunk*. I believe that if the slaveholder would be sober for a moment—would consider the sinfulness of his position—hard-hearted as he is, I believe there is humanity enough if we could get him sober—we could get a public opinion sufficiently strong to break the relation of master and slave. *All great reforms go together*.”[100] Douglass’s speech exposes the unfeeling hypocrisy that bestowed universal humanity with one hand and withheld it from chattel slaves with the other. But it also implies a particular theory of history. To speak of “mankind” as having been drunk is to indict the “progress” of white Western civilization; it construes the past as neither guide nor precedent for the present. The speech imagines neither a prior state of enlightened sobriety from which subsequent generations have deviated nor a future ideal of sobriety toward which everyone must aspire; rather, it critiques the Enlightenment past for having permitted chattel slavery as the result of continuous drunkenness. In Douglass's vision, the intemperance of chattel slavery is more than an embarrassing blemish on Enlightenment progress; it is rather a modern characteristic.

Douglass's temperance rhetoric diverges from other noted orators and writers, such as Abraham Lincoln and, interestingly, Walt Whitman. Lincoln imagines the triumph of temperance as the triumph of reason in his "Temperance Address," and he links it, in an unbroken chain, from the national founding to a future in which chattel slavery will end: "Its march cannot fail to be on and on, till every son of earth shall drink in rich fruition, the sorrow quenching draughts of perfect liberty. Happy day, when, all appetites controlled, all passions subdued, all matters subjected, mind, all conquering mind, shall live and move the monarch of the world. Glorious consummation! Hail fall of Fury! Reign of Reason, all hail!"[101] Lincoln's address references the familiar dichotomy between the passions of the body and the sober enlightenment of the mind; for progress to enthrone reason, the public must be physically purified. Timothy Hickman writes that Lincoln's address insisted "on the necessity of self-possession for the production and maintenance of what he saw as a fully functional and distinctively American political subjectivity."[102] This political subjectivity posited the moral freedom of temperance, to which Lincoln added, at the end, the political freedom of abolition. In keeping with the cultural logic of the metaphor of the slavery of drink, however, temperance comes first: the body, detoxified of passion, intemperance, excess, and habit, will guarantee the sovereignty of the mind and create a transparent public sphere in which reason glows. For this to happen, however, every individual of the social body must first become temperate. Whitman imagines this literally taking place in the final scenes of his temperance novel *Franklin Evans* (1842), when the last drunkard takes the teetotal pledge: "Victory! victory! The Last Slave of Appetite is free, and the people are regenerated!"[103] Douglass's speech sounds similar, since he suggests achieving sobriety first, then abolition; but it is more strategic, asking only for a sober moment and only for those segments that tend to represent "mankind," the masters. Douglass's African-American temperance perspective is a valuable corrective to mainstream temperance ideology and its twentieth- and twenty-first-century successors, because it insists on temperance's embeddedness within social contexts of freedom, not an abstract and totalizing ideal that makes moral purity dependent on physical purity and collective identity dependent on the elision of individual difference.

The site of Douglass's speech—Cork, Ireland—is also important for rethinking the relationship of the history of addiction to modernity, antislavery, and anti-imperialism. Douglass traveled to Ireland during 1845 and 1846, giving lectures on temperance and abolition; other former slaves such as Joseph Woodhouse and Benjamin Benson traveled around Ireland under the auspices of the Belfast Total Abstinence Association and the Irish Temperance League.[104] The Irish temperance movement, both in its early phase in the 1840s and again during its resurgence in the 1880s and 1890s, also characterized Ireland's colonized status as intemperate slavery. Father Mathew, who traveled the countryside converting millions of Irish to teetotalism and who administered the pledge to Douglass himself, notably refused to link teetotalism to nationalist politics; but the Young Ireland movement led by Thomas Davis hitched national self-fashioning to teetotal aspirations, as Elizabeth Malcolm has shown, most notably in the slogan "Ireland sober, Ireland free."[105] The alternative of intemperance as colonial subjection was explicitly figured as slavery. According to George Bretherton, a brief parable told at a Dublin temperance meeting in 1837 was repeated far and wide within the movement: "The ancient Spartans, it seemed, at certain appropriate times exhibited drunken helots to their children so that they might be taught to recognize and despise true servility. The Spartans had created a class of drunken, fawning slaves to serve them; the Irish upper classes had done no less to their fellow countrymen."[106] Observing similar rhetoric, Lloyd comments, "The autonomy of the politically free citizen and nation was opposed to the absolute instantiation of heteronomy, the slave."[107]

Here we might profitably borrow Lloyd's identification of Irish drinking as a practice of "countermodernity" to think about the ethics of addiction surrounding Prue and the resistive figure of the habitually drunken slave. "What determines cultural difference is not its externality to modernity nor the persistence of a premodern irrationality, but rather the mutually constitutive relation between the modern and the countermodern."[108] In other words, neither Ireland nor the space of the plantation should inhabit the tacitly primitivized space of a "drinking culture" where the "modern" phenomena of intemperance and addiction do not exist. Rather, the exchanges and engagements between minor temperance movements and allied political movements such as abolitionism and Irish nationalism show that the metaphor of intemperate slavery mobilized countermodern critiques throughout the Atlantic world. Their "countermodernity" inheres in their departure from the overconfident idealizing of a pure, detoxified body politic as the locus of reason. If "addiction" designates the genealogy of ethical deficit of the normative, white Anglo-American modern consumer, its nineteenth-century histories of politicized links to movements for reform and freedom show us alternative trajectories toward a different kind of sobriety, one not reducible to physical purity.

As loci of addiction, the plantation and the colony appear again in chapter 6, where I analyze the rise of eugenic ideas about addiction and the vampiric fictions that map them onto the metropole-colony relationship. There, the far smaller potential for countermodern critique lies in the representation of imperial dependency upon the colony as an addicted dependency, one that circulates through images of blood-drinking and, as we will see, nursing. The eighteenth-century teacup overflowing with the sugary blood of slaves and the nineteenth-century drunken overseer, whip in hand, will become more familiar figures; in one novel, their mingled consumption and violence will even be presented as heroic. Accordingly, the political stakes of representations of addiction and race will shift away from the "slavery of drink" metaphor and its attendant institutional politics of reform and toward a discourse that more explicitly relates social and biological death through the metaphor of "living death." The whiteness of addiction will remain, but it will begin to reshape itself under the demands of racial purity inherited from the era of plantation slavery. Before we can reach this point, however, we need to see how the "slavery of drink" adapted to cover a new phenomenon of the 1870s and 1880s: addiction to hypodermic morphine.

3

IMPOSTORS OF FREEDOM

Hypodermic Morphine and the Labors of Passing in E. P. Roe's *Without a Home*

As I look back to 1842,—twenty-seven years ago,—it seems almost a hideous dream; I can hardly realize my identity with the staggering, hopeless victim of the terrible vice of intemperance; but the scars remain to testify the reality; yes, scars and marks never to be eradicated; never to be removed in this life.
John B. Gough, *Autobiography and Personal Recollections*

"Slavery" and National Memory

The "slavery of drink" metaphor long outlived its vehicle, chattel slavery. Once slavery had been outlawed in the U.S., its metaphorical uses became less urgently politicized and found a wider usage than abolitionist-temperance activism. Henry G. Cole, author of *Confessions of an American Opium Eater: From Bondage to Freedom* (1895), compared his liberation from hypodermic morphine to "the first few months of liberation from a life of slavery's curse after the Emancipation Proclamation."[1] Cole's subtitle, like that of Leslie E. Keeley's *The Morphine Eater; or, From Bondage to Freedom* (1881), mimicked the title of Frederick Douglass's second autobiography, *My Bondage and My Freedom* (1855). Psychologists used the metaphor widely in their early explanations of addiction: "Man longs to be free . . . to secure a respite from the pains of existence—to lose himself; hence his resort to the use of narcotics. Sad delusion! The greatest slave of all is he who seeks his freedom in these deceptive agents."[2] At the same time, habituations described as self-enslavement acquired the additional negative connotation of really belonging to a shameful, primitive past.

The conceptualization of habituated compulsion as throwback behavior was curious, because it pertained to modern habituations that began to appear in the 1860s and 1870s. In this period, the newly widespread use of the hypodermic syringe to inject morphine produced the first recognizable cohort of addicts. The first U.S. novel about hypodermic addiction, Edward Payson Roe's *Without a Home* (1881), adapts the "slavery of drink" metaphor to describe its protagonist, the Confederate veteran Martin Jocelyn, as an "opium slave," with constant references to its protagonist's "chains," "bondage," "enslavement," and "thralldom."[3] Because the metaphor began to be used widely in medical writings, Roe could even blandly use it to describe his research: "I have conversed with many opium slaves in all stages of the habit" (*WH* xi).

And yet the entire nineteenth-century discourse of addiction was marked by inconsistent terms: just as De Quincey referred to laudanum as opium, so too did Roe and others use "opium" and "morphine" interchangeably, referring to "opium eating" when they really meant "hypodermic morphine injecting." Perhaps to mark the break with the past suggested by the new technology of the needle, Cole noted that by the late nineteenth century, there were no longer any literal opium eaters.[4] The slavery metaphor cut through this terminological disarray, unifying disparate habituations under the same ironic sign of self-destruction.

On the slavery metaphor's wide application to a variety of white masculine behaviors, Russ Castronovo comments that "such sensational conclusions were standard fare in a nineteenth-century rhetorical universe where self-reliance as a corporeal principle became a national concern."[5] Indeed, other temperance and addiction novels of the time deployed the language of slavery. But *Without a Home* distinctively maps the emerging disease of addiction onto the South's primitive past of chattel slavery. Just as southern slave mastery now belonged to the past, so too did opium "slavery" need to be relegated there, where it could not impede the nation's industrial progress. *Without a Home* thus claims our interest because it performs three significant pieces of cultural work. First, it links the discourses of intemperance, traditionally focused on alcohol, to those of narcotic dependencies on substances such as morphine and cocaine which we now categorize as illegal "drugs." Second, it frames the early medical and popular thinking about addiction as such—including the major question of whether and how addicts were responsible for their condition—within the cultural memory of chattel slavery and the Civil War that ended it. Finally, while the novel continues to represent addiction as an irony of white masculinity, it develops that irony in terms of labor and class in northern industrial modernity in ways that *Uncle Tom's Cabin*, with its antebellum southern settings, could not.

Without a Home reads much like the subgenre of "dark temperance" described by David S. Reynolds, in which sensational homicides, brutality, and insanity helped convey the horrors of habitual drunkenness.[6] Similar spectacles of degradation pervade the genre of the first-person drug memoir in the early twentieth century, such as MacMartin's *Thirty Years in Hell* (1921), which—in spite of its comic panache—nevertheless depicts an underworld landscape littered with corpses; or the anonymous *No Bed of Roses: The Diary of a Lost Soul* (1930), with its tales of prostitution and violent crime.[7] Often these accounts were mediated by a social scientist narrator; journalists like Fred V. Williams and Winifred Black also presented first-person drug stories in texts such as *The Hop-Heads* (1920) and *Dope: The Story of the Living Dead* (1928), respectively.[8] Roe's *Without a Home* unites these historical genres because it weaves the shocking spectacles of dark temperance with the medico-scientific research of the later social science narratives. In so doing, it also attempts to mediate between an earlier nineteenth-century view of habituation as a moral failing or vice and an emergent postbellum view of addiction or "inebriety" as an uncontrollable disease and social problem.

Roe does not entirely pull off this balancing act. For example, in keeping with the novel's temperance roots, Jocelyn's self-destruction drives his genteel family from its comfortable home to a filthy tenement and his non-working daughters Mildred and Belle from domestic feminine propriety to physical and moral exploitation as department store saleswomen. The novel's title and its tenement plot signal the characteristic pleasurable fear that motivates the reading of temperance fiction, the possibility of losing "an adequately prosperous home."[9] At the same time, however, Roe develops awkward, polemical subplots indicting the corporate maltreatment of shopgirls and the filth of tenements. Roe's tenement setting and shopgirl plot display many of the same features of poverty soon to be exposed by Jacob A. Riis in *How the Other Half Lives* (1890), and Roe researched this angle by visiting tenements himself.[10] Yet because Roe makes Jocelyn's addiction the shameful cause of these degradations, he blunts his own denunciation of them as social evils with wider causes.

Roe was typically a master of the sentimental novel who could combine sensation with didacticism, and he used *Without a Home* to frame the new phenomenon of addiction for his vast reading public. Although he authored some of the period's bestselling novels, such as *Barriers Burned*

Away (1872), about the great Chicago fire, and *Opening a Chestnut Burr* (1874), which featured a shipwrecked ocean liner, Roe has been largely forgotten.[11] When he died seven years after the publication of *Without a Home*, his combined sales were estimated at 1.4 million, not counting pirated editions and translations.[12] An earlier generation of critics, leaning heavily on Roe's own remark that his novels were an extension of his Presbyterian ministry to the masses, dismissed his novels as didactic.[13] Yet as a novel and social document, *Without a Home* offers a context for comprehending the overlooked literary tradition and cultural formation relating slavery in general—and the historical past of U.S. chattel slavery in particular—to addiction as a degraded ethical state.

Roe's protagonist, Jocelyn, is a descendant of Simon Legree, but with crucial differences. His slave-owning past is implied rather than represented within the novel's narrative action, which dwells instead on his past as a Confederate soldier; his predisposition toward morphine is represented as an effect of his southern identity, not slave mastery; and his primary dependency on hypodermic morphine—a new drug treatment and a cutting-edge medical technology—connotes pathology more than it expresses the starker moral deficit associated with Legree's cruelty and alcoholic vice. Slave mastery remains with the postbellum addict in the trope of an inherent incapacity for labor, since the long dependency on slaves has undermined what would normally be a physiology of self-reliance. The rhetoric of self-enslavement to narcotics thus indexes a wider discursive question about the fate of the white southern elite after the demise of chattel slavery. Chattel slaves had been emancipated, at least nominally; but if their masters had formerly been imagined to be ethically degraded through their complicity with commercial vice, could they now be regenerated? And if—as we might easily suspect—they could not, then how did the inevitability of their demise complicate the central irony of the temperance plot, namely, the protagonist's gradual loss of capital, social standing, and psychological plenitude?

Appearing at the threshold of a sociological view of alcoholism and drug use as deviance, Jocelyn therefore also prefigures a mid-twentieth-century U.S. literary and theatrical tradition of depicting white alcoholism and addiction as forms of melancholy self-medication to assuage guilt for past transgressions touching the core of elite white southern identity. Roe's Jocelyn falls between forthright depictions of southern drunkenness as a metaphor for racism in, for example, Twain's *Adventures of Huckleberry Finn* (1885) and early to mid-twentieth century treatments of it as part of psychologically layered, class-inflected investigations of the southern past in, for example, the novels of William Faulkner and the plays of Tennessee Williams.[14] More generally, by exploring the attendant reversals whereby the white man becomes "enslaved"—racialized and feminized in his abjection—*Without a Home* stages a transformation that plays to the fears of dispossession and failure governing white heteronormative masculinity in U.S. culture. The shameful marks of an addictive past, to which the temperance lecturer John B. Gough alludes in the epigraph to this chapter, are not so abstract; Roe fleshes them out in racial and gendered terms. In tracing such transformations, models of passing and queer sexuality suggested by Robyn Wiegman and Eve Kosofsky Sedgwick can be brought to bear on representations of addiction in productive and illuminating ways.

That the first U.S. novel about addiction should frame that condition as an outcome of white involvement in chattel slavery is of vital and overlooked importance, to the history of both addiction and slavery. *Without a Home* reframes the pressing late nineteenth-century question of whether addiction was a vice or a disease as a question of whether the South's ravaged postwar condition was the consequence of its own depravity or merely the result of an unfortunate affliction. To the extent that addiction represents vice, the addict is responsible for his condition, much the same way that the South was perceived to cause its own downfall. On the other hand, if addiction is a disease, then it might be curable; by analogy, the South could also be reincorporated into the productive, northern-dominated national body. But because the hypodermic syringe must not be used to bring the debilitated southern body into compliance with the demands of a nerve-wracked industrial modernity, *Without a Home* suggests that an addicted, enfeebled white southern manhood cannot be recuperated within the sweep of history that northern progress was making. By contrast, Roe valorizes the self-reliant northern manhood of Roger Atwood, the farmer's son from upstate New York who befriends the Jocelyns and courts Mildred, as the engine of the national future. As before the war, the ignoble white individual metaphorically enslaved to alcohol, opium, or morphine symbolically challenged the racist order by revealing his or her own experience of freedom to be deficient. After the war, however, the metaphoricity of his "enslavement" produced a discourse in which he could potentially free himself, quite paradoxically, by mustering unspecified psychological resources to assert his damaged will. In this period, the narrative outcomes of an individual's addiction—recovery or death—rehearse a drama in which white freedom is imperiled or rescued, notably without the vast legal, social, and cultural change effected by abolition and the Civil War.[15]

The Nervous Credit Economy of Hypodermic Morphine

Having migrated north from his devastated plantation after the war, Jocelyn acquires his dependency on hypodermic morphine in a desperate effort to quell pain and remain productive in his job at a New York City iron firm. Although his predisposition to addiction lies in his southern plantation background, his strivings in the commercial sphere of the modern industrial North develop it. The treatment of nervous diseases such as neuralgia with the new technology of the hypodermic syringe helped workers appear productive and efficient in spite of pain. The hypodermic syringe, introduced into medical practice in the 1860s and 1870s, was far speedier and more efficacious in delivering narcotic relief from pain than the older method of ingestion.[16] Physicians prescribed it to the middle class, particularly women, for numerous aches and pains, but it also became the treatment of choice for an emergent northern professional class, the very social segment which Jocelyn aspires to join. According to the physician and writer Silas Weir Mitchell, "insatiate commerce" had compromised mental stability: "The cruel competition for the dollar, the new and exacting habits of business, the racing speed which the telegraph and railway have introduced into commercial life . . . have brought about some great and growing evils."[17] The neurologist George Beard similarly attributed his version of the illness, "neurasthenia," to a lack of nerve-force found in the "brain-workers" of the hypermodern northern regions of the United States.[18]

Beard, Mitchell, and other writers used financial metaphors of speculation and credit to describe the nervous professional body; as Mitchell put it, "It is making money fast and accumulating a physiological debt of which that bitter creditor, the future, will one day demand repayment."[19] The anonymous author of *Back from the Mouth of Hell* (1878) explained how speculation and drinking reinforced each other through the same addictive influence: "Every devotee of the game can tell how one game leads to another; one drink entails repetition; how the loser 'sours,' loses his 'nerve' and self-possession; how each consecutive discomfiture adds to his bitterness; and how, to steady his nerves, and indulge his angry, inflamed appetite, he swallows glass after glass of liquor."[20] This nervous logic is the same one that governs addiction; Roe points out the similarity between financial and physiological credit and debt in his description of Jocelyn's addicted physical economy:

> [His partners] had been strong, and had endured the evil times for years without wavering, but now were compelled to obtain a credit more and more extended, in the hope of tiding themselves over the long period of depression.
>
> This increasing business stagnation occasioned a deepening anxiety to her husband and a larger resort to his sustaining stimulant. While he had no sense of danger worth naming, he grew somewhat worried by his dependence on the drug, and it was his honest purpose to gradually abandon it as soon as the financial pressure lifted and he could breathe freely in the safety of renewed commercial prosperity. Thus the weeks and months slipped by, finding him more completely involved in the films of an evil web, and more intent than ever upon hiding the fact from everyone, especially his wife and children. (*WH* 25)

Just as the firm must rely on credit rather than capital, so too does Jocelyn rely on the physical credit represented by morphine, which gets him through his pain, but in the process expends his personal physical capital by making him utterly dependent on its artificial sustenance. As one physician of the day put it in a treatise on addiction, "Like a bad debtor, [narcotics] promise much and pay little."[21] In a description that closely mirrors Jocelyn's part in the plot, the physician T. D. Crothers wrote that "opium, like a bank defaulter, both makes and masks the mischief done, which may be kept concealed so long as he stays in the institution."[22] This observation about concealment demonstrates that the addict's success in remaining undetected is governed by the same narrative logic as credit: it extends good faith into an uncertain future, when the debt may be called in and the deception exposed.

The hypodermic syringe complemented this kind of physiological credit economy because it offered a far faster and smoother amelioration of withdrawal pains than did ingestion and epidermal administration, the traditional modes. One physician wrote that "with a good needle the pain is much less dreaded by the patient than the trouble of being raised and the nausea of being dosed."[23] Another characterized its instantaneous effect: "At the touch of the hypodermic syringe, the tortures of neuralgia, the pangs of colic, the suffocative paroxysms of asthma, vanish as if by magic."[24] Smaller quantities of hypodermic morphine could also produce the same effect as larger quantities of opium taken orally. Roe narrates Jocelyn's switch from morphia powders to hypodermic morphine in order to accentuate its efficiency in relieving his depression about his debts: "Throughout the entire winter he had been under a severe strain of business anxiety, and then had come the culminating scenes of failure, loss of income, and enforced and unhappy separation. . . . Ordinary remedies not giving speedy relief, his physician injected into his arm a few drops of the solution of morphia. . . . Now every day was precious, and he felt he could not give himself up to pain and patient waiting until the disease could be conquered in a slow, legitimate way, when by a wound no more than a pin-prick he could obtain courage, happiness, and prospects illimitable" (*WH* 108–9). Roe's representation confirms the medical establishment's consensus that hypodermic morphine was faster, more efficient, and easier to use than opium in curing neuralgia, Jocelyn's disease. But far from helping Jocelyn's faltering body keep pace with the economic demands of what Beard called "a new and productive country," the syringe merely institutes its own regime of credit and debt. In Roe's account of Jocelyn's transition from morphia powder to hypodermic morphine, any lingering associations of such narcotics with the intoxicated Orientalist visions of Thomas De Quincey and Fitz Hugh Ludlow vanish. In chapter 1, we saw that U.S. writers such as Bayard Taylor and Ludlow mimicked De Quincey's hallucinatory visions; by the time of the anonymous *Opium-Eating* (1876) and Cole's *Confessions of an American Opium-Eater* (1895), De Quinceyan visual disorientation had been supplanted by a thematic of self-reform through work. The immediate cause of Jocelyn's addictive behavior is his need to keep pace with the new business class. In the United States, the syringe at first seemed like an innovative tool of postwar capitalist efficiency for businessmen prone to neuralgia and neurasthenia.

Within this analogy of addiction and credit, the addict also screens the creditors—in this case, the medical establishment. Yet the syringe fast became the subject of great controversy in medical journals and newspapers in both the United States and Britain in the 1870s and 1880s, when it became clear that patients had developed debilitating dependencies on it. The withdrawal symptoms that attended habituation were horrible: "I have not attempted to describe the dreadful hankering of the body, blood, bones and sinews, for the injection, after the habit has been established, and the time comes to discontinue it. It is indescribable."[25] Roe similarly represents Jocelyn's withdrawal: he enters "a region of unimaginable horrors, dying ten thousand deaths in the indescribable anguish of his mind and body" (*WH* 287). The recognition of addiction threatened an as yet unconsolidated medical power. Physicians had caused the first wave of hypodermic morphine dependencies by freely prescribing morphine and syringes; as they recognized their error and attempted to reform, they made patient self-use illicit. It quickly became a commonplace of the medical literature that physicians should not prescribe syringes to the patients; by controlling both the new technology and the dose of morphine, doctors would manage the debacle and reap the benefits of the miracle technology. Hence S. W. Caldwell, writing in the *Mississippi Medical Monthly* in 1885, told his fellow physicians to "give a person suffering with that torturing disease [cholera] a puncture of morphia and atropia if you want him to rise up and call you blessed forever" but also warned, "never place a syringe in the hands of one of your patients for them to use unless it be one afflicted with a painful and incurable disease."[26] *Without a Home* begins to align itself with medical authority when it notes that "having obtained the syringe and a vial of the solution of morphia, [Jocelyn] injected into his arm a much larger quantity than the physician would have dreamed of employing" (*WH* 109). At this moment, Roe's text performs a signature paradox of addiction discourse: the moment that the addict's behavior is clearly pathologized by medical authority is the same moment in which he appears to be acting intentionally. This paradox reflects the hefty moral quotient of medical knowledge during the period. Medicoscience reorganized elite white masculinity into two categories, those with healthy wills and those with diseased ones.

The paradox that the addict's self-representation is both diseased and vicious plays out in the common belief that addicts are notorious liars. Conventional wisdom had long held that opium-eaters and alcoholics lied often; now the charge that hypodermic morphine users were habitual liars became a commonplace of medical and mainstream literature.[27] In *Doctor Judas: A Portrayal of the Opium Habit* (1895), William Rosser Cobbe wrote that "opium is a deceitful, sneaking wretch who communicates of his spirit to those he has enthralled."[28] Keeley put it less dramatically: "The opium eater almost invariably understates the extent of his habituation. It is only after he has been restored to a normal condition that he will admit the truth."[29] Roe deploys this trope as part of Jocelyn's attempt to conceal his condition from his family by having him tell his naive wife that his track marks are the result of a blood ailment: "He, who had once been the soul of honor and truth, had lied that day again and again, and the thought pierced him like a sword" (*WH* 283). Excavating the trope of the habitué as pathological liar, one finds a contest for authority between addicts attempting to navigate the social pressures surrounding their compulsion and physicians attempting to preserve their cultural authority in the face of scandal.

The contest cut both ways, since some writers characterized the physicians as the deceivers: the narrator of *Opium-Eating* (1876) compares himself to "the notorious fly, invited into the parlor of the deceitful spider, and met with something like the same sad fate": only to have his physician "dupe and deceive" him by giving him "bare morphia by way of a syringe"—after expressly requesting no narcotic treatment.[30] In her novel *A Voice in the Wilderness* (1895), Maria Weed creates a deceitful physician, "Dr. Lyman," who secretly habituates his patient, Helen Mathews, and then abruptly foists her off on another doctor.[31] Roe reproduces this side of the debate by having Jocelyn, exposed one day at work when a visiting physician notices his track marks, display an addict's indignant anger at medical malfeasance: "It was through one of your damnable fraternity that I acquired what you are pleased to call my chains, and now you come croaking to my employers, poisoning their minds against me" (*WH* 280). Having originally "poisoned" his body, physicians now seem to poison his livelihood—a charge that may seem paranoid but that also articulates a widespread and well established distrust of the medical profession in the late nineteenth century. The historian of medicine Roy Porter links this mistrust, along with the actual lack of progress in curing diseases rather than merely treating symptoms, to the growing popularity of habit-forming sedatives.[32] Although his morphine plot would have been far less plausible to late nineteenth-century readers had it not acknowledged such outrage against doctors, Roe falls far short of indicting the medical profession, instead finding a more compelling villain—Jocelyn himself.

Indeed, *Without a Home* joins the wider discursive use of the metaphor by ultimately ratifying medical authority and assigning responsibility for addiction to the addict. Although his condition was caused by medical treatment and is intelligible only to a medical professional, and although the physician represents a medical cure as the only possible liberation from Jocelyn's metaphoric "enslavement," the text does not position its addict as a sufferer of a disease who requires sympathy. Instead, it construes his problem as his own "folly and weakness" (*WH* 280). In doing so, it aligns itself with the conventions of temperance fiction, in which young, white, middle-class men destroy their own prospects for success by taking the first sip of alcohol. Such characters become alcoholics and addicts primarily through ignorance and incompetence at managing the interfaces between desire and necessity, or consumption and labor, characteristic of modern consumer life. Like other temperance plots, Roe's plot can be read as the systematic deflation of C. B. Macpherson's possessive individual: first the possessions are pawned, but then the body's capacity to work is lost; with it go the prerogatives of kinship reproduction and the right to membership in the social body.[33]

Without a Home thus takes the temperance maxim that young men must make their own way in the world and transfers it to the new phenomenon of drug addiction: the addict must keep up with industrial modernity—and must renounce any artificial help. In a key moment in the novel, the physician who pulls back Jocelyn's sleeve and fingers him for "an opium-eater" also tells him that "if you ever wish to break your chains you had better tell doctors the truth. . . . No physician ever advised the destroying vice you are practicing" (*WH* 280). Roe uses this exchange to exonerate the medical profession and place the blame squarely on Jocelyn's shoulders, a point driven home by his immediate firing. Jocelyn incites readerly skepticism by resisting the slavery metaphor itself, instead referring to his habit elliptically, as "what you are pleased to call my chains." The medical literature repeatedly used the metaphor of self-enslavement, in no small measure because it absolved doctors of blame and emphasized their indispensability to a cure: "Link by link the 'devil's chain' of [the patients'] thralldom is forged . . . a slavery from which, unaided by the physician's art, there is no escape."[34] The novel stages this resistance to discursive "enslavement" as Jocelyn's unconsciousness of his very real lack of freedom. It represents Jocelyn's habit as a self-destructive vice that will, in disqualifying him from the workplace, destroy the family that depends on his income. The outcome of the neuralgic businessman's nervous economy, propped up by the false credit of morphine, is thus his failure in the modern, urban industrial economy—a failure for which no one else can be blamed. In a late nineteenth-century culture in which free labor was a guarantee of postwar national reconsolidation, only a white, male, heteronormative body free of morphine and, as I will next demonstrate, untainted by the shame of chattel slavery, could achieve the moral purity requisite for industrial progress.

"True Southern Blood": Addiction, Identity, and Freedom

By representing the lingering influence of chattel slave mastery as the condition of susceptibility to addiction, *Without a Home* deploys a longstanding abolitionist trope. As I demonstrated in chapter 2, in the abolitionist imaginary, southern white men of the planter class had long been depicted as habituated to luxury and inactivity, since they lived off the stolen labor of their slaves. Expanding the frame of reference for such tropes from planters' bodies to the region at large, contemporary historians claimed that slavery had "paralyzed invention and commerce . . . prevented manufactures and the general introduction of railroads . . . [and] stunted all the energies of the people."[35] Ronald Walters notes the popular abolitionist concept of the South as "an economically backward region, building neither factories nor railroads, seldom even paying its debts. Progress, in fact, could not long continue in a region where man lost control of himself."[36] Roe's depiction of Jocelyn's habit fits with these views by relating his morphine-dependent physical economy to the slave-labor dependent southern financial economy. Having ruined his new start at the iron firm, Jocelyn attempts to cure himself by discarding his syringe and returning to the South, but once there he renews his habit in order to ward off withdrawal symptoms, keep up appearances, and find work. Yet his effort is futile, because the South under Reconstruction has little to offer: "His quest of employment was naturally unsuccessful. The South was impoverished. Weak from the wounds of war, and the deeper enervation of a system that had poisoned her life for generations, she had not yet begun to rally. There was not enough business in the city for the slow and nerveless hands of its citizens, therefore there was little prospect for the new-comer, unless he had the capital and energy to create activity in the midst of stagnation" (*WH* 405). According to this critique, white southerners cannot integrate into a modern industrial economy because their dependency on chattel slavery has incapacitated them for labor. In the throes of withdrawal after the end of chattel slavery, the southern economy crawls along insensibly, its life "poisoned," just as Jocelyn "poisoned his system." (*WH* 146). Under the influence of his morphine habit, Jocelyn's palsied, "spasmodic" efforts lead him only to "drift on in the old way," like the atrophied South itself. Unlike the dynamic economy of the industrial North, with its nervous fast pace, the South is "nerveless"; newcomers could reinvigorate it, Roe suggests, but only if they introduce "capital and energy," two things that Jocelyn, a returning native, lacks.[37] Just as Jocelyn's morphine-induced lassitude makes his life a burden to himself and to his family, so the South's systemic dependency makes it a burden on the North. *Without a Home* grounds Jacques Derrida's observation that drug use is always associated with "irresponsibility, nonwork, irrationality, unproductivity, delinquency, promiscuity, illness and the social cost it implies"—all qualities mapped onto the South.[38]

Opium, as well as hypodermic morphine, were tailor-made to serve as combined symbols of white southern torpidity and postwar desuetude. Keeley, architect of the infamous "Keeley Cure," wrote that "the Southern states contain so many who are addicted to the use of opium. The ruin wrought by the war . . . has caused many a bereaved and despairing woman, many a man, ruined in property and hopeless of regaining the wealth and position he has lost, to endeavor to dull all their feelings and make life endurable by the use of the drug."[39] Although soldiers from both sides took morphine to ease the pain of their wounds and although many developed addictions to hypodermic morphine as the result of their treatment, Confederate soldiers and veterans were thought to be particularly in its thrall.[40] Indeed, southern land itself was used to grow poppies to supply Confederate troops with opium during the Union blockade.[41]

Roe makes use of these associations by metaphorically restaging the Civil War on the ground of Jocelyn's broken body: "He surely had the will and the strength to give up a mere drug. He who had led charges amid the smoke and thunder of a hundred canon, and had warded off sabre-thrusts from muscular, resolute hands, was not going to be pricked to death by a little syringe in his own hand" (*WH* 139). Roe's analogy flaunts the success of northern strength and resolution—precisely the qualities that Roger Atwood possesses and Jocelyn lacks. As he spirals downward into the throes of his dependency, Jocelyn's confidence in his own manly resolution becomes obviously fallacious. He may have escaped the Civil War with only "a few slight scratches" (*WH* 22) at the time, but the repeated, self-inflicted scratches of the syringe will mark him fatally. Jocelyn's morphine habit assumes one of the functions of the Civil War in the abolitionist imagination: to purge deficient, unproductive southern manhood from the nation. In this formulation, southern manhood is based on premodern qualities: "Many a time during the long civil war he had smilingly led charges wherein the chances of death were greater than those of life, but neither then nor since had he ever displayed any great aptitude for quiet endurance and self-control" (*WH* 109). A modern industrial economy requires personal discipline, not reckless derring-do, but Jocelyn carelessly behaves as if it's still wartime: he "had fallen into rather soldier-like ways, and after being so free with Confederate scrip, with difficulty learned the value of paper money of a different color" (*WH* 23). The thoughtless wartime habits of the Confederate army often included the outright appropriation of goods, a theft of others' labor and property that echoed the abolitionist critique of slave mastery itself. To become modern and adjust to the standards of the North, Jocelyn must recognize the superiority of capitalist exchanges over feudal expropriation and accept "paper money" over a simplistic sensual desire for goods. Above all, just as Jocelyn must give up morphine, so must the nation renounce its unnatural reliance on chattel slavery.

Jocelyn's morphine habit is therefore associated with profligate expenditure, excess, and an inability to think abstractly, traits thought to be underwritten by the chattel slavery system. These qualities also lead to magical thinking, since under morphine's influence, Jocelyn has proud delusions that his poverty is temporary rather than systemic and profound: "What does it signify that we are poor for the moment? True Southern blood is in our veins, and I have a dozen plans for securing large wealth" (*WH* 117). Roe's irony equates the "truth" of southern blood with morphine, that other infamous substance coursing through Jocelyn's veins as he speaks. In the same utterance, southern pretensions to recover wealth and standing are exposed as delusion and disease. Moreover, this delusion is so intrinsic to white, southern, elite manhood that it can be found in the very bloodstream itself. Morphine alters the addict's consciousness of his own reality, but its contamination of the physiological medium of racial truth—blood—also suggests a more profound dispersal of identity. Jocelyn's delusion about what his southernness can achieve activates a much broader skepticism about the prospects of a formerly elite class when its financial and social edifice has vanished.

Doubtful about reincorporating the feudal vestige of an outmoded economic model that Jocelyn represents, *Without a Home* suggests that the prognosis of his addiction is bleak. Given the slavery metaphor, a cure would represent self-liberation and transformation from aristocratic privilege to citizenship based on self-reliant labor, but this is not a vision that the novel's critical utterance can countenance. Indeed, Roe replicates the sensual aristocrat's demise in the figure of Vinton Arnold, Roger's rival for Mildred's affections, who sickens and dies because he fails to forge an independent career. Significantly, by having addiction kill Jocelyn, the novel activates the lay pessimism of the day toward medical promises of cures for addiction or "inebriety," particularly in treatment homes, asylums, and institutes.[42] Such venues for the treatment of addictions sprang up in New York, Massachusetts, and England; patients could receive medical care under strict surveillance and with great discretion; almost all early issues of the American Association for the Cure of Inebriety's *Proceedings* advertise them. As John Crowley and William White characterize these early rehabilitation centers, "To the extent that inebriety was viewed as a disease in these homes, it was deemed a disease of the will, best treated in environments and by methods that would rehabilitate the inebriate's power of self-control."[43] Although Roger finances Jocelyn's stay in such a home, he relapses and commits suicide in the very next chapter. Roe himself felt powerless to write a different outcome for his character: "I felt from the first that Mr. Jocelyn was going to ruin and I could not stop him, and suffered much with him."[44]

Roe's sense of the addict's inevitable end reproduces the old temperance axiom that some habitual drunkards were unreclaimable, but the fatalism of Jocelyn's conception echoed the inevitability of the South's defeat in the northern imaginary, since it is committed with "his cavalry revolver—the one memento left of his old heroic army life," on the steps of their New York home (*WH* 489). This building was a subdivided, ramshackle Revolutionary-era mansion that Jocelyn has admired for its architectural similarities to southern mansions and its Gothic associations with colonial and antebellum pasts (*WH* 140). This disparaged gothic residue fits with Donald Ringe's assessment that postwar northern industrialism and urbanization had "profoundly transformed American consciousness," reinforcing "the fundamental rationalism of the American mind" and leading to future-oriented, realist fiction based on European models.[45] Jocelyn's nostalgia reflects his addictive leanings: his relationship to history is cyclical rather than linear and progressive. Rather than success in the new market, his fondness for the house and all it represents indicates a longing for old economies—not just chattel slavery, but colonial dependency itself. If Jocelyn's morphine habit represents the long, slow suicide of the South under slavery, his suicide on this particular site reveals southern heroism as a tragically empty, spectacular degringolade. The idea that the South vanquished itself resonates more meaningfully within this cultural history than the reality of its military defeat by the Union: self-destruction proves that the South was too weak to survive in a northern-dominated modernity. Addiction as southern self-defeat, far from a moral repudiation of slavery as an inhumane system, functions as an ethical rebuke of slavery as a backward, effeminate economic model that keeps its white masters paradoxically dependent. In the historical moment of *Without a Home*, U.S. culture produces addiction in order to separate and cast off the memory of white male slave mastery.

Unable to exploit others, the addict as former slave master unproductively exploits himself in an inversion of the bourgeois norm of accumulation through labor; the economy of pleasure and pain intrinsic to chattel slavery as a commercial institution runs instead through the closed circuit of the addict's body and mind. The suffering of enslavement manifests as the anguish of self-consciousness, so that the abjection of this particular form of metaphorical "slavery" inheres less in the compulsion to drink or inject drugs than in the self-reflective awareness of it: "It is not inability to comprehend his degradation, his danger, his utter loss of manhood, which opium imposes on its wretched slaves, but an impossibility to do aught except gratify the resistless craving at any and every cost. All will-power has gone, all moral resistance has departed, and in its place is a gnawing, clamorous, ravening desire. The vitiated body, full of indescribable and mysterious pain, the still more tortured mind, sinking under a burden of remorse, guilt, fear, and awful imagery, both unite in one desperate, incessant demand for opium" (*WH* 329). Compromised manhood means that slaves lack the natural resistance of men; they must obey the commands of their master, opium. The slaves' emasculated abjection reduces their bodies and minds alike to desire itself; this is voiced internally as an "incessant demand" that, lacking its object, gnaws at itself. This essential desire that defines the slave corresponds to the origin of Jocelyn's habit, an unnamed "painful disease, the evil effects of which did not speedily pass away"—the ailment for which he is first prescribed morphia, before his neuralgia develops (*WH* 23). Roe's decision to leave the original disease that incurred Jocelyn's habit unnamed seems to imply that elite white southerners are inherently flawed in their misdirected, insatiable desires.

But Roe's prose does more than merely racialize and degender the white male addict by comparing him to a chattel slave. In addition, it plays on the very irony of the comparison, accentuating the opium slave's compulsion to *gratify* his desire, unlike the chattel slave, whose desire is always violently squelched. The white, male opium user should be the iconic U.S. version of the liberal subject, free to pursue happiness by satisfying his cravings; yet because this gratification comes to be compelled, he becomes the deeply ironic figure of the metaphorical slave. This irony corresponds most closely to the temperance and abolitionist critique of chattel slavery's effect on its white masters, who gratify their cravings to a point beyond which they can no longer choose to do so. This figure, of which Jocelyn is a significant example, exposes the white master/addict as an impostor of freedom.

Because slavery as a metaphor applies largely to whites—and mainly to men, who are normally their own masters—their potential exposure as secret black "slaves" becomes an overwhelming cultural and narrative anxiety. Writing about the slavery metaphor in early temperance fiction, Gretchen Murphy notes: "For a sentimental male hero to become a 'slave,' to be capable of losing his self-directed manhood, a bodily difference . . . must be presupposed, in order to reassure the reader that no self-possessing man can lose his freedom. But this results in a more threatening implication: that no difference separates the bodies of black and white 'slaves.' "[46] Even after the official end of chattel slavery, such an implication would have threatened the racist imaginary. With respect to addiction, Murphy's observation points us toward a principal anxiety, namely that addicts' bodies might not differ from non-addicted ones. As with race, this anxiety operates according to the panoptic logic of visual modernity, which Robyn Wiegman describes as organizing epistemologies in the era of Reconstruction: "The binary cleavage of race to which this panoptic system applies radiated its significatory value through the ever-present production of community gazes, inscriptions that read and rendered the truth of the body, and in doing so, produced the experiential truth of the subject as well."[47] Could the physical differences that bespoke addicted identity be detected? In *Without a Home*, such questions are inseparable from the more familiar nineteenth-century plot of the discovery of secret racial identity.

As in plots of racial revelation, Jocelyn's metaphorical slavery is perceived to be intensified by exposure: "The vice was already stamped on his face and manner, so that an experienced eye could detect it at once; soon all would see the degrading brand" (*WH* 283). This anxiety extends to Jocelyn's daughter Mildred, whose prospects of marrying the wealthy Vinton Arnold, already damaged by the family's bankruptcy, are scotched by the revelation of Jocelyn's habit: "The truth that my father is an opium slave can never be hidden" (*WH* 325). The anxiety that Jocelyn's metaphorical slave status—which now carries the weight of his experiential "truth" as a subject—will be made public discloses the shame of reversals of racial, gender, and class privilege. The possible revelation of his "slavery" threatens not only his own identity but all of the exogamous property relations touching his family too.

In the discourses that include *Without a Home*, then, clandestine morphine "slavery" is a raced, gendered, sexualized, and classed concept, and the narrative anxieties about its concealment can be productively interpreted through a critical discourse of passing. As Elaine K. Ginsburg notes, passing historically denoted the assumption of white identity by someone defined as black; it disclosed a sense of trespassing upon a domain of privilege normally reserved for others. But as the essays in Ginsburg's volume attest, passing was, and is, a multifarious phenomenon; it can disguise "other elements of an individual's presumed 'natural' or 'essential' identity."[48] First, in spite of its absence from allegedly natural racial taxonomies, "morphine addict" functions as a racial identity category, as I have suggested, because morphine contaminates the purity of the addict's blood and thereby redefines its racial truth.[49] The addict becomes a defective version of whiteness, a disadvantageous mutation that appears white and yet signifies a hidden lack of autonomy coded black. This hybrid racial identity overlaps with a class identity, since the novel performs the work of naturalizing the unnatural substance coursing through his blood as a sign of southern incapacity to labor. On the job in the new, nerve-wracked sphere of northeastern commerce, which is keen to dominate the crumbled South, Jocelyn fails to pass as a competent worker who can open up his native land to northern markets. This failure reveals his essential southernness or, in other words, his inability to shift allegiance, and incapacity for industrial commerce. Since modern workers are supposed to cultivate a psychological and physical fitness, drug dependencies must be kept secret; hence the recourse to passing for healthy, where health is defined as the body's freedom from chemical assistance. The national ideal of free labor, so recently—and for many emancipated African Americans, only nominally—obtained, entails a self-reliance so scouring as to exclude dependence on any external help. The new national body had to be clean and sober in order to purge the memory of the South's compulsively self-destructive past. The failure of Jocelyn's passing for "straight" or unaddicted threatens the myth of individual self-reliance as well as the fantasy of national dominance it conditioned. The figurative purge of premodern, addicted whiteness from the larger, modernizing national white body also spoke to the material fact that nineteenth-century African Americans tended to lack the cutting-edge medical care that would have introduced them to the syringe in the first place.[50]

Accordingly, *Without a Home* also reveals the gendered and sexual aspects of the impostures of mastery, demonstrating that addiction can be interpreted as a related mode of sexual and gender passing. As Eve Kosofsky Sedgwick has noted, the taxonomic regimes of addiction that blossomed alongside those of gender and sex at the fin de siècle oblige us at least to consider addiction in terms of queer sexuality, especially since its regulation of desire appears to suspend or exclude reproductive heterosexuality and kinship norms.[51] I theorize this possibility at length in chapter 5. In the novel, Jocelyn's all-consuming desire for morphine causes his failure to fulfill masculine and heterosexual roles, bringing about a form of shame, which, though it lacks homosexual content, appears somewhat queer.[52] Indeed, the shame of his racializing, emasculating desire keeps Jocelyn from sleeping: "He often lay awake . . . trembling and cold with apprehension of the hour when she would become aware that her husband was no longer a man, but the most degraded of slaves" (*WH* 285). His wife's possible knowledge of his condition degrades him by threatening the intimate discovery that he is merely posing as a man—now no longer only a public identity, but also a private, sexual one. For she would not discover merely the apparent emasculation of the man unable to perform his heterosexual desire, but that very lack of desire itself, since Jocelyn's sole preference is for the syringe. Jocelyn becomes "queer" not by virtue of any same-sex desire, nor simply because Roe's prose feminizes him, but because his addicted desire violates the heterosexual norms governing marriage bed and public life alike.

What Jocelyn's wife, and the world at large, cannot know about him—his secret morphine slavery—carries both emasculating and racializing effects that have no clear order of causal priority: he is disqualified as patriarch of his family and of his lost plantation by virtue of either, or both. Before this exposure, however, Jocelyn attempts to conceal the habit that enables him to function in the social position left to him, family breadwinner. The four modes of passing—racial, economic, gendered, and sexual—are inextricably linked; together they promote a masculine ideal of accumulation through the wise investment of physical capital, demonizing addiction as an abnormal form of self-squander. *Without a Home* demonstrates that addiction's rehearsal of personal failure as destiny is really a failure to pass.

Addiction and Labor: Cultural Amnesia and Cultural Memory

In the period between *Without a Home* and the next significant novelistic treatment of morphine addiction, William S. Burroughs's *Junky* (1953), addiction became the signature condition of a criminal urban underclass that appeared to have made itself unfit for labor and integration into bourgeois society. The very term *junkie* illustrates a parasitic lack of productivity: the term arose when addicts in New York City in the 1920s began scavenging metal scraps of industrial refuse and exchanging them for heroin. As David Courtwright notes, the term signaled addiction's swift shift "from the office and parlor to the desolate piles of urban debris."[53] Assisting this metamorphosis was the metaphor of addiction as self-enslavement: by conflating master and slave, it forgets or obscures the relations connecting labor, capital, and consumer. David Brion Davis comments, "Analogies with chattel slavery may also have retarded the development of a vocabulary that could depict more subtle forms of coercion, oppression, and class rule. To be a free worker was to be as unlike a Negro slave as possible."[54] Conversely, it also became much more difficult to pursue addiction as a political issue, unlike agitation stoked by other contemporaneous metaphorical invocations of chattel slavery, such as the scandals of urban prostitution ("white slavery") and the agitation against low factory wages ("wage slavery"). Addiction could be fashioned as a problem of neither labor nor disability. In addiction narratives, the condition's origins and causes, if not submerged, tend to be dispensed with quickly, so that the addict's inability to be productive within society seems like a tragic flaw of her personhood. Addiction as self-enslavement became the primitive past of an industrial modernity that only the physically able could inhabit; in this formulation, the original ailment for which addicts sought pain relief was actively forgotten, as it is in Roe's novel. This amnesia, combined with the persistence of temperance notions of vice and villainy within the emergent medical concept, meant that addicts could be reviled for vicious throwback behavior. Such a common attitude merely reflected a progressive, liberal vision of the future of the United States in which new technologies such as the syringe would be properly deployed to secure national efficiency, not to foster debility and weakness.

Without a Home constructs another plot around the metaphor of "wage slavery"; this sequence of events remembers chattel slavery briefly, only to forget it again. In this second plot, Jocelyn's morphine habit and unfitness for work causes his daughters, Mildred and Belle, to take up retail drudgery as shopgirls. In the preface and an appendix, Roe polemically decries their working conditions: the new department stores forced young girls to stand all day in unforgiving heat under the surveillance of floorwalkers Roe compares to slave drivers (*WH* 276). In keeping with the cult of true womanhood, the Jocelyn women are too frail to work: Mrs. Jocelyn never attempts it; delicate, slender Mildred faints on her first day; and even the stout, hearty Belle gradually wears herself out performing her job.[55] Roe assigns his critique to Mildred's beau, Roger Atwood, who is distressed at his beloved's predicament: "It's not the work that's harming her so much as the accursed brutality which permits more cruelty to white women than was ever inflicted on black slaves. If the shopkeepers owned these girls who serve their counters, they would provide them seats instantly, on the same principle that some of your Southern people, who had no humanity, cared well for their human property; but these fellows know that when a girl breaks down they can take their pick from twenty applicants the next morning" (*WH* 300–301). By extending the metaphorics of slavery beyond Jocelyn's morphine addiction to the shopgirls' labor, Roe actually replicates proslavery critiques of northern exploitation of poor laborers, referred to as "white niggers" or "pallid slaves."[56] Since he is claiming that chattel were better cared for than wage "slaves," Roe must be quick to emphasize that this superior "care" was merely instrumental to capitalist efficiency rather than the expression of human kindness. For Roe, northern industrialism is still preferable to the southern plantation system—though it must constantly be reformed to avoid lapsing into a resemblance.

Putting this critique in the mouth of Roger, who ardently protects Mildred from capitalist depravity at every opportunity, Roe implicitly advocates a different model of human property, a traditional patriarchal system in which fathers and husbands insulate their daughters and wives from the ruthless touch of the profit motive; Roger more ably fulfills this function than the dependent, effeminate Mr. Jocelyn. When Mildred briefly becomes a nurse at the novel's end, her work is represented not as labor but as the natural outgrowth of her feminine disposition to care. Jocelyn's "enslavement" to morphine thus proliferates, infecting his daughters with "wage slavery"; in the process, chattel slavery is remembered fleetingly in a way that veers close to proslavery arguments that, whether chattel slaves were treated with sentimentality or not, they at least received superior care to northern workers. Indeed, in this period, corporations began to adopt temperance as a style of corporate care: realizing that sobriety enhanced worker productivity, they began to forge alliances with the temperance movement.[57] Addiction remained a matter of individual responsibility, but to the slight extent that it was viewed as a collective problem, it was in the context of corporate management and not labor politics.

The lost politics of addiction in the United States are tellingly illuminated by the counterexample of British history. The social changes attending the Industrial Revolution happened far earlier in Britain than in the United States, with the result that habitual drinking rather than morphine addiction brought reform movements into conjunction with labor advocacy in the 1830s and 1840s. Since most urban working men could not vote—the Reform Act of 1832 established voting rights only for those men who met property qualifications, which excluded the urban working class—the question of their potential freedom from the "thralldom" of drink activated questions of suffrage and citizenship without intensively invoking the racial valences of chattel slavery, as in the United States. As Catherine Gallagher has demonstrated, the "wage slavery" metaphor was used by three different groups in Britain: proslavery polemicists such as William Cobbett, industrial reformers, and Chartists, the working-class radicals who demanded suffrage.[58] Industrial reform, Chartism, and temperance could invoke "wage slavery" and the "slavery of drink" together in a political alliance against industry and the state. Workers were urged to sell themselves to no one: not to their greedy employers, not to the publican, not to the government that taxed beer, and, in the purple prose of *Teetotaler* editor G. W. M. Reynolds, putting to use his expertise as a writer of "penny dreadfuls," not to "the demon of intemperance" and "the Satan of alcoholic hell":

> And why are you more enslaved, then, than the working classes of those nations which are upon an equal footing of civilization with yourselves? The answer is ready,—because you have sold yourselves to the demon of intemperance . . . because you give way to a degrading habit, instead of keeping your intellects free and unimpaired to watch over your political interests with vigilance and effect; because you pass your time in the public-house instead of improving your minds and adapting them to the rational enjoyment of that liberty which you have a right to demand.[59]

Rhetoric like this implied that working men would have to demonstrate their rationality and sobriety—indeed, their exercise of freedom—before they could be awarded the formal freedom guaranteed by full membership in the national civil body.[60]

Accordingly, working-class advocates who were also teetotalers built libraries, Mechanics' Institutes, and coffee rooms, where the respectable working class could enjoy what Peter Bailey has called "rational recreation."[61] The brief fusion of teetotalism and Chartism in the early 1840s flaunted working-class sobriety in order to decry the hypocrisy of middle-class electoral drunkenness, in which votes were bought with drink.[62] Similarly to William Whipper's strategy of demonstrating black temperance and readiness for citizenship through temperance and moral reform,

British working-class advocates felt that they had to defend themselves against the perception that they were too drunk and irrational to be entrusted with the franchise. In its alliance with the "wage slavery" metaphor, the "slavery of drink" muted the idea of self-enslavement and voiced instead a critique of the industrial capitalist system and the British nation's political organization. Only by grouping together to avoid the pub could workers begin to free themselves; liberation from the "enslavement" of addiction was less a matter of individualist self-making, as it was in the United States.

This different politicization of drunkenness on class lines helps to explain the major English novelists' relative aloofness from the topic, and tendency to reproduce working class stereotypes during this period. Novels in which central characters were drunkards or addicts risked resemblance to temperance and teetotal propaganda and their class politics. As we have seen, temperance narratives characteristically substituted individualizing narratives of personal choice and class descent for systemic analysis of the relationship between intemperance and class. Temperance ideology ran directly counter to Charles Dickens's novelistic analyses of corrupt or malfunctioning social systems such as poor relief, the Yorkshire schools, and the law courts. Amanda Claybaugh demonstrates how Dickens, as he metamorphosed from a sketch writer to reformist novelist, appropriated the temperance narrative's form as individualizing narrative, while rejecting its faulty notion that drinking caused poverty in favor of the insight that poverty created the conditions for habitual drinking.[63] As a result, Dickens's most extensive commentary on intemperance can be found in several brief pieces collected in *Sketches by Boz* (1836), and in his parodies of the temperance movement in *The Pickwick Papers* (1837), not in his more mature and emblematic work.[64]

By contrast, middle-class moralism underwrote both temperance fiction in general, and the conceptualization of opium use and intemperance in novels such as Elizabeth Gaskell's *Mary Barton* (1848) and Anne Brontë's *The Tenant of Wildfell Hall* (1848). Such novels were more multidimensional and insightful than either the ordinary crop of temperance fiction or other industrial novels, but they tended to promote middle-class ideals of domestic propriety, thrift, and accumulation. As a result, the most memorable drunkards of mid-century British novels—such as Grace Poole in Charlotte Brontë's *Jane Eyre* (1847) or John Raffles in George Eliot's *Middlemarch* (1871)—occupy minor roles and confirm an unanalyzed association between intemperance and the working and serving classes. For example, in spite of the unusual terms of Grace Poole's employment, *Jane Eyre* manages to naturalize her drinking; it was "a fault common to a deal of them nurses and matrons—she kept a private bottle of gin by her, and now and then took a drop overmuch. It is excusable, for she had a hard life of it, but still it was dangerous."[65] Indeed, Grace's drinking leads directly to the destruction of Thornfield Hall, since her inebriated slumbers give Bertha Rochester the chance to escape from the attic and burn down the house. Her drunken incompetence cites a common representational trope in English fiction, which temperance fiction accentuates. For example, within the first few chapters of Ellen Wood's *Danesbury House* (1860), a drunken nurse accidentally poisons the baby, and a drunken hand causes a coach accident that kills the lady of the house. The novel extends this association to the workers in the Danesbury factory, who must be taught by their paternalistic employer to favor his new company coffee house over the pleasures of the pub. For the most part, intemperance characterizes the working class across English fiction in a manner that dispenses with psychological detail.

Because the slavery metaphor of habitual drunkenness in Britain invoked the class politics of "wage slavery" rather than chattel slavery, it also unfolded a different representational logic of race and national memory. In this slightly later discourse, excessive drinking belongs to a preindustrial English "drinking culture" unregulated by modern capitalism and therefore expressive of a nostalgic version of white ethnicity. Thomas Hardy's *The Mayor of Casterbridge* (1886) is the best social document of this vision: in its pages, excessive drunkenness belongs to a disappearing bucolic folk-world of county fairs and seasonal labor. The drunkenness of its protagonist, Michael Henchard, is linked to an energy and impulsiveness no longer useful in a modern world of industry that favors punctuality over imprecise timekeeping, written contracts rather than word-of-mouth agreements, measurement over estimation, and calculation instead of explosive reaction. With this novel, Hardy both sidesteps the modern discourse of the syringe and buries the temperance plot of individual struggle against alcohol: his protagonist's flaw is his chaotic temperament rather than his drinking. In keeping with the novel's motto, "character is fate," Henchard becomes a tragic hero because he represents the cultural loss associated with the passage of time within industrial modernity, whereby English drinking customs reappear as signs of degeneration rather than as expressions of community. Hardy's England is like Roe's South, unable to compete in the new economic regimes; like Jocelyn, Henchard is marked by a repetitive compulsion that writes him out of the future. But Hardy wistfully interprets the rush to modernization and attempts to memorialize its losses through recourse to a cultural nationalism not quite available to Roe.

Hardy's novel reveals how much twentieth-century assessments, like that by E. P. Thompson in *The Making of the English Working Class*, are contiguous with the late nineteenth-century ethos of progress: "The passing of Gin Lane, Tyburn Fair, orgiastic drunkenness, animal sexuality, and mortal combat for prize-money in iron-studded clogs, calls for no lament."[66] Drunkards, quite unlike "the poor stockinger, the Luddite cropper, the 'obsolete' hand-loom weaver, the 'utopian' artisan, and even the deluded follower of Joanna Southcott" are not worthy of the act of historical rescue Thompson wishes to make "from the enormous condescension of posterity."[67] Hardy, of course, felt otherwise; and yet in celebrating drunken excess as the lost domain of sociable animal spirits and community ritual, he bestows the aura of cultural authenticity upon it. Sobriety was a function of the new, rational modernity on both sides of the Atlantic; but whereas Roe's *Without a Home* attempted to forget the shameful national past by writing addicted individuals out of the national future, Hardy's *Mayor of Casterbridge* remembered them as remnants of a unified, if waning, culture.

Between the white U.S. model of cultural amnesia and the white British model of cultural memory, a third strategy for thinking about addiction—call it countermodern—activates a wealth of critically neglected texts and traditions, such as the writings and oratory of African-American temperance. *Without a Home* fashions the "slavery of drink" as a phenomenon of white individualism by converting the real racial, gender, and sexual relations of chattel slavery into metaphorical ones; as I have shown in chapter 2, counternarratives that invert the metaphor characterize addiction as a social and political problem explicitly related to chattel slavery. For example, *Free at Last* (1896), a late temperance novel by Jane S. Collins, features an African-American protagonist, George, who is the antithesis of Roe's Jocelyn. When George travels north after the Civil War to bring the temperance message from Tennessee to Washington, D.C., he encounters white condescension and bibulous excess. Whereas in *Without a Home* emancipation exposes the addicted white elite's incapacity for labor and imagination in rebuilding the nation, in *Free at Last* it reveals the teetotaling African American's superior intellect and self-discipline in solving the social problem of drunkenness for everyone.

"He delighted in tracing the analogy between [intemperance] and slavery. . . . He thought that possibly God had a purpose in freeing them at the time. Was it that they might enlist in the glorious warfare against the liquor traffic?"[68] In this inverse formation, intemperance and addiction represent a collective social and political problem.

African-American temperance, of which Collins's novel is arguably a part, could be productively read as a precursor to the tradition Paul Gilroy describes, in which "the memory of slavery . . . helped [blacks in the West] to generate a new set of answers" to "what the best possible forms of social and political existence might be."[69] Given this definition, Collins's novel might be countermodern, but that does not make it politically or aesthetically sophisticated. Indeed, it is worth studying precisely because of the tortured difficulty with which it produces its doubled critique of post-Reconstruction racial exclusion and intemperance.[70] As Denise Herd's work attests, the political shifts that realigned anti-liquor activism with white supremacy, and the disenfranchisement of African-Americans through Jim Crow laws, spelled the effective demise of African-American temperance as a political force in this period.[71] Roe's novel helped addiction substitute for and obscure guilt over chattel slave mastery as a pressing problem for the white ethical subject; by contrast, Collins's novel frames addiction as a collective problem consciously informed by the history of slavery. Whereas addiction tended to remain an effect of the white masculine transcendence of social limitations, this alternative trajectory represented an unchosen path, by which its relationship to history, culture, and politics might have become a larger part of public discourse.

II

DISEASE, DESIRE, AND DEFECT

4

NEEDLING DESIRES

Women, Morphinomania, and Self-Representation in Fin-de-Siècle Britain

> And my arm was pricked. The drug ran through my veins. I felt the colour come into my cheeks, and instinctively I knew that a feverish sparkle was in my eyes. I had been haggard and my face drawn and bloodless, now a warmth and brilliance came to me, and the pain died, and then came sleep. Now answer me my question. Did my responsibility begin then?
>
> Richard Pryce, *An Evil Spirit* (1887)

WHEN THE governess Isabel Gordon recounts her introduction to the hypodermic injection of morphine in Richard Pryce's novel *An Evil Spirit*, she poses a challenge to the readers of her fictional diary. By requesting them to assign her responsibility for her morphine habituation to a precise moment in her narrative, the text defies them to assign responsibility to her at all. Whereas temperance fiction had conjured the drunkard's responsibility for his own degradation, Pryce's novel signaled a turn away from such moralistic conceptualizations of intemperance. As we have seen in chapter 3, in *Without a Home* (1881) the U.S. novelist E. P. Roe had engaged the problem of viewing the new personage of the hypodermic morphine habitué with sympathy, as the victim of an illness, but ultimately framed him as responsible for his own malady. In the 1870s and 1880s, the British reading public was also learning of this new phenomenon that appeared primarily to afflict bourgeois urban women. Variously termed "morphinomania" and "morphinism" in Britain, this new disease was the same compulsive, clandestine use of up-to-date hypodermic technology to inject morphine, a recently isolated alkaloid of opium. Roe's bestseller had featured a male protagonist even though the population of early hypodermic morphine habitués in the United States was overwhelmingly female; the novel traced his feminization and racialization as he became hysterically dependent upon, and significantly "enslaved" by, the needle. In Britain, when the story of hypodermic morphine habituation migrated from the pages of medical journals to mainstream reviews and novels, it revolved almost entirely around women. Whereas De Quincey's *Confessions of an English Opium-Eater* had advertised his masculine scholastic and empirical authority to supply the deficiencies of a scanty medical literature, texts about women's morphinomania were largely written by doctors and their popular interpreters, whose analysis mixed scandalized morality and scientific suggestion as they began to articulate a disease model of "inebriety." More than their German and U.S. counterparts, British physicians built an overarching concept of inebriety, later formalized as "addiction," on the perceived similarities between the covert use of morphine and alcohol, a scandal of the same period that also implicated women.[1] In Britain, as the early- and mid-nineteenth-century dominance of the temperance metaphor of self-enslavement unevenly began to give way to a metaphor of disease, women moved from the role of long-suffering drunkard's wife into the discursive locus of a frightening and modern self-relation.

This shift was uneven, drawing issues of self-representation, medico-scientific and cultural authority, and women's rights into complex relation with femininity. Histories of addiction in British culture tend to sketch these episodes without fully analyzing the politics of representation that inform them. For example, Virginia Berridge and Griffith Edwards report that "conventional ideas about the weakness of the female sex were also soon linked with the spread of morphia use."[2] Yet a major feature of this weakness was deception: as in the United States, morphine users were routinely portrayed as liars who would say anything to obtain a dose. Physicians, keen to absolve themselves of responsibility for having prescribed hypodermic morphine and inadvertently turning their patients into addicts, described their patients' inability to represent themselves straightforwardly as "pathological." Both narrowly, to conceal the habit, and more generally, lying became a physical symptom of the compulsive use of alcohol, opium, and morphine. Testifying before a parliamentary committee, the Scottish psychologist Alexander Peddie stated that the habitual drunkard "will tell the most shameful lies, for no truth is ever found in connection with the habitual drunkard's state. I never yet saw truth in relation to drink go out of one who was a dipsomaniac."[3] One physician wrote that opium-eaters are "given to romancing, exaggeration, wide and wild assertions or absolute falsehood."[4] And in popular periodical pieces, the claim was repeated often enough to become a maxim: "Untruth is second nature with them."[5]

Lying emasculates the male protagonist of Roe's *Without a Home*, since a southern man's honor was supposed to be based on his truthfulness. But lying engaged a different cultural logic with respect to women. Although all addicts were characterized as liars, this deficiency of self-representation had special resonance for female addicts, since it reproduced a conventional fascination with the deceptive potential of women. The same fascination also motivated the recent popular emergence of sensation fiction, which often constructed lurid plots of insanity, bigamy and adultery around a calculating villainess who had invaded the domestic sphere. As the figure of the femme fatale began to take hold in literature and culture, lying to conceal a secret shame seemed to fit perfectly with women's skill at manipulating appearances. Some of these writers broadened this commonplace into an argument against women's collective self-representation. Nineteenth-century British texts that describe key features of an emergent disease model of addiction also vehemently refute women's capacity for and right to political self-representation.[6]

Pryce's morphinomaniac Isabel Gordon as well as later fictional morphinomaniacs like Valeria Ismey and Julie Thibaud, created by Robert Hichens and Eliza Margaret J. Humphreys ("Rita"), respectively, also exhibit the pathological lying commonly ascribed to morphine users in the medical literature.[7] Pryce directly confronts the challenge of making a pathological liar a sympathetic protagonist by having Isabel narrate part of the story. Her untruthfulness challenges the traditional protocols of readerly sympathy and the flow of narrative information. Although only Isabel can tell the truth of her own experiences, her status as an addict renders all of her statements suspect. Simultaneously admitting that she is a liar and confessing her true crimes, Isabel sabotages her own coherence as a character. More significantly, she embodies a crucial representational paradox at the heart of addiction: as the people who experience addiction firsthand, addicts are the best source of information about the condition, yet the experience itself is thought to destroy their ability to comprehend and represent it faithfully to others. That is, only after they have exhibited other signs of having reformed their behavior, and their speech conforms to normative expectations of remorse, can their self-statements be accepted. In the 1930s, Alcoholics Anonymous invented a formula for the production of personal oral narrative about addiction that generally guarantees its veracity, but in the nineteenth century, no such conventions existed. The daughter of a recently bankrupted parvenu, Isabel is like the upper-class female hypodermic morphine users whose veracity the emergent medical establishment challenged. The form of Pryce's novel directly engages the extraliterary discourses of women's morphinomania.[8] This new species of addiction was broadly similar to other women's pathologies of the late nineteenth century, such as anorexia and hysteria, but its dynamics differently configured women's bodies and subjectivities in relation to habit, consumption, dependency, and most of all, representation.[9] Because the actual experience of addiction converts one into a liar who cannot re-present the experience honestly to others, knowledge about addiction must be produced through practices of reading. The act of consuming the novel—of learning about the latest mode of modern degradation—also aligns actual readers with the fictional readers of Emily's diary and with a putatively non-addicted culture attempting to "read" and know the new disease.

The trope of feminine lack of self-control and mendacity was readily available in midcentury culture and literature, particularly in sensation fiction. Wilkie Collins, who himself used the syringe to self-medicate, gave his anti-heroine Lydia Gwilt of *Armadale* (1866) a fondness for drops of laudanum, stopping short of having her inject herself with morphine.[10] Collins experimented with a narrative about drug use in the detective novel *The Moonstone* (1868), creating a doctor, Ezra Jennings, who takes opium; a single instance of laudanum use also creates a rift between the novel's hero, Franklin Blake, and his sweetheart, Rachel Verinder. With these sympathetic characters, Collins domesticates drug use; but he is more interested in exploring unconsciousness than habituation: Blake cannot lie about his theft of Rachel's diamond because, having been secretly dosed with laudanum, he wasn't aware of it.[11] It took Pryce, writing a generation later, to explore the implications of the deceptions of women morphine users for novel form. Pryce's novel uneasily straddles the genres of sensation fiction, detective fiction, and even—in its reception—the newly scandalous naturalism, with its detailed portrayals of modern degradation. Borrowing from Lawrence Rothfield's archaeology of the literary-medical relations that helped produce these genres, I describe *An Evil Spirit*'s narrative innovations as a conflicted response to the new disease model of morphinomania.[12] Pryce used the novel to explore the question of how one could feel sympathy for a sufferer whose primary symptoms were mendacity and subterfuge.

Ultimately, these scandals did their part to change gendered social relations. Midcentury Victorian femininity had turned self-denial and submission to external authority into virtues; women's autonomy was not the transparent execution of their spontaneous wills but subservience to the appropriate influences. Women's covert habituations and dependencies were scandalous only because women appeared to be permitting a degrading influence to shape their characters. Addiction was thus demeaning to womanhood not because it interfered with self-reliance but because it appeared to produce self-gratification, a phenomenon with the potential to reshape gendered politics radically. Within temperance and mainstream discourses, women were supposed to help manage men's morals, especially when it came to the promotion of sobriety. For women themselves to appear susceptible to tippling or—more horrifying—the uncharted territory of drug-taking was to render them unfit for that important social role as well.

"Shameless and Most Skillful Liars": The Gendered Politics of Morphine, Alcohol, and Self-Representation

By the late 1860s, physicians in London, France, Germany, and, as we have seen, the United States increasingly administered medicine via syringes to relieve neuralgia.[13] A London surgeon, Charles Hunter, introduced the term *hypodermic* in an 1863 paper that sparked a contentious disagreement with Edinburgh physician Alexander Wood about how the process affected the body. Wood held that the injection had to be made at or near the painful body part, but Hunter recognized that remote injection would relieve pain just as well, since the effect was systemic. This debate was still going on in the 1880s. The former president of the Royal College of Physicians of London, Thomas Watson, had decried the woeful lack of standardized knowledge of drugs: "To me it has been a lifelong wonder how vaguely, how ignorantly, and how rashly drugs are often prescribed."[14] A new journal, *The Practitioner*, aimed to dispel such therapeutic ignorance. "By purely empirical inquiry we have got possession of a few remedies—such as cod-liver oil, chloroform, iodide of potassium—which are of the greatest value; but it is none the less certain that an exact knowledge of the mode of handling remedies does not exist," wrote the journal's co-founder and co-editor Francis Edmund Anstie in the inaugural 1868 preface.[15]

One of the first steps the journal took to ameliorate the situation was to publish Anstie's unqualified praise for the hypodermic syringe. Characterizing those physicians ignorant of its benefits as technophobes, Anstie recommended hypodermic injection over old-fashioned digestion because of its increased ease, efficacy, and permanence. Indeed, this was the medical explanation given to Collins, who explained to a friend in 1869, "I am stabbed every night at ten with a sharp-pointed syringe which injects morphia under my skin—and gets me a night's rest without any of the drawbacks of taking opium internally."[16] Anstie's praise for morphine injections was ringing: its advantages "are such as would be a priori incredible, nor can they as yet be fully explained."[17] Other physicians extolled its use in cases of mental disease and dyspepsia. The prominent physician T. Clifford Allbutt, soon to become George Eliot's model for Tertius Lydgate in *Middlemarch*, wrote that hypodermic effects "are greater than we dream of as yet . . . its power is something far wider in its bearings than we can at present formulate, or, indeed, conceive."[18] In a piece rushed to publication, Allbutt panegyrized the new technology for allaying the suffering of patients undergoing the torments of terminal heart disease: "From small and timid beginnings I have gone forward with this marvellous remedy, until I find myself now justified in using it fearlessly in any form and in any stage of heart and aortic disease. No matter how swollen the limbs, no matter how agitated the pulse, no matter how blue and how turgid the face and lips, I now never hesitate to inject morphia, and scarcely ever fail, even up to the time of the dying agonies, to give relief decided enough to earn the warm gratitude of the patient. At such times one feels the blessing of being a physician."[19] Allbutt depicted himself as a medical adventurer battling the menacing symptoms of heart disease to bring his patients peace. This embedded narrative, the story of the physician's emotional reward, culminates in an affirmation of his professional identity of metaphysical proportions. Beyond even its therapeutic value to the patient, the administration of hypodermic morphine brings the individual man into complete harmony with his social role as physician. Allbutt's enthusiasm for hypodermic morphia was not idiosyncratic. British physicians prescribed it for unusual ailments such as chorea and mundane ones like hiccups.[20] It must have seemed that there was nothing hypodermic morphine could not remedy.[21]

Yet no sooner did this idyllic harmony come to pass than it was undone by the patients themselves. Just a few months later, Allbutt published a paper detailing the negative effects of hypodermic morphine. Amazingly, he was suddenly attempting to distance himself from its use: "Although I may . . . seem to have used morphia very extensively, yet I cannot compare myself with those practitioners of whom the syringe and phial are as constant companions as was the lancet to their fathers."[22] Anstie leapt at this opportunity to temper his own earlier advocacy and revise the rules for hypodermic use. What could occasion such an obvious and embarrassing about-face? Allbutt, Anstie, and other physicians had been supplying syringes and morphine to their patients and allowing them to inject themselves or to have their servants inject them. Yet the original ailments—abdominal, uterine, facial, and back pain—persisted. For a while, Allbutt could not see a need to forbid repetitions of morphia; after all, they temporarily eased his patients' pain, and withholding it made them suffer. Yet eventually he came to understand that his patients had become dependent on the morphine injections, which "create the same artificial want and gain credit for assuaging a restlessness and depression of which it was itself the cause."[23] Hypodermic morphine was reproducing a decades-old suspicion of the medical profession itself—that it exacerbated existing ailments, or even caused new ones, in order to promote its own business.

Doctors needed to shed this old image of charlatanism for one of professional competence and expertise; the needle, which had seemed like the perfect way to modernize their knowledge and enhance their cultural authority, was now threatening both. British doctors had more to lose than their U.S. counterparts: though far from organized, by the late 1860s, their profession was more consolidated and regulated, less susceptible to the outright quackery that continued in the United States until well into the twentieth century. The gendered dynamic whereby a male medical profession seemed to be preying upon upper-class female patients worsened the fiasco; especially in delicate female cases, such as hysteria, the syringe had to be "used carefully in a moral as well as in a medical sense."[24] From the vantage of hindsight, physicians were responsible for turning their female patients into the first cohort of drug addicts. Yet their victims could not voice this perspective on the event at the time, since the disease model of addiction had not yet been accepted and since their behavior did seem synonymous with a reprehensible lack of self-control. Instead, their voices were enlisted in the medical identification of tolerance and withdrawal: "They seem as far from cure as ever they were, they all find relief in the incessant use of the syringe, and they all declare that without the syringe life would be insupportable."[25] This declaration itself became a symptom of the dependency that must be eliminated; in other words, the patients' claim could not be allowed to come true, for the syringes must be surrendered without loss of life. The phenomenon of addiction thus requires physicians to interpret their patients' self-statements to make a diagnosis; as I will demonstrate, readers of fiction narrated by addicts would also be obliged to adopt this practice.

The gendered politics of the hypodermic fiasco remained a subtext in the medical literature but arose in the mainstream press at almost precisely the same time with respect to alcoholism. Doctors had been prescribing alcohol widely since the 1830s, when the Brunonian system of medicine replaced bloodletting.[26] An 1871 *Saturday Review* piece warned that drunken habits were "notoriously on the increase, and . . . threaten to degrade women even of the well-born and educated classes."[27] Because the article attacked doctors in a vulnerable spot, underlining a longstanding claim that they made their patients into drunkards by prescribing "stimulants" too frequently, it inspired Anstie to reassert medical authority, once again, in the pages of the *Practitioner*. Anstie conceded that medical carelessness was partly responsible and needed reforming, thus creating an opportunity for further discipline- and profession-building.[28] But in defending the profession, he also mounted the following sensational counterattack: "The fact is that all tipplers become more or less untruthful, but that female tipplers invariably become shameless and most skilful liars. And the favourite lie which they invent as an excuse for their habits, is an apocryphal medical order 'to take plenty of support and stimulants.' We have personally detected the manufacture and skilful dissemination of this particular falsehood in several instances, and the practice is notorious to physicians who see much of nervous diseases."[29] The scandal of upper-class women's drinking replicated the contest for authority about hypodermic morphine. As with morphine, physicians' disinterested knowledge—signified by Anstie's corporate "we"—and efficacy of treatment were presented as being in stark contrast with women's susceptibility to secrecy and deception. *The Lancet* complained: "It is a shabby thing to attribute to the profession the creation of intemperate habits. . . . [I]n too many cases the doctor is unjustly made the scapegoat."[30] One doctor wrote: "People who drink do so knowingly. . . . They will, of course, try to shift the blame upon their Doctors."[31] The sharp defensiveness of these medical writings was occasioned by the generalized prejudice against physicians, who were still perceived as profit-seekers intent on keeping their patients sick and thus dependent on them. Physicians also had to fight the teetotal campaigns that had challenged the medical efficacy of stimulants from the 1830s through the 1870s.[32]

The scandals of iatrogenic hypodermic morphine dependency and alcoholism shared the same narrative feature, a contest for credibility between women and their physicians. Terry Parssinen describes the British medical establishment's attempt to pathologize such habituations as "part of [an] aggressive thrust" of new cultural authority; I contend that it coincided with the erosion of a transparent model of middle-class femininity that safeguarded the domestic sphere of private life. This episode is part of a cultural split that Kathy Psomiades has described as occurring, within bourgeois femininity, "between surface and depth, knowable exterior appearance and unknowable interior desires."[33] As physicians cast their patients as vicious, intemperate women who used their prescriptions as pretexts for secret self-indulgence, so too did they cast themselves as experts on the proper administration of medicines, once a matter of feminine, household expertise. With the same maneuver, physicians successfully subsumed moral judgments into their medical diagnoses: if addictions were vices, then physicians were merely abetting sin; but if addictions were diseases, with shameless lying as a symptom, then physicians were desperately needed—not merely to cure them but to restore their patients' moral integrity too. The logic of this phenomenon was contradictory but effective: suggesting that addictions were diseases entitled physicians to pronounce upon them; retaining the shock of moral scandal gave them a mandate to do so. Physicians used this maneuver to conceptualize an ambivalent new figure to whom a unified medical and moral charge could stick, the morphinomaniac, who became a subspecies of the "inebriate," "narcomaniac," and "addict." As Richard Davenport-Hines remarks, "addiction became identified with gender; the hypodermic habit was feminised."[34] Because a major feature of the public discourse of hypodermic morphine was the gendered contest for cultural authority that I have outlined, the politics of gender representation should be central to the history of addiction.

"Oh Doctor, Shoot Me Quick!": Narrating Hypodermic Desire

In Maria Weed's novel *A Voice in the Wilderness* (1895), published in the U.S., a widow named Helen Matthews becomes habituated to hypodermic morphine during treatment following a train wreck, but her doctor keeps her dependency a secret from her.[35] After filling her in on her shameful condition, he abruptly leaves the country on a long voyage at sea, consigning her case to his protégé, the young and handsome Dr. Stanley. Lyman's excuse for foisting his patient off on another doctor is itself suspicious, since long sea voyages were frequently recommended as cures for habitual drunkenness.[36] Predictably, Dr. Stanley falls in love with the vulnerable but courageous Helen, who reminds him of his wife, Leila: a woman who—rather ominously for Helen—had perished from a morphine overdose while under his care. Since Stanley's only hope of saving Helen depends on her being honest with him about how much morphine she is injecting, her potential for deception coalesces all the ambivalence of his transgressive erotic attachment to her. Deceit within the doctor-patient relationship is complexly layered, disclosing a highly developed narrative of disturbing power dynamics in a way that Roe's novel could not. On Stanley's first night as her doctor and houseguest, he waits for Helen to come to him for her dose of morphine—but it seems that she is ready to administer it herself, retrieving the syringe and morphine from its spot over the living room mantle: "Then with womanly deftness she unfastened the buttons upon the outside of the sleeve—which until then he had, with manly ignorance, supposed to have been intended for purely ornamental purposes. This done the drapery fell back, disclosing to Stanley's gaze her exquisitely beautiful arm. He was spell-bound by her manner and appearance as one in a dream, seemingly unable to stir. If she could deceive them in this way, her case was hopeless" (*VW* 30–31). In keeping with the heavy-handed gendering of this passage, Helen's feminine beauty is a function of her ability to deceive—indeed, mesmerize—Stanley with the concealment and revelation of her body as she prepares to inject herself. In the next moment, Helen proves her honesty by breaking down in front of the portrait of her dead husband, sobbing that she cannot go through with so deceitful an act, before fainting. But it is the spectacle of her imagined dishonesty—her power to conceal or reveal both her body and her depravity—that arrested Stanley's gaze and makes her desire—which is also her disease—appear momentarily resistant to heroic medical effort. The passage reveals a fantasy of a woman who can experience not just relief but also pleasure and even euphoria at her own hands, but at the last moment concedes her desperate need—less for morphine than for masculine medical help. The imagined private moments in which women perform their addictions become the scene of a new kind of erotic spectacle.[37]

The cultural history enfolding this moment is one in which women are represented as addicted *to* mass culture at the same time that their images circulate *as* mass culture's addictive material.[38] Since the eighteenth century, women have been represented as the excessive consumers of novels, romance narratives, fashion, tea, chocolate, and other frivolous luxuries, a phenomenon that constructs their capacity for addiction as fundamental lack; yet women also represent the very addictiveness of mass culture, in heteronormative scenarios, to men. Hence Helen's desire both represents her own craving for morphine and relays Stanley's desire for her.

Weed intensifies the eroticism surrounding the surrogate phallus of the needle, creating a scenario that graphically enacts the sexual fantasies of power underlying much of the gendered discourse of hypodermic morphine. For when the medical man takes his cue to leap into action, his use of the needle is an act of penetration that resembles both rape and murder: "Then the wicked instrument was handled with a much firmer grasp, the needle plunged into the snowy arm and removed, Stanley placing his finger over the punctured flesh until the slowly beating heart had permitted its servants to appropriate the drug, while the quivering eyelids and quickened pulse indicated that the medicine was doing its work, and the struggle for that night was over" (*VW* 32). Here the hypodermic needle becomes the ultimate alibi for a violent masculine desire lurking within the practice of medicine, since it permits Stanley to penetrate Helen's beautiful, racially clean flesh in the name of curing her withdrawal symptoms and giving her comfort. In the passage's sexual economy, Helen's painful symptoms are the analogues of a sexual desire that only Stanley, the physician, can legitimately satisfy.

Yet the morphine injection is itself the cause of Helen's physical distress, a fact that licenses a performative logic of repetition and replication, since Helen refigures Stanley's dead wife. *A Voice in the Wilderness* thrives on this repetition of masculine power: Stanley is repeatedly late with Helen's dose, increasing the sharpness of her cravings and the pleasure of her relief. With this motif, the novel recapitulates a feature of the medical reportage: the physician H. Gibbons, writing in the *Pacific Medical and Surgical Journal*, had documented a similar case of a nervous woman who required injections twice a day: "The suffering was more and more aggravated. Most impatiently did she await the injection, morning and evening, often crying like a child, and always exclaiming, as I entered, 'Oh doctor, shoot me quick!' "[39] How many other physicians hurried to and fro around the fin-de-siècle streets of London, New York, San Francisco, and other cities, syringes weighing heavily in their pockets, as they delivered the very latest in medical technology to their demanding patients? The scandal of women secretly dosing themselves found legitimacy under the disciplinary sign of medicine, a phenomenon positioning women's potential for deception at the crux of medical and novelistic discourse.

Meanwhile, the German physician Edward Levinstein suggested that alcohol and morphine dependency were causally connected, some patients resorting to alcohol to ward off the desire for morphia.[40] Levinstein's *Die Morphiumsucht* (1877; English trans. *Morbid Craving for Morphia*, 1878), the first major scientific treatise on the condition, warned physicians that their otherwise respectable patients "will so far forget themselves as to lie willfully."[41] In the case of "Mrs. von C.," admitted to a hydropathic institution to cure her morphine habit, he noted that "as the patient could move about freely both inside and outside the Institution with her own attendants, she injected secretly during the night the same dose as before."[42] By the 1880s, the indulgence of society women in this secret pastime had become a sensational topic: "Ladies even, belonging to the most elegant classes of society, go so far as to show their good taste in the jewels which they order to conceal a little syringe and artistically made bottles, which are destined to hold the solution which enchants them! At the theatre, in society, they slip away for a moment, or even watch for a favourable opportunity of pretending to play with these trinkets, while giving themselves an injection of morphia in some part of the body which is exposed, or even hidden from view."[43] This passage demonstrates that as the issue moved from medical to more general-interest British periodicals such as *The Nineteenth Century*, the accusation of lying developed into a more salacious portrait of generalized deception. The idea that these women were engaging in penetrative, covert self-pleasuring in public was scandalous and monstrous. Of course, such wantonness also required a nefarious, careless, or naive physician-supplier, but this figure could fade to the background, since the real attraction was the female body as ground of a bizarre new secret self-relation.

The idea that women were lying to cover vices was subsumed into a broader cultural thematic of women's inherent disposition toward false appearances, especially as they aged: "It is then that she has recourse to those foul and fatal expedients of which we have heard more than enough in these latter days. She will not try simplicity of living, natural hours, wholesome occupation, unselfish endeavour, but rushes off for help to paints and cosmetics, to stimulants and drugs."[44] In France, morphine and syringe became the emblems of a new version of the femme fatale, the *morphinée*, but, as Liedekerke reports, "fashionable woman or courtesan, fake duchess or real countess, actress, theater-type, call girl or bluestocking, today's woman injects herself with morphine."[45] Even the decadent Arthur Machen complained of "your fine City dames . . . who, in the privity of their chambers, will stupefy themselves with chloral or morphia and the like."[46]

An Evil Spirit squares neatly with these views. The doctor who first hooks Isabel Gordon is perhaps too trusting—he extracts her promise to follow his orders to the letter—but he is not at all careless or malignant. Rather, he merely falls prey to Isabel's deception:

> "You need not be afraid," I said; "I think I am fairly strong-minded. I will do exactly as you tell me. Now will you not trust me, and let me take these with me?" I put my hand on the vial and needle-squirt as I spoke.
>
> "Very well, Miss Gordon, I will trust you," he said; "but let me warn you that if you use this often you will become a slave to it. People have gone to their ruin before now by giving themselves over to its power. It will absorb your vitality, and you will lose your youth and appearance. So that I can only give it to you on the promise that you will keep rigidly to my directions."[47]

In this exchange, Isabel proves to be untrustworthy, and the doctor joins the ranks of Isabel's dupes. Pryce dramatizes Isabel's mendacity by letting his physician off the hook. But in fictional writing, establishing a narrator as a liar creates problems for readers who rely on her for narrative information. Isabel's narration requires the reader to infer the appropriate moral relationship to her, but this process is vexed by the ambiguous status of the habit, as vice or disease.

The demand for readerly inference is most pronounced in Isabel's "Record," with its haunting demand, "How far am I responsible?" (*ES* 2:67) Isabel begins her "Record" to confess her crime but assigns blame more to her "devils" than to herself. The plot alternately suggests she is victim and aggressor: when her fiancé Geoffrey Howard leaves for India to earn enough money to marry her, the debilitating pain of a neuralgic attack inspires readerly sympathy; when she later pushes him off a cliff in a fit of jealous rage over his apparent attentions to her rival, Grace Carruthers, readers naturally resist sympathy by reading against the grain of her narration. The narration thematizes this instability: "How far am I responsible? That is the question which night and day is before me. I ask it again and again, and I answer nothing. I ask another: If I am at all responsible, when did my responsibility begin? Is it that I cannot answer these things, or that I dare not face them? Ah, this is maddening! Let me escape! Let me not listen to these voices! They follow me, and it is vain. Then let this Record answer for me" (*ES* 2:67–68). The closer the text verges toward a direct statement about Isabel's moral responsibility for her acts, the more it shies away, referring back to itself as her "answer." This answer functions less as an apology or an explanation than as the performance of fictionality itself. Rather than actually judging if Isabel is responsible or not, the reader is asked to decide when the "real" Isabel is speaking and when the narrative voice is narcotized. Readers assume the role of the physician, who must interpret their patients' statements to figure out their physical states.

This literary collision with the medical produces even more contradictions, since the novel must establish Isabel as a character who both possesses and lacks agency and intent. Isabel's retrospective narration of her arrival at Manor House to become the Carruthers's family governess reveals these fault lines: "I was very happy; and surely, surely this must be a proof of how unrealizing was my folly when I opened the door to my devils! Surely it must be seen that it is not probable that I should of my own free will jeopardize this happiness. Was I in any way responsible?—if so, at what point? But should circumstances ever occasion that this diary be my confession, my confessor must judge for himself" (*ES* 2:53). This is a familiar plea for Isabel's nonresponsibility, but in making its argument for her unknowingness, for the lack of intentionality with which she gave up her happiness as she embarked upon a morphia habituation, it makes another and more complex case. It seems to be arguing for Isabel's coherence as a character, one that behaves freely and rationally so that readers can follow the plot as the consistent effect of her intent. Yet this normal state of affairs is eclipsed by the story's requirement to represent Isabel's habit, which deviates from the typical bildungsroman plot of upward mobility through hard work and marriage by actively thwarting her own best interests. Accordingly, Isabel's narration must flaunt her unknowingness and lack of agency in order to gain the sympathy normally accorded to a novel's protagonist. In performing this operation, the text constantly risks reminding the reader of Isabel's fictionality; to prevent this from becoming a distraction, it places the responsibility of judgment on the reader, cultivating a metanarrative. Perhaps this constant pressure against fictional conventions, along with the process of readerly diagnosis, prompted a reviewer's complaint that the novel read like "literature for medical students."[48]

The narration's demand for diagnosis results in more awkward negotiations between the literary and the juridical. As a morphia habitué, Isabel cannot be truthful, for she must lie to hide her habit, a familiar example of the discourse detailed above: "I lie quite easily now. At first I found it hard. I reddened, and I contradicted myself; now it is different" (*ES* 2:48). Yet as the narrator of events that take place over years, and which must be seen by the reader to confirm the other characters' versions, she must be truthful enough to be accurate: "I could give the exact dates for everything in this journal of mine, for it has been my habit always to keep a note-book, and to put down facts as they occur. From these notes, then, I am compiling this record" (*ES* 2:50). Isabel must be seen to lie, yet the "Record" she writes must be trustworthy. The best example of the text's tortured questions about its own status comes in Isabel's rationale for writing her confession: "Hence my diary. Will it ever, I wonder, answer its purpose and be my confession? Will it justify its own *raison d'être*? I mean to conceal nothing, not my crime even, which not a soul suspects. It is therefore a gratuitous confession, but I shall carry it out to the bitter end. In these days of novel writing, when this diary might be well thought an MS., they could scarcely convict me on my own writing" (*ES* 2:44). Activating the metanarrative, this passage brazenly reminds the reader that he is indeed reading a text that was once a manuscript rather than a legal confession. This reminder helps readers to locate themselves in the proper realm of fiction and sympathy, where judgment is most expansive and lenient, rather than in the legal world, where Isabel's crime would presumably require no explanation at all, merely confirmation of its occurrence.

Isabel's exemption from the law is also thematized in the plot, when Grace Carruthers, having witnessed the murder, refuses to turn Isabel over to the police. Isabel's rescue from legal power, combined with the readerly process of diagnosis, forces readers to suspend judgment. One can only continue reading the texture of her confession against itself. After all, the "confession" marks itself as "gratuitous" or uncompelled, a gift to a stranger who turns out to be Emily Howard, Geoffrey's interfering aunt, and, through her, the reader of the novel. The invitation to read is an invitation to infer and diagnose. D. A. Miller's model of power in the Victorian novel would interpret Isabel's exemption from formal prosecution as the condition of readers' inculcation of a generalized "discipline"; it would also conjure the reader's suspension of judgment as a compulsive activity akin to addiction itself.[49] Neither of these formulations is attuned to the specific cultural status of morphinomania in the late 1880s, when it was consciously and ambivalently positioned between morality and medicine, castigation and sympathy.

The tergiversations accompanying the reading of the addict's first-person narration were not typically required by the nineteenth-century realist novel or even by the sensation novel, and its frustrations may have informed the negative review of *An Evil Spirit* that appeared in *The Saturday Review*. This reviewer felt that literature and medicine should be kept as far apart as possible: "[The novel's] author, 'Mr. Richard Pryce,' has been foolish enough to write a preface to this story in which he states that the truthfulness of his book must be its own apology for existing, forgetting that mere correspondence with the facts of life does not make a work of art, and that what may be excellent in the *Lancet* may be detestable in literature."[50] This complaint echoed those of horrified critics of sensation novels a generation earlier: before novels began to depict such awful crimes and outrageous behavior, this complaint ran, the preponderance of dry reading made people "welcome as excitements they might almost be grateful for, what we are in the habit of regarding as the 'horrors' of the times."[51] But the reviewer's critique also resembled a new critical position on contemporary fiction, Oscar Wilde's half-serious remark two years later, about another text featuring compulsive, secretive consumption and metamorphosis: "the transformation of Dr. Jekyll reads dangerously like an experiment out of the *Lancet*."[52] Wilde was arguing against modern writers' "careless habits of accuracy" that made their novels about social problems dreary with detail. The *Saturday Review*'s similar complaint might have been bolstered by increased commentary on the medical accuracy of novels by physicians such as Norman Kerr, the president of the Society for the Study and Cure of Inebriety.[53] Ultimately, however, the *Saturday Review*'s frustration with Pryce's disclaimer was less an objection to "literature for medical students" than a complaint that the novel turned all of its readers into medical students learning to diagnose the narration as a symptom of narcosis and feeling sympathy for a character engaged in a repulsive new form of self-abuse. The difficulty of reading the novel's contorted form reflects both an affective problem about proper sympathy and judgment and a cognitive one about how to value narrative information. Ultimately *An Evil Spirit* educates its readers in a profound cultural ambivalence about hypodermic morphine habituation; the only concrete lesson is technical—how to recognize a body under the influence of morphine.

Detecting the Morphinized Body

Such new interpretive practices are required to diagnose habituated female characters through their narration and their bodies. Women's bodies figured in physicians' responses to the awkward problem of controlling the use of the syringe. Like their patients, physicians balked at giving up hypodermic morphine altogether. Its almost magic capabilities put it in the same technological echelon as gaslight and the railway, "one of the most valuable inventions of the century."[54] The instant relief of pain was too good to renounce altogether, especially when it could stand as a defining medical contribution to the times. Anstie solved the problem by revising the rules for its administration, recommending only small doses, from 1/12 to 1/4 of a grain, which would relieve pain and induce sleep "*without producing either stupor, contracted pupil, or subsequent constipation of bowels or burning of tongue*. Here is no vestige of *narcotic* action . . . no depression, no indescribable uneasiness, no yawning or sighing, no craving for the repetition of the dose."[55] Here Anstie crafts a norm for distinguishing the proper patient from the badly regulated one, whose narcotized body would manifest signs of morphine intoxication, a sure sign of a habit. One quarter of a grain became the threshold of visibility of the habituated body, because it was just enough to readjust that body to its "natural" processes.

Anstie's calculation was also motivated by anxieties over another elusive, less visible effect of morphia—pleasure. "The ease and recreation which naturally follows the arrest of intense pain, has passed by insidious gradations into a substantive sensation of well-being, of conscious activity, and of cheerfulness . . . which is more . . . than the mere recovery of natural elasticity on relief from pain."[56] Anstie is describing a surplus of pleasure extending far beyond the elimination of pain that would restore the patient to the desired, healthful equilibrium. If a generalized Victorian idea of health could be described as "life being pleasant," as Anstie had put it in a piece for the *Cornhill Magazine*, then this was to be distinguished from the old, eighteenth-century model of the libertine's "life with many pleasures."[57] Several significant characteristics distinguish women's imagined morphine and alcoholic pleasures from those of men in temperance and other narratives. The most important is secrecy, since solitary substance use directly violated the communal, public, social, and therefore legitimate pleasures of men's drinking in company at the pub. Second, this secrecy was far too similar to illicit sex. If women were pleasuring themselves, or if physicians were pleasuring their female patients rather than restoring their health, then such pleasure had to be detected and eliminated. Third, the grounding of such pleasure in a substance that women inserted into their own bodies was grossly offensive, because it brought women's bodies too much into the commercial sphere as an instrument of consumption. Perhaps the most illustrative poetic allegory of women's addiction, Christina Rossetti's *Goblin Market* (1862), combines all of these elements. Moreover, its central plot point—the same fruit that makes Laura waste away with desire also cures her—is a textbook illustration of addictive consumption.[58]

The marks of this obscene pleasure were accordingly ugly. The shockingly self-mutilated body of the morphine user and the scandalous ineptitude of her physician both emerged into medical and popular discourse throughout the 1870s and 1880s and continued to dominate drug narratives into the twentieth century. Stories circulated about patients pockmarked with abscesses from repeated injections, the result of careless physicians' "rash experiment[s]."[59] A woman who had injected herself twenty-four times in as many hours was reported to be "covered with tumours, some hard, others suppurating."[60] Harry Hubbell Kane, a prominent American expert on hypodermic morphine, catalogued "abscesses . . . in every stage. . . large and small cicatrices, reddened, bluish, hardened or doughy lumps; ecchymoses; patches of gangrene of various sizes cover[ing] the body everywhere, 'leaving,' as some of my correspondents express it, 'hardly a spot of healthy skin, large enough to be covered by a dime.' "[61] *The Lancet* reported with disgust that "a middle-aged lady, who has been in the habit of administering it to an invalid sister for some years, rewards herself at the same time with a dose in the neck, which is seamed with ugly scars from the frequent repetition of an operation conducted too often in very close propinquity to the external jugular vein."[62] Keen to standardize professional practice in a sincere attempt to quell the problem, medical writers catalogued the signs of hypodermic abuse so that they might be easily detected. Fictional accounts convert these clinical descriptions of sepsis into depictions of personal filth, suggesting that the practice of repeated morphine injections was less reprehensible than its untidy management. Robert Hichens's *Felix* (1902) frequently refers to its protagonist Valeria Ismey's hands as unimaginably, shamefully dirty; her young *amour*, the eponymous Felix, begs her to wear gloves.[63] In Rita's *Queer Lady Judas* (1905), the morphine addict Julie Thibaud "thrust out one bare, thin arm with an imploring gesture. . . . From shoulder to wrist it was all punctured with the needle marks. Some were inflamed and some discoloured, and she had evidently lacked courage to cleanse the arm."[64]

Medical journals drew the moral that "physicians ought never to trust the morphia syringe either to patients or their friends, and they should also be cautious in the use of this remedy."[65] As David Trotter comments, "the gendering of these morphia narratives was further reinforced by avid attention to the body of the addict."[66]

In *An Evil Spirit*, the physician's task of surveillance is taken over by Emily Howard, who functions as a bumbling amateur detective. Isabel's monstrous body is first presented through her deformed thumbs, which Emily, knowledgeable about chiromancy, notices in a tea shop: "A healthy hand closes so—the thumb outside, which shows that the will is firm. In the thumb is denoted the will. That woman has no control over herself, or I know nothing of palmistry. Her power of will and self-control are *nil*" (*ES* 1:30). This foreshadowing suggests that Isabel's morphine habituation is the specific fulfillment of a more generalized characterological defect, detectable by an updated version of that old mainstay of Victorian fiction, physiognomy. Isabel's thumbs and her generally gray, bloodless skin tone confuse Emily when she later encounters her at a society dinner; she even wonders if Isabel could be the same woman. The text appears to borrow a protocol of detective fiction described by Rothfield, wherein the body "is not an organized totality of qualities woven biologically into a person . . . but a corpus of isolated, discrete elements, a congeries or consilience of particulars . . . left on the material world by parts or extensions of the body—the foot, the elbow, the finger."[67] The obscure knowledge of chiromancy that allows Emily to read Isabel's thumbs and help identify her resembles a convention of detective fiction.

Yet this generic classification fails, because it cannot account for a strange scene of self-surveillance in which Isabel enjoys watching the drug take effect in her mirror and, in the process, recites the signs of morphine intoxication. Here is Isabel in her diary:

> I have never been vain, but it was with an acute sense of delight that, after I had used the drug, I used to sit before the looking-glass and watch it work its changes in my face. First there would come a glow—a wholesome and healthy glow into my cheeks, and this would warm gradually to a deep and beautiful pink, like finest rouge. My lips would get red as the colour of ripe cherries. My eyes would grow clear then as crystal. At first the pupils would shrink rapidly, then the irises would slowly distend as I have seen those of an excited animal, and the pupils, as if taking advantage of the greater space, would dilate, and encroach upon the grey. At these moments from being pretty I be-

> came beautiful. I have sometimes laughed with joy at this unreal brilliance which I had the power to develop. The doctor was right. He had put a potent charm into my hands. (*ES* 2:76–77)

The analogy of morphine and cosmetics is significant, because it creates a discourse of narcissism and artificiality that is distinctively feminine and reinforces an old moral about the rewards of dissimulation. It also notably violates the detective fiction model by having Isabel revel in her own apparent anatomization. Rothfield writes, "From the detected person's standpoint, identification separates one's body not so much from other bodies as from one's own self-possession."[68] But Isabel has already ceded her self-possession, to morphine and to the eroticized feminine image it produces. Unlike the deceivers that detective fiction exposes, Isabel is not motivated by simple social or financial gain but by and through her addiction and its transformative power.

The delight Isabel takes in the physical metamorphosis morphine offers turns to despair when Geoffrey returns unexpectedly and calls on her while she is in a state of narcotized desuetude. In a frenzy to improve her disheveled and haggard appearance, she guzzles brandy and applies too much rouge. When Geoffrey appears, finding her drunk and garishly made up, he becomes horrified and leaves. This episode sparks Isabel's jealousy of Grace Carruthers and her murder of Geoffrey in a psychotic fit, all of which is expressed through shame over her own appearance: "He had come from India after four long years, and I had greeted him, drunk! The sight of my besmeared face, my unsteady eyes, my tumbled hair, must have been revolting enough! What wonder if he turned for comfort to the beautiful creature beside him? What wonder? I was untidy, faded, worn. She was young, clean, smart" (*ES* 2:127–28). Grace's healthier, more hygienic body has more value within the marriage plot than Isabel's monstrous one. More significantly, Isabel's metamorphoses under the influence or withdrawal from morphine are more egregious than those produced by makeup, because they are more physiologically grounded—they represent a more extensive instance of unnatural meddling with one's body.

Indeed, with respect to addiction, deception became a physical property. Only two years later, the physician T. S. Clouston listed "physiological lying" as a symptom associated with morphinomania.[69] Clouston's notion, that the body compels verbal acts of misrepresentation, locates dissimulation *inside* the body's systems rather than in a single part or on the surface. His term begs the question of how physicians or readers could detect a "physiological lie." Emily's anatomizing view allows her to read Isabel's thumbs, but how can she read her bloodstream? Since Isabel's looks change with the hidden rhythms of her dependency, how can Emily read her physiological vagaries? Pryce realizes Clouston's notion of "physiological lying" in his portrayal of Emily's interpretive difficulties, one shared by physicians and readers. He satisfies these difficulties by producing Isabel's "inside" first-person narration of her subjective state; this narration makes the novel significantly different from detective fiction, which can detect anatomical evidence and disguises but not physiological lies.

The confusing task of reading a morphinomaniac's body, which changes appearance with the rhythm of addiction, put the reader/physician in scary proximity to the addict's dangerous knowledge. Pryce's novel represents this problem by drawing an analogy between Emily Howard's fascination with Isabel and Isabel's fascination with morphine. Emily's obsession and her quest across London to discover Isabel's secret casts her in the numerous roles that brought English women onto the underground railway and into the city streets in the 1880s: the female *flâneuse*, the lady shopper, the social worker, and the lady detective.[70] Harangued by her more conventional sister Constance, who fills her time—and her own diary—with the humdrum details of household management, Emily longs for a more interesting life and uses Isabel's enigmatic allure to realize it. She is initiated into the mystery when, at a society dinner, she observes Isabel undergoing withdrawal symptoms that transform her entire physical appearance. She realizes that the elegant Miss Gordon is the same violently ill woman to whom she had given half a crown in a confectionary only a few days earlier:

> From that moment Miss Howard knew that the woman of the incident at the confectioner's and Miss Gordon were the same, and that she herself had seen a glimpse of some terrible mystery. It was as if, in an express train, she had passed a station at full speed, and had seen the board on which the name of the place was written—nay, more, had even seen the form of the name—but had not been able to read it. More than once that evening she saw Miss Gordon by fearful effort brace herself together, and each time it was as if in her mind's eye she had seen once more the shape of that name, the number of its letters even; but the name itself! Should she ever read it? (*ES* 1:45–46)

This passage is intriguing because it dramatizes the position of the uninitiated into the knowledge of addiction, a condition so new that it even lacks a name. This position of unknowing and the condition's nameless status are historically self-conscious; they are features of the technologically sophisticated nineteenth century, with its express trains that speed people from place to place—and that transport Emily from her routine existence in suburban Bayswater to the drama of Soho and the East End—but that fail to heighten knowledge commensurately. One might analogize this new technology to that of the hypodermic needle, which speeds morphine through Isabel's veins but clouds her own moral perception and self-knowledge. Compared to opium-eating and epidermal forms of drug administration, the hypodermic injection of morphine produced somatic effects instantly, leaving no time for comprehension.

Significantly, Emily's unknowingness is figured as lacking the time to read, a deficiency fulfilled when Isabel finally gives her—and the reader of *An Evil Spirit*—her "Record." Reading, a safer self-reflexive and enlightening activity than using the syringe, yields knowledge rather than the disorganized, animalistic sensations and perceptions that Isabel experiences. Reading brings one closest to addiction without actually giving one over to the experience of it, an event that would forever compromise one's ability to know. Emily, physicians, and all who read representations of addiction are caught in its peculiar paradox: in the tradition of British empiricism, the surest knowledge of a thing is unmediated experience, but in the case of drug addiction, firsthand experience forfeits the ability to comprehend and re-present the experience to others. Hence the truth of Isabel's condition can only emerge in the space between her own narrative and Emily's—the space of Isabel's narcotized body, which substitutes for the drug as Emily's object of fascinated pursuit and reading. This body cannot be read in parts; its total condition can only be understood through the addict's self-statement. The difficulties of reading addiction thus correspond less to an older anatomical model that would gain new heuristic life in detective fiction and more to a physiological model as it was coming to be viewed by the emergent medical field of therapeutics.

New Women and Morphine in *Felix and Queer Lady Judas*

This paradox at the heart of addiction generated problems for self-representation, both in ordinary life and in politics. Unlike men, whose social authority stemmed from their capacity to accumulate wealth through labor in the public sphere, bourgeois women derived their social authority from their domestic virtue and influence; the scandal of their secret addictions to alcohol and morphine eroded it. "A habit that isolates and degrades her, while at the same time she retains her rank as wife and mother, is not only dangerous to her individually, but to society," commented the author of "Drawing Room Alcoholism" in the *Saturday Review*.[71] The feminist idea emerging in the 1860s that women should operate in the public sphere merely by virtue of being citizens broke this traditional logic. Accordingly, arguments against women's use of hypodermic morphine in medical and popular literature link recent arguments for suffrage—as well as advances in marriage and property rights—to drug use. The medicalization of morality that I have been tracing even led writers to question women's cognitive abilities. Since addicted women were clearly acting against their own best interests, and since they seemed to be living proof that women were peculiarly susceptible to addiction, they appeared to be defective liberal subjects and were cited in arguments that women should be disqualified from formal political representation. "There is at present a singular push for power among women which suggests rather a deterioration than a development of the female intellect and will. This feverish self-assertion is a confession of weakness."[72] With this tactic, the *Saturday Review* attempted to neutralize women's collective political will by citing their individual mental incapacity and susceptibility to habitual drunkenness.[73] The French writer Jules Clarétie made a similar link between morphine and women's rights; women "who exultantly call for their rights, are acquiring a new one . . . the right to morphine."[74] Opponents of changes in women's roles could always invoke the plight of the individual female habitual drunkard, usually luridly represented as a descent into poverty and prostitution.[75] The radical political implications of female morphine and alcohol use spurred its antagonists to define it as a self-destructive habit, a vice, and a disease.

From this point of view, early medical definitions of addiction were elucidated and put forth as arguments against women's right to self-representation. Isabel's exculpatory query—"How far am I responsible?"—is actually the implied argument against women's claims for expanded rights and responsibilities. The opposing argument, that women should suffer no special social opprobrium for drinking and using drugs, was relegated to the most esoteric of venues, such as Alice Ilgenfritz Jones and Ella Merchant's feminist utopian novel, *Unveiling a Parallel: A Romance* (1893). In this science fiction text, women drink champagne and smoke valerian through "vaporizers" with impunity—on Mars.[76]

Here we can demarcate a major difference between Pryce's novel and the earlier texts—the intervening discourse of the New Woman in the 1890s, which debated not only women's claims to representation but their own representative function in society. Before the New Woman movement, Pryce's heroine's habit is a tragedy, exiling her from marriage and sentencing her to death; this is a classic enactment of Michel Foucault's concept of biopolitics, in which biological life is valued only insofar as it conforms to the heteronormative and reproductive coercions of the state.[77] As Grace tells Isabel of Geoffrey, "You had his love and you did not value it. You have poisoned yourself with drugs till you are fit to be no man's wife" (*ES* 2:132–33). Isabel also becomes unfit for her single career option, governessing, and is expelled from the Carruthers household for setting a bad example. Isabel is a defective model of bourgeois femininity because she is dependent on the wrong things; likewise, her dependency makes her too much a victim and a sufferer to inhabit the sensation fiction model of Collins's wicked Lydia Gwilt.

After the turn of the century, writers could invoke New Woman discourse as a way of making sense of morphine and other addictions, whether they perceived such afflictions to be the result of emancipation or, as Hichens apparently did, of conventional femininity. Hichens's *Felix* gave voice to the older, married, upper-class woman who has missed out on New Womanhood and, lacking the supporting ideology of Victorian domesticity, drifts into anomie. Although Valeria Ismey is well enough read to help her husband with his publishing business, she never performs this work and has no professional identity. Her room, like her friend Lady Caroline's, is scattered with messy writing tables and ink-stained books, but these literary labors are supplanted by her more fascinating acts of fiction-making, her deception of Felix as she attempts to hide her habit: "Morphia bred in her a passion for subterfuge. It had become an instinct in her to pretend that she had given up the mania which governed her whole life—an ineradicable instinct" (*F* 403). Here Hichens repeats the familiar trope of lying as the overarching trope of feminine subjectivity, but elsewhere he complicates this image by giving Mrs. Ismey a rather feminist-sounding declaration: "I sometimes think that a woman who tells the truth is fit only for a madhouse. It's all very well for men. People expect the truth from men. From women they don't. And if you give people what they don't expect from you they nearly always hate you" (*F* 277) With this insight, Hichens transforms *Felix* into a thoroughly modern, post–New Woman novel. Mrs. Ismey's story ultimately becomes Felix's, since her lying and, indeed, her morphia habit itself provide the raw material of his personal experience, which helps him mature as a man and as a writer. But instead of maintaining feminine addiction solely as erotic spectacle, masculine proximity to it also functions as a kind of witnessing of women's living through a series of fin-de-siècle double binds, of which morphia becomes the symbol. Hichens has Lady Caroline express it in a startling formulation:

> "Look here! I'm the last woman to make excuses for my acts, but you don't know what morphia means to some of us, many of us, modern women without professions, without beliefs. Morphia makes life possible."
>
> "Hideous!" he said.
>
> "Possible. It adds to truth a dream. What more does religion do?"
>
> "Oh!" he exclaimed.
>
> "I shock you. What I mean is that truth alone is both not enough and far too much for us." (*F* 383)

New Womanhood underwrites Lady Caroline's exposure of the modern bourgeois woman's alienation; it cannot recuperate morphine habituation as an emblem of independence, but it mobilizes it as evidence of intolerable social conditions.[78]

Whereas Hichens uses his morphine plot to mobilize sympathy for the ideals of New Womanhood, Eliza Margaret J. Humphreys, who wrote under the name "Rita," enlisted the narcotic in an attack on New Womanhood in her strangely wonderful novel, *Queer Lady Judas* (1905).[79] The narrator, Madame Beaudelet, arrives in London to set up shop selling beauty treatments to an aristocratic set that interprets New Woman ideals to license its fox-hunting, motorcar-driving, cigarette-smoking ways while its members fret about the effect these activities will have on their visual appearance, particularly their skin. With financing from the exceedingly ugly but highly fascinating Lady Judith Vanderbyl, who goes by the nicknames "Queer Lady Judas" and "Lady Ju," the narrator becomes the purveyor of an array of treatments, one of which contains a secret drug supplied by a French chemist, Monsieur Thibaud. The novel develops an analogy between the habitual use of morphine by New Women and their compulsive consumption of cosmetics. But it shifts the focus from women's deception of men to their self-deception, which appears to define womanhood: as one of her clients, Lady Ormaroyd, exclaims, "Oh! That's just the way with women. We try a thing for an experiment, or because all the other women we know are trying it, and then we find me must go on. It's like drug-taking. You think you can leave off when you like—but you can't. So with beautifying. You try one thing, and then another" (*QLJ* 58). But Madame Beaudelet becomes a pusher in more than just a metaphorical sense, since, in endeavoring to cure her supplier's daughter, Julie Thibaud, of her morphine addiction, she begins to control her supply and regulate her intake. (We will see more of the queer erotics produced by Madame Beaudelet's "enslavement" of Julie in chapter 5.) Julie is a cross between the typewriter girl of the 1890s and T. S. Eliot's typist from *The Waste Land*: having ventured out into the office work force, she makes friends with a chorus girl, Ada St. Vincent, who introduces her to the *piqure* (needle) and makes her a *morphineuse*, but the habit turns her into an automaton.[80]

Madame Beaudelet is thus well positioned to critique New Womanhood as a license for the vapid life of the thrill-seeking aristocracy, and as it constitutes a petit-bourgeois work force that brings young girls into dangerous contact with vicious influences. Indeed, she frequently launches into conservative meditations in which drug addiction figures as the delirium of modernity: "To such a pitch had civilization arrived that, with all good gifts of life and wealth at its disposal, it must needs fly to abnormal vices, filthy sins, sensual degradation of past centuries, for its excitements or pleasure" (*QLJ* 171). Not surprisingly, the cause of this decadence is the New Woman's sense of freedom, which only leads to drug habits and vanity: "The new century was essentially a clamorous, an exacting, and a selfish one. And foremost in the ranks of noisy progress stood woman. . . . A sisterhood of pleasure, sacrificing on their own selfish altars a sisterhood of pain" (*QLJ* 25). The wide disparity between Hichens's feminist leanings and Rita's anti–New Woman screed shows that morphine had become a powerful symbol of the dilemmas over women's roles and of the ambiguous meaning of their freedom. In *The Gender of Modernity*, Rita Felski reads this turmoil through the crisis provoked by women's new status as consumers, but she could also be describing their new identity as addicts when she writes, "Perhaps, once awakened, this appetite would have disturbing and unforeseeable effects, reaching out to subvert the social fabric and to undermine patriarchal authority within the family."[81]

The cleverest post–New Woman narrative about hypodermic morphine use (and an excellent short story in its own right) is Mary Cholmondeley's "The Lowest Rung."[82] Cholmondeley's narrator, a middle-aged woman writer of trite spiritual wisdom who comically lacks self-awareness, shelters a woman tramp during a rainstorm; the tramp proceeds to tell her a long, melodramatic story about her descent from middle-class domestic life to the hell of morphine addiction. The realistic details of this story are overwhelmed by the generic tropes of addiction plots: the narrator recounts "having my hands beaten from each rung, one after another . . . sinking lower and lower yet" and suffering "the flame of hell which is thirst."[83] Predictably, her story includes the confession that, when caught with the "infernal machine" of the syringe, she lies to protect herself. What makes Cholmondeley's story so smart, however, is that its conclusion reveals the tramp's morphine tale to have been a ruse, merely a way to play to the obtuse narrator's cultural assumptions about class, femininity, and drug use. By telling a story about lying, Cholmondeley highlights what by 1908 had become a well-known cultural discourse linking women's capacity for fiction-making to addiction. Yet "The Lowest Rung" redeems its storytelling tramp, linking her persuasive abilities not to mendacity, subterfuge, or superficiality but to an exposure of class hypocrisy and short-sightedness.

My exposure of morphinomania's historical emergence in the context of arguments against women's political advances might be construed as a way to set the stage for an alternative version of addiction authored by the women who experienced it, but it is not.[84] Sympathy for the suffering of that original cohort of bourgeois lady morphine addicts comes too late; nor is it worthwhile to recover their voices in order to valorize their experiences as a form of resistance to medical power. That physicians' accounts of morphinomania were ideologically inflected does not nullify their descriptive value: morphine addiction can indeed disfigure and harm bodies; the women who first experienced it very likely lied to conceal and maintain their dependencies. It is neither possible nor desirable to use the exposure of medical science's cultural investments as a springboard for the denial of the horrible reality of addiction. Rather, this exposure obliges us to produce new ways of understanding the nature of addicted abjection by considering its cultural history from the oblique angle of the countermodern.

It is in this context that "disease" became a metaphor for addiction in the late nineteenth century—and even governed novelistic representations of it—without rendering it a fictive or illusory phenomenon. That the disease model was deployed with different emphasis in the United States, where, as we saw in chapter 3, it inscribed addiction on the white, southern, male body in order to forget the shameful past of chattel slavery, shows that it is neither a politically neutral nor a politically uniform metaphor. As Michelle McClellan and others have shown, the disease model revived again in a different time and place to reconfigure the gender of addiction in relation to women's imagined capacity for freedom.[85]

Indeed, in order to better understand the history of addiction, the starkness of the dichotomy between truth and deception in the discourse on morphinomania cannot be unthinkingly reproduced within the critical framework. Rather, recognition of the discourse's cultural investments invites us to note how quickly and intensively that very competition for truth status takes hold—how swiftly the information that counts as "knowledge" of drug addiction becomes polarized, constructing the authoritative realm of the disciplined expert and the counterdiscourse of experience assigned to the addict. This split can be understood as a question about who is "really" free enough from coercion—whether ideological or biochemical—to tell the truth.

5

"AFFLICTIONS À LA OSCAR WILDE"

The Strange Case of Addiction and Sexuality in *Dr. Jekyll and Mr. Hyde*

> Remember, reader, that the great majority of our law-makers, both State and National, know no more about the physical, mental and moral influences of opium over its victims than a goose does about God. And yet they essay to make laws on the subject! Their knowledge of the subject has, in the main, been gained from what little contact they may have had with Chinese opium-smoking joints, or with "hop heads" and "coke fiends" of the tenderloin districts. Hence, they look upon all such addictions as merely vicious habits, persisted in for the physical pleasures to be derived therefrom; and therefore, catalogue them along with afflictions à la Oscar Wilde, and other abnormalities.
>
> John Harrison Hughes, "The Autobiography of a Drug Fiend" (1916)

John Hughes's complaint that addiction is not sufficiently distinguished from foreign customs or homosexual practices implicitly attempts to construe it as a preserve of whiteness and heteronormativity—in other words, *not* the grounds of deviance, but also, interestingly, not the scene of pleasure, either. In the last chapter, I showed how medicalizing discourses implicated women's capacity for self- and mutual pleasure via the hypodermic needle as part of the disease of addiction. In this chapter, I analyze the curious conflation of, and often stranger attempts to differentiate, addiction and homosexuality. Hughes's reference to Wilde as well as his trailing, vague citation of "other abnormalities" perform what Ed Cohen has described as the "condensation of knowledge effects" that "(re)produce 'Oscar Wilde' as an index for a variety of 'unspeakable' male homoerotic practices and desires."[1] The same logic allows Hughes to dispatch with his own gender and sexual identity in the broad, silent strokes of patriarchal manifest destiny: "I started November 1, '85, for 'The Land of Sunshine, Fruits and Flowers,' where I landed in due time on a government claim of land in a sparsely settled community. By this time my total worldly possessions were a wife, two children, and $250 in cash."[2] Reproductive masculine heterosexuality, of course, is the *other* sexuality that doesn't speak its name, in this case because, since it is so easily voiced in terms of property rights and the self-making attendant upon manifest destiny, it goes without saying. Yet, as the titular "drug fiend," Hughes straddles both the power conferred by these norms and the deviance that resists their legal and taxonomic force, a balancing act common to addicts, and which most closely resembles closeted homosexuality.

Indeed, heterosexuality is clearly not the mode of greatest libidinal investment in Hughes's story, whose narrator recounts his insatiable obsessions—mainly with hypodermic morphine, but also with cocaine, chloral, and alcohol. Though he mentions youthful heterosexual flirtations in passing, Hughes's narrative is motivated primarily by his relations with the men who introduce him to morphine's seductions, supply him, keep his habit secret, attempt to cure him, and ultimately betray him, particularly the effeminate and ingratiating "Dr. B": "He was pompous. He was dignified. He was handsome. He was physically well-proportioned. The embonpoint of his middle was just sufficient to make his white vest fit well and add to his dignity. He was between forty-five and fifty years of age. His dark hair and mustache were slightly tinged with gray. He was of florid complexion. He had a soft voice, a winning smile, and a sympathetic and paternal bearing that won your confidence at once." Whereas Hughes's wife is never mentioned again, his attachment to "Dr. B," who promises him a cure for his morphine addiction, is intensely developed: "I fell so completely under the influence of this new-found friend-in-need I would have done anything he said."[3] Because so much narrative energy and erotic description attends his relations to Dr. B., Hughes's sexuality seems only nominally straight. Yet it is in the space between heterosexual text and homosexual subtext that certain questions arise. After all, Hughes's most insatiable desire—the one that authorizes this self-defining narrative—is for morphine. The story of succumbing, body and soul, to the sway of a powerful new charm imbues Hughes's drug autobiography with intense physiological desires, pleasures, and gratifications that often seem manifestly erotic but are directed neither toward women nor men. Neither quite straight nor exactly gay, the addict Hughes obliges us to find new interpretive tools to configure his identity, desire, subjectivity, and habit.

"Autobiography of a Drug Fiend," a late but fairly characteristic example of drug autobiographies from the period from 1880 to 1920, raises the question of its narrator's sexuality in a way that unfolds a larger conundrum, the relationship of addiction to sexuality. Putting addiction into a meaningful relationship with sexuality already implies a certain malleability within both terms, deriving from Michel Foucault's generative insight that sexuality is foremost a technique of social power rather than an essential, biological orientation or a simple reaction to repression, and taking up the subsequent work of both gay and lesbian history on the one hand, and queer theory on the other. Gay and lesbian histories are entangled with the history of addiction: they run parallel to it, but they also significantly cross it. Numerous critics have pointed out the simultaneous articulation and taxonomization of homosexuality and addiction by medical professionals in the period from 1870 to 1925.[4] Then "disease" and "disorder" gained significant ground as the metaphors that explained both phenomena. Case studies, textbooks, medical societies, journals, and conferences began to circulate etiologies to classify sexual proclivities and drug habituations as varieties of compulsive, unnatural behavior. Magazine pieces, stories, and novels reframed them as their sufferers' secret problems, in conflict with the protocols of kinship such as marriage and reproduction. As sources of intense pleasure and ambivalence, both homosexual and addicted activity incited more confessional discourse that, under the imprimatur of medicine, began to transform acts into identities: in the same way that sexologists such as Karl Maria Kertbeny, Karl Heinrich Ulrichs, Edward Carpenter, and Havelock Ellis respectively invented identities such as "monosexual," "urnings," "the third sex," and "inverts" to describe people who deviated from the state that would only later come to be known as heterosexuality, medical researchers and other writers invented new identities for drug users suffering from: "alcoholmania, opiomania, morphinomania, chloralomania, etheromania, chlorodynomania, and chloroformomania."[5]

Legal constructions of identity have also been central both to the history of sexuality and to the history of addiction. Although gay history is increasingly turning to other sources and methodologies, it often cites the British Criminal Law Amendment Act of 1885, which outlawed sodomy committed in private, as a sign that homosexual identity held new cultural currency.[6] Similarly, in the United States before the 1880s, consensual sodomy was not widely prosecuted, but by the end of the century, New York law, for example, had criminalized it in response to fears of pathologized homosexuality.[7] As with sodomy, excessive habitual public drinking had a long legislative history in Britain and the United States, but in the final third of the nineteenth century, the Habitual Drunkards and Inebriates Acts began to restrict its private occurrence, a process that had the effect of creating the new identities of "habitual drunkard" and "inebriate" for the addict. In 1879 the Habitual Drunkards Act made provision for middle- and upper-class people to have themselves declared habitual drunkards and, with their consent, incarcerated in licensed homes in an attempt to cure them. The Act was renewed and updated in 1888 and 1898, and given the more scientific-sounding title of "The Inebriates Act," which seemed more sympathetic and amenable to self-identification than "habitual drunkard."[8] Just as the criminalization of sodomy inaugurated the heightened self-policing of sexual behavior, so too did the criminalization of habitual drinking foster new discipline in the habitual consumption of alcohol.

These parallel discursive productions of addicted and homosexual identities crossed, reinforcing each other. Medical researchers and shapers of drug policy such as William Wilcox and Sir Malcolm Delevingne of Britain's Home Office made public statements linking drug addiction with "unnatural sexual vice" and addicts' cross-recruitment of "perverts."[9] Most forcefully, psychoanalysis often articulated homosexuality as the secret lurking behind addiction. Karl Abraham suggested that "in every public-house there is an element of homosexuality. The homosexual components which have been repressed and sublimated by the influence of education become unmistakably evident under the influence of alcohol."[10] Wilhelm Stekel illustrated the way in which psychoanalysis implants "the truth" of addiction within deep subjectivity such that it inevitably calls forth homosexuality: "Narcotomaniacs, not only drinkers, but all who are addicted to the use of drugs for whatever reason, are trying to run away from some truth"; for Stekel, this truth partook of various taxonomies but was at bottom homosexual: "Drunkards suffer from serious paraphilias (sadism, necrophilia, paedophilia, zoophilia, etc.); nearly all of them are latent homosexuals."[11] In twentieth-century clinical accounts, homosexuality would detach from addiction, which would nevertheless retain its status as symptom of a buried truth, usually a childhood trauma disclosed through analysis or other form of therapy. What is perhaps even more remarkable than homosexuality's role as the secret truth of addiction, however, is the common operation of the hermeneutics of suspicion for both identities: each one is thought to exist far below the threshold of social visibility or personal recognition, awaiting disclosure through intervention and confession. Behavior is mortised to identity with a finality that permits no other relationship; as Sadie Plant writes, "By the turn of the century, using drugs was something only addicts were supposed to do, just as gay sex was confined to homosexuals. Occasional flirtations with life beyond the straight lines of normality were no longer legitimate options."[12]

Homosexuality and addiction also crossed in the space of urban subcultures, beginning at the fin-de-siècle but continuing long afterward.[13] The journalist and dramatist George R. Sims could nonchalantly slip from one to the other as he traced the footsteps of *The Devil in London*: " 'Yes, this is the age of eccentric clubs. A little time ago there was a Morphia Club. Some daring spirits not long since so far exceeded the wildest dreams of the Bloomerites as to start a small and particularly private club in which all the members were to be dressed in male attire when on the club premises. It was to be called 'The Rosalind.' "[14] In *Felix*, Robert Hichens's description of the Parisian morphia club haunted by the addict Mrs. Ismey similarly resembles subcultural queer spaces: in "a horrible, dreary quarter beyond Montmarte . . . down a narrow dark passage" ending at a "mean little door," Mrs. Ismey finds women lying on divans, "staring at each other in the firelight with hollow, expressionless eyes. . . . Two or three of these women were trembling. . . . Another was holding an unlit cigarette between her teeth and stretching out her arms. . . . There was one woman who was beautifully dressed, a real *mondaine* of Paris. She had torn open all the front of her gown, and—but I can't tell you everything."[15] The seedy urban location, filled with women whose subjectivity appears oddly evacuated, and yet who also are trembling with desire and pleasure; the beckoning embrace of the underworld; the veil of propriety rent asunder; and above all, the seemingly unnatural exchanges taking place as women penetrate themselves and each other with the needle, signify queerly because homosexuality and addiction shared a common descriptive vocabulary and emplotment of deviance. Gay and lesbian spaces and those of addiction were thus connected both analogically and metonymically.

The word *queer* also supplied a semantic connection between addiction and homosexuality. "Queer" acquired the connotation of same-sex desire late in the nineteenth century, but it also meant "drunk" throughout the century. The common meaning was in a subjective feeling or appearance of deviant ill health: the *OED*'s second definition for *queer* is "Not in a normal condition; out of sorts; giddy, faint, or ill: esp. in phr. to feel (or look) queer. Also slang: Drunk."[16] Thomas Hardy used it with this meaning in mind in *The Mayor of Casterbridge*, when the eponymous Henchard, having sold his wife while drunk on furmity spiked with rum, complains, "She wasn't queer if I was."[17] Arthur Symons, translating Émile Zola's *L'Assommoir*, also deployed it when Coupeau, describing his delirium tremens, says, "Ah! yes. . . . I was a bit queer. Fancy! I saw rats!"[18] Coupeau's understatement—his hallucinations are the symptom of full-blown alcoholic degeneration, not an isolated episode of intoxication—demonstrates how "queer" could mean addicted at fin-de-siècle, particularly in the mingled air of literary naturalism and decadence.

This shared sense of feeling or seeming off-kilter, skewed, and even radically disconnected from the world of normality, reconnects our discussion to the present deployment of "queer" within cultural theory and history, where this position often doubles as subjective experience and source of critique.[19] Although I am not attempting structurally to replicate queer academic politics within the domain of addiction, I find the critical displacements of time, space, and other structures of normality common to queer theory useful for thinking deconstructively about the identity of the addict. For example, Judith Halberstam, beginning *In a Queer Time and Place* by outlining the ways in which the pace of many queer lives departs from the characteristic unfolding of straight lives in normative time, invokes addiction: "Within the life cycle of the Western human subject, long periods of stability are considered to be desirable, and people who live in rapid bursts (drug addicts, for example) are characterized as immature and even dangerous."[20] Halberstam goes on to specify queer times and spaces within postmodernism, queer subcultures, and popular culture; but her analysis can also be used to reorient our approach to the historical emergence of addiction within subcultures. Elizabeth Freeman likewise distinguishes queer time as that lived by "those forced to wait or startled by violence, whose activities do not show up on the official time line, whose own time lines do not synchronize with it."[21] Addiction, regulated by the overlapping temporalities of individual physiology and often underground global and local supply chains, only ever appears on such official time lines as a catastrophic interruption; it more characteristically dwells in those time lines' hidden and increasingly disappearing nooks. As Jennifer Terry writes of "deviant subjects" more generally: "They are in the complicated position of having to negotiate the intricate and contradictory relationships between, for example, the rules of the courtroom and the semiotics of the street, the conventions of the clinical confession and the limitations to self-knowledge, the demands of the desiring body and the probabilities of risk."[22] Especially with respect to addiction, the kind of historical recovery required to see and value such divided experience cannot be one that keeps its subjects' identity uninterrogated; as I have been arguing, the identity of the addict functions instantly to weld together the pieces of a cultural logic that are more productively imagined apart.

Thus the parallelisms and crossings between gay and lesbian history and the history of addiction offer a necessary but partial picture of the relationship between sexualities and addiction. The rest of the picture falls into view when we use the tools supplied by queer theory, particularly its characteristic unthinking of identity, and its founding assumption that sexuality is an effect, rather than a cause, of discourse. One of the more radical consequences of these critical processes has been the chance to jettison sexuality's basis in genitality. Eve Kosofsky Sedgwick limns this intervention in the first two of her axioms in *Epistemology of the Closet*: "Even identical genital acts mean very different things to different people," and "To some people, the nimbus of 'the sexual' seems scarcely to extend beyond the boundaries of discrete genital acts; to others, it enfolds them loosely or floats virtually free of them."[23] With this intellectual and political gesture, sexual orientation can detach from the binary of heterosexuality and homosexuality; brought into relation with a variety of objects and practices, it comes to resemble both fetishism and addiction, revising both conventional and radical understandings of sexuality. Some of the most interesting new work in the history of sexuality avoids the monolithic heterosexual/homosexual divide, contending instead that heterosexual norms and institutions such as marriage have been hospitable contexts for queer experiences, relationships, and desires. Such work, by Sharon Marcus, Holly Furneaux, James Eli Adams, and others, applies new pressure to refine descriptions of sexualities as embedded social relations.[24] Taking this work on board, we can observe addiction and sexuality informing each other, rather than conflating or reducing either of them.

More specifically, using a critical queer lens, we can see the ways addiction resisted norms of sexuality, kinship, class, and race in the nineteenth century, without crudely confusing it with the same sex desire that frequently seems to accompany it in literary representations. Then and now, narratives about addicts characteristically show them demurring, faking, destroying, or otherwise sabotaging possibilities for heteronormative romantic love and kinship and the bourgeois striving that underwrites them. In the conventional wisdom, addiction destroys families; to reference the masculinist and heteronormative terms of Alcoholics Anonymous, addiction gives rise to "financial insecurity, disgusted friends and employers, warped lives of blameless children, sad wives and parents."[25] Since the earliest teetotal confessions and temperance novels, a legion of fictional and real habitual drunkards had marched through the nineteenth century, seemingly compelled by the pleasure of alcohol, and the homosocial milieu of the pub, club, or gentleman's rooms in which to drink it, over the domestic joys of heterosexuality. In the last quarter of the nineteenth century, real and fictional middle-class women addicted to hypodermic morphine and other drugs appeared to prefer their bouts of euphoria and withdrawal among each other to romance and marriage, made newly mundane by the thrilling possibilities of New Womanhood. Yet these resistances are by no means queer by virtue of any resemblance to same-sex desire. To suggest so would be to instantiate a homophobic model of same-sex desire as failed heterosexuality; it would also flatten a varied historical terrain. Rather, these examples constitute a series of queer refusals unassimilable to sexual identities conventionally understood.

Other models of sexual identity have been proposed as analogues of the addict, and it is worth briefly describing them in order to eliminate their conceptual residue. For example, in a late letter to Wilhelm Fleiss, Sigmund Freud conjectured that "masturbation is the one major habit, the 'primary addiction,' and it is only as a substitute and replacement for it that the other addictions—to alcohol, morphine, tobacco, and the like—come into existence."[26] Indeed, the language and assumptions of the antionanist movement had resembled those of the temperance movement in the nineteenth century: both addiction and masturbation were considered solitary, secret, compulsive, debilitating vices. "Children who are addicted to such habits like to be in solitary places, where they can indulge their vicious propensities. They like to sleep late in the morning and nevertheless feel unrefreshed and heavy on getting up," wrote the surgeon George Calhoun in 1858, sounding very much as if he were describing habitual drunkards or drug addicts.[27] Thomas Laqueur's recent cultural history of masturbation even posits addiction as an underlying conceptual model, although it more convincingly links the discursive emergence of masturbation to the rise of credit culture in the late eighteenth century.[28] While the politics of self-pleasure inform representations of addiction, as I demonstrated in the previous chapter, masturbation cannot be the conceptual model for addiction, particularly since it obscures its connections to an extra-bodily materiality and economy, and elides technical explanation of it as a habituation or dependency. And the identity of the "masturbator," which neither inspired medical, juridical, political, and economic controls nor saturated and exhausted identity as completely as "addict" did, does not begin to illustrate addiction's cultural grip.[29]

A second model relates addiction to heterosexual obsession, passion, or overfulfillment. This model, typified by iconic myths of grand, destructive fascinations such as those of Tristan and Isolde, obscures addiction's longstanding associations with solitude, deviance, and resistance to bourgeois norms. For at least two centuries, it has also been applied unequally, and misogynistically, to mock heterosexual women's immersion in the trivial romance narratives of mass culture.[30] A third, racist model likens addiction to generalized "Eastern" luxury, perversity, sensuality, and idleness. For example, in spite of much empirical evidence that opium habituation tended to blunt sexual appetite and enjoyment, a retired surgeon-general writing in 1882 claimed that it "intensifies the mere animal gratification arising from the sexual *congrès*." As an example, he recounted an anecdote of "an Indian nobleman, who was in the habit of taking opium to increase the pleasure of the sexual act" and who requested chloral hydrate from his doctor as another sexual enhancer. The writer concluded, "The case of this voluptuary is but one of many in the East."[31] Tales of the Chinese sexual sadist who beat the young English women he had addicted to opium also circulated through Thomas Burke's *Limehouse Nights* and Sax Rohmer's *Dope*.[32] In such texts, racism structures many of the vulgar characterizations of addiction as sexual perversity.

Perhaps the most recent problematic configuration of addiction and sexuality has been the invention of "sex addiction" in the 1990s. This taxonomic designation proposed that sex could be a compulsive behavior on which individuals grew dependent, to the detriment of other areas of life and the exploitation of others. Yet, as Helen Keane has pointed out, the discourse of sexual addiction is skewed toward the preservation of companionate heterosexuality and marriage; all of its "addictive" properties are the ones traditionally considered deviant by homophobic culture.[33] Similarly, Janice Irvine associates the rise of sex addiction discourse with pervasive cultural panic over AIDS, including a right-wing backlash against the sexual revolution and feminist gains of the 1970s.[34] Finally, addiction cannot be considered a mode of asexuality or the absence of sexuality without obscuring the erotic meanings that subtend any representation of social exchange.

Instead, if addiction can be best described as a mode of queer conduct that can seem to signify same-sex desire without actually identifying it, then we can deepen and enrich our readings of fin-de-siècle and early twentieth century popular literature, especially one of its more enduring icons, Robert Louis Stevenson's *The Strange Case of Dr. Jekyll and Mr. Hyde* (1886). In recent years, due to the insightful work of Wayne Koestenbaum, Stephen Heath, Elaine Showalter, and George Haggerty, this text has become part of the gay canon.[35] Generally speaking, in this interpretation Hyde functions as the ambivalent sign both of Jekyll's interiorized homophobia and of his disavowed erotic desire. Showalter, emphasizing the former, writes: "The reaction of the male characters to Hyde is uniformly that of 'disgust, loathing, and fear,' suggestive of the almost hysterical homophobia of the late nineteenth century. In the most famous code word of Victorian homosexuality, they find something *unspeakable* about Hyde 'that gave a man a turn,' something 'surprising and revolting.' "[36] And yet Jekyll cannot give up Hyde and finally even acknowledges him as he acknowledges his homosexual identity: "And yet when I looked upon that ugly idol in the glass, I was conscious of no repugnance; rather a leap of welcome. This, too, was myself."[37]

Yet, as I will demonstrate, the critical evidence used to support conventional queer readings of the text can also be persuasively deployed to contend that Jekyll, by the standards of 1886, is an addict.[38] Mounting such a reading requires the suspension, rather than the replication, of the hermeneutics of suspicion that characteristically interprets signs of "deviance" as the exclusive signs of masculine homosexuality. As Eli Adams has suggested, "It is of course the case that male-male desire throughout the Christian West has tended to be cloaked in secrecy, but this does not entail—as a good deal of recent literary and cultural criticism tends to assume—that secrecy always speaks of homoerotic desire."[39] With respect to both Stevenson's story and its historical moment, Sedgwick formulated addiction as "both a camouflage and an expression for the dynamics of same-sex desire and its prohibition."[40] My aim is neither to fulfill this maxim nor to reverse its hierarchy and make same-sex desire into the screen for addiction as the story's "real" meaning. The latter especially would perform the sort of paranoid reading that queer theory and criticism have begun to question.[41] Rather than demote or efface the conventionally "queer" reading, I want to use the story's striking resemblance to the strange case of addiction to generate a more nuanced historical understanding of both identities.

By admitting more than one referent to the hermeneutics of the "unspeakable," we can generate a denser depiction of both the story's own unease with regimes of identity and the period's anxious attempt to reconfigure identity, desire, and compulsion. Accordingly, the first section of this chapter, "Epistemology of the Needle," demonstrates how the representational strategies of popular fiction conflate homosexuality and addiction under mobile signs of nameless vice and disease. The second section, "Rewriting the 'Slavery' of Drink," shows how *The Strange Case of Dr. Jekyll and Mr. Hyde* can be read as a story about both addiction and gay identity. Stevenson's story offered doctors and the wider culture an allusive shorthand for addicts' compulsions, habituations, secrecy, and, most of all, their apparently dual personalities; however, the story also represents a lament about a white masculine embodiment made increasingly uninhabitable under the representational pressures of addiction.

Epistemology of the Needle

In turn-of-the-century popular fiction, queer sexualities and addiction are both represented as mysterious, barely intelligible secrets; within the hermeneutics of suspicion, they frequently become interchangeable. In chapter 4, I presented Rita's *Queer Lady Judas* (1905) as a text that argued vociferously against New Womanhood by associating it with morphine addiction. In just one of the novel's queer subplots, the narrator and beauty guru Madame Beaudelet cures her chemical supplier's morose young daughter, Julie Thibaud, of her morphine addiction. Madame Beaudelet first becomes interested in Julie when she fails to diagnose the source of her sullenness: "She held for me a curious pathological interest. She was young—yet so old. Ill—yet without a pronounced disease. Melancholy—with no apparent reason for unhappiness. And to all life and to all affection she seemed indifferent."[42] In this passage, Julie's unspecific, undetectable illness engages all the tropes of decadent, degenerate sexuality. Interesting because she both inspires and defies classification, Julie, like Walter Pater's Mona Lisa, is vampiric—old but young, obscurely ill, nurturing a hidden sadness, contemplating death rather than life. The same trope opens Guy Thorne's *The Cigarette Smoker* (1902), a novel for which the addicted identity "nicotomaniac" only very thinly screens a homicidally ambivalent same-sex desire, when the hale young protagonist Uther Kennedy can't quite put his finger on what's wrong with his old friend: "Léopold suggested the *absintheur*, *enervé* by his vice, and yet in some points there was no resemblance to that grim ghost of the cafés. He bore the imprint of many vices, though he had the distinguishing characteristics of no single one. It was strange, and chilling."[43] The multiplication and dispersion of vice into unintelligibility suggests the cultural code of homosexuality, but the secret in each case is addiction.

The same trope operates with respect to Hyde in *The Strange Case*: at the outset, the man-about-town Enfield declares that Hyde is all but indescribable, and Jekyll's servant Poole goads his lawyer, Utterson, "You must know as well as the rest of us that there was something queer about that gentleman—something that gave a man a turn—I don't know rightly how to say it, sir, beyond this: that you felt in your marrow kind of cold and thin" (*JH* 46). Of course, in this story the "vice" is doubly unguessable: Jekyll's compulsive transformations into Hyde are absolutely idiosyncratic, and Hyde's sensual indulgences are never specified—the trampling of little girls and beating of old men notwithstanding, since they seem to happen either en route to other assignations, or without premeditation. And yet consider the way that, in *Queer Lady Judas*, Madame Beaudelet's speculations take the same "queer" turn that also describes Jekyll's condition: "And once again my suspicions wandered into that queer channel of a hospital experience; of cases that had puzzled doctors. Of queer contorted phases of the mind acting on the body, and producing results, monstrous as are some tropical plants, evil as a hidden vice. Was this girl the victim of some such obsession of the senses? Had she been tempted by the poison of an insidious thought, and yielded herself as a slave to a taskmaster?" (*QLJ* 159–60). In this passage, medical knowledge becomes the new context of the slavery metaphor, and produces queerness in the suspended space of diagnosis. The master-slave relationship, now long deracinated from both chattel slavery and wage slavery, takes on the sexual overtone of "insidious" influence, such as Lord Harry Wotton's over Dorian Gray; the menacing tropical plants index the decadence of bizarre collections and arcane poisons that deform the mind and in turn, the body. Such language speaks directly to Jekyll's warping obsession with his own moral purification, which leads him to produce and reproduce Hyde. In both texts, "queerness" remains inexplicable, mysterious. In Julie's case it turns out to be her desire—not for other women but for morphine; in Jekyll's, the desire is for the powder that literally transforms him.

Addiction takes on the alluring mystery of a vice that cannot be specified—a tantalizing formlessness that, upon disclosure and medical scrutiny, can be diagnosed using the new profusion of clinical taxonomies. M. Kellen Williams links the text's inability to designate Hyde's exact mode of deviance to "a radical degenerating of the representational medium itself, the complete erosion of what in its barest, most basic form would be narrative's communicative capacity."[44] I will take up the social effects of this narrative degeneration later in this chapter. For now, I want to note that when addiction is not disclosed, the language used to describe its mystery looks a lot like that used to describe that other secret desire, homosexuality.

Addiction further organizes representations of same-sex eroticism as relations of power. When addiction becomes the explicit plot, then the subtext appears queerer. In both *The Strange Case* and *Queer Lady Judas*, same-sex eroticism is never far behind the actual secret. In the latter novel, Madame Beaudelet decides to cure Julie, a project that requires her to dole out her supply in ever-dwindling doses. By becoming the sole source of Julie's morphine, Madame Beaudelet insists on an exclusive relationship of the most intimate kind—one that extorts a promise of fidelity from her young object of conquest. Given this context, the following passage reads like an erotic encounter:

> "Look at me," I said, suddenly. "My will is stronger than yours."
>
> I pressed my hand heavily on her shoulder. I forced her to look into my eyes. I brought every force and energy of mine to break down the weak barriers of her enfeebled mind; as she ceased to resist, the more I dominated.
>
> When her eyes closed, and she seemed about to sleep, I put the question I had determined to put. Feebly and reluctantly she groped about with those weak, thin hands. Then from the bosom of her gown she took out a little case.
>
> I seized it.
>
> "Come to me when you want it," I said. "I am not going to force you away from the poison at once. But promise me that from this moment you will not use the stuff unknown to me." (*QLJ* 167)

Queerness operates in this passage in several ways. The female narrator's characteristically New Woman, "masculine" activity and directness assumes a particular sexual force, and Julie becomes a more than usually abject species of femininity, the woman who not just has been enthralled by morphine but now also finds herself dominated by a mannish woman. Here, the language of mental and physical contest that pervades descriptions of conventional sexual trysts is adapted to the plot of resistance, indulgence, desire, and prohibition surrounding morphine. Julie becomes the fantasy of the woman whose excessive craving for sex has been contractually disciplined and regulated by masculine-controlled access to the phallus, represented here as the quasi-institutionally controlled needle.

The novel stages this intimacy as a banal mixture of repulsion and desperation when Julie arrives for her morning fix and the narrator makes her bathe first; wrapped in a towel and sitting on the bathtub edge, Julie "thrust out one bare, thin arm with an imploring gesture. . . . Her eyes devoured my face with a fearful eagerness. I said nothing, but applied the *piqure*" (*QLJ* 173). What is the nature of this eroticism, particularly when Julie, covered with abscesses, presents such an abject spectacle of self-damage? Whereas in the previous passage, Madame Beaudelet had been the powerful one, subduing Julie and forcing her to fulfill her cravings only through her, here the addict becomes the more powerful partner, since her voracious desire must, after all, be satisfied. From the narrator's point of view, the *piqure* or hypodermic needle becomes a lesbian phallus, when faced with the intensity and apparent bottomlessness of Julie's desire.[45]

The same power struggle governs the narrative in *The Strange Case*, which resolves it by answering the question of whose will, and whose desires, are stronger, Jekyll's or Hyde's. If the potion and the powders that compose it are the analogue of Julie's *piqure*, then the friends who find themselves involved in its procurement occupy the same mixed position of pity, revulsion, and false power as does Madame Beaudelet. Hence Utterson's pity when confronted with Jekyll's note to his chemist, in which, "with a sudden splutter of the pen, the writer's emotion had broken loose. 'For God's sake,' he added, 'find me some of the old' " (*JH* 66). Lanyon's reaction, when Hyde importunes him for the powder, is less sympathetic: " 'Have you got it?' he cried. 'Have you got it?' And so lively was his impatience that he even laid his hand upon my arm and sought to shake me. I put him back, conscious at his touch of a certain icy pang along my blood" (*JH* 78). Just as Madame Beaudelet forces Julie to bathe before giving her morphine, so Lanyon enjoys his power over Hyde, making him sit down and be civil before giving him his fix. Rita discreetly omits the spectacle of Julie getting high, but Stevenson relishes delivering the full extent of his crypto-addict's revenge on his supplier: Hyde "uttered one loud sob of such immense relief that I sat petrified"; rather than be satisfied with having helped him, Lanyon gives way to "the greed of curiosity" and is appropriately rewarded with "a mind submerged in terror," a condition that kills him. If, following Foucault, it has become a contemporary banality that the exchange of power produces sexuality, the application of this insight to addiction, a narrative formation governed by the physiological rhythms of power and powerlessness, has been a less explored but no less meaningful possibility.

Narratives of addiction resemble narratives of queer sexualities when they emplot the transfer of power through the addict's confession. The typical protagonist's secret problem operates the way that Foucault has described all sexuality, as "a furtive reality" that must be discovered for the truth to come out.[46] This usually happens when the addict confesses to someone with a medical background who understands the problem; in *Queer Lady Judas*, it is Madame Beaudelet, with her past experience working in a hospital. Throughout the Victorian period, the power of the family doctor to keep secrets or spread gossip was formidable. As Samuel Guy wrote in the preface to a series of medical tales titled *The Doctor's Notebook* (1864), "I have had the knowledge, too, of a shameful secret—a secret to all but me and the persons themselves—which would blast the honour of more than one noble family."[47] The possible contents of such a secret are fairly limited: before the 1890s and the emergence of male homosexuality into mass public discourse, habitual drunkenness would have been the leading candidate; afterwards, supplemented by drug habituation, it would have remained high on a list that also included abortion or contagious sexual disease. Given the physician's immense power, the drunkard or addict's confession to him is particularly fraught. Addiction narratives typically stage this confession between the members of an intensive homosocial friendship. Coke Richardson's novella *Horace Saltoun* (1861) has the eponymous brilliant young medical researcher confess his family curse of dipsomania and subsequent sins to his medical school friend Paul, who serves as narrator; not even his mother and sister have such intimate knowledge of him. Paul's friendship with Horace motivates him to keep quiet and help Horace's medical career where he can.[48] This plot device greatly resembles the way the work of maintaining Jekyll's secret falls to his homosocial milieu; in Stevenson's text, men keep each other's secrets and intimacies, and their disclosures and surveillances resemble the curious passion engendered through the confession of addiction.

The same plot contours John Saunders's *The Tempter Behind* (1919), in which the novice Anglican priest Wade Concannon confesses his habitual drunkenness to Dr. John Goodge, a prickly Independent Church member who nevertheless wells up upon hearing of Concannon's plight. The two form an impassioned friendship based on the disclosure and Concannon's pledge to be honest with him.[49] In Kate Jordan's "The Grey Land of Drugs," a similar lesbian trope surfaces explicitly, forming the ground of the disclosure. The narrator is pursued by her childhood friend Amy, a professional nurse with whom, as a girl, she had been in love; Amy combines the powerful surveillance of a masculine medical gaze with the homoerotics of schoolgirl intimacy: "Each time [Amy] sought me I could feel her studying me. Each time, after she left me, I was haunted. 'She knows,' I would say, and then: '*Does* she know?' " When Amy confronts her about her problem, it is in intimate terms: " 'I know the signs. Oh, come! Open your heart to me!' . . . I begged her to help me—asked her to let me see her every day. How tenderly she kissed me as she went away!"[50] Here the lesbian relationship becomes the basis on which the confession of addiction can emerge.

As with non-normative sexualities, the desire for drugs is abhorrent because it is thought to be unnatural, whereas natural desires are heteronormative ones that promote kinship. Sedgwick notes that in both queer and addicted taxonomies, "the old antisodomitic opposition between something called nature and that which is *contra naturam* blends with a treacherous apparent seamlessness into a new opposition between substances that are *natural* (e.g., 'food') and those that are *artificial* (e.g., 'drugs')."[51] The conflation of multiple substances into a prohibitive discourse on "drugs" is a twentieth-century phenomenon, but its roots can be found in the late nineteenth century, when the disgust for alcohol and drug dependencies coalesced around their putative degenerate artificiality. In this formation, the term *morbid* crosses between medical and mainstream print culture, usually to designate bizarre cravings. This formation features queerly in Thorne's *The Cigarette Smoker*, when Kennedy confesses to Dr. Wriggel that his thoughts "tend towards a loathsome morbid cruelty. I watch my wife in horrible torments without any wish to help her. I contemplate coldly—Oh, I can't go on." Rather predictably, his wife cannot help him at all with the source of this unnatural feeling, his overwhelming desire for nicotine: "I cannot conceive of any more fearful craving. It is never satisfied. It grows and grows till it becomes absolute torture."[52] Not just bizarre or mysterious cravings, but the state of craving itself is unnatural to a well-regulated nineteenth-century body. The deficiency signals a disordered physical system, one lacking the staples of "fresh air, exercise, natural rest, temperance, quietude of mind" that will maintain people "vigorous in mind and body, so as to be always fit for work and ready for enjoyment," wrote Francis Anstie, describing a mid-nineteenth-century ideal of health.[53] A "natural" nineteenth-century body had no cravings.

In this period, addiction and same-sex desire produced informal intimacies characteristic of underground communities rather than kinship relations. Indeed, alcohol and drugs routinely mediated same-sex intimacy and eroticism in fiction from this period. Jordan's "The Grey Land of Drugs" links addiction with lesbian desire, since the narrator begins taking morphia pills to blunt the grief of widowhood and "escape from eating loneliness," only to watch her addiction become the center of a homoerotic triangle. On the one hand, she attempts to hide it from "the woman who was to be the good angel of my life," Amy, with whom, years earlier, the narrator "had been chums of the romantic sort—had exchanged locks of hair, 'would have died for each other' " ("GLD" 301–2). On the other, there is temptation in the figure of a "full, soft, Spanish-type" actress acquaintance she makes at a boarding house, Mrs. Layton, who seduces the narrator with her "languorous southern charm":

> She began to notice me. There was no speed limit to my friendly overtures. Before I had been there a week we were sharing the same table. She told me she was an actress, and spent about twenty weeks of the year on tour; that she was a "heavy," and generally found a berth in melodrama or farce. I gave her an embellished account of myself—a pudding of truth with raisins of lies. I began to wonder if she were not, like myself—*queer*. Later, she told me that she had "spotted me" from the first time she spoke to me.
>
> Physicians say that perverted beings of every sort discover each other by instinct, even in crowds, and come together as surely as the steel to the magnet. ("GLD" 304)

Jean takes an apartment with "Mrs. Layton," who teaches her how to use a syringe to inject morphine rather than swallow morphia tablets. This initiation is similar to a sexual one: "It is true a twinge of my native fastidiousness made me shudder when I first saw the secret parts of her body lacerated and green from a thousand needle pricks, with scattered inflammations and small ulcers; but this oozed away, as did all normal sensations" ("GLD" 306). Mrs. Layton's racialized body is revealed to be both a ruined monument to excessive heterosexual violations, since it has suffered from "a thousand . . . pricks" and something oddly alien, a secret, green object of the narrator's abnormal sensations. Both bizarrely embellished and nearly invisible as it disappears inside the stock roles of "the heavy," Mrs. Layton's crypto-lesbian body functions like the hypodermic morphine, to draw the narrator deeper into her own nearly fatal identity. Here the story plainly conflates lesbian desire with addiction under the sign of queerness as just another sort of "perversion" identified by physicians. The narrator's overarching choice is not between "morphine" as a metonym for lesbianism or "no morphine" as a signifier of straight-and-narrow living. Rather, the choice is "morphine" as metonym for the raunchy, racialized, Bohemian, queer sex associated with the theater, or "recovery" as a signifier of the wholesome, healthy, committed relationship with the wifelike Amy. In "The Grey Land of Drugs," each side of its love triangle vibrates with homoerotic frisson.

In the completely different context of the lawless spaces of the closing U.S. frontier of the 1880s, D. F. MacMartin's memoir *Thirty Years in Hell* similarly stages a mutual attraction ostensibly about addiction but conjuring a secret intimacy that also connotes gay desire. In a chapter titled "My First 'Shot,' " MacMartin has been on an alcoholic bender, in his words, "swine drunk," when he finds himself in a bar the next morning with other "human driftwood," and he connects with one of them in a passage worth quoting at length:

> There was a certain fascination about him which I could not resist, altho' had I been normal, I would have known it to be only a veneer for demonology. Leaving his position against the wall where he had been posing as a mural lizard, he flashed me a wireless radiogram to follow him and as a nod is as good as a wink to a blind man, I obeyed this telepathic message. When we reached the tap room of this barrel house, he seemed after a few moments' conversation already installed in my intimacy. We had evidently reciprocal sympathy and similar tastes. In fact, he began by saying that he believed we were both born under the same planet. Very readily he came to the point when he confided to me that he had it within his power to steady my nerves, and immediately transform me from a shivering disciple of John Barleycorn to a status where I would loll in a veritable heaven of ease and exhilaration.[54]

What begins as a seedy bar pickup and proceeds as flirtation turns into a different kind of transaction: the means by which MacMartin is promised "ease and exhilaration" is not sex but hypodermic morphine. The initially wordless exchange proceeds along the unvoiced, invisible, and therefore unpoliced lines of radiograms and telepathy—media that use the arcane new technology of electricity to flash secret messages. Even the astrological allusion represents an alternative form of sympathy and kinship between two "abnormal" or alien creatures finding each other in an infernal frontier. That this moment also represents MacMartin's break with alcohol, personified as "John Barleycorn" and his introduction to a new love, hypodermic morphine, can be read as an analogue for the tryst that converts the nominally straight man to queerness. Later on, MacMartin will describe another shot in terms of ending innocence—"I suddenly slipped the little sting of steel, sweeter than the first kiss of love to the innocent"—which underlines his lifelong erotic attachment: "I was not married, except to drugs."[55] Versions of this comment crop up repeatedly in twentieth-century drug narratives, as wry parodies of "normal" kinship relations.

Indeed, alcohol and drug addiction is often represented supplanting or ruining marriage. Like "inverts" and "homosexuals," intemperates, habitual drunkards, inebriates, and addicts were each marked by the desire for a substance that seemed to surpass the desire for the conventional social bonds of kinship and citizenship and by an apparent rejection of the dominant ideologies of class mobility, reproductive sexuality, and gender compliance. The marriage ruined by a spouse's habitual drinking was perhaps the most popular addiction plot in Victorian realism, spanning major authors and texts throughout the period, such as Anne Brontë's *The Tenant of Wildfell Hall* (1848), Charles Dickens's *Hard Times* (1854), George Eliot's *Scenes of Clerical Life* (1857), and Thomas Hardy's *The Mayor of Casterbridge* (1886). Among these, I'd like to take up *Tenant*, because it most vividly demonstrates how same-sex intimacy emerges from the gendered segregation of pleasure in drinking.

Brontë's heroine, Helen Graham, is trying to make her young son Arthur a teetotaler by teaching him to abhor the smell and taste of alcohol; as one of her neighbors, Mrs. Markham, chides her, "Well, but you will treat him like a girl—you'll spoil his spirit, and make a mere Miss Nancy of him."[56] Mrs. Markham's objection stems from the conventional expectation that men were supposed to meet and resist temptation. "What is it that constitutes virtue, Miss Graham?" asks Gilbert Markham. "Is it the circumstance of being able and willing to resist temptation, or having no temptations to resist?" (*TWH* 31). This objection articulates the conventional wisdom of two powerful overlapping discourses: midcentury liberalism and midcentury masculinity, in which the putatively masculine self meets, surmounts, and commands the influences of the commercial and public sphere.[57] Brontë, in critiquing this position, offers a characteristic blend of feminism and temperance, which develops as the backstory of

Helen's nefarious husband unfolds. Arthur Huntingdon was a malign influence on his habitually drunken friend, Lowborough, constantly plying him with brandy and steering him back to the club where their friends wallow in dissolution. Huntingdon himself figures less as a habitual drunkard than as a libertine or rake with multiple sexually deviant overtones: "I like to enjoy my life at all sides and ends, which cannot be done by one that suffers himself to be the slave of a single propensity—and moreover, drinking spoils one's good looks" (*TWH* 194). Indeed, Huntingdon looks so good that he curiously appears to substitute for alcohol in Lowborough's economy of addicted desire. For example, when Lowborough tells his friend that he intends to abstain, and Huntingdon replies that he's heard *that* before, Lowborough claims, "Yes, but you wouldn't let me; and I was such a fool I couldn't live without you" (*TWH* 195). Is it brandy or Huntingdon without which Lowborough cannot live? The narrative of addiction is ensconced within the context of a homosocial affection so intense, it resembles homoerotic desire.

In such a gendered and sexual emotional economy, women are neither desirable nor desiring subjects but rather managers of consumption. Thus Lowborough explains the necessity of a wife to his plans for self-reform: "For I can't live alone, because my own mind distracts me, and I can't live with you, because you take the devil's part against me. . . . But if I could get a wife, with fortune enough to pay off my debts and set me straight in the world. . . . And sweetness and goodness enough . . . to reconcile me to myself" (*TWH* 195). Heterosexual desire depleted by his brandy and laudanum debauches, Lowborough wants a wife only in order to manage his errant desires, to "set [him] straight," both as a heterosexual credential and as a means of restoring his lost character. "I shall never be in love again, that's certain," says Lowborough; but it hardly matters: he just needs someone to pull him out of his addicted abyss, a task to which his fellows could hardly be worse suited (*TWH* 195). Since, as the conventional wisdom went, men were typically more susceptible to dissipation than women, women were better at regulating men's desire and, sometimes, at being the sensible substitutes for it.[58]

In his attachment to Huntingdon, Lowborough vividly illustrates the overlapping of homoeroticism and addicted desire, but this imbrication results from the gendered segregation of pleasure so characteristic of the mid-nineteenth century. Part of women's expected management of men's consumption included making the home a pleasant, enjoyable place without the assistance of alcohol so that the domestic sphere could compete with the pub for men's leisure hours. "My good women . . . how many of you have done anything to induce your husbands not to tope—except in the way of scolding and abuse? Have you . . . made his home comfortable and peaceable? Have you kept it clean and cheerful? Have you ever met him with kind words? I fear not," chided Mr. Danesbury in Ellen Wood's *Danesbury House* (1860).[59] In these endeavors, both working-class and middle-class women faced an uphill challenge. Within more prosperous homes, women were excluded from the after-dinner conviviality men characteristically shared over alcohol and tobacco—and to which the prohibitions of temperance or teetotalism sounded a dissonant note. The English bourgeoisie typically drank wine with dinner but restricted drinking as its own activity to the postprandial hours and to male company.[60] Women were to content themselves with conversation, sewing, and other tame pursuits. And they were also excluded from alcohol-saturated male camaraderie and bonhomie located at the pub, club, and university.

The social context of drinking and tobacco smoking, which increasingly covered for it, was thus male homosocial intimacy of the kind imagined by, for example, W. M. Thackeray in *Vanity Fair* (1848): a thunderstorm "obliged the young people, perforce, to remain at home. Mr. Osborne did not seem in the least disappointed at this occurrence. He and Joseph Sedley drank a fitting quantity of port-wine, tête-à-tête, in the dining-room, during the drinking of which Sedley told a number of his best Indian stories; for he was extremely talkative in man's society."[61] Because drinking almost exclusively takes place within male homosocial contexts, it will always appear on the gamut of masculine friendship, mutual pleasure, intimacy, and homoeroticism. The characteristic heteronormative telos from a young man's carousing and camaraderie to marriage and respectable comportment also traces an arc from the convivial, public life of social drinking to private, domestic, soberer pleasures. By contrast, as we have seen in Rita's *Queer Lady Judas* and Kate Jordan's "The Grey Land of Drugs," the overlap between women's addictions and queer desire develops in private, where friends, female relations, or maids start dosing each other. Lacking an origin in a public social ritual like drinking, women's addictions emerge from private to public once women abandon their mid-nineteenth century social role of domestic and moral management in favor of mutual self-gratification.

In the 1880s, popular fiction built on these social contexts, adapting the plot to drug addiction, dispensing with the typical temperance-influenced moralizing, and preserving addiction's characteristic interruption of the marriage plot. We have already seen how, in *An Evil Spirit*, Isabel Gordon's morphine addiction leads to the demise of her engagement and how, in *Without a Home*, Martin Jocelyn's hypodermic habituation destroys his marriage and family. In Walter Besant's *The Demoniac* (1890), in which, feeling uneasy upon hearing the news that his New Woman fiancée Elinor will be joining him at Cambridge when she enrolls at Newnham, George Atheling experiences a mysterious thirst that can only be slaked by multiple tumblers of whisky, launching him on an alcoholic career that scuttles his engagement.[62] The same plot governs Coulson Kernahan's story "A Literary Gent: A Study in Vanity and Dipsomania" (1895), in which the narrator's budding alcoholism ends his marriage prospects.[63] In domestic novels about wifely disappointment such as F. Mabel Robinson's *Disenchantment: An Everyday Story* (1886), the protagonist discovers her husband to be a habitual drunkard and feels disgusted by him; this is also the plot of Mary Lake's *The Drug Slave* (1913), except that the husband is addicted to morphine.[64] On her wedding eve, the incipient nausea of Lake's heroine is curiously presented: "As I stood watching his tall, graceful figure by the table, a queer feeling swept over me, bringing all sorts of ugly, slimy fears in its wake."[65] The narrative assigns the cause of the protagonist's sudden repulsion toward her husband-to-be to the natural disgust generated by the spectacle of drug use. Addiction intervenes in these narratives, either to thwart a doomed marriage from taking place or to play out the horror of being married to a person who cannot love their spouse, or respect the institution of marriage, enough to quit their habit. The ubiquity of this plot suggests that addiction thrives on the ruins of heterosexual alliances—sometimes even to epic proportions: at the end of *Dope-Darling* (1919), a novel by David Garnett written under the pseudonym Leda Burke, Roy Gordon reflects on his failed project of marrying Claire Plowman in order to get her off cocaine, ruefully musing: "What I feel about Claire is what we soldiers keep saying about the war. If we had known in 1914 what we know now, we should have done things very differently."[66] Like the survivors of the Great War, those who emerge from the rubble of heterosexual institutions destroyed by addiction are left shell-shocked.

Garnett's allusion to the war notwithstanding, addiction and same-sex desire share a final representational strategy, their seeming trajectory toward death. In keeping with their biopolitical framing as deviant, both modes of conduct compulsively represent the mass death of the social body as incipient in the individual, a subject handled in further detail in chapter 6 and the afterword. For now, however, it seems clear that for reproductive heterosexuality to maintain power through a valorizing discourse on life and health, its implicit antonym, homosexuality, must remain an abject condition through an association with disease culminating in death. Adapting the psychoanalytic model of the death drive, Lee Edelman writes that it "names what the queer, in the order of the social, is called forth to figure: the negativity opposed to every form of social viability."[67] Similarly opposed to conventional kinship and to its allied activity, the accumulation of wealth for future generations, the figure of the addict shares this comprehensive negativity with the queer.

Indeed, considered as a cultural trope rather than any psychic disposition, the death drive can be properly said to describe the foreclosure of the future that makes addicts and queer people each seem like, in Jeff Nunokawa's phrase, "a population doomed to extinction."[68] Radclyffe Hall observed this similarity in two moments in *The Well of Loneliness* (1928). In the first, Stephen Gordon finds herself in Alec's, a Parisian gay bar, "that merciless, drug-dealing, death-dealing haunt to which flocked the battered remnants of men whom their fellow men had at last stamped under; who, despised of the world, must despise themselves beyond all hope, it seemed, of salvation."[69] Of the "drink-sodden, doped" men dancing there, one approaches her with "a grey, drug-marred face with a mouth that trembled incessantly" to claim a solidarity that Stephen only grudgingly gives.[70] In the second moment, the spectral quality of the drug-ruined gay men returns to haunt Stephen's lesbian circle in the figure of the drunkard Wanda, whose contagious alienation threatens to poison Mary Llewellyn in the form of brandies and soda.[71] In Hall's novel, such addictions function as gravestones for people who are already socially dead. So too in narratives of addiction: death is one of two available conclusions to the addict's downward spiral. Either the addict recovers, or he dies from an overdose, illness, or accident associated with his addiction. Saunders's *The Tempter Behind* articulates the irony of the drunkard's self-imposed demise when the church bell-ringer tells one of the characters, "A queer fish was the man I'm ringing for. He came here only yesterday to ring his own knell, and then went home, and actually drank himself to death."[72] The specter of death carries over to fiction about drugs, often in heavy-handed excurses such as those of *Dope-Darling*: "At eighteen, Claire Plowman . . . had had varied and horrible experiences, and had contracted one of the most terrible vices in the world. Sniffing cocaine is one of the most terrible, the most dangerous and horrible habit that can be formed. The devotees of cocaine all end under sentence of early death. In a girl of Claire's age there is practically no hope."[73] Underneath the conventional wisdom that drugs kill lies the imagined death-driven sexuality of addicts, whose abnormal desires cause them to destroy themselves incrementally—in the words of one nineteenth-century medical writer, "suicides who poison themselves."[74] It is not merely that addicts, like homosexual characters, must be eliminated from normalizing narratives; rather, they must be seen to eliminate themselves because they are essentially diseased or abnormal—not well enough to participate in the healthy practices of kinship.

Throughout this section, I have been describing the strategic similarities between representations of same-sex desire and of addiction, but there is an important exception to these parallel cultural logics that helps bring them both into more vivid relief. Aestheticism and decadence provide a context of arcane connoisseurship for the pleasures of intoxication and of homosexual desire aligned *against* discourses of addiction. Sedgwick to the contrary, "Dorian Gray" names an important locus of *incommensurability* between homosexual desire and addiction in this discussion. The crucial eleventh chapter of Wilde's novel opens with his protagonist's "addiction" to a book, Huysman's *Au Rebours*: "For years, Dorian Gray could not free himself from the influence of this book. Or perhaps it would be more accurate to say that he never sought to free himself from it."[75] Wilde's equivocation is crucial: it emphasizes Dorian's choice to remain influenced rather than his incapacity to escape influence. Wilde clearly enjoyed playing with—and significantly, challenging—the new idea that people were compelled, diseased, and unable to choose their "unnatural" vices and sins. Indeed, the eleventh chapter of *The Picture of Dorian Gray* is full of Dorian's obsessive fixations with everything from Catholic ornamentation to narratives about jewels to foreign musical instruments precisely because Wilde wanted to mock the inflated menace of the "unnatural," tacitly conceived of as the unusual. For example, Dorian "found a curious pleasure in tracing the thoughts and passions of men to some pearly cell in the brain, or some white nerve in the body, delighting in the conception of the absolute dependence of the spirit on certain physical conditions, morbid or healthy, normal or diseased" (*DG* 147). In this joke on materialism and degeneration, Wilde casts the theoretical reduction of human behavior to physiological causes as itself an unhealthy tendency. He parodies the ideal of "nature" as the masquerade of social hegemony. The scientifically describable operations of natural gray matter are less interesting and important to Wilde than their potential within Aestheticism and intellectual history.

Wilde continues his jest by staging Dorian's relationship to opium to parody habituation: Since Dorian is never represented smoking or eating it—he takes it out of its lacquered box, leers at it greedily, then puts it away—its effects on his brain and behavior are nil. Indeed, given the novel's premium on Aesthetic judgment, the best way to appreciate opium is *not* to eat it, since doing so would fog his delicate sensibilities. Opium does not even produce pleasurable intoxication. When he observes the opium smokers in their den, Dorian "knew in what strange heavens they were suffering, and what dull hells were teaching them the secret of some new joy. They were better off than he was. He was prisoned in thought" (*DG* 179). Here Wilde takes pains to identify and then distinguish Dorian's "imprisonment" from that of opium addiction. As Curtis Marez's insightful work on Wilde's relationship to opium has shown, the drug is valued for its Aesthetic, Orientalized provenance, not for its addictive properties. In Marez's interpretation of this passage, opium becomes a metonym for Wilde's homoerotic, Orientalist desire: "Wilde called attention to the 'open secret' of British imperialism: the fact that it often depended on homoerotic fantasies about the laboring Chinese male body."[76] The substance opium may be linked to homoeroticism in the mingled air of Orientalism and Aestheticism that Wilde breathed, but he distinctly did not link it to opium *addiction*. The sole image of addiction in *The Picture of Dorian Gray* is a distinctly English, uncultured, class-marked, degenerate one, taking place when Dorian, fresh from the disappointment of Sibyl Vane's atrocious performance, walks the London streets, encountering "Drunkards . . . reel[ing] by cursing, and chattering to themselves like monstrous apes" (*DG* 86).[77]

By deflating the materialist discourses of the brain and its morbid cravings, Wilde "made science underwrite an argument for its own inadequacy."[78] For Wilde, the modes of defining "the unnatural" were more interesting as cultural distinctions grounded in social power than as descriptive realities. Wilde exposed the discourses of degeneration as fictions about diseased wills designed to smother Aesthetic delight and pleasure, including elite homosexual desire. Wilde's philosophy and politics were plainly aligned against the new regime of identities, which were the instruments of the medico-scientific, taxonomizing force of psychiatry.[79] It was in this mode—essentially as a historian of his own present—that Wilde became the patron saint of modern gay sexuality, by linking the freedom of self-development central to liberalism to the legitimation of gay pleasure as intellectual, spiritual, and cultural pleasure.[80] As Linda Dowling puts it, "Here may be glimpsed the roots of the modern homosexual identity, for during this period the notion of Greek pederastia made so vivid by Oxford Hellenism persuaded many late-Victorian 'inverts' that the homoerotic emotions they themselves had felt in fearful isolation or confused disgust might instead belong to human experience in its fullest historicity and cultural density."[81] The nature of Aesthetic experience that Wilde used to validate gay desire required a basis of cognitive and physical freedom from which one could flirt with intoxication as a figure of delirious submission to influence—not the specter of addiction that could erode subjective plenitude.

John Addington Symonds felt the same way: "Vice only comes into the matter when the man who gives does so for the sake of gain. It is the same with wine. There is no evil in moderate indulgence. The dedication of the higher self to lust or drunkenness, the immersion of the personality in either pursuit, is ruinous."[82] Like Wilde, Symonds identifies addiction with drunkenness and an effacement of subjectivity via the blunted perception typically thought to accompany the habitual rough use of mental faculties. Habituated perception was the bane of the Aesthetic worldview. In his famous conclusion to *The Renaissance*, Walter Pater had recently figured "habit" as anathema to Aesthetic delight: "In a sense it might even be said that our failure is to form habits: for, after all, habit is relative to a stereotyped world, and meantime it is only the roughness of the eye that makes any two persons, things, situations, seem alike."[83] The exaltation of crude habit to the status of identity was antagonistic to Wilde's and other Aesthetes' intellectualized conceptualization of pleasure as varied and multiple.

Like Wilde, Stevenson wanted to conduct a more complex investigation of desire, identity, compulsion, and power than was typically represented in the fiction discussed in this chapter. While *The Strange Case* keeps Jekyll's condition "nameless" in ways that allow it to approximate both addicted and same-sex desire, it also articulates a more complicated response to the emerging politics of addiction, and the role of white, masculine embodiment within them.

Rewriting the "Slavery" of Drink: Pleasure, Compulsion, and the Hermeneutics of Suspicion

Stevenson's story consistently represents Jekyll's signature ritual as a combination of moral failing, compulsion, and illness—the same overlapping conceptual rubrics applied to the new "conditions" of homosexuality and addiction at fin de siècle. By these means, the metaphor of the diseased will came to regulate suspicious forms of desire and behavior. *The Strange Case* is amenable to both readings, not least because it remains silent on the precise nature of Jekyll's "nameless situation" as well as on Hyde's crimes. Hyde's abnormality cannot be pinned down, though it repulses everyone who meets him; Stevenson manipulates the hermeneutics of suspicion, as readers wonder about the secret cause of the instant hatred Hyde inspires. In this and several other ways, *The Strange Case* matches the common features of the popular fiction I just surveyed, making it amenable to both conventionally queer and addicted interpretations: Jekyll's strange secret is kept and revealed through the power relations of a small homosocial network; his self-revelation occupies the doubled position of confession and case study; Hyde's unnaturalness conjures degeneracy and mass death that threatens the future; and, most obviously, the psychic splitting between the two of them can be read as the vicissitudes of addiction or homosexual self-denial.

All of these qualities, which make narratives of addiction and homosexuality echo each other, culminate in their common crisis of the self: are the problematic desires and activities—same sex intimacy and addiction—chosen or compelled? This is the crux of Stevenson's investigation into human nature, since Hyde, especially when he appears unbidden, represents the usurpation of Jekyll by his "lower" nature. The same line of questioning propels addiction narratives such as Ellen Pinsent's *No Place for Repentance* (1896): "What if after all the Freedom of the Will was but a delusion on the human brain? Impossible—life would be a constant terror, and yet—it was strange, this feeling of impotent captivity—was he free to act as his better nature directed him?"[84] Such questions certainly echoed Symonds's struggle with his homosexuality, his feelings of being "innocent . . . yet haunted by a sense of guilt and dread of punishment."[85] In the late nineteenth century, this was a question of character, of personal and social responsibility, but it was metamorphosing into one about diagnosis, individual repression and expression, and taxonomy, what we have come to call "identity." For example, in a letter to Stevenson, Symonds once complained that "physical and biological Science on a hundred lines is reducing individual freedom to zero, and reducing the sense of responsibility. I doubt whether the artist should lend his genius to this grim argument."[86] Stevenson, particularly in *The Strange Case*, agreed with this sentiment more than Symonds realized: although dissatisfied with the old regime of character, Stevenson also rails against the new one of identity. He does this by appropriating the hermeneutics of suspicion to expose its own shortcomings. The text tries to universalize this problem, but it sabotages its own effort: Hyde may be a dimension of Jekyll's personality, but because he is also a classed and raced figure, and because his relationship to Jekyll is described in political terms, he reveals the reliance of unmarked subjects on the social order. *The Strange Case* thus furthers the history of addiction by ambivalently exposing the traditionally white, masculine, bourgeois addict's futile struggle to liberate himself from his inner "slave" or "demon" in a way that will make a heterogeneous, fragmented social order unify and cohere.

When Stevenson references the "slavery" and "freedom" of Jekyll's indulgence in sin through Hyde, he deploys the metaphor familiar from temperance and mainstream nineteenth-century discussions of addiction: "My new power tempted me until I fell in slavery. I had but to drink the cup" (*JH* 85). The language of slavery and freedom also captures the rhythm of the habitual drunkard's urges in Jekyll's waxing and waning conscience: "But time began at last to obliterate the freshness of my alarm; the praises of conscience began to grow into a thing of course; I began to be tortured with throes and longings, as of Hyde struggling after freedom; and at last, in an hour of moral weakness, I once again compounded and swallowed the transforming draught" (*JH* 90). This is precisely the rhythm of addiction: the end of the sober interval becomes the moment of crisis, as resolve erodes. The passage also underscores a familiar teetotal concept of temporality, in which it only takes a short amount of time, such as "an hour," to undo years of difficult self-management. In the narrative economy of temperance fiction, the smallest amount of drink or the most customary toast is a test the protagonist is likely to fail; as Jekyll puts it, "In my case, to be tempted, however slightly, was to fall" (*JH* 90). Jekyll also directly compares himself to a drunkard in the context of the failure to calculate when drunk: "I do not suppose that, when a drunkard reasons with himself upon his vice, he is once out of five hundred times affected by the dangers that he runs through his brutish, physical insensibility; neither had I, long as I had considered my position, made enough allowance for the complete moral insensibility and insensate readiness to evil, which were the leading characters of Edward Hyde" (*JH* 90). This passage suggests quite clearly that Stevenson is mobilizing the old temperance model of "vice" in conceptualizing Jekyll's temptation and repeated indulgence. It also demonstrates that Jekyll's failure, like the drunkard's, is his own: a failure to anticipate in advance the effects of his altered sensibilities. To the considerable extent that the story is about Jekyll's ethical dilemma, these backslidings and failures form the tragedy; to Hyde, though, they are of course a triumph: "I knew myself, at the first breath of this new life, to be more wicked, tenfold more wicked, sold a slave to my original evil; and the thought, in that moment, braced and delighted me like wine" (*JH* 84). Jekyll's intemperance is Hyde's intoxicated delight; Jekyll's self-enslavement is Hyde's mastery. Stevenson invokes the "slavery of drink" metaphor, but he innovates upon it by conjuring the pleasure, rather than just the horror, of abandoning oneself to vice.

Like the promising young men who become drunkards, Jekyll, falling prey to his secret vice, begins to lose his reputation and his wealth; he has a brief period of reform but then tragically succumbs more fully to his compulsion. But Stevenson—like E. P. Roe in *Without a Home*—does more to play out the dramatic irony whereby the white, privileged man is transformed into the abject slave through capitulation to his own desire. Hyde at first seems like Jekyll's slave or tool, which, combined with the powder and the potion, allows him to indulge his taste for the unnatural, but as Jekyll loses control of the process, he becomes Hyde's unwitting instrument in the same way that the habitué becomes the servant of alcohol or drugs. Unlike temperance fiction, however, which devised plots to display this ironic transformation, *The Strange Case* renders those transformations in class and status at the level of metaphor: Jekyll's spiritual powers are "dethroned from their supremacy," usurped by Hyde, who "bore the stamp of the lower elements in my soul" (*JH* 83). Jekyll's fate plays out through the familiar master/slave, monarch/subject, lofty/debased, soul/body binaries, so that, seeking freedom for his soul, he inadvertently imprisons himself in his body, which no longer obeys his direction, but transforms and indulges itself. The text's marking of Hyde as simian, "abnormal and misbegotten," and suited for abjection and servitude, yokes the language of medico-scientific racism embedded in the idea of "abnormality" to an older model of fateful physical deficiency, the quality of being "misbegotten" (*JH* 78).

Using this strategy, the text engages the discourse of degeneration, a prevalent theme in addiction explored in chapter 6; however, the Jekyll-Hyde split corresponds to a generalized nineteenth-century notion of an individual mind divided between higher sensibilities that checked lower, animal impulses. Alcohol was thought to suppress the higher faculties and allow the lower ones freer reign.[87] In his influential *Stimulants and Narcotics* (1864), Francis Edmund Anstie recategorized alcohol from its status in Brunonian medicine as a stimulant to a narcotic that destroyed the brain's capacity for moral and intellectual activity and unveiled the lower part of human nature.[88] By making Hyde an aspect of Jekyll's personality but also a classed and raced figure, Stevenson links these medical ideas to a political order; as other critics have shown, he makes explicit the contingency of the unmarked subject's self-rule on class, racial, and imperial order.[89] The reversal whereby Jekyll becomes Hyde's minion reveals how the compulsions of habitual drunkenness, inebriety, and addiction threatened the underpinnings of nineteenth-century British identity.

Queer readings of *The Strange Case* tend to interpret the story's disruption of the social order as the tantalizing prospect of homosexual intimacy, using the scene in which Jekyll wakes up as Hyde in Soho, and the scene in Regent's Park in which Jekyll turns into Hyde without first taking the potion. George Haggerty, for example, notes that "the horror Jekyll experiences when he realizes he is turning into Hyde without willing to do so is uncannily sexual."[90] Thus read, the park scene is also full of Jekyll's sexual excitement as a strange hand appears on his knee:

> a qualm came over me, a horrid nausea and the most deadly shuddering. These passed away, and left me faint; and then as in its turn faintness subsided, I began to be aware of a change in the temper of my thoughts, a greater boldness, a contempt of danger, a solution of the bonds of obligation. I looked down; my clothes hung formlessly on my shrunken limbs; the hand that lay on my knee was corded and hairy. I was once more Edward Hyde. A moment before I had been safe of all men's respect, wealthy, beloved—the cloth laying for me in the dining-room at home; and now I was the common quarry of mankind, hunted, houseless, a known murderer, thrall to the gallows. (*JH* 92–93)

But the passage equally conjures addiction. In temperance fiction, the turning point in the protagonist's transformation is usually a moment of intense shame from public intoxication. Jekyll's involuntary metamorphosis into Hyde is strikingly similar, for it is then that he no longer controls his self-indulgence. Aside from its phenomenological resemblance to sensations induced by drink or a drug after a period of abstinence, this passage also hits all the notes of temperance characterizations of lower-class drunkenness. A well-respected public man, once given over to his secret vice of drinking or drug-taking, becomes a universally despised figure subject to criminal justice, all within a moment of backsliding. False courage and total disregard for familial relationships were signature features of this drunkard-protagonist of temperance fiction. When Jekyll observes his "shrunken limbs" and a hand whose flesh cannot conceal its inner parts, he is witnessing both the worker's muscular physique and the bourgeois habitual drunkard's emaciation simultaneously. Hyde, after all, in spite of being small and malformed, is also preternaturally strong, but these are qualities of laborers—not to mention degenerates—and not those of professional men. Jekyll also repeatedly refers to losses in his "stature" when he becomes Hyde—a reference both to Hyde's stunted growth and to his lower public standing. Such allusions are often read as cross-class eroticism, but they just as easily suggest the horror of recognizing oneself sliding down in society that was part of the thrill of temperance narratives. The horror of realizing that one has become the detested Other closely corresponds to the dramas of self-transformation by which middle-class professional men ruined themselves through drink.

Stevenson borrows the language, plot, and social anxieties of temperance fiction, but he does so in order to expose their inadequacy to psychological realities and thereby transform them. The newer phenomenon of drug addiction made the old tempted and trembling sinner of temperance fiction seem even more wooden and simplistic than, to many critics, it already was. By the 1880s, temperance fiction in both Britain and the United States was treated with the contempt of too-long familiarity. Stevenson's generic innovations, by contrast, update the conceptual horizon of intemperance by incorporating elements of more recent narratives of drug habituation, a new, modern reality not yet widely found in novels. For example, a feature of drug use long familiar from De Quincey's *Confessions of an English Opium-Eater* was the alternation between pain and pleasure; the newer technology of the hypodermic syringe compressed the transition into a sudden moment when euphoria succeeds pain. Stevenson's text replicates this compression in the description of Jekyll's transformation into Hyde:

> The most racking pangs succeeded: a grinding in the bones, deadly nausea, and a horror of the spirit that cannot be exceeded at the hour of birth or death. Then these agonies began swiftly to subside, and I came to myself as if out of a great sickness. There was something strange in my sensations, something indescribably new and, from its very novelty, incredibly sweet. I felt younger, lighter, happier in body; within I was conscious of a heady recklessness, a current of disordered sensual images running like a mill race in my fancy, a solution of the bonds of obligation, an unknown but not an innocent freedom of the soul. (*JH* 83)

Queer readings take these sensations as the euphoria of liberation through freer sexual expression, but they can also be read as evidence of a chemically altered state. One critic has even posited that this giddy, energetic sense of power may reflect Stevenson's experience of the cocaine he may have been taking for his respiratory ailments.[91]

More convincingly, however, what appears to be the most implausible aspect of the story—Jekyll's transformation—was actually the strangest element of the new cultural narrative of habituation: the formation of a newer, freer feeling of personhood as the result of taking a drug and the foundation of this feeling on the elimination of pain. This formation accordingly corresponds to the most illogical, fairy-tale–like aspect of the story, namely, that the same potion that turns Jekyll into Hyde also works in reverse, to restore Jekyll to himself.[92] This paradoxical plot element makes perfect sense within the logic of addiction, in which, as Clifford Allbutt first observed, the drug has the capacity to alleviate the symptoms it has itself produced.[93] As with habit-forming alcohol and drugs, tolerance eventually reduces this magical efficacy, so that Jekyll is no longer able to orchestrate his own transformation: "I had been obliged on more than one occasion to double, and once, with infinite risk of death, to treble the amount" of the drug (*JH* 89). Temperance fiction, which put tremendous narrative pressure on the first taste, often seemed oblivious to the gradual process of habituation to alcohol. Narratives about drug habituation, on the other hand, began to represent phenomena such as withdrawal, tolerance, and overdose. Stevenson's citation of these phenomena updated the older model of intemperance, making it more topical and menacing.

Jekyll's condition reflects the uneasy transition between vice and disease as the conceptual paradigm of addiction. As I have been arguing in the previous two chapters, medicalization was a partial process that left a good deal of moralizing intact in the concept of addiction. In the historical moment of *The Strange Case*, then, the medical discourse of habituation was combining with the older temperance model to produce a proliferation of terms—Stevenson uses "malady," "madness," "cerebral disease," "disgrace," and "evil"—and a failure to specify Jekyll's "nameless situation," situated somewhere between vice and disease. Utterson conjectures to Poole that Jekyll "is plainly seized with one of those maladies that both torture and deform the sufferer; hence the mask and the avoidance of his friends; hence his eagerness to find this drug, by means of which the poor soul retains some hope of ultimate recovery" (*JH* 66). Stevenson could easily have been referencing alcoholism or another debilitating habituation, especially since their ravages were thought to effect physical transformations so thorough that family members could not recognize their sufferers. Lanyon also predictably voices the medical view: "The more I reflected the more convinced I grew that I was dealing with a case of cerebral disease" (77). The earliest British medical researchers into addiction, such as Norman Kerr, Francis E. Anstie, and Allbutt, made this case, arguing that habituation altered brain structure and function. Jekyll also describes his condition as "sickliness" and the drug as his "medicine" (*JH* 95, 65). The concept of "sickliness" rather than "sickness" reveals another layer of ambivalence in describing habituation as an illness: it still seemed like a simulacrum of a real illness to those who held that it was a moral failing. In *The Strange Case*, medical references are scant compared to the language of temptation, sin, and confession, but what Stevenson achieves by medicalizing Jekyll's condition, even to a small degree, is crucial. He manages to postulate Jekyll's state as a kind of moral illness or, as addiction would soon come to be theorized, as a "disease of the will." That is, although Jekyll's problem is, like habitual drunkenness, a self-caused behavioral problem, it also is the expression of an immanent defect, Jekyll's "impatient gaiety of disposition," which in this tale becomes a predisposition.

Indeed, Stevenson's story became an easy byword for theorizations of addiction split between moral and medical frameworks. Writing about inebriates, Kerr, then president of the Society for the Study and Cure of Inebriety, alluded to the book: "With all this confused disturbance of perception, sensation, and reason, the 'ego' is an *alter ego*, a false man and not *the true*; a Mr. Hyde, not the original Dr. Jekyll."[94] Although Kerr wanted to establish inebriety as "a true disease, as unmistakably a disease as is gout or epilepsy or insanity," he was also keen to explain that inebriates' "moral faculties are even more deadened by the poison, than are their intellectual."[95] Hughes himself referenced Stevenson: "Even at the height of such a mad mental revelry I seemed to realize just what was causing it. There seemed to be a separate me watching and studying the effects of the drug I had taken—a Dr. Jekyll, as it were, compelled to witness, but powerless to prevent, the insane acts of a Mr. Hyde."[96] In addition to his unattributed ransacking of Stevenson's text, MacMartin also alluded directly to *The Strange Case* in a chapter titled "Jekyll and Hyde": "I injected an extraordinarily copious 'shot' of morphine, blended with a homeopathic quantum of cocaine, and I slyly slid out of that house forever. Before I was Dr. Jekyll, the creative; now I was his *alter ego*, Mr. Hyde, the resolvent soul."[97] The incompatible coexistence of the scientific and moral epistemologies had led Kerr and other writers to posit two beings in one to explain the condition. A sober inebriate may resolve not to drink, but once he has imbibed, another existence takes him over: "he is now not his own master, his good resolutions (whether of moderation or abstinence) are swept away in the tidal wave of an overwhelming flood of another and degenerate, though evanescent, existence. The gallant resolve is the act of one person, the breakdown the act of a different person. The former person can make a good resolution, which the latter cannot keep."[98] Kerr's reasoning slides over the logical difficulty at the center of both his theorization of addiction, and of *The Strange Case*: for the breakdown to be the second man's act, he must already have been called into existence by the first man's act of weakness. Does Jekyll weaken, or does Hyde gather strength and emerge unbidden? The logical problem whereby addiction is both a disease and a moral failing is recapitulated in the awkward doubling of the addict's personhood. Stevenson's story offered theorists of addiction an easy way to explain the inherence, in one individual, of two persons.

As one might expect, notorious grammatical difficulties inhere in this model of doubled subjectivity. The major fault line of this kind of narration is that one narrator, designated by a consistent first-person pronoun, must record intoxicated exploits that seem to belong to someone else. *The Strange Case* emphasizes this paradox of the drunkard's confession by playing up its grammatical challenges: late in his "full statement of the case," while narrating Hyde's activities, Jekyll breaks down and writes, "He, I say—I cannot say, I" (*JH* 94). As Judith Butler explains the use of the first-person singular pronoun, "Where there is an 'I' who utters or speaks and thereby produces an effect in discourse, there is first a discourse which precedes and enables that 'I' and forms in language the constraining trajectory of its will."[99] The rough grammatical texture of *The Strange Case* exposes and partly undoes this very effect. One discourse that precedes and enables Jekyll's speech is the temperance confession, which establishes psychic unity through the temporal arc of sin, confession, and forgiveness. "Jekyll" thus becomes, in the first person, both an index of that discourse and the trace of its own partial undoing, the possibility that the subject "I" has a defective will backing it up. Hyde's debased narration survives only as obscure, profane footnotes to this text because there is no available discourse to authorize the speech of a discontinuous, meandering will. Peter K. Garrett points to the descriptions of Hyde's voice as "not only hellish but inorganic," as "the slime of the pit . . . utter[ing] cries and voices," and "a dismal screech, as of mere animal terror" as noises that undo the binding force of language itself.[100] In my reading, this is the incoherence of a possible voice—one that exists as glossolalia or noise because it lacks a supportive discourse and authentic personhood.

The alternative is for the addict to be transformed from speaking being to gibbering degenerate, the fate of the eponymous alcoholic of *Horace Saltoun*; if we look into Horace's darkened house, the narrator tells us, "you may see a fantastically attired, restless being, talking perpetually and incoherently. . . . Sometimes he will make a brilliant metaphor, or begin to quote a fragment of some fine passage, but invariably relapses into vapid nonsense before he can finish it."[101] This counterexample suggests why Stevenson chose not to have Hyde narrate any of the story: his own voice would have undermined his status as fragment or "false man," and construing him as his own person would nullify his status as Jekyll's symptom. The second man, who cannot occupy the position of the second person, "you," thus remains in the limbo of grammatical difficulty and, within theories of addiction, as a defective aspect of the first person's will. Stevenson's story engages and promotes the abiding wisdom, which the medical model preserved from temperance, that addiction was a problem of individual moral self-division, rather than an intersubjective or collective phenomenon—a truly radical countermodern refiguring. Modernism is usually characterized by psychic fragmentation, but compared to the prospect of considering an addict as two people, it seems quite psychically unified. In order to preserve this psychic wholeness from disintegration, Stevenson employs a literary technique of the narration of addiction: he produces Jekyll's "full statement" or retrospective confession at the close of the story to reassert psychic continuity. With respect to addiction, this psychic unity fits perfectly with the idea that addiction was a disease that made an individual temporarily behave *like* someone else.

Jekyll's doubleness corresponds neatly to another aspect of addiction discourse, the figure of the habituated doctor.[102] This real and fictional character foregrounded a different kind of irony from the temperance character of the middle-class man who has squandered his prospects in drink. From the 1860s, doctors had ample access to new opium alkaloids and the cheap hypodermic technology with which to inject them. The pages of *The Lancet* in the 1870s and 1880s are sprinkled with stories of doctors, chemists, doctor's wives, and medical students—people expected to know better—overdosing on morphine and laudanum. It was likely with such episodes in mind that George Eliot had Tertius Lydgate, the emblem of modernizing medicine in *Middlemarch* (1871), dabble in opium. Virginia Berridge and Griffith Edwards note the perception of the medical profession's susceptibility to hypodermic morphine habituation.[103] "Even the possession of technical knowledge does not always qualify a practitioner to deal with his own ailments," *The Lancet* reminded its readership.[104] A piece in the neuroscience journal *Brain* sketched a vision of poetic justice for iatrogenic misdeeds: "If medical men are charged—and it is to be feared, justly—with the propagation of [morphinism], owing to their carelessly, or for mere convenience' sake, leaving morphia and subcutaneous syringe with the patient, it may be regarded as their punishment that the demon morphinism finds among them his favorite victims."[105] *Horace Saltoun* also illustrates this idea, but *The Strange Case* offers us the self-experimenting doctor par excellence. Addicted doctors like George Harley were both figures of modernity and the primitive past lurking inside it; true to their fin-de-siècle origins, they sow the fields of Victorian promise with the seeds of its own destruction. Jekyll embodies this division between a professional expertise derived from Enlightenment science and private, subjective knowledge of pleasure as the failure to fulfill that expertise. Like the syringe itself, the doctor-addict represented the defeated promise of modern technology to alleviate suffering and the spectral rise of degeneration. Like Roe's Martin Jocelyn, he is an impostor of freedom; more important, he is an impostor of knowledge. Moreover, he threw the entire project of medico-scientific progress into doubt. Addiction demonstrated that doctors needed doctors—or, in the words of *The Lancet*, "A fully trained practitioner, other than the patient, is obviously the only natural guide as to treatment."[106] The physician

Morris F. Baldwin wrote, "A person should not, under any circumstances, try to treat his own case, for the opium or morphia habit."[107] Yet, since any doctor could be an addict, the promises of medical progress seemed either false or unattainable.

Through the figure of the doctor-addict, *The Strange Case* produces white, middle-class masculinity anew. In keeping with the cultural politics of the "slavery of drink" metaphor, the production of Hyde out of Jekyll has the interiorized "slave" take shape, emerge, and act freely and chaotically. This was a problem not only for white men per se but also for a transparent, autonomous public sphere that reflected their abstract, unmarked subjectivity. For the other significant dimension of Stevenson's story—the one that makes it really interesting—is the way that Jekyll's divided psychology is reflected in the cosmopolitan social body of the East End. Showalter interprets Utterson's cab ride to Hyde's house through the imagery of anality: "the 'chocolate-brown fog' that beats about the 'back-end of the evening'; while the streets he traverses are invariably 'muddy.' "[108] But there's a more critically productive spectacle to be observed there: "The fog lifted a little and showed him a dingy street, a gin palace, a low French eating house, a shop for the retail of penny numbers and twopenny salads, many ragged children huddled in the doorways, and many women of many different nationalities passing out, key in hand, to have a morning glass" (*JH* 48). Stevenson's numerous images of variety and multiplicity—penny periodicals, salads, rags—culminate in the women's multiple nationalities. The text explicitly connects this to Jekyll's divided psyche when he speculates that "man will be ultimately known for a mere polity of multifarious, incongruous, and independent denizens" (*JH* 82). By virtue of both their gender and their national affiliations, the women collected near Hyde's house are denizens rather than citizens; they are the human flotsam that introduces the opacity of difference into what would otherwise be a transparently homogeneous, legitimate social body. The same is true for Hyde, who has taken up residence in Jekyll's character as the "second person" to Jekyll's first; he remains a second-class citizen, of a "lower" political and biological order, not a full subject. As Simon Petch reminds us, "the language of civil order here storms 'the very fortress of identity' from within: a denizen is an alien with the right of residence."[109]

Stevenson's favorite word for the problem of the abstract, only tacitly white male citizen's encounter with multiplicity and difference, is *incongruous*: "It was the curse of mankind that these incongruous faggots were thus bound together," he writes (*JH* 82). Jekyll also refers to himself as an "incongruous compound," distinct from Hyde's purity of evil (*JH* 85). Indeed, the entire premise of Jekyll's original experiment was to purify his own identity: "If each, I told myself, could be housed in separate identities, life would be relieved of all that was unbearable; the unjust might go his way, delivered from the aspirations and remorse of his more upright twin; and the just could walk steadfastly and securely on his upward path, doing the good things in which he found his pleasure, and no longer exposed to disgrace and penitence by the hands of this extraneous evil" (*JH* 82). This was a problem of white masculine self-difference: not just between surface and depth, public and private, but a problem of overcrowding within the subjective unit, one reflected in the social geography of London. By now it should not be surprising to find that the symbol of this sudden lack of social and self transparency is also the sign of feminine addiction to alcohol: women drinking their morning glass of gin. The problem of being either homosexual or addicted at fin de siècle was a fear that one had lost one's character, considered both as the transparent self-knowledge and the autonomy derived from self-unity, to the compulsions and passions of the body. This required a representational process of turning the unmarked, abstract subject inside out and revealing his feminized, racialized interior.

As a final example of the way that addiction and homosexuality inhere together, consider the story's other protagonist, Utterson. The story's famous marginalization of women means that Utterson takes over their role as the manager of men's consumption, though he takes up his duty belatedly, serving as the "last good influence in the lives of down-going men" (*JH* 29). Utterson does this with great ambivalence, seen in his reference to himself as Cain: he doesn't quite, he claims, "incline toward Cain's heresy," which would make him a murderer of Abel/Jekyll. Does he want the men around him to sink into the dissipation and death normally associated with drink, or does he want to regenerate them? What kind of erotic dynamic does he play, vis-à-vis his friends' likely alcoholic desires? But Utterson himself also engages in a solitary addiction: "He was austere with himself; drank gin when he was alone, to mortify a taste for vintages" (*JH* 29). Utterson's behavior here corresponds to the late-century logic of substitution governing addiction: gin serves as the poisonous cure for wine, the remedy that is its own habit. As we saw in chapter 4, this was also a feminine mode of addiction, since it took place as a form of medication and in private: mortification is the shame that kills. Within the history of addiction assembled in this book, this is simultaneously the killing shame of female desire, queer desire, and addicted desire.

But this shame does not comprehensively describe Utterson's own self-division; he is, after all, human—which is to say, an abstract person—and as such, he drinks socially: "At friendly meetings, and when the wine was to his taste, something eminently human beaconed from his eye" (*JH* 29). Here Stevenson configures humanity as the element released by the pleasure of wine consumed in good company; but it is also, in this era, the practice of men. He repeats this figure when Utterson drinks with his closest friend and head clerk, Mr. Guest. Here, the wine that "had long dwelt unsunned in the foundations of [Utterson's] house" has the power to dissolve Utterson's characteristic control and reserve, a mellowing process explicitly likened to liberation: "The acids were long ago resolved; the imperial dye had softened with time, as the colour grows richer in stained windows; and the glow of hot autumn afternoons on hillside vineyards, was ready to be set free and to disperse the fogs of London. Insensibly the lawyer melted. There was no man from who he kept fewer secrets than Mr. Guest" (*JH* 53–54). The evocative imagery of intoxication becomes charged with the closest approximation Utterson can make to intimacy, the relative absence of secrets. The "imperial" discipline and self-control that normally marshals an individual's resources and instantiates hierarchies is lifted. This kind of homosocial drinking is a mode of pleasure in conviviality, the delight in hosting a guest without the pressure exerted by either the temperance model of moderation or the disease model of addiction, in which too much imbibing might be the sign of inebriety.

The new regime of identities and identifications did not allow white, middle-class men to define themselves and enjoy their pleasures. The central crisis of *The Strange Case* is their new susceptibility to the hermeneutics of suspicion that attended the taxonomic imperative. To identify someone as belonging to a medico-legal classification, be it homosexual or inebriate, was altogether different from appreciating their character. Indeed, when reflected onto the social body as a whole, it meant that white men could no longer enjoy the privileges of abstraction; to represent the social body as it actually existed—complete with foreign prostitutes and homicidal maniacs—required their own identities to become merely one of many, even to vanish. Writing about the way in which male-male eroticism and love is frequently associated with apocalypse in Gothic literature, Haggerty notes: "To identify Jekyll is to destroy him. To push for this clarity leads to dissolution."[110] Such destruction through identification, I contend, is related to the naming that, to writers of the late nineteenth century, killed pleasure. Whether as queer or addicted, to identify an act was to mark it as behavior and hence as potentially pathological. This was a full century before the queer political equation of silence with death; it was not then clear that public self-naming might lead to liberation. Quite the contrary, for elite white men, it meant sacrificing the multiple sources of social power that created the context for a gamut of same-sex pleasure ranging from conviviality to sex. As H. G. Cocks reminds us, for most of the nineteenth century, the very namelessness of sodomy "did provide certain paradoxical opportunities for homoerotic expression."[111]

So although Stevenson's tale plainly functions as an argument against repression and segregation, both psychic and social, it also anticipates Wilde's *Picture of Dorian Gray* in defending pleasure against the "mortifications" of addiction. Aligned with this mortification are the medico-legal regimes of identity that require not merely the exposure of private pleasures but also their conceptual eradication under the sign of compulsion. Stevenson keeps Jekyll's secret, his condition "nameless" for much of the story; when he finally reveals it, he makes it utterly idiosyncratic, a chemical quirk that can never be replicated. These choices fueled the critical tendency to *identify* Jekyll/Hyde, whether as gay, addict, syphilitic, degenerate, criminal, and so on, as a way of completing a particular hermeneutic circle. But this reflex—one that I have obviously found irresistible too—performs a new cultural trend Stevenson himself bristled against, the hermeneutics of suspicion. Stevenson rejected the essentially scientific bent of literary realism, which he aptly limned "a fine intemperance" that "will not suffer the presence of anything so dead as a convention"; such writing was "all hot-pressed from nature, all charactered and notable, seizing the eye."[112] As Williams contends, Stevenson's impatience with scientifically observed and defined identities led him away from realism in *The Strange Case*. Ultimately, Stevenson saw this new world of taxonomic identities as one at least as lonely as Utterson's solitary austerity; his ambivalence can be seen, on the one hand, in the idiosyncrasy of Jekyll's vice, which no one else can replicate and which thereby resists a community of like people; and on the other, as the telling of the story in the newly available forms of the case study and anonymous public confession.

Stevenson thus alludes to the discursive forms of identity and identification—the scientific reification of character—in order to make a case against them. By doing so, he hoped to preserve a mode of homosocial conviviality, signaled by the loosening pleasure of alcohol, in which men could share unguarded intimacy. Against the medico-scientific regime in which pleasures are identified, catalogued, and pathologized, and in which addiction functions similarly to homosexuality, Stevenson defended the prerogatives of white masculine anonymity, the "something eminently human" that beacons from Utterson's eye when drinking wine in good company. Such a stratagem protected both elite white masculinity, and its heightened potential for queer acts and identities, from emerging into the uncertain medico-scientific light of classification. This was perhaps the only social position from which to make the strangest of cases on behalf of unclassified pleasure.

6

UN-DEATH AND BARE LIFE

Addiction and Eugenics in *Dracula* and *The Blood of the Vampire*

Narcotic intoxication, in which the euphoric suspension of the self is expiated by deathlike sleep, is one of the oldest social transactions mediating between self-preservation and self-annihilation, an attempt by the self to survive itself. The fear of losing the self, and suspending with it the boundary between oneself and other life, the aversion to death and destruction, is twinned with a promise of joy which has threatened civilization at every moment.

Theodor Adorno and Max Horkheimer, *Dialectic of Enlightenment* (1944)

Illness is the night-side of life, a more onerous citizenship.

Susan Sontag, *Illness and Metaphor* (1978)

DRACULA DOES not smoke. He doesn't eat. Nor is he seen drinking—alcohol, at least. These minor observations of Jonathan Harker indicate the intuitive resemblance of vampirism to a singular addiction that obliterates all other desires, needs, compulsions, habits, and affections. Bloodsucking has had long associations with the metaphor of intemperance as a supernatural parasitism.[1] Christopher Craft, whose influential reading inaugurated almost a quarter century of critical enthusiasm for Stoker's novel, elaborated this insight: "Dracula has a spirit's freedom and mobility, but that mobility is chained to the most mechanical of appetites: he and his children rise and fall for a drink and for nothing else, for nothing else matters."[2] In the moment of the vampire's bite, a liberating experience of sensual intoxication masks the imprisoning compulsion underlying it. The same irony organizes what Robert T. Eldrige has dubbed "the other vampire novel of 1897," Florence Marryat's *The Blood of the Vampire*, in which Harriet Brandt, who longs only for the transcendent emotional fulfillment that comes from love, cannot help but drain the vital energy from everyone to whom she becomes close.[3] As with the ironies of addiction, in these novels and in the general cultural disposition of vampirism, the most intensely felt need is discovered to be depraved desire; the most intimate choice is revealed to be the servant of a far more powerful and alien mechanism; and the putatively autonomous self is transformed into a monstrous parasite. Since vampire narratives perform the legerdemain of transforming the terror of the temperance narrative—namely, the protagonist's loss of his individuality, autonomy, and status—into a pleasurable seduction, they perform the distinctively new thrill of imagining oneself to be a vampire or addict. Both conditions fulfill an unusual desire to be freed of the normative obligations of freedom. The cultural density of vampirism thus affords perspective on the recognizably modern ambivalences of addiction: that a lifetime of compulsion contains moments of intoxicating freedom; that horror and pleasure can coincide; that an imprisoning loss of identity can be temporarily liberating. The modern ironies and paradoxes governing vampirism also structure addiction, constituting the secret of the hold that both discourses have on the twentieth- and twenty-first-century imagination.

In *Dracula* (1897) and *Blood of the Vampire*, the metaphors of exile, self-enslavement, disease, and sexual desire in nineteenth-century narratives of addiction combine to form something new. In the emergent genre of drug autobiography described in chapter 1, we saw that the Romantic intoxication of opium and hashish generated fantastic visions of imperial travel to exotic locations and across the U.S. frontier, before the underside of this experience, addiction, transformed that ideal of mental travel into a modern figure of disenchanted exile in a paradise turned dystopia. Fin-de-siècle vampire fictions compress and transform this sequence. Dracula embodies both the freedom of travel—he can shape-shift, fly, crawl up and down walls, even enter into the minds of others—and its sense of exile, his addictive condition of death-in-life that separates him from the human family. As Nina Auerbach has noted, Dracula observes more taboos than he breaks: as with addiction, the vampiric habit proscribes his movements and activities, squelching any spontaneity under its massive domination.[4] Although appearing as a cosmopolitan émigré, he must bring boxes of dirt with him in which to sleep. Similarly, Harriet Brandt is a wealthy traveler with the world all before her, but she can only destroy the people she meets and loves. Like the narrator-addict of

D. F. MacMartin's *Thirty Years in Hell*, each vampire can travel the world in search of "life" and love, but meeting the needs of their condition makes every place seem just the same. Unlike Fitz Hugh Ludlow's narrative of hallucinogenic manifest destiny, in which the intoxicated self ventures forth to find itself in the act of colonization, each vampire travels from the periphery of civilization or, quasi-synonymously, the British Empire—Dracula from a Transylvania frequently interpreted as a coded Ireland, Harriet Brandt from Jamaica—to its center, seeking to feed off the life teeming in the metropole.[5] As Stephen Arata's notable essay first suggested, fin-de-siècle popular fiction rehearses a cultural narrative of "reverse colonization": "In the marauding, invasive Other, British culture sees its own imperial practices mirrored back in monstrous forms."[6] Vampiric identity represents not just a frightening contamination by the colonies but a terrifying reversal of the geopolitical order of things. The same reversal structures the turn from intoxication to addiction.

It is not difficult to read vampirism and other, realistic forms of addiction as signs of this reversal and of the implosion of the military and commercial British imperial projects. The identification of inebriety at century's end meant that the veil of propriety drawn over the problem in various areas of British life could be torn away. For example, Hesketh Bell, straying from the ostensible topic of *Obeah: Witchcraft in the West Indies*, put his finger on a larger illusion of colonial conditions: writing about plantation overseers and managers of the past, he claimed, "To hard drinking . . . ought mainly to be ascribed the evil reputation of the West Indian colonies; these young English and Scotch immigrants, long before they were acclimatized to the tropics, would indulge in unlimited quantities of the poisonous common rum manufactured on the estates, and in many cases would generally be carried off by delirium tremens. The cause of their deaths would never be reported home under its true name, but rather as 'fever' and 'the effects of this deadly climate!' "[7] At the same time that assertions such as Bell's were beginning to shift perceptions of the inherent dignity of the imperial mission, so too did fictional representations, particularly of Rudyard Kipling's habitually drunken, often violent soldiers in texts such as "The Mark of the Beast." Examining stories such as B. M. Croker's "The Khitmatgar" (1893) and Kipling's "The End of the Passage" (1890), Marlene Tromp shows how their representations of addiction expose the bad faith of empire: "In spite of the shipments of beer and ice and the doses of morphine, nothing can erase the haunting presence of violence and exploitation."[8]

Addiction was becoming an apt metaphor for the ennui of maintaining the empire; it certainly changed perceptions of colonial space. By the 1890s, the old temperance hope that one could be cured by a long sea voyage on a temperance ship or emigration to a colony had begun to seem naive; Walter Besant even emplotted the failure of such an attempt in his 1890 novel *The Demoniac*.[9] Yet the cultural logic by which the colonies signified the possibility of inebriate reformation—as well as the undifferentiated elsewhere into which British social problems might obligingly disappear—persisted: one of the letter-writers to the *Daily Telegraph*'s ongoing public forum on "The Slavery of Drink" in 1891 suggested that a colony in northwest Canada might be founded for the rehabilitation of habitual drunkards.[10] A good deal of *Dracula*'s cultural resonance at the time lay in the explosion of the assumptions underlying such a proposition. The novel uses vampirism as an analogue for addiction to engage the burgeoning doubts about the motives and functions of the empire. *The Blood of the Vampire*, a far more politically retrograde narrative, nevertheless also casts the colonies as the space of imperial laxity and compulsive disease. These vampire narratives intervene in the cultural history of addiction by decentering the addicted subject's conventionally metropolitan identity and refracting it through the colonial periphery.

This anxiety of reverse colonization, in which colonial habituations, compulsions, and dependencies appear to parody metropolitan ones, inevitably draws racial identity into its purview. The whiteness of addiction, which I have been demonstrating throughout this book, begins to appear more explicitly, and to deform, under the pressure of its metropolitan position within the Empire. I have been contending that throughout the nineteenth century, addiction was an implicitly white phenomenon because it drew on the following things: a fantasy of imperial mastery of the scholarly archive assisted by opium; a related fantasy of self-fulfillment via hallucinogenic manifest destiny; anxieties surrounding the metropolitan consumption of colonial goods; guilt over the European seduction of African elites considered to be innocent savages; and shame over the extraction of black slave labor on plantations. After the official end of chattel slavery in the United States, the figure of addiction coded the apparently persistent dependence of southern whites on slave labor. *The Blood of the Vampire* and *Dracula* engage and reinvent different pieces of this lineage.

Marryat's novel locates the origins of Harriet Brandt's compulsive parasitism both in her Jamaican planter family's history of sadistic violence against their slaves and in its racial contamination through miscegenation with them. Harriet's miscegenated, vampiric identity indicts the rapacity not only of the sadistic excesses of chattel slave owners and overseers but also of the erstwhile innocent longings of feminine, bourgeois imperial appetites. *The Blood of the Vampire* engages and updates the "blood sugar" discourse of the 1790s, which I discussed in chapter 2. Like the English ladies who would not stop drinking the blood of slaves from their teacups, Harriet Brandt performs the shame of imperial mastery as the shame of addictive consumption. But—also like those genteel eighteenth-century tea drinkers—she embodies repulsion at racial contamination. Both positions could be inhabited simultaneously; as Orlando Patterson suggests, the figure of parasitism—which comes to shape addiction as a social problem—helps to comprehend "the complexities of dependence" within the master-slave relationship too.[11]

Likewise, Dracula's vampirism also performs both the shame of imperial dependency and its repulsion at colonial contamination. As numerous critics have shown, *Dracula* is a tale of degeneration, the late Victorian discourse about the racial and cultural decline of the British people into atavism, because the vampires sap English blood and convert the English social body into their own kind.[12] Like its fictional analogue, compulsive and habituated dependency on the blood of others, addiction was newly generated through popular and medical discourses of degeneration. Viewed through the lens of degeneration, addiction begins not merely to afflict unfortunate individuals but to threaten the entire social and racial body as well. In this subtextual project, vampirism is not the only instance of habituated dependency in Stoker's novel, which also indicts the relative meaninglessness of its white characters' dependent, habituated existences, before they combine forces to destroy Dracula. Hyper-civilized and "up-to-date with a vengeance," Seward, Jonathan, Mina, and Lucy are all figured as nervously habituated to and dependent upon the frequently mentioned technologies they use to hunt Dracula: not just the typewriter, the gramophone, and the Kodak camera, but also, tellingly, the new medical technologies of chloral hydrate and blood transfusion. On one level, then, Dracula represents a straightforward threat of addiction as racial invasion of the body politic via the feminine conduits of Lucy Westenra and Mina Harker; but on another level, the novel is keen to suggest that white imperial dependency and enervation is a sign of its own racial degeneration and enfeeblement, that is, its own collapse from internal pressure rather than an invasion from without. The novel thus helps articulate the problem that addiction might also be a side effect of the empire on its masters—a deadening condition of white modernity and civilization in its attempt, to borrow Adorno and Horkheimer's phrase, to survive itself.[13]

How do these novels resolve the complex geopolitical and subjective problems they unleash? Traditionally, nineteenth-century narratives about habitual drunkenness and inebriety had ended in the protagonist's death or, less frequently, in recovery. Stoker's and Marryat's novels expand on this trope by creating vampires as figures of "un-death" or incipient death; this paradoxical category echoes the vexed biological status of addicts in the popular imagination. In 1828, Heman Humphrey characterized victims of intemperance as fleshless, "panting skeletons"; in 1836, Charles Dickens imagined "The Drunkard's Death" by drowning as a metamorphosis from human being into "a swollen and disfigured mass"; and in 1895, William Rosser Cobbe described how opium den habitués languished in "a stupor that has all the appearance of death."[14] One Spiritualist case study of a vampire involved a drunkard who, spurned by the woman he loved, shot himself and returned to her as a vampiric incubus.[15] This trope continued well into the twentieth century. In Edith Blinn's *The Ashes of My Heart* (1916), the anti-heroine, addicted to gambling and opium, withers away: "What an appalling aspect, to lie there and watch her own body slowly die."[16] When the popular journalist Winifred Black wanted to sensationalize the "dope fiends" of San Francisco in the 1920s, she referred to them as "the living dead."[17] With every drink, Upton Sinclair warned in 1931, "you throw the dice with death."[18] William S. Burroughs, perhaps the century's most astute literary analyst of addiction, often described his junkies as ghosts. At its most extreme manifestation, throughout the nineteenth century and arguably the twentieth, addicts were not really or fully alive; conversely, as Mark Seltzer puts it with respect to the "wound culture" of the United States, "from the turn of the century on, the living dead subject . . . is at once generalized and pathologized . . . precisely as the subject, or quasi-subject of addiction."[19] The vampire gorged with blood and resting in his coffin evokes the satiated death-in-life of the iconic heroin addict whose world had been apparently depopulated and reduced to similar proportions.

These figurations of addicts as un-dead or incipiently dead have geopolitical and racial ramifications that both novels develop. Having reconstituted the problem of addiction as an imperial and racial one, Stoker and Marryat turn to an idea that was increasingly gaining purchase in both the theorization of addiction and late nineteenth-century social discourse in general: the racial death posited by eugenics, a racial science designed to apply principles of natural selection to human populations so that the unfit or defective could be allowed to die, and healthier ones to thrive. The "un-dead" quality of vampires and addicts is an equivocation of biological status, but as such it is also an ambivalent racial and political category, concealing a broad fantasy of white racial decline, purging, and expiration. Harriet Brandt, the anti-heroine of *The Blood of the Vampire*, takes her own life in order to forestall her destructive, deracinating influence on those around her; her suicide note, as we will see, reads like eugenic propaganda. *Dracula* exploits the concept of un-death so that the first "death" operates as racial conversion and the second as an execution staged as eugenic extermination. Eugenic fiction erects a narrative in which alcoholics, vampires, and other social parasites pose a reproductive threat to society that must be contained, either by their own self-expiration, or—as in the case of *Dracula*—by execution.[20] Their "un-dead" or incipiently dead nature must be narratively resolved by a more absolute or permanent death: racial flaws, unlike sins, cannot be forgiven; unlike diseases, they permit no recovery. In Sontag's formulation, illness and disease are "onerous" forms of citizenship because their land lies in the shadow of health and life; for addiction and its analogue, vampirism, this citizenship is so attenuated it creates a supernatural, other world.[21]

Addiction becomes more than just a disease at fin de siècle; it also becomes a racial defect for which mass extermination is an imagined possibility. As such, it shifts the biopolitical meanings of death and life. "Biopolitics" is the name Michel Foucault gave to the new set of calculations of the value of biological life arising from the state's emerging interest in promoting the health of its population.[22] Recently, theorists as diverse as Giorgio Agamben, Zygmunt Bauman, Russ Castronovo, Achille Mbembe, and Nikolas Rose have revised the concept, introducing concepts such as "bare life," "necro citizenship," "necropolitics," and "emergent life" in order to explain the relationship between biological and political life in modern liberal states.[23] I conclude this chapter, and, in the afterword, this book as a whole, by joining this critical conversation, because it helps reveal the looming shape of the twentieth-century history of addiction. The vampires' "un-dead" status illuminates addicts' unfolding categorization as shadowy denizens or "necro citizens" of a racialized, criminal, degenerate underworld. Because they cannot join the social body without destroying it, they inhabit a half-life in the subcultural spaces underneath it. In this way, they also resemble the queer denizens of underground clubs such as "The Rosalind" described in chapter 5. As my afterword contends, the stakes of addiction become particularly acute, intensively attuned to the apparent health of liberal democracies, because at any given moment, anyone living a "normal" life might succumb and fall into this zone of "bare life." Stoker's and Marryat's fictions bring us to the brink of this subsequent reality, in which many of us are arguably still living.

Degeneration, Eugenics, and Imperial Parasites

When medical approaches to alcohol and drug habituation came into vogue in the 1860s and afterward, such conditions were increasingly reconceptualized from foreign customs or personal habits to behavioral symptoms of inherited biological differences. Virginia Berridge notes that "the influence of heredity was important; alcoholic heredity manifested itself in the transmission of the drink crave itself; in defective mental and physical development; in weakened will power and general nervous instability."[24] Addiction became a disease that was also, strangely, a sin or moral failing; it could both be inherited from one's parents and induced in oneself. Articulating this widely accepted idea, Scottish alienist Thomas S. Clouston referred to the causes of inebriety as "ancestral and personal." But the emphasis began to shift to the alarming implications of heredity: Clouston, for example, claimed that, having never tasted alcohol, children of alcoholic inebriates could experience a drink crave.[25] Norman Kerr, the founder of the Society for the Study and Cure of Inebriety, described such hereditary inebriates in an 1888 position paper: "There are persons born into the world with an innate susceptibility to narcotic and anaesthetic action. If they so much as taste any intoxicant, their whole organization is, as it were, set on fire, without their consent."[26] This formulation significantly undermined the temperance narrative's characteristic framing of the first sip of alcohol as a moment of individual consent to sin. Conventional wisdom had long held that habitual drunkenness was a family affair, but as the culture began unevenly to absorb the implications of Darwinian evolution, the narrative models of temperance, with their emphasis on personal striving and salvation, came to seem less relevant than newer fictions that could account for biological inheritance. As medical writers and the reading public began to apply new biological ideas of disease, morphological change, adaptation, and the struggle for existence to the problems of habitual drunkenness and inebriety, they opened addiction to an entire field of racial theory. From this point on, the term *intemperance* would sound increasingly unscientific and outdated.

As medical writers and others began to apply their new conceptual tools to the problem of inebriety, they increasingly turned to the discourse of degeneration. Degeneration began as a biological theory of hereditary decline promoted by Benedict Morel in *Traité des Dégénérescences* (1857), that an organism or an organ could become altered in structure and so assume the forms of less developed types.[27] This simple definition seemed eminently amenable to the disease of inebriety, which appeared to change the structure of its sufferer's organs, particularly—and most mysteriously—the brain and nerves. The British psychiatrists who were most influenced by Morel's theory of degeneration as a disease were Henry Maudsley, David Skae, W. H. D. Sankey, and Clouston.[28] All proposed that alcoholism was an example of degeneration, and all theorized it as an acquired characteristic that nevertheless could shape-shift in extremely unspecific ways.[29] To the familiar notion that inebriety was one of many nervous diseases of modern life, Kerr added the idea that it was a racial inheritance: inebriety "has largely been developed from the increasing nervous exhaustion consequent on the wear and tear, the bustle, the pressure, and worry of modern civilised existence, combined with the accumulated heredity (neurotic and narcotic) of our ancestors."[30] Inebriety embodied the paradox of degeneration: it was at once a hypermodern disease afflicting those on the cutting edge of modernity, and at the same time, it represented the survival and recrudescence of ancestral primitivism.

Marie Corelli had represented this paradox evocatively in her 1890 novel *Wormwood*, depicting a young boy whose grandfather was an erudite materialist scientist and whose father became an *absintheur* and lunatic. Within one generation, Corelli claimed, absinthe could cause man to regress to "Stone Age" savagery: living on rats he catches in the Paris gutters, the boy can barely speak or think. "I think I know now how we can physiologically resolve ourselves back to the primary Brute-period, if we choose,—by living entirely on Absinthe!" declares André Gessonex, Corelli's degenerate artist and the young troglodyte's mentor.[31] To cultural conservatives such as Corelli and Max Nordau, the terrifyingly addictive absinthe perfectly signified the strange mixture of nervous modernity and primitive regression.[32] As Patrick Brantlinger notes, fears that whites—grouped together in their own race—were declining, to be surpassed by other races, suggested that "through the civilizing process itself, the white race was committing suicide."[33] Absinthe, hypodermic needles, and soporifics such as chloral signified the new, bleeding edge of modernity.

Eugenics refocused and refined degeneration along the lines of natural selection, but with respect to addiction, it emphasized August Weismann's theory that alcoholic heredity was transmitted to progeny through the prenatal environment of the mother's body rather than through the inheritance of maladaptive alcoholic traits.[34] Indeed, habitual drunkenness and inebriety formed the crux of the theoretical development of eugenics by its British architect, Francis Galton. Writing in *The Fortnightly Review* about the observation that the children of drunkards suffer from nervous disorders and idiocy, Galton conceded, "Here, then, appears an instance . . . in which an acquired habit of drunkenness, which ruins the will and nerves of the parent, appears to be transmitted hereditarily to the child."[35] But he quickly revealed this to be a fallacy, offering an explanation based on Weismann's theory: "For my own part, I hesitate in drawing this conclusion, because there is a simpler reason. The fluids in an habitual drunkard's body, and all the secretions, are tainted with alcohol; consequently the unborn child of such a woman must be an habitual drunkard also. The unfortunate infant takes its dram by diffusion, and is compulsorily intoxicated from its earliest existence. What wonder that its constitution is ruined, and that it is born with unstrung nerves, or idiotic or insane?"[36] This theory focused attention on the problem of sexual reproduction by inebriate parents, creating acute consternation about the problem of inebriate women and their careless propagation of an out-of-control population of inebriates.[37] In the 1880s and 1890s, Weismann's and Galton's ideas were debated in the meetings of the Society for the Study of Inebriety (SSI).[38] In one of the discussions, "a lady member expressed her belief in the hereditary transmission of acquired inebriety and expressed the opinion that a woman who bore a child to a drunken father was guilty of a crime against society."[39]

This discussion merely reflected a larger cultural conversation about the problem of maternal drinking of the sort put forward by William Booth in his jeremiad on degeneration, *In Darkest England and the Way Out* (1890): "There are thousands who were begotten when both parents were besotted with drink, whose mothers saturated themselves with alcohol every day of their pregnancy, who may be said to have sucked in a taste for strong drink with their mothers' milk, and who were surrounded from childhood with opportunities and incitements to drink."[40] Similarly, Andrew Mearns's pamphlet *The Bitter Cry of Outcast London* described "the child-misery . . . inherited from the vice of drunken and dissolute parents, and manifest in the stunted, misshapen, and often loathsome objects that we constantly meet in these localities."[41] As David Gutzke has shown, over the next decade maternal drinking would become central to eugenic discussions and national policy about the possibilities for stemming inebriety's destructive social influence and improving hygiene and efficiency.[42] I will return to this important point when I take up the images of vampiric nursing central to the novels' theories of addiction.

Degeneration and eugenics were racial discourses, but they extended and transformed earlier class-based fears of habitual drunkenness. Angelique Richardson has argued that the racialization of class anxiety motivated eugenics.[43] More specifically, the remaking of intemperance into the inherited condition of "inebriety" grafted fears of national weakness rooted in a generalized class anxiety onto fears of collective racial disease and degeneration.[44] The public drunkenness of the poor—who could not, unlike the middle and upper classes, drink comfortably at home—had been viewed as a social problem since the eighteenth century's laments about "Gin Lane."[45] Throughout the nineteenth century, middle-class exposés of poverty's seedy habits by Booth, Henry Mayhew, James Greenwood, and G. R. Sims, a member of the SSI, reanimated the specter of a degenerate criminal class out of control with drink.[46] Far from being a purely medical endeavor, the SSI actively pushed legislation for the compulsory incarceration of habitual drunkards, but this was inevitably class-based legislation.[47] Because drunkenness itself could not be considered a crime, habitual drunkenness became a kind of crime through repetition or, in other words, a term for the repeated contact with the law that came with living in public urban spaces. Women such as Tottie Fay and Jane Cakebread became minor celebrities for their prodigious number of arrests for public drunkenness and for their drunken courtroom mirth.[48] For the middle class, habitual drinking and other addictions were essentially private and family matters, in keeping with the middle-class abhorrence of publicity and consequent avoidance of the police described by D. A. Miller.[49] The eugenic interpretation of inebriety therefore represented a desire to purge the increasingly visible disorderliness of the poor from an organized social body, since the public/private class divide was not wide enough for middle-class comfort.

Complaining that legislation had not done enough to stop the infectious drunkenness of the poor, Alexander Peddie claimed that their alcoholism jeopardized the middle and upper class: "There are in [the lower classes] also a greater number of the worst type of Inebriates, namely genuine Dipsomaniacs, dragging down to beggary and wretchedness numbers of those who are well-to-do; and thus largely increasing disease, destitution, and crime, and consequently continuous gravitation to our Hospitals, Poorhouses, Asylums, and Prisons, imposing a correspondingly heavy burden on local taxation, and the funds of the Nation."[50] Arnold White and others indicted drunkenness as a factor in imperial dereliction.[51] Such complaints echoed older ones but significantly enlisted the new medico-scientific categories "inebriates" and "dipsomaniacs" within a model of social infection that taxed the economic health of the nation and empire in specifically eugenic terms. "Those of us who know that the foundations of any empire are living men and women, and that, to quote Mr. Kipling, 'when breeds are in the making everything is worth while,' . . . especially those of us who know what alcohol costs in life, feel a momentary recession of our faith that Great Britain need not now be writing the last page of her great history," wrote SSI member and eugenicist Caleb Saleeby in *Parenthood and Race Culture*.[52] As inebriety hit the crime, disease, and racial defect trifecta, its status as a rational lower-class strategy for staving off hunger and alleviating misery became increasingly obscure and incomprehensible.

Dracula fits into this social schematic, if not perfectly. A minor debate within *Dracula* criticism pits his aristocratic identity as a count, left over from an earlier Gothic tradition, against his resemblance to the usual degenerative and eugenic suspects, "syphilitics, alcoholics, cretins, the insane, the feeble-minded, prostitutes."[53] Croley assimilates these to the category of "the poorest of the poor—not the industrious artisan but the vagrant, not the respectable working class but its supposedly shiftless, slum-dwelling underclass."[54] These interpretations are built on the novel's infamous invocation of the principal two architects of degeneration, Max Nordau, the German author of *Entartung* (1892; English translation, *Degeneration*, 1895), and Cesare Lombroso, the Italian founder of criminology, who in the early 1860s began to advance the theory that criminals were recognizably atavistic, essentially insane humans. Stoker puts this associative diagnosis in Mina's mouth, in a conversation with Van Helsing: "The Count is a criminal and of criminal type. Nordau and Lombroso would so classify him, and *qua* criminal has to seek resource in habit."[55] Far from insignificant, Mina's point invites readers to conceptualize vampirism as a habitual compulsion. Van Helsing further elaborates this criminal habit as a racial defect and the ruins of reason: "The criminal always work at one crime—that is the true criminal who seems predestinate to crime, and who will of none other. This criminal has not full man-brain. . . . To do once, is the fulcrum whereby child-brain become man-brain; and until he have the purpose to do more, he continue to do the same again every time, just as he have done before!" (*D* 439). Updating an early nineteenth-century concept of monomania, the unvarying behavioral symptom of an *idée fixe*, Van Helsing construes Dracula's blood drinking as a crime of irrational, infantile repetition.

As with more properly degenerationist and eugenic accounts of criminal behavior, such as habitual drinking, the question of motive is entirely beside the point. In spite of the similarities to a psychoanalytic concept of neurosis, Dracula's signature behavior is sublimely superficial and more or less purposeless; like the drinking habits of the poor, the needs it might fulfill do not have to be taken seriously. My point is not only that Dracula's blood drinking resembles addiction because its authorizing discourses, degeneration, eugenics, and criminality, all emphasize the constituent role of compulsive habit, but also that the habitual quality of addiction itself could easily have furnished the epistemic framework for fin-de-siècle theorizations of degenerative criminality, particularly the trendy new way to characterize class behavior in the 1890s, recidivism.[56] At the bottom of the incessant "othering" of the poor via the conceptual tools of addiction lay a distinction between the spontaneous use of reason to inform action and the compulsive dependence on unreasoning habit.

But the novel's critical utterance on this point is sharper than many critics have imagined, because it does not fully or simply credit Mina's and Van Helsing's characterization of Dracula as degenerate. Indeed, the narrative suggests an awareness and exposure of the hypocrisy at the heart of the class and racial meanings of addiction that I have been describing. As William Greenslade has pointed out, within two years of its 1895 translation into English and phenomenal print run of seven editions, Nordau's *Degeneration* "was the subject of lengthy critiques and vigorous denunciation, and in due course its fate was ironic dismissal."[57] This would have taken place, of course, during Stoker's composition of the novel, which may therefore reflect a more dynamic cultural relationship to Nordau's ideas. What other positions were available, then, for thinking about disease, degeneration, and inebriety? The new disease model of addiction offered a way to unite the social phenomenon of lower-class, public inebriety with the individualistic, middle- and upper-class, private inebriety of the women and men who had become habituated to alcohol, morphine, and other drugs prescribed by physicians. For middle-class writers, the conceptual proximity of lower-class drinking and the nervous illnesses of the over-civilized, professional segments of the population became threateningly close. Rather than simply racialize its vampire-addicts, *Dracula* commented upon the whiteness and attendant middle-class quality of addiction, which made for a very interesting ambivalence.

Indeed, *Dracula* builds an entire critique of its hypermodern characters' habits and dependencies on various technologies. Its most explicit reference to addiction comes when Seward considers taking chloral hydrate, one of the new habit-forming drugs: "I am weary tonight and low in spirits. I cannot but think of Lucy, and how different things might have been. If I don't sleep at once, chloral, the modern Morpheus—C_2HCl_3O-H_2O! I must be careful not to let it grow into a habit. No, I shall take none tonight! I have thought of Lucy, and I shall not dishonour her by mixing the two. If need be, tonight shall be sleepless" (*D* 136). Chloral hydrate had been in demand as a palliative for insomnia since it was isolated in 1869; it was thought to be a safer alternative than opiates.[58] As with hypodermic morphine, it appeared to have become a habit of middle-class women and physicians; it was also widely used in insane asylums to placate patients, which explains its presence in Seward's hands.[59] As early as 1875, the physician Gordon Stables had drawn popular attention to chloral's addictive ravages in a first-person tell-all for *The Pall Mall Magazine*, predictably titled "The Confessions of an English Chloral-Eater." Stables and his friend became "chloralists" in 1871, when "little was then known of the after effects of chloral even by medical men. It was a new medicine, and worked wonders—they lauded it to the skies. We know better now."[60] His friend dies of an overdose after a few months; after sinking into the agony and despair of a habit "more tempting than alcohol, more insinuating than opium, and more terrible in its effects that either," Stables finally receives a remarkable cure.[61] Henry Lyman's handbook *Artificial Anaesthesia and Anaesthetics* (1881) noted tersely that "the prognosis in chloral inebriety is variable, and generally unfavorable."[62] Seward's enthusiasm for this "modern Morpheus"—which leads him to recite its chemical formula into his phonograph diary—would thus have signaled his enthrallment to modern medical technology, his susceptibility to addiction, and his struggle to keep separate the debased world of addiction and the authentic world of noble love.

Stoker assigns the same gesture to Renfield, in a speech in which he appears to speak quite sanely about his own insanity. "The doctor here will bear me out that on one occasion I tried to kill him for the purpose of strengthening my vital powers by the assimilation with my own body of his life through the medium of his blood, relying of course, upon the Scriptural phrase, 'For the blood is the life.' Though, indeed, the vendor of a certain nostrum has vulgarized the truism to the very point of contempt. Isn't that true, doctor?" (*D* 273). Different editors identify different manufacturers of blood tonics as the vendor in question; these patent medicines purported to cure everything from piles to Saint Vitus' dance by strengthening the blood and restoring the energy dissipated by modern nervous exhaustion.[63] With this speech, Stoker has Renfield issue a wry critique of bourgeois English life, although—coming from the mouth of a supposed lunatic—it may be difficult to appreciate at first. The novel clearly suggests that Renfield's own consumption of insects, mice, and—he hopes—a kitten is pathological; it is likely inspired by medico-scientific accounts of psychopathology such as W. A. F. Browne's "Morbid Appetites of the Insane," which describes a desire for "living flesh" that led patients to eat "live kittens and rats" as well as cases "where live mice, frogs, beetles, and worms were devoured."[64] At the same time, the novel also pokes fun at Seward's obtuse ambition to taxonomize Renfield: "My homicidal maniac is of a peculiar kind. I shall have to invent a new classification for him, and call him a zoophagous (life-eating) maniac" (*D* 95). John Greenway comments that "Renfield's experiments fascinate him, but he is content to label it 'zoophagy' and not pursue its logic."[65] As Stoker's subtle parody of the materialist strain of the medical establishment, Seward's push to classify Renfield, which includes cruel dreams of letting him "complete the experiment"—via cannibalism and vivisection—is meant to be ridiculed. Seward exclaims: "Men sneered at vivisection, and yet look at its results today! Why not advance science in its most difficult and vital aspect—the knowledge of the brain? Had I even the secret of one such mind—did I hold the key to the fancy of one such lunatic—I might advance my own branch of science to a pitch compared with which Burdon-Sanderson's physiology or Ferrier's brain knowledge would be as nothing" (*D* 104). Seward's valorization of the vivisectionists John Burdon-Sanderson and David Ferrier would have sufficed to make readers blanch. But Stoker characteristically pushes this unease over the top, since Seward is clearly fantasizing about first letting Renfield ingest human blood or flesh, then vivisecting him to examine his brain. Renfield's madness and Seward's mixture of scientific curiosity and megalomania combine in a folie à deux.

In turn, readerly scorn for Seward calls into question Mina and Van Helsing's easy dismissals of Dracula's behavior via Nordau and Lombroso's classifications. Renfield's mockery of patent medicines, combined with Seward's own susceptibility to a chloral habit, points the finger back at the nervous British middle class, and its habituation to prescription anodynes to perform the natural function of sleep. This gesture invites readers to draw a comparison between the compulsive self-medication of vampiric blood-drinking, and the banal nervous compulsions of middle-class British life. If the nervous practices of mass consumption and industrial modernity create insatiable, addicted appetites, where can they come to a resting point? Renfield's madness shapes itself into an oppositional critique along these lines when he asks Seward the question, "And doctor, as to life, what is it after all? When you've got all you require, and you know that you will never want, that is all" (*D* 347). Through Renfield, Stoker illuminates the artificial quality of addicted needs and links it to the modern conceptualization of "life" itself as insatiable desire.

Stoker's novel indictment of white dependencies and habituations is more expansive than this handful of references suggest. After all, longing for sleep becomes one of the novel's themes: vampiric sleep may be unnaturally altered, but the white characters are similarly estranged from their own blood, out of sync with its life-regulating rhythms. Though he retreats from the brink of an addiction, Seward is also blind to the symptoms of Lucy's growing vampirism: watching over her rest, he mistakes it for "a deep, life-giving, health-giving sleep" in the same way that thousands of Britons had mistaken chloral-induced sleep for the real thing (*D* 161). Because her blood has already been chemically altered, by the puncture of both Dracula's fangs and Van Helsing's needle, Lucy is heading toward a dark, Keatsian narcosis. The degenerate, daytime sleeping of vampires, itself a figure for the death-cravings of addicts, resonates through the apparently ordinary characters' cravings for sleep. Sleep, Seward reminds us, is "the boon we all crave for" (*D* 161); yet neither the vampires nor their hunters appear able to achieve it naturally. The novel is larded with artificial sleep and stimulation: Lucy gets hypodermic morphine; Mina and Renfield are given opiates; Van Helsing prescribes port wine for Holmwood and Seward after the transfusion; Lucy's mother takes laudanum, which knocks out the servants the night of Dracula's attack as a wolf; Mina plans to ask for chloral and also undergoes hypnotic sleep. As new medical technologies, chloral hydrate and hypodermic blood transfusion function in the novel just as Jonathan's Kodak, Seward's phonograph, and Mina's typewriter: they are another of the self-consciously up-to-date technologies that made the novel so topical, eliciting *The Spectator*'s complaint that they "hardly [fit] in with the mediaeval methods which ultimately secure the victory for Count Dracula's foes."[66] In his 1884 handbook on transfusion, the London obstetrician Charles Egerton Jennings gloried in the syringe as "a very beautiful instrument, the most complex and ingenious that modern science has as yet produced" and narrated the daring procedure of "immediate transfusion," as Stoker had, with brio.[67]

Yet the contrast between antiquity and modernity has a more specific critical purpose. The vampire hunters are dependent on their gadgets in order to collect data to defeat Dracula; insofar as these metrological weapons are extensions of themselves, they become mechanically habituated to them.[68] Stoker's point about technological dependency becomes even clearer when *Dracula* is compared to Wilkie Collins's *The Moonstone* (1868), a text that Stoker references in his prefatory note on the novel's form as a series of documented testimonies. Whereas Collins's novel is merely composed of different statements, Stoker's foregrounds the recording and transcribing technologies used to reproduce them. Noting the context of the mass emergence of unemployed women into office bureaucracies as "typewriters"—the term denoting both the machine and the woman who operated it—Friedrich Kittler has interpreted Mina's role in the novel as "the central relay station of an immense information network."[69] Indeed, Mina transcribes and then retypes all of the evidence they have collected, making her the ostensible editor of the novel. " 'What does a woman want?' " echoes Kittler. "In the discourse network of 1900 the alternatives are no longer motherhood or hysteria, but the machine or destruction"—in other words, Mina's fate, or Lucy's.[70] The characters' immersion in media—recorded sound, photographs, self-typed manuscript, chemical sleep—produces a welter of mediation that connects them to the vampiric world but that inevitably also mechanizes them, making their actions compulsive rather than volitional.

Given this context, Jonathan Harker's peculiar failure to fulfill his ostensible narrative function as the hero is marked enough to become part of the text's critical utterance. Although he is introduced in the capacity of the hero, Jonathan's distinct lack of self-reliance precludes spontaneous action. Jonathan refers to his sanity through mechanical metaphors; it's the habit of keeping his diary that lulls him back into working order: "For now, feeling as though my own brain were unhinged . . . I turn to my diary for repose. The habit of entering accurately must help to soothe me" (*D* 68). In another moment of epistemic crisis, Jonathan observes, "Not knowing what to trust, I did not know what to do; and so had only to keep on working in what had hitherto been the groove of my life. The groove ceased to avail me, and I mistrusted myself" (*D* 225). The mechanical connotation of a "groove" as a rut had already been current since the 1840s, and by this time, the term was acquiring a new meaning, the spiral cut in a phonograph cylinder in which the needle travels.[71] Jonathan identifies the monotony of his life with the technologies on which the vampire-hunters depend. Even the premier piece of everyday personal technology in industrial modernity, the pocket watch, signals Jonathan's habitual fastidiousness and boring regularity: awakening after his orgiastic dream, he finds his "clothes . . . folded and laid by in a manner which was not my habit. My watch was still unwound, and I am rigorously accustomed to wind it the last thing before going to bed, and many such details" (*D* 72). As E. P. Thompson has shown, the watch was the first thing a downsliding habitual drunkard would pawn, and the first thing a recovering drunkard would purchase with his newfound disposable income.[72] Jonathan, of course, is the exemplary white-collar worker, but the price of keeping time or of staying "nineteenth-century up-to-date with a vengeance" is the dull routinization of life known as habit.

Indeed, to say that Jonathan is a slave to habit at the outset of the novel may not be an overstatement: right after Dracula makes a grab for his bloody throat, and then settles for throwing his mirror out the window, which he shatters in the process, Jonathan crowns his narration of these startling events with the observation, "It is very annoying, for I do not see how I am to shave, unless in my watch-case or the bottom of the shaving pot, which is fortunately of metal" (*D* 57). The reviewer for *The Athenaeum* complained that "the people who band themselves together to run the vampire to earth have no real individuality or being."[73] Yet, far from an aesthetic flaw in the novel, the bloodlessness of the British characters is part of the text's critical utterance, against the hyperconsumption and techno-dependency draining the life from modern metropolitan existence. The text begins to imagine addiction more broadly, as one of many compulsive, mechanized habituations and dependencies inhabited by white middle-class professionals, not just racially marked, deviant supernatural beings.

The scene in *Dracula* that depicts most vividly the imperial and racial ambivalences of addiction is the scene of Mina's vamping; its most remarkable aspect is that she is made to drink his blood as if she were nursing. The scene is narrated twice, once from Seward's point of view, and once from Mina's. In her more detailed version, Dracula explains the motives of his vengeance: "But as yet you are to be punished for what you have done. You have aided in thwarting me; now you shall come to my call. When my brain says 'Come!' to you, you shall cross land or sea to do my bidding; and to that end this!' With that he pulled open his shirt, and with his long sharp nails opened a vein in his breast. When the blood began to spurt out, he took my hands in one of his, holding them tight, and with the other seized my neck and pressed my mouth to the wound, so that I must either suffocate or swallow some of the—Oh my God! My God! What have I done?" (*D* 328). Craft deftly describes the various displacements whereby "blood, milk, and semen forcefully erase the demarcation separating the masculine and the feminine."[74] Likewise Judith Halberstam notices its transposition of sexual meanings, as it inverts Mina's maternal impulse: "The woman who, by day, nurtures all the men around her, by night drinks blood from the bosom of the King Vampire himself"; this makes Dracula's masculine sexuality the procreative force, especially in comparison with Lucy's predatory relationship to children.[75] For our purposes, however, the domination enacted here has another valence not exhausted by gender and sexuality alone: when Mina recounts her forced consumption of Dracula's blood, she is telling the story of her literal addiction. From that moment, he tells her, she will belong to him and perform at his command: she has been enslaved. Thus when Burton Hatlen writes that "the force of Stoker's book lies in its capacity to mobilize the feelings that surround the master/slave relationship," he is close to identifying the power dynamics at work in this scene, of which erotics are merely the side effect (*D* 96). As with alcohol in the temperance imaginary, one exposure to Dracula's blood is enough to establish this psychic bondage; if not for the interruption by the Crew of Light, Mina's formal and physiological devotion would have been complete.

To be sure, as a scene of addiction, this melodramatic tableau is also polymorphously gendered—Dracula's body becomes the characteristically feminine addictive substance; Mina, a good woman with a "man brain," could be its masculine or feminine consumer. It also performs a racial reversal, the enslavement of the white bourgeois woman to the degenerate, habitual criminal. In this way, of course, Dracula hopes to enact revenge on the masculine vampire hunters by compromising their precious asset, the racial purity of their line of descent. By appealing to what he imagines to be her own desire for revenge against them—"You shall be avenged in turn; for not one of them but shall minister to your needs"—he imagines Mina vampirizing the Crew of Light, enslaving and addicting them in turn, provoking an even more extensive vampiric chain reaction (*D* 328). This threat is carried by a potential form of mass communication: Mina's literal addiction or dedication to Dracula establishes their telepathic connection, a communication medium that Garrett Stewart has described as "the necromantic counterpart of the new technologies of telegraphy and phonography . . . along with their mediumistic displacement of origin: the very technologies that labor along with written text to outmode and obliterate him."[76]

The context of revenge, combined with the force feeding of blood, suggests an ironic re-enactment of imperial dependency. For as long as Britons have depended on their colonies, they have taken their resources without acknowledgment; as Dracula describes this politically devious relationship: "Whilst they played their wits against me—against me who commanded nations, and intrigued for them, and fought for them, hundreds of years before they were born—I was countermining them" (*D* 328). On the eastern fringe of Europe, one imagines, Dracula protected Britain by keeping eastern hordes at bay; he thus figures as an exploited colonial resource. Bloodsucking was a familiar metaphor for this kind of imperial rapacity; Thomas Carlyle cited it defensively: "Not by drinking, cannibal-like, the blood and fat of Ireland, has England supported herself hitherto in this universe, but by quite other sustenances and exertions."[77] The metropole-colony dependency worked both ways: when Dracula sucks Mina's blood, he also performs the role of the parasitic colony, draining the motherland's resources. From Dracula's point of view, this is a form of revenge—a theft of the Crew's belonging as compensation. The visual frisson of Mina's sucking his breast emphasizes the violence of something new, at the verge of recognition. The quality of exposure is enhanced by Mina's "pallor which was accentuated by the blood which smeared her lips and cheeks and chin" (*D* 323): the doubled dependency spreads all the blood on the outside of the body, but it is not Mina's blood—it signifies the blood of Others. In this scene, Britons are figuratively revealed as the true bloodsuckers, sapping the vitality of the colonial peoples upon whom they have always depended, and repudiating the dependency.

Marryat's Plantation Vampires

In contrast to the spurting, polyvalent blood/milk/semen smeared on Mina's face in *Dracula*, the blood of *The Blood of the Vampire* is tidily kept within the skin: Marryat's anti-heroine Harriet Brandt is a psychic vampire. Fangless, she metaphorically sucks the vital energy from all who come near her; yet, unlike other the other female vampires populating fin-de-siècle fiction, Harriet is unaware of her compulsive dependency. The other notable fictional vampires of this period are scheming dowagers: Mary Elizabeth Braddon's "Good Lady Ducayne" (1896) literally steals her young servant's blood via nightly transfusions; the eugenist physician and novelist Arabella Kenealy's Lady Deverish, in "A Beautiful Vampire" (1896), is another psychic vampire requiring only proximity to youth and health; and Arthur Conan Doyle's Miss Penelosa, the eponymous villain of "The Parasite" (1894), uses mesmerism to control her victim. By contrast, Harriet's ignorance of her effect on others allowed Marryat, by 1897 an accomplished and prolific writer of sensation fiction, to play Harriet's femininity along the genre's characteristic opposing lines of femme fatale and ingénue.[78] It also allowed her to eschew the supernatural and criminal epistemologies at work in *Dracula* for purely medical explanations that produce Harriet's vampirism as a racial defect. Indeed, these explanations conflate the inherited effects of a vampire bite with her plantation past and quadroon identity so that Harriet's vampiric dependency on white life becomes a eugenic threat that the narrative must eliminate. In her very first novel, *Love's Conflict* (1865), Marryat had depicted the degeneration of a working-class male habitual drunkard.[79] In keeping with the 1890s shift toward eugenic discussions of inebriety as a crime of inebriate maternity, *The Blood of the Vampire* makes Harriet's mother the monstrous half-caste glutton, whose insatiable addiction to blood Harriet inherits. With this plot, Marryat, like Stoker, grafts the parasitic dependency of addiction onto the imperial-colonial context.

Fascinatingly, although this neglected novel is about vampirism, it is not a supernatural novel: Harriet's "proclivity" is rigorously elucidated via medical science. Marryat medicalizes Harriet's vampirism by having the physician Dr. Phillips solve the mystery of her strange effect, as he repeatedly warns the other characters against her fatal influence, flaunting his medical authority and rehearsing his diagnosis with variations in racial emphasis. When Harriet, newly sprung from a decade-long confinement in a Jamaican convent following her parents' deaths, ingratiates herself with a vacationing Margaret Pullen, her aggressive snuggling makes Margaret feel "as if something or some one, were drawing all her life away. . . . [B]ut Harriet Brandt seemed to come after her, like a coiling snake."[80] With her ophidian, "boneless," tropical body and its evil power, Harriet has a similar effect on others: "a terrible oppression as though someone were sitting on my chest," "a general feeling of emptiness," "as if I had been scooped hollow" (*BV* 37, 29). Although it is Harriet who is habituated to the life of others—when Margaret leaves, she feels "a cold empty feeling in her breast, as though, in losing her hold on Margaret Pullen, she had lost something on which she depended"—she also functions as an addictive substance for them, enjoyable but nauseating (*BV* 31). Margaret confesses that she likes Harriet, but that "her company enervates me—I get neuralgia whenever we have been a short time together—and she leaves me in low spirits and more disposed to cry than laugh!" (*BV* 68). Ralph Pullen, Margaret's brother-in-law, whom Harriet rather easily seduces away from his uptight fiancée Elinor Leyton, confesses that "only speaking of her seems to have revived the old sensation of being drawn against my will—hypnotized, I suppose, the scientists would call it—to be near her, touch her, to embrace her, until all power of resistance is gone" (*BV* 265). So Harriet's addictive condition is twofold: she is dependent on physical intimacy with others, from whom she draws vital energy, and she accordingly makes them sink into the desuetude characterized by the nervous illness of neuralgia, a smothering paralysis they undergo against their better judgment. Harriet functions in the novel as both addicted subject and object.

Accordingly, when Dr. Phillips explains Harriet's condition to her, he addresses her as if she personified a drug: "After a while, having sapped their brains, and lowered the tone of their bodies, you will find their affection, or friendship for you visibly decrease. You will have, in fact, *sucked them dry*" (*BV* 298). Harriet's transmission of the energy of others to herself therefore dries up their blood within their own bodies; for *Dracula*'s revised Christian equation that "the blood is the life," it substitutes a more medico-scientific formulation, namely that energy is life. This idea spoke to a central tenet of classical eugenics: as Galton wrote in *Inquiries into Human Faculty* (1883), energy "is the measure of the fullness of life; the more energy the more abundance of it; no energy at all is death; idiots are feeble and listless. . . . Energy is an attribute of the higher races, being favoured beyond all other qualities by natural selection."[81] Here, incidentally, Galton expresses a significant piece of the cultural illogic of eugenics, whereby "higher" races are somehow more fully alive than "lower" ones. As we will see, Harriet's lower racial identity means she must steal energy from others. She thus comes to embody an addictive substance that drains away energy and life, turning her victims into emaciated corpses.

Energy was "life," but it was also crucial to character and manliness: James Eli Adams defines "the Victorian conception of 'character' " as "the maintenance of a stable, autonomous fund of purposeful energy—as a leading masculine virtue."[82] Harriet's personal addictiveness—her feminine sexual appeal—thus has the power to melt character and masculinity, too. The physician Franz Hartmann, writing in W. T. Stead's popular occult periodical *Borderland* in 1896, explained the psychic economy whereby a woman enslaved by a vampire or "dual," must "vampirize everybody with whom she comes into contact to make up for this loss."[83] A Spiritualist, Marryat herself was accused of psychic vampirism, as Sian MacFie and K. Octavia Davis each note; a medium's spirit guide told her, "You draw people to you, and live upon their life; and when they have no more to give, nor you to demand, the liking fades on both sides. . . . You draw so much on others, you *empty* them, and they have nothing more to give you." The same guide informed Marryat that she was haunted by an evil genius who "is addicted to drinking. I see her rolling about now under the influence of liquor."[84] The idea that vampiric women must make up their lost energy by depleting those around them was not merely an idiosyncrasy of Spiritualism, however: it overlapped with the cultural figure of the woman as carrier of infectious disease. The woman whose energy is depleted gains not merely the motive but also the capacity to compel others to cede their energy to her. Thus the addict becomes herself the mystified facilitator of the addictions of others, replicating her own condition in a kind of lateral or simultaneous transmission of traits.

But Phillips's most scandalous explanations have to do with Harriet's blackness, inherited from her slave grandmother and mulatta mother. Here Phillips relies not only on his medical knowledge but also on his personal observations as a soldier "stationed in Jamaica with my regiment . . . when this little girl was a child of six years old, running half naked about her father's plantation, uncared for by either parent, and associating solely with the negro servants" (*BV* 137).[85] Harriet's mother, Phillips goes on to explain, "was the daughter of a certain Judge Carey of Barbadoes by one of his slave girls"; according to the local lore, during her pregnancy Carey's slave "was bitten by a Vampire bat, which are formidable creatures in the West Indies, and are said to fan their victims to sleep with their enormous wings, whilst they suck their blood' " (*BV* 137, 122). Here Marryat stages the secret scandal of Harriet's parentage both as her descent from slaves and as the accident of the bat bite, equating blackness with animality, as Davis also notes. And yet, as Brenda Hammack observes, the absurdity of the bat story, with its "cross-species transmission of characteristics," is soon dropped in favor of recounting her parents' depravity, especially her mother's gluttony. In Phillips's words: "She was not a woman, she was a fiend . . . a revolting creature. A fat, flabby half caste, who hardly ever moved out of her chair but sat eating all day long, until the power to move had almost left her! I can see her now, with her sensual mouth, her greedy eyes, her low forehead and half-formed brain, and her lust for blood" (*BV* 122). Phillips's standard Victorian physiognomic practice of adducing moral and mental qualities from physical characteristics is overlaid with the racist and sexist caricature of women of color as sexually voracious: "Gluttonous and obese—her large eyes rolling and her sensual lips protruding as if she were always licking them in anticipation of her prey" (*BV* 137). Ultimately, Phillips's descriptions have a eugenic function, to keep black blood from contaminating white English lines of inheritance: "The fact is, I knew her parents in the West Indies, and could never believe in anything good coming from such a stock. Whatever the girl may be, she inherits terrible proclivities, added to black blood. She is in point of fact a quadroon, and not fit to marry into any decent English family!" (*BV* 213).

Though updated by the addition of eugenic language, this longstanding cultural fear had structured an earlier novel's plot of imperial dependency as colonial and racial contamination, that of Charlotte Brontë's *Jane Eyre* (1847). As Rochester, defending his imprisonment of his mixed-race wife, explains: "Bertha Mason is mad; and she came of a mad family; idiots and maniacs through three generations! Her mother, the Creole, was both a madwoman and a drunkard! . . . Bertha, like a dutiful child, copied her parent in both points."[86] As with Harriet, Bertha's Creole blood carries addiction as an infectious racial pathology; both women inherit their conditions from their mothers; and both possess enough wealth and personal charm to lure their unsuspecting white male victims into relationships of dependency. Brontë even references the vampiric connotations of Bertha's alleged habitual drunkenness, having Jane describe her as "the foul German spectre—the vampire."[87] In this way, Creole matrilineal relations are thought to replicate colonial parasitism, but this is a convenient screen masking imperial dependency on plantation wealth, and repulsion at Creole proximity to enslaved blacks. All of these associations are condensed into the figure of the Creole woman's excessive consumption. Marryat burnishes Brontë's Caribbean gothic plot with eugenic science, leaving its racial and sexual fears intact.

At the heart of Marryat's conceptualization of Harriet's mother's miscegenated identity is her constant eating. Her mammoth bulk literalizes the massive anxiety about biological reproduction between masters and slaves and expresses a white fear of being devoured by a voracious black appetite. Approaching the Miltonic figure of Sin, Harriet's mother's massiveness indicates her capacity to give birth to an entire population of similarly dependent, compulsive, habituated monsters, of which Harriet is one. Phillips warns the smitten, too open-minded socialist Anthony Pennell against Harriet: "I can tell you by the way she eats her food, and the way in which she uses her eyes, that she has inherited her half-caste mother's greedy and sensual disposition. And in ten years' time she will in all probability have no figure at all! She will run to fat. I could tell that also at a glance!" (*BV* 138–39). Taken with Phillips's other references to Harriet's sinuous bonelessness, this imagery aligns blackness with the tropical snake's skeletal absence and, with this lack of human structure, a fat that terrifyingly defies form and strains the bounds of representation, predicting for Harriet a menacing absence, "no figure at all." This out-of-control fat literalizes the bottomless appetite of the addict, who, by virtue of her very identity, cannot limit her consumption. And, since Harriet's "proclivity" manifests itself as a longing only for love—"to come out into the world and find some one to be a friend, and to love me, only me, and all for myself!"—Marryat links the coarseness of this appetite to women's putatively self-centered and delusional romantic and sentimental desires (*BV* 59). Indeed, Davis contends that "the novel, in fact, depicts all women and effeminate beings as living parasitically off their environments."[88] Here, the novel lays the groundwork for its eugenic representation of Harriet's vampirism as the racial inheritance of addiction, a compulsive, even unconscious gluttony that performs love as a destructive practice of consumption.[89] Moreover, Marryat's vision of addiction yokes the anxiety about women's monstrous sexualized appetites and the imperial fear of a contaminating, overwhelming nonwhite dependence upon fragile white resources.

As I have shown, Marryat's vampire signifies distinctly as black, but in the tortured, ambivalent late nineteenth-century logic of race engaged by

Marryat's novel, she also embodies the white legacy of plantation violence discussed in chapter 2. Marryat reinvents the iconic cruel, drunken slave owner who "drinks his slaves' blood," blending this figure with the more up-to-date one of the sadistic vivisectionist intoxicated by esoteric, unholy knowledge. These figures mingle in the character of Henry Brandt, Harriet's English father, who has studied medicine in Swiss hospitals—noted bastions of the "branches of science that gratify the curiosity and harden the heart of man"—where he experiments on and kills patients; even by these dubious standards of civility, Henry Brandt's "barbarity" causes him to be "expelled with ignominy" (*BV* 120). In what must be a unique plotline in nineteenth-century British literature, Brandt takes his private fortune to Jamaica, buys a plantation, and becomes a planter and human vivisectionist. "Brandt did not confine his scientific investigations to the poor dumb creation. He was known to have decoyed natives into his Pandemonium, who were never heard from again" (*BV* 120–21).

From her father, Harriet inherits a love of cruelty toward slaves; here the odd veil of vivisection disappears, and the older model of overseer cruelty reemerges. Harriet recounts an experience that pains the more sensitive, humane Margaret: "When I was a little thing of four years old, Pete [the overseer] used to let me whip the little niggers for a treat, when they had done anything wrong. It used to make me laugh to see them wriggle their legs under the whip and cry! . . . [T]hey deserved it, you know, the little wretches, always thieving or lying or something! I've seen a woman whipped to death, because she wouldn't work. We think nothing of that sort of thing, over there" (*BV* 27–28). Harriet's clearly pathological violence is meant to inform her psychic vampirism, but its relationship to the bat bite, and to her mother's gluttony, convolutes the novel's racial and imperial politics. By transforming the older trope of intemperate slave mastery into vampirism, Marryat reflects a shift from the long-standing genre of abolitionist novels for children, in which West Indian heiresses, like Harriet, return to Britain but find that their insensitivity to suffering, learned through their intimate contact with chattel slavery, socially handicaps them. Over the course of such novels, the West Indians' friendships with English children help reform their manners, so that, for example, they no longer abuse their black servants. As Katie Trumpener observes, "Optimistic about the chances of personal and thus imperial reform, this children's literature stresses individual transformation over systemic change, abolitionist sentiment over abolition."[90] By contrast, Harriet's unconsciousness of her vampirism mirrors her lack of awareness of her own former callousness to her slaves, but neither can be cured—even nominally—by emerging into her consciousness.

Indeed, because the inheritance of a white compulsive, heinous appetite threatens to attenuate Harriet's inheritance of her mother's monstrosity, Marryat reinserts her in the narrative of Henry Brandt's madness. Not only is she a glutton for food, she is also afflicted with a bloodlust that feeds on the scraps of her husband's more erudite, scientific fascination: "It was said that the only thing which made her laugh, was to watch the dying agonies of the poor creatures her brutal protector slaughtered. But she thirsted for blood, she loved the sight and smell of it, she would taste it on the tip of her finger when it came in her way" (*BV* 121–22). In a description that grimly parodies the ceremonial refinements of tasting sugar for tea on the fingertip, Marryat focuses Harriet's mother's generalized gluttony on a specific, compelled thirst for blood. Far from remaining a simple figure of black contamination of the white English social body, she also comes to signify the commercial and techno-scientific imperial rapacity that feeds on the blood, sweat, and tears of chattel slaves.

Harriet's mother's mixed-race pathologies, with their dual tropical and European origins, engage eugenics' obsessive focus on maternity, especially with respect to inebriety. As in *Dracula*, the trope of nursing is conflated with vampiric bloodsucking and helps unfold the dynamics of raced dependency underlying the novel's imagination of addiction. Harriet's psychic vampirism means that instead of drawing appropriate nourishment from her nurse's breast, she exhausts and kills the nurse. Since her own mother operates by the same principle of parasitic overconsumption, she cannot feed her daughter; so the job falls to a succession of slaves: "I can remember now hearing old Pete say, that when I was born, I was given to a black wet nurse, and after a little while, she was taken so ill, they had to send her away, and get me another, and the next one—died! Pete used to laugh and call me the puma's cub, but I didn't know the meaning of it, then. And—O! . . . there was a little white child, I can see her so plainly now. They called her little Caroline, I think she must have belonged to the planter who lived next to us, and I was very fond of her" (*BV* 302–3). Harriet's fatal dependency thus takes the lives of two slave women, but they become indistinguishable, merely elements of a vast, undifferentiated reservoir of black labor, when compared to the supposedly greater crime of sucking the lifeblood of a named, loved white child. This passage maximizes the ambivalences of Harriet's miscegenated identity: when she kills the black nurses, she represents the rapacious overdependence of a whiteness that lives off and uses up its black colonized material. But when she kills Caroline, she functions as the contaminating death of a terrifying proximity to blackness. This ambiguity is signaled by her identification of the characters' races: the speaker of the sentence "I was given to a black wet nurse" is putatively white, whereas a speaker who identifies her playmate as "a little white child" is presumably not white herself. Harriet's vampirism thus signifies both an imperial dependency coded as white and a colonial dependency figured as black and enslaved; both are fatally devouring forces. The scene of Mina's addiction in *Dracula* conflates nursing with fellatio, but it stages the same racial and imperial ambivalences: when Mina appears to be nursing, she is the white child feeding off of foreign resources; when she appears to be performing fellatio, she represents the reversed order of powerful colonial ascendance and imperial decline.

Thus both novels—as well as other fin-de-siècle vampire fiction—demonstrate the threatening biopolitical reversal of vampiric nursing, when the "puma cub" grows up and nurses white children to death. Marryat richly imagines this plotline, having Harriet take an intense and sinister interest in Margaret Pullen's baby, Ethel, the sight of whom "drive[s] Miss Brandt wild" (*BV* 21). In keeping with the racial problematics of the novel, Harriet prefers white children to black: "I love little white babies! I adore them. They are so sweet and fresh and clean—so different from the little niggers who smell so nasty, you can't touch them! We never saw a baby in the Convent, and so few English children live to grow up in Jamaica! O! let me hold her! Let me carry her! I *must*!" (*BV* 21). Whereas one might reasonably suppose that for a psychic vampire, any living human prey would do, white babies are preferable because their ostensible freshness signals the purity and strength that Harriet's quadroon constitution craves. Black children, by contrast, signify the odor of death that pervades the colony and proves fatal to little white children; in Harriet's capacity as black vampire, she has this effect on Ethel. Harriet's traveling companion, herself a victim, figuratively links Harriet's desire for children to the specter of cannibalism: "She wants to kiss [every child]. Sometimes, I tell her I think she would like to eat them. But she only means to be kind" (*BV* 102). A similar trope operates in Kenealy's "A Beautiful Vampire," in which Lady Deverish demands that children be brought to her so that she can augment her own vitality with theirs: " 'Get me healthy children,' she cried; 'I must have health about me.' "[91] In *Dracula*, Lucy pursues more delicious white English children, using her physical appeal—she is, in the imagined cross between street dialect and infant lisping, the "bloofer lady," meaning "beautiful lady"—to lure them along for a walk. The children to whom the text imagines Lucy gravitating would most likely be lower-middle-class, "grubby faced" ones who play without supervision on Hampstead Heath. They all, of course, sport bite marks on their throats, including the most recent one detailed under the headline, "Extra Special: The Hampstead Horror," who is additionally "terribly weak, and looked quite emaciated" (*D* 215). These examples of defective maternity, in which the mother destroys rather than nurtures children, emplots the eugenic specter of the inebriate woman, whose alcoholized womb saturates and deforms her progeny.

Nothing signals *The Blood of the Vampire*'s definitive break with conventional mid-Victorian novelistic concerns of unknown parentage and class identity better than its neat substitution of biological inheritance for property inheritance. Illegitimacy is the least of Harriet Brandt's problems. Hence Marryat signals her naïveté by having her demand of Phillips, "I *must* know the truth—I will not leave the house until you tell me! Were they married? Am I a—a—bastard?" (*BV* 294). But the truth of Harriet's identity is medical rather than contractual; the sins of her parents have to do not with unsanctioned but with socially irresponsible procreation. In thinking back on her parents' profligacy in bearing her, she voices the outrage of rational eugenicists at century's end—the kind of people who railed against the specter of inebriates and other mental defectives reproducing and passing their deformities along to their children: "How had they *dared* to bring her into the world, an innocent yet hapless child of sin—the inheritor of their evil propensities—of their lust, their cruelty, their sensuality, their gluttony—and worst of all, the fatal heritage that made her a terror and a curse to her fellow-creatures? How dared they? *How dared they?*" (*BV* 324). The logical consequence, of course, is suicide, which Harriet achieves, significantly, with an overdose of chloral. Her suicide note is thus also a eugenic manifesto: "My parents have made me unfit to live. Let me go to a world where the curse of heredity which they laid upon me may be mercifully wiped out" (*BV* 345). Harriet Brandt's self-authored demise thus enacts the fantasy of "negative" eugenics, namely that defectives might auto-expire, dying off through their very unfitness; at the same time, however, since Harriet takes her own life, her suicide can be read as the activism of "positive" eugenics, a kind of self-extermination. Both fantasies also inform the eugenic figure of the addict viewed as a gradual suicide. Harriet, like other addicts who die of their disease, brings the death inside her out into the open, realizing its incipience. From the eugenic point of view endorsed by the novel, her birth and survival is not just unnatural but also an accident to be corrected.

Like Martin Jocelyn's, however, Harriet's survival is also an accident because she has outlived the plantation violence that the novel would like to confine to the past. The novel's racial loyalties are therefore riven with ambivalence. On the one hand, feeling readers are calculated to despise Brandt for torturing and killing chattel slaves for his own "civilized" gratification; on the other, Harriet's mother's similarly barbaric bloodlust appears as an organic force erupting from a tropical, colonized landscape of bats and blacks. Because she is herself half-black, that she enjoys tasting the blood of vivisected slaves crystallizes a white impulse to represent a blackness that, having trespassed on white power, turns back and devours itself. Harriet's parentage motivates both a critique of white power submerged in familiar sentimental accusations against unfeeling science and a more free-ranging racist delight in spectral black monstrosity.

This ambivalence culminates in the most apocalyptic violence the novel represents, the slaves' revolt against the Brandts' sadistic rule and burning of the plantation. The novel's omniscient narration endorses the character Phillips's approval of this retaliation as just punishment: "I am glad to say that his negroes revolted, and after having murdered him with appropriate atrocity, set fire to his house and burned it and all his property to the ground. . . . [H]e richly deserved his fate, and no torture could be too severe for one who spent his worthless life in torturing God's helpless animals!" (*BV* 120–21). Although the natives wrongly blame Brandt's experiments on Mrs. Brandt's reputation for obeah, her heinous bloodlust nevertheless legitimates their reciprocal acts of torture and murder: "When they got her in their clutches, I have heard that they did not spare her, but killed her in the most torturing fashion they could devise" (*BV* 137). Although the novel approves of the slave rebellion, it justifies it only by the Brandts' extravagant and unusual cruelty, not by the mundane violence of slavery's structural inequalities. But since the rebellion is elicited by that brutality and mirrors it, it also figures white anxiety about the possibility that black retaliatory violence could be just compensation for white chattel slave mastery. Because these racial ambivalences surround the causes of Harriet's vampirism—her parasitic dependence on and unconscious murder of her acquaintances, friends, and lovers—they are at the root of its resemblance to addiction. The narration states repeatedly that Harriet would herself have been murdered if her friend the overseer had not spirited her away to his cabin and then placed her in the convent. Harriet's survival is thus a kind of racial accident: as the vestige of multiple, conflicting kinds of racial shame and hatred, she persists as both a black blot on whiteness and a uniquely white blot on imperial power. As Patterson has commented on the parasitic ideology sustaining chattel slavery, those "forced to examine the realities of their dependence on slaves—and its ideological underpinnings—simply turned away from the truth and ended up with hopelessly contradictory positions."[92] As fin-de-siècle readers looked back on an earlier era of plantation slavery, they grafted older racial fears and desires onto newer ones, using both to imagine addiction as a racial defect.

In the process of neatly tying up her eugenic plot, Marryat leaves one telling loose end. Before she overdoses on chloral, Harriet leaves Margaret her fortune. This is clearly Harriet's attempt to expiate her guilt for killing baby Ethel, but it opens a wider ethical and historical problem. By recirculating the ill-gotten wealth of slave ownership back into the British economy, Harriet leaves behind a poisoned gift. Indeed, since this money could be viewed as payment for Ethel, the novel drops the faint suggestion that British homes and bodies are still all too easily susceptible to the addictive enticements of intemperate slavery.

"Bare Life" and "Un-Death"

I have been relating eugenic theory and policy to the politics of colonial and imperial dependency in order to illustrate the powerful cultural logic beginning to shape addiction at fin de siècle. On the one hand, addiction was a disease of modernity, striking nervous, "up-to-date with a vengeance" English types who couldn't sleep without chloral hydrate or make a move without recording it in their diaries. On the other, addiction was a recrudescence of irrational, savage appetites that threatened to deracinate and destroy the social body. All through the nineteenth century, the temperance insistence that habitual drunkenness transcended class differences, along with the medical articulation of it as a disease, held out the possibility of producing a universal model of addiction that would dissolve all of its social differences. Instead, the technical, professional expertise of medicine and law were remotivated to instantiate and reify those differences, a phenomenon that only intensified the paradox whereby addiction is simultaneously individualized according to ideologies of freedom and abstract self-making, and collectivized by recourse to conventional racism, homophobia, and sexism.

When the racial dichotomy between white, abstract, individual models of addiction and embodied, collective ones was mapped onto the metropolitan-colonial relationship, particularly the memory of chattel slavery and mastery, it dredged up old fears of colonial parasitism upon the civilized metropole, but it also exposed the metropole's parasitic, infant nursing upon the colony. Addiction thus bore the shame for the bad faith of modernity. This failure to acknowledge imperial dependency on its colonies as anything other than debilitation was grounded in the colonies' symbolic status as a realm of death: a tropical climate that kills whites, a black land populated by the socially dead, and a land of the past no longer animated by its own energy, the substance powering modernity, progress, and empire. Precisely in order to maintain the fiction of progressive metropolitan Enlightenment modernity, the metropole's complicity in the propagation of death in the colonies must never be acknowledged. Addiction is the side effect of this refusal. If intoxication represents the unconsciousness of imperial rapacity, the enchantments and charms of the exotic goods it brings back to the imperial seat, then addiction registers but displaces the awareness that these enchantments are really compulsions, expensive and onerous to maintain and ultimately fatal. The narrative trajectory through addiction to death relocates death from the colony back to the metropole, the home, and the imperial modern body.

In the late nineteenth century, degeneration and eugenics biologized these imperial inequities. Eugenics, however, offered a series of policies for attempting to realize a national body free of the contamination of death. Within an empire, whose great status and great instability both inhere in the multiplication of internal borders, this task takes on a particular urgency. As an allegory for addiction, vampirism exposes the ambiguity of imperial and colonial parasitism and dependency; but through its close association to eugenics, it turns that confusion into one between life and death, most notably represented by Stoker's concept of "un-death." The un-dead or incipiently dead vampires of Stoker and Marryat represent those parasitic segments of the population who, from a eugenic viewpoint, should not be alive. In this way, they fit neatly into Giorgio Agamben's model of "bare life" articulated in *Homo Sacer*: biological life that is excluded from political relevance and that accordingly "may be killed and yet not sacrificed."[93] Existing in the un-dead world below the threshold of citizenship, the vampire becomes "bare life" insofar as he is endlessly available for execution. The seemingly bottomless appetite for vampire narratives in the century-plus of popular culture since *Dracula* attests to the intensive elaboration of this fundamental biopolitical calculation. The vampire's comebacks and executions eternally rehearse the urgent threat posed by the subnational populations that constitute "bare life" and their imperfect containment by state forces. As with addicts, the normal population waits in vain for them to expire, but the processes of natural selection are too slow. For these reasons, eugenics dictates their extermination.

Stoker's concept of the "un-dead"—an idea so important to the novel that Stoker almost picked it to be the title—is its most far-sighted conceit. Rather than a simple synonym for *alive*, it references a twilight zone of negation—neither dead nor alive. Defined by their habit, vampires exist in what Craft calls "an eternity of sexual repetition"; although they possess some of the hallmarks of life—bodies, animation, cognition, consciousness—they lack the dynamism or spontaneity that makes life, in the conventional phrase, "worth living."[94] Zygmunt Bauman describes this biopolitical calculation when he articulates the nation's need to obtain its own immortality by killing the representatives of death, decay, degeneration, and disease in its midst: "Killing the disease-and-degeneration carriers, as killing the bacteria or viruses, is a life-serving and life-enhancing exercise. One does not think of it as murder, but as of life-saving. The lives destroyed are 'lives devoid of value'; they are also lives inimical to life, lives which have to be killed so that they shall not kill. . . . Killing of the appointed disease-carriers is a symbolic surrogate of death-killing."[95] This formation appears in *Dracula* when Van Helsing tries to convince Arthur Holmwood and the others that decapitating the un-dead Lucy and driving a stake through her heart is a mercy that "live" Lucy would have wanted. This ritual must be performed to release Lucy's soul into a Christian afterlife: "Instead of working wickedness by night and growing more debased in the assimilation of it by day, she shall take her place with the other Angels. So that, my friend, it will be a blessed hand for her that shall strike the blow that sets her free" (*D* 253). With this sentiment, Van Helsing voices the biopolitical calculation that Lucy's un-dead life is not worth living; in keeping with the paradox engendered through the demand for national immortality, the Crew of Light must kill a being who is already nominally dead. Here, un-dead Lucy inhabits Agamben's zone of "bare life": since her "life" is not worth living, she can be "killed" without being sacrificed.

"Live" Lucy, of course, was really *English* Lucy: her first death has not completely killed her but only deracinated and denationalized her, making her a "foul thing," her virtuous English self, the embodiment of "unequalled sweetness and purity," no more. Her execution at Arthur's hands, with its screeching, writhing, and spurting blood, is frequently interpreted as an orgasm; yet for our purposes, it more obviously registers the throes of racial extermination. Lucy's first death becomes the boundary crossing that separates her not from the living but from humans. As a vampire about to be exterminated, she signifies "The Thing," a veritable animal, which we know because she emits a "screech," her teeth seeming "to champ," and her mouth "smeared with a crimson foam" (*D* 254). The second death thus functions to eradicate the biological and racial alterity she represents and her inevitable deracinating effect on Britain's future, as she drinks the children's delicious blood. This, of course, is her biopolitical threat. Van Helsing, with his usual bluffness, does the eugenic math for Seward: if left unchecked, Lucy "must go on age after age adding new victims and multiplying the evils of the world; for all that die from the preying of the Un-Dead become themselves Un-Dead, and prey on their kind. . . . The career of this so unhappy dear lady is but just begun. Those children whose blood she suck are not as yet so much the worse; but if she live on, Un-Dead, more and more they lose their blood, and by her power over them they come to her" (*D* 252–53). In other words, vampiric reproduction is geometrical; it outstrips ordinary human sexual reproduction by continuing forever, eventually converting the entire population to the status of "un-dead."

Van Helsing's explanation for why Lucy must die an additional death is an argument about controlling an undesirable population that will communicate its racial difference to everyone else. That this eugenic procedure is performed without the up-to-date modern technologies that had been employed to maintain Lucy's biological life—she cannot be killed again, for example, by injecting her with poison—is telling. Un-dead Lucy has become a primitive, atavistic force, committing her vampiric crimes with the low-tech weapon of her own teeth; she therefore must be exterminated and dismembered with commensurately primitive tools, a stake and knife. Furthermore, the appearance of the host during this ritual tellingly aligns it with Christian funerals and suggests how much eugenic extermination merely recapitulates the modern conceptualization of death as social exclusion. Bauman, referencing Jean Baudrillard's pithy observation that the village cemetery was "the first ghetto, prefiguring every future ghetto," elaborates: funerals "proclaim the dead abnormal, dangerous, those to be shunned. . . . Through applying to the dead the same technique of separation as they do to the carriers of infectious diseases or contagious malpractices, they cast the dead among the manageable threats that lose their potency if kept at a distance."[96] Dracula may have claimed Lucy's life, but in managing her un-dead existence, the Crew of Light remains in control of the national social body.

At fin de siècle, the biopolitical drive to purify state populations that culminated with the Holocaust began; for Bauman and others, this drive arises from the internal contradictions of the state.[97] Suppressing its own ambivalence, nationalism projects it onto internal others: "Lest they should suffocate under the rising mounds of ambiguity, nations are called to be vigilant against the strangers in their midst, those false pretenders who claim the soil and blood that are not their own."[98] Dracula fits this paradigm neatly, both as an immigrant planning to purchase real estate in London but more obviously in literally claiming British identity by laying invalid claim to its distinctive racial material, blood. In this way, the state's futurity is contingent on the Crew's campaign of purification against the vampire. The novel quite obviously endorses this viewpoint, since Dracula loses his desires; but it also allows him to voice a different, older paradigm. In Bauman's scheme, states are intent on "banishing the *strangers* rather than *enemies*,[99] but for Dracula, who recites the long history of the Szekeley family's battles against European tribes such as Magyars, Lombards, Avars, Bulgars, and Turks, the nation is not an operative concept. Dracula's pre-modernity honors a history of a "whirlpool of European races"—a mixture that modernizing nations prefer to homogenize (*D* 59). Why, then, must the Crew of Light pursue Dracula back to Transylvania, when his departure appears to have secured the English mainland? Elucidating the supernatural lore of the vampire, Van Helsing explains that it is to rescue Mina from his telepathic clutches; but from the point of view of eugenic politics, it is to eliminate the threat of the stateless being. Since his people are an antique race, already extinguished by the modern national reorganization of Europe, Dracula represents a kind of refugee whose home sanctuary is limited, precarious: with only one coffin's worth of soil left, he has to be back in his castle by sundown. Furthermore, he is aided by another set of paradigmatic modern stateless people, considered equally disposable by the vampire hunters, the gypsies known as the Szgany. Agamben, referencing Hannah Arendt, reminds us that "the very figure who should have embodied the rights of man par excellence—the refugee—signals instead the concept's radical crisis."[100] In other words, because the modern Western state—originating in Rousseau's and Locke's articulation of the social contract—has the ultimate power to recognize and to take biological life, the person without a national identity becomes the locus of tremendous—frankly supernatural—resistive power.

Perhaps the most significant way in which Dracula's death represents a eugenic fantasy is that, because he is the last surviving member of his race, his execution represents a relatively easy genocide.[101] Indeed, that Dracula's actual spread of his racial alterity was limited to Lucy, Mina, and the three female vampires in Castle Dracula suggests that his threat always loomed larger in the minds of the Crew of Light than in any demonstrable reality. Unlike the self-exterminating Harriet, Dracula represents the vampire-addict who must be zealously pursued far beyond national and imperial borders in order to be exterminated. Because his un-dead "life" exists beyond the bounds of any state, he represents the unthinkable: biological life without political sanction, beyond the social contract, beholden to no one. This is the real secret of the vampire's power—and of the addict's threat: as the "living dead," they exist in an underworld as their own life form and have their own social order; if they do not autodestruct through their own fatal habits, they must be eliminated. *Dracula*'s concerns with eugenics and genocide anticipate some of the twentieth century's conceptual frameworks of race and addiction, part of the reason why the vampiric meta-discourse it spawned across popular culture has so endured.[102] In the afterword to this book, I show how this biopolitical management increasingly turned to the control of drug supplies under an ascendant U.S. imperialism in the first two decades of the twentieth century.

AFTERWORD

The Biopolitics of Drug Control

Beginning around the time of *Dracula* and continuing into the twentieth century, addicts increasingly inhabit urban underworld zones of "bare life," into which their seemingly predatory motives suck unsuspecting citizens. This anxiety structures the most common narrative context of addiction in the years 1900–1920, the seduction or rape of vulnerable white women by men of color and their consequent contamination by foreign deathliness.[1] For example, in London in 1918 and 1922, the fatal overdoses of actress Billie Carleton and dancer Freda Kempton spawned media sensations and made death seem to lurk in every prick of the syringe or sniff of cocaine. Yet as Marek Kohn's analysis has shown, these Englishwomen's flirtations with death were also eroticized encounters with dark figures from a shadowy underground, suppliers such as Brilliant Chang and Edgar Manning. These episodes, and their fictionalized and cinematic counterparts, updated the opium den fascination that started in the 1870s by sexualizing narrative relations between white women and racially marked men. Edith Blinn's *The Ashes of My Heart* (1916), Thomas Burke's *Limehouse Nights* (1916) and *More Limehouse Nights* (1921), D. W. Griffith's film adaptation *Broken Blossoms* (1919), Sax Rohmer's *Dope* (1919) as well as his seemingly endless string of Fu Manchu novels (published between 1913 and 1973), and Lady Dorothy Mills's *The Laughter of Fools* (1920) used opium, cocaine, and heroin to bring white Anglo-American women into degrading, deracinating intimacy with Chinese and Afro-British men.[2] "I fear he is going to put me to sleep forever," declares the gorgeous but decaying opium addict of her Chinese American lover, Foo Gum, in *The Ashes of My Heart*.[3]

In contrast to this model of being lulled to death by Chinese narcotics, the association of African Americans with cocaine led to fears of explosive, fatal violence toward whites, often toward white women and often inciting brutal retaliatory lynchings.[4] "Most of the attacks upon white women of the South are the direct result of a cocaine-crazed Negro brain," wrote Dr. Christopher Koch in the *Literary Digest* in 1914.[5] In keeping with the supernatural paradigm set by *Dracula*, southern blacks were thought to acquire the superhuman power of being immune to police bullets.[6] Such mythology flourished with respect to a historically disposable population that, not long before, had been nominally included within the norms of citizenship, and yet was still violently under threat of racial extermination. Finally, in the same period, the various wings of the U.S. temperance movement began attacking poor and working-class European immigrants in northern cities in racist terms, for their allegedly addictive use of alcohol. "Besodden Europe, worse bescourged than by war, famine and pestilence, sends here her drink-makers, her drunkard makers, and her drunkards, or her more temperate and habitual drinkers, with all their un-American and anti-American ideas of morality and government," wrote Alphonse Alva Hopkins.[7] In all of these ways, even though the typical U.S. addict was still a white, native-born man, the racial valence of addiction began to reverse. Gone were the days when temperance tales told of promising young white men falling into the clutches of drink, physicians dabbled with the instruments of their profession, and upper-class society ladies injected themselves with morphine. Medical, legal, and public health authorities, as well as professionalizing social scientists, began to take new notice of those less-than-fully franchised subjects, to pathologize and criminalize their customs and habits, and to invent habits to police where none had existed. All of these actions were justified, within this racist ideology, because the groups had been deemed to be parasites on the purer social body.

Elaborating such vampiric imagery, addiction narratives increasingly conjured urban "drug undergrounds," where white drug use could flourish on the fringes of poor communities, communities of color, queer subcultures, criminal networks, avant-gardes, Bohemias, and other outcast milieux. Each of these possess varying degrees of potential for countermodern perspectives on addiction; some are more contiguous with bourgeois culture than others. Virginia Berridge emphasizes the Decadent Rhymers' Club, the occult circles surrounding Aleister Crowley, and the hallucinogenic experimentations of Havelock Ellis and Silas Weir Mitchell as the 1890s origins of a British drug scene.[8] Marek Kohn focuses on the music hall, theater, café, and nightclub spaces. In the United States, Caroline Jean Acker locates the origins of "junkie" culture in the urban entertainments frequented by working-class men: "pool halls, bars, brothels, restaurants, theaters, dance halls, and perhaps a racetrack."[9] We can see the beginnings of this kind of underground community, which organizes itself in opposition to the mainstream norms of kinship and bourgeois accumulation, in *Dracula*: Lucy casts her vampiric spell over the grubby tots of Hampstead Heath, who, far more than the wolves Dracula mentions, become the novel's true "children of the night."[10] At first, Lucy's malign influence appears to be their game, since they emulate her by luring each other away; but when the psychological and physical extent of her influence becomes clearer, the vampiric threat becomes more alarming: at North Hospital, Dr. Vincent tells Van Helsing and Seward that "even this poor little mite, when he woke up today, asked the nurse if he might go away. When she asked him why he wanted to go, he said he wanted to play with the 'bloofer lady.' "[11] In this way, a single vampire-addict can replicate exponentially, transforming a susceptible population into an entire subcommunity intoxicated with delinquent delight. The terrifyingly expansive reach of the racial defects of vampirism thus appear to exceed the sexual reproduction that would be normally necessary to transmit them.

The same is true of addiction, which, in the logic of both degeneration and eugenic theories at the century's end, could be transmitted through "personal or ancestral" causes: it could be acquired and passed on through a kind of decadent pedagogy, as one addict might train another in the use of the needle or pipe. Lodged in the commercial hearts of urban centers, these shadowy communities represented the consolidation of the parasitic, eugenic threat on the life of the national body. The anxieties focused especially on children and youths, who, in Lee Edelman's trenchant queer theoretical critique, become emblematic of a mythic "child [who] remains the perpetual horizon of every acknowledged politics, the fantasmatic beneficiary of every political intervention."[12] As Edelman theorizes, since "the Child" must be protected in order to guarantee the national future, children become fraught symbols of national and social purity who must be kept free from sexual, and therefore, racial contamination at all costs. On the other hand, the "children of the night" represented by vampires and addicts are parented by evil forces that are outside politics and its future orientation. Inhabiting a twilight of "un-death," they grow only backward, toward greater depravity, expanding their zone of abjection—if left unchecked.

The need to control these threats to bodies politic led to an era of international narcotics control beginning in the early twentieth century, a point at which the global history of drugs begins to supersede the history of addiction. The ascendancy of U.S. imperialism, with its distinctive style of biopolitical management, ushers in this history. In 1898, Spain ceded the Philippines to the United States as a result of losing the Spanish-American War. The Spanish had profited from contracts for the supply of opium to the seventy thousand Chinese living in the Philippines, with the stipulation that Filipinos be prohibited from purchasing it.[13] Combining idealism with arrogance, the United States decided to end these contracts and cut off the opium supply entirely; this immediately led to an underground market and use by Filipinos. The U.S. response was an escalating attempt to control the opium traffic. The United States was eager to distinguish its imperial approach to opium from that of Britain: Britain had fought two wars (1840–43 and 1856–60) to keep Chinese markets open to opium grown in India and to make China its economic satellite. By the 1870s, a vociferous anti-opium movement within the United Kingdom had gathered critical mass, arguing that Britain was morally responsible for the moral degradation of innumerable Chinese: "Year by year the deadly drug is poisoning the very life-blood of the Chinese nation. . . . Year by year England becomes more deeply involved in the trade, and year by year it is more difficult for her to extricate herself from the web of her own weaving."[14] Subsequent research from the Chinese perspective has shown this hand-wringing to be detached from the political and cultural realities of opium use in China, where the attempts at suppression by the Chinese emperor Daoguang and others were instances of policing the lower classes, which had recently taken up a formerly elite custom. The specter conjured by anti-opium propaganda of emaciated, addicted Chinese peasants shivering for a fix in sinister dens bore little resemblance to reality.[15] Yet this was the scourge that the United States felt motivated to eliminate, as it eagerly took up what Kipling called "the white man's burden"; not for nothing does the poem of the same name take the subtitle, "The United States and the Philippine Islands."[16] Charles Henry Brent, the Evangelical Bishop of the Philippines, described it succinctly: "Our desire is to give the Orient civilization."[17] Whereas the British had let the Chinese molder in a narcotic stupor, the United States would uplift and civilize its imperial subjects. Although an earlier and more pragmatic proposal, to reinstate the monopolies and fund public education with the revenues, had been considered, the specter of "a government pandering to opium craving by degenerate races" took precedence, and the resulting strategy of total enforcement became the law.[18] Underlying this plan was the confidence that drug supplies could be easily stopped; when this happened, addiction would become a thing of the past. Mingled with this naivete, however, was a certain biopolitical ideal: that individual physical Filipino and Chinese bodies reflect the purity of the civilizing mission of the United States.

At the end of the century, U.S. imperialism, along with the international and national controls it spawned, helped to shift the status of addiction to a medical condition that was also a crime. To bolster its imperial authority in its attempts to ban opium smoking throughout the Far East, the United States pushed through the Smoking Opium Exclusion Act in 1909, which regulated opium within its national borders. Motivated by these gains, Brent led the U.S. delegation to the 1909 Opium Commission, convened by U.S. president Theodore Roosevelt in Shanghai, and chaired the International Conference on Opium at the Hague (1911–12), both focused on suppressing opium smoking and the international opium trade. Two further conferences in the Hague, in 1913 and 1914, put pressure on the United States to regulate its own pharmaceutical production and distribution of cocaine and heroin, which it eventually did through the Harrison Act, passed in December 1914. As David Musto notes, "Here was one more instance in which enactment of exemplary domestic laws became necessary in order to avoid international embarrassment."[19] The Harrison Act, which was in effect until the Nixon administration launched the contemporary "war on drugs" in 1970, required everyone but the consumer to document their role in the import, production, and sale of opium and coca products, which were still perceived to have medicinal uses. Possession of the drugs without a prescription effectively indicated violation of the Harrison Act. Glossing the effect of such drug control legislation, Davenport-Hines writes, "Addicts (rather than addiction) were soon being represented as a contagious disease."[20] In order to stop addiction, legislators attempted to stop the unregulated global circulation of the substances; this had the effect of creating a criminal component of identity for individual addicts and shifting the disease metaphor from individual habituation to social infection.

Significantly, the partial transition of drug dependency from condition to crime also pried apart the conceptual unity of alcohol, morphine, and cocaine under the medical notion of "inebriety," since the public debate surrounding the prohibition of alcohol, and especially its repeal, in the years between 1920 and 1933, had the effect of categorizing alcohol as a substance that could be moderately consumed by ordinary middle-class people. Heroin and cocaine, by contrast, were drugs thought to be taken only by criminal degenerates. U.S. aspirations toward global hegemony, especially the desire to assert international moral leadership on the topic of addiction, helped to construe addiction as a crime as well as a condition. Under the Harrison Act, the ambiguity over physicians' prescriptions to relieve withdrawal symptoms—actions that construed addiction as a disease with symptoms—was cleared up when the Supreme Court ruled against maintenance prescriptions in 1919, as Musto points out, against the backdrop of an aggressive and anxious nationalism fueling the Red Scare and Prohibition.[21] Thousands of people who had been made drug-dependent through medical prescription became criminals embodying a pernicious social disease.

The British approach to addiction in this period both resembled and departed from the United States' insistence on drug-free bodies. The resemblance inheres in the hysteria over war, sex, and cocaine. Britain, the largest manufacturer of morphine, had been obliged by the international agreements to control opium and morphine smuggling, but the traffic continued, filtering into the United States, Japan, and other points in the Far East.[22] Uncontrollable smuggling raised national security issues, especially at a time of war; Sir Malcolm Delevingne of the Home Office brought the matter under the jurisdiction of the Defence of the Realm Act (DORA) in 1916. Delevingne was also concerned about cocaine, which was so unregulated that retailers advertised it as a good present for British soldiers headed to the front. When Canadian soldiers in Folkestone were found to have picked up the cocaine habit from prostitutes, who had given it to them to help remedy hangovers, fears mounted that British soldiers would take up the habit, compromising their fighting efficiency and national security. The eugenicist Caleb Saleeby wrote that "hundreds of soldiers" would be driven "mad" unless the traffic in cocaine were stopped.[23] Cocaine was thus included under the DORA regulation.

As in the United States, Britain also needed to overcome international embarrassment, in its case over its nineteenth-century opium policy. In 1895, the Brassey Report to the Royal Commission on Opium had definitively repudiated the anti-opium argument, claiming that opium smoking was not the abject, degrading practice that depictions of dens had fixed in public consciousness. *The Lancet* had backed up this professional opinion, mounting a telling cross-cultural comparison: "If we reverse the situation and suppose that the natives of India had sent a commission to this country to inquire into the drink question—into the sum spent per head by our population on alcohol, and the degradation, misery, and crime which are too often the outcome of it all—can there be any reasonable doubt that the evils traceable to alcohol here would appear to such a commission enormous, and those arising from the abuse of opium there, in India, altogether insignificant in comparison with them."[24] But in the new era of international control spearheaded by the United States, such opinions were merely taken as signs of European decadence and racist neglect. In 1919, the Treaty of Versailles entrusted the League of Nations with general supervision of the international narcotics agreements; it also enacted the Hague Conventions, which had not been fully and formally adopted. Versailles influenced the hard line taken by the Dangerous Drugs Act of 1920, which extended DORA and remained the most significant control on drugs in the United Kingdom for much of the century. The Dangerous Drugs Act regulated morphine, cocaine, and heroin and prohibited the sale and smoking of opium. The British departure from the U.S. model of total enforcement came in the episode of the Rolleston Report of 1926, which reasserted the medical authority that had been displaced throughout the wartime bans and international agreements.[25] The Rolleston Report helped establish the medical maintenance of morphine and heroin that had seemed so unthinkable under the drive toward criminalization; it struck a victory for the disease model on the premise that the relief of overpowering cravings was fundamentally a medical intervention.

Most drug historians are critical of the international and U.S. regimes of law enforcement throughout the twentieth century, because they seem to have created far more human misery than addiction, had it been left unchecked or treated differently, might otherwise have.[26] As usual, Berridge provides the most nuanced opinion, cautioning against the impression that the more medically oriented British approach was humane to addicts, whereas the more criminal justice-oriented approach of the United States was not. Such an opinion overlooks the realities of the broad institutional and disciplinary partnership between medicine and the law to manage addicts in the Foucauldian sense of care as coercion. Furthermore, "medical humanitarianism was maintained only so long as there was a limited, middle class and respectable addict clientele."[27] The criminal model, especially as it unfolded in the United States, requires urgent critique; nonetheless, at its origins, both its proponents and those writing from the medical perspective assumed that addiction was going to be a short-term problem. "In future the cocaine habitué will be dependent for his supplies of the drug on clandestine sources, and as it is no doubt correct to assume that special efforts will be made to prevent smuggling, we may take it that the cocaine habitué will soon be almost an extinct type in this country," predicted *The Lancet* in 1916.[28]

In the gray zone that combines the medical and criminal conceptualizations of addiction, the illness indeed becomes, in Sontag's words, a "more onerous citizenship." Sontag's phrase touches Agamben's concept of "bare life," in which the biological ground of political citizenship erodes. That is, because addicts are not simply criminals but also possess a pathologized status somewhere between criminal and diseased, they are not simply transgressors of the law whose violations and punishment strengthen its hold on the entire population. Rather, addicts signify as the weak appendage of the ordinary population: they are sick, but because they appear to have given themselves their illness, they are easily disqualified from health insurance and legal provisions for disabilities, susceptible to unusual punishment, and deprived of other minor civil rights. They thus remain a kind of collateral damage in the war on drugs that intensified the international prohibitions and regulations on substances. Although the "criminal model" may appear to dominate, the disease model still inheres in it, motivating it to curb addiction's threat to bodies politic.[29]

But what happens when the concept rhetorically proliferates, as it has since 1980? In the introduction, I reframed the question of how individuals become addicts to ask how the concept of addiction suits an overdeveloped, contemporary middle-class society, such as exists in the United Kingdom and the United States. Having surveyed the history of addiction through the early part of the twentieth century, we are in a position to assess its relevance for the early twenty-first century. After all, rather than throwing one into an underworld of "bare life" on the threshold of extermination, "addictions" to things like yoga and caffeine are more often the signs of middle-class social success and self-regulation. Yet when addiction operates most obviously as a metaphor, it actually helps sustain its more seemingly literal applications. When the entire population appears to be susceptible to addictions that range along the spectrum from pitiable self-devastation to ironic sign of self-care, then the concept so saturates the culture that nearly every utterance of it reinforces rather than destabilizes its social power. Hence, when William Whipper characterized addiction as a kind of democratic force, making no discriminations, he recognized that the whole social body is susceptible to it. Intemperance, he wrote, "is found in the palace; it exists in the forum; it mingles with society; its abode is by the fireside; it is felt in the sanctuary; it despises the prejudices of caste; it seeks its victims alike among the learned and the ignorant, the poor and the rich."[30] From a Foucauldian perspective, this depth of penetration incites discipline, but it has the more insidious effect of construing the whole population as vulnerable to a covert process of denationalization and extermination. The middle class can continuously monitor itself for "serious" addictions while simultaneously and casually characterizing its acts of compulsive consumption, practices of self-care, hobbies, rituals, and other activities as "addictive," borrowing the allure of a dangerous habit.

But that everyone feels "addicted" does not lead to new, intersubjective relationships or coalition politics, only to individualized recoveries or deaths. Because the rhetoric of addiction and recovery posits an inner self that is endlessly available to be "worked on," as Helen Keane puts it, as an ongoing, quasi-aesthetic project, each of us merely waits for others to retake similar control of their own lives.[31] Conceptualizing addiction as any compulsive consumption redefines "life" itself as a kind of extended, pleasurable suicide or "un-death"; in this way, middle-class westerners become participants in a kind of thanato-politics. That is, what distinguishes addicts from other forms of "bare life," such as refugees or populations at risk of genocide from ethnic hatred, is their apparent enjoyment of their own vulnerability to death. The discursive spread of addiction has promulgated this fatal flirtation to the point of utter banality, in which death lurks in ordinary items of food or acts of media consumption. Addiction thus rewrites freedom not as the unique fulfillment of an individual's biological life but as a negative freedom, the freedom from death. Thus distracted by individual efforts to achieve freedom, understood as some version of sobriety, biological purity, health, or maximum performance, middle-class consumers rarely join together to address the heinous social ills that have arisen from the restriction of drugs in our name: poverty, war, political repression, commercial exploitation, and environmental destruction. Both "serious" addicts and more clearly "metaphorical" ones both fail to perceive their own perilous proximity to these larger, collective snares.

Metaphors and narratives have the ability to shape individual and collective lives—indeed, to reinvent the very concepts of life and death. I have shown how metaphors of addiction structured social meaning in the nineteenth century, and how the invented identity of "the addict" destabilized those of master and slave, consumer and producer, men and women, straight and queer, white and raced, citizen and pathological criminal. But the history of addiction is much longer and broader than the episodes chosen to represent the century covered by this book. How has addiction continued to reinvent the public sphere and the global consumption taking place within it?

NOTES

Introduction: Addiction and History

1. Describing his relief from eye pain, Harley reported, "The feeling the opiate produced was heavenly. It lifted me from purgatory into paradise, and I made to myself a vow never to be hard upon an opium-eater after having myself tasted of its bliss. Once having begun the sleeping-draught, I took regularly ⅙ grain of morphia with ½ grain of quinine every six hours, so that I was always more or less under the influence of the drug, sometimes being sound asleep and at other periods in a state of conscious divine beatitude. What a blessed change from the torments of the damned that I had previously suffered!" See Mrs. Alec Tweedie, *George Harley, F.R.S.: The Life of a London Physician* (London: The Scientific Press, 1899), 176–79.

2. John R. Reed, *Victorian Will* (Athens: Ohio University Press, 1989), 83–84.

3. John W. Crowley and William L. White, *Drunkard's Refuge: The Lessons of the New York State Inebriate Asylum* (Amherst: University of Massachusetts Press, 2004), 41. Crowley and White are quoting Edward Turner's *History of the First Inebriate Asylum in the World* (New York, 1888), which, in turn, quotes physician and temperance activist Reuben Dimond Mussey.

4. For a similar story involving amputation, see W. J. Rorabaugh, *The Alcoholic Republic: An American Tradition* (Oxford: Oxford University Press, 1979), 199.

5. Henceforth, I use *addict* and *addiction* to include a compulsive habitual relationship to alcohol, except where noted, for the sake of convenience.

6. Oxford English Dictionary, Third Online Edition.

7. Sarah Stickney Ellis, "A Voice from the Vintage," in *Guide to Social Happiness* (New York: E. Walker, 1850), 145.

8. For an analysis that distinguishes between the non-profit, decentered fellowship of twelve-step philosophy and the celebrity- and expert-driven discourse of the recovery movement, see Helen Keane, *What's Wrong with Addiction?* (New York: New York University Press, 2002), 160. For critiques of the recovery movement, see David Forbes, *False Fixes: The Cultural Politics of Drugs, Alcohol, and Addictive Relations* (Albany: State University of New York Press, 1994), esp. ch. 8; and Helena Michie and Robyn Warhol, "Twelve-Step Teleology: Narratives of Recovery/Recovery as Narrative," in *Getting a Life: Everyday Uses of Autobiography*, ed.

Sidonie Smith and Julia Watson (Minneapolis: University of Minnesota Press, 1996), 327–50.

9. Eve Kosofsky Sedgwick, *Tendencies* (Durham: Duke University Press, 1993), 130.

10. The overwhelming historical and cultural-studies consensus is that addiction is a side effect of modernity. Richard Davenport-Hines assesses opium use in ancient Egypt, Greece, and Rome, but like most other drug historians, dates the emergence of addiction to the eighteenth and nineteenth centuries. See Davenport-Hines, *The Pursuit of Oblivion: A Global History of Narcotics* (New York: W. W. Norton, 2002), 30–32. The immense and detailed research of Virginia Berridge also establishes the modernity of addiction; see especially "Dependence: Historical Concepts and Constructs," in *The Nature of Drug Dependence*, Society for the Study of Addiction, Monograph No. 1, ed. Griffith Edwards and Malcolm Lader (Oxford: Oxford University Press, 1990), 1–18; "The Society for the Study of Addiction, 1884–1988," special issue, *British Journal of Addiction* 85 (1990); and, with Griffith Edwards, *Opium and the People: Opiate Use and Drug Control Policy in Nineteenth and Early Twentieth Century England*, rev. ed. (London: Free Association Books, 1999). See also Alina Clej, *A Genealogy of the Modern Self: Thomas De Quincey and the Intoxication of Writing* (Stanford: Stanford University Press, 1995); David Courtwright, *Forces of Habit: Drugs and the Making of the Modern World* (Cambridge: Harvard University Press, 2001); Geoffrey Harding, *Opiate Addiction, Morality and Medicine: From Moral Illness to Pathological Disease* (New York: St. Martin's Press, 1988); Barry Milligan, *Pleasures and Pains: Opium and the Orient in Nineteenth-Century British Culture* (Charlottesville: University Press of Virginia, 1995); Terry Parssinen, *Secret Passions, Secret Remedies: Narcotic Drugs in British Society, 1820–1930* (Manchester: Manchester University Press, 1983); Dolores Peters, "The British Medical Response to Opiate Addiction in the Nineteenth Century," *Journal of the History of Medicine* 36:4 (October 1981): 455–88; Sedgwick, "Epidemics of the Will," in *Tendencies*, 130–42; Maria Valverde, *Diseases of the Will: Alcohol and the Dilemmas of Freedom* (Cambridge: Cambridge University Press, 1998); and, most recently, Timothy Hickman, *The Secret Leprosy of Modern Days: Narcotic Addiction and Cultural Crisis in the United States, 1870–1940* (Amherst: University of Massachusetts Press, 2007). For insightful analyses that find addiction or aspects of addiction in earlier periods, see Jessica Warner, "Before There Was Alcoholism: Lessons from the Medieval Experience with Alcohol," *Contemporary Drug Problems* 19:3 (Fall 1992): 409–29; idem, "'Resolv'd to Drink No More': Addiction as a Preindustrial Construct," *Journal of Studies on Alcohol* 55:6 (November 1994): 685–91; and Deborah Willis, "*Doctor Faustus* and the Early Modern Language of Addiction," *Placing Christopher Marlowe*, ed. Sara Munson Deats and Robert Logan (London: Ashgate, 2007).

11. Courtwright, *Forces of Habit*, 2. On spices, see Wolfgang Schivelbusch, *Tastes of Paradise: A Social History of Spices, Stimulants, and Intoxicants*, trans. David Jacobson (New York: Vintage, 1992); on sugar, see Sidney W. Mintz, *Sweetness and Power: The Place of Sugar in Modern History* (London: Penguin, 1985); on tobacco, see Jordan Goodman, *Tobacco in History: the Cultures of Dependence* (London: Routledge, 1993); on chocolate, see Sophie D. Coe and Michael D. Coe, *The True History of Chocolate* (London: Thames and Hudson, 1996); on coffee, see Mark Pendergrast,

Uncommon Grounds: The History of Coffee and How It Transformed Our World (New York: Basic Books, 1999); on tea, see Piya Chatterji, *A Time for Tea: Women, Labor, and Post/Colonial Politics on an Indian Plantation* (Durham: Duke University Press, 2001); on rum, see Ian Williams, *Rum: A Social and Sociable History of the Real Spirit of 1776* (New York: Nation Books, 2005).

12. On the relative acceptability of upper middle-class "luxurious" use of opium, see Louise Foxcroft, *The Making of Addiction* (London: Ashgate, 2007), 3, 32. Berridge and Edwards note that "self-medication was the most common reason for opiate use . . . at all levels of society, opium and laudanum were commonly and unself-consciously bought and used." Berridge and Edwards, *Opium and the People*, 49.

13. Foxcroft, *Making of Addiction*, 37. Standard analyses in this tradition include Jeanette Marks, *Genius and Disaster: Studies in Drugs and Genius* (New York: Adelphi Company, 1926), M. H. Abrams, *The Milk of Paradise: the Effect of Opium Visions on the Works of De Quincey, Crabbe, Francis Thompson, and Coleridge* (1928; repr., Folcroft, PA: Folcroft Press, 1969); Elisabeth Schneider, *Coleridge, Opium, and Kubla Kahn* (Chicago: Chicago University Press, 1958); Alethea Hayter, *Opium and the Romantic Imagination: Addiction and Creativity in De Quincey, Coleridge, Baudelaire, and Others*, rev. ed. (1968; Wellingborough: Crucible, 1988). An indispensable reference for the literature of addiction as well as of intoxication is Marcus Boon, *The Road of Excess: A History of Writers on Drugs* (Cambridge: Harvard University Press, 2002). Sadie Plant, *Writing on Drugs* (London: Picador, 1999), is also insightful.

14. The most detailed political history of the temperance and teetotal movements in Britain remains Brian Harrison, *Drink and the Victorians* (London: Faber and Faber, 1972). See also Lillian Lewis Shiman, *Crusade against Drink in Victorian England* (New York: St. Martin's Press, 1988). For historical analyses of temperance in the United States, see Joseph R. Gusfield, *Symbolic Crusade: Status Politics and the American Temperance Movement* (1963; repr., Urbana: University of Illinois, 1986); Ian R. Tyrrell, *Sobering Up: From Temperance to Prohibition in Antebellum America, 1800–1860* (Westport, CT: Greenwood Press, 1979); and Ronald G. Walters, *American Reformers, 1815–1860* (New York: Hill and Wang, 1978), ch. 6. For more recent scholarship, see Michael Warner, "Whitman Drunk," in his *Publics and Counterpublics* (New York: Zone, 2002); Elaine Frantz Parsons, *Manhood Lost: Fallen Drunkards and Redeeming Women in the Nineteenth-Century United States* (Baltimore: Johns Hopkins University Press, 2003); David S. Reynolds and Debra J. Rosenthal, eds., *The Serpent in the Cup: Temperance in American Literature* (Amherst: University of Massachusetts Press, 1997); Carol Mattingly, *Well-Tempered Women: Nineteenth-Century Temperance Rhetoric* (Carbondale: Southern Illinois University Press, 1998); Gretchen Murphy, "Enslaved Bodies: Figurative Slavery in the Temperance Fiction of Harriet Beecher Stowe and Walt Whitman," *Genre* 28 (Spring/Summer 1995): 95–118; and Amanda Claybaugh, *The Novel of Purpose:Literature and Social Reform in the Anglo-American World* (Ithaca: Cornell University Press, 2007), chs. 3 and 4.

15. See Anna Alexander and Mark S. Roberts, eds., *High Culture: Reflections on Addiction and Modernity* (Albany: State University of New York Press, 2003).

16. The standard history on opium and hypodermic morphine remains Berridge and Edwards, *Opium and the People*; other works include David Courtwright,

Dark Paradise: A History of Opiate Addiction in America (Cambridge: Harvard University Press, 1982); Peters, "British Medical Response"; Harding, *Opiate Addiction*; Davenport-Hines, *Pursuit of Oblivion*; Hickman, *Secret Leprosy*; Foxcroft, *Making of Addiction*; and Caroline Acker, *Creating the American Junkie* (Baltimore: Johns Hopkins University Press, 2002). For an account of the history of addiction that makes alcohol central, see Valverde, *Diseases of the Will*.

17. For more on the Society for the Study and Cure of Inebriety, the British professional medical organization devoted to studying addiction founded by, among others, George Harley in 1884, see Berridge, "Society"; the unpublished proceedings of the Society are housed in the Royal Society of Medicine library. The American Society for the Study and Cure of Inebriety, founded by Thomas D. Crothers in 1874, published *The Quarterly Journal of Inebriety* from 1876 to 1906.

18. Several historians point to the origin of the disease model in Thomas Trotter's *Essay, Medical, Philosophical, and Chemical, on Drunkenness* (1804), well before it really began to gather consensus. Roy Porter, noting that precursors such as Bernard Mandeville and George Cheyne had made similar claims, nonetheless cautions against an earlier dating, because the term still connoted "disorder or distemper," rather than "a distinct ontological entity." See introduction to Thomas Trotter, *An Essay, Medical, Philosophical, and Chemical on Drunkenness and Its Effects on the Human Body*, ed Roy Porter, Tavistock Classics in the History of Psychiatry (London: Routledge, 1988), ix–xl: xxiii–xiv.

19. Berridge, "Society," 1018. For the mid-twentieth century revival of the disease model, see E. M. Jellinek, *The Disease Concept of Alcoholism* (New Haven: Hillhouse Press, 1960).

20. See Davenport-Hines, *Pursuit of Oblivion*, chapter 8.

21. Several critics have observed similarities between aspects of the nineteenth and twentieth centuries of the history of addiction, including Harry Gene Levine, "The Discovery of Addiction: Changing Conceptions of Habitual Drunkenness in America," *Journal of Studies on Alcohol* 39:1 (1978): 166; Katherine A. Chavigny, "Reforming Drunkards in Nineteenth-Century America: Religion, Medicine, Therapy," in *Altering American Consciousness: The History of Alcohol and Drug Use in the United States, 1800–2000*, ed. Sarah W. Tracy and Caroline Jean Acker (Amherst: University of Massachusetts Press, 2004), 118–19; and Robyn Warhol, "The Rhetoric of Addiction: From Victorian Novels to AA," in *High Anxieties: Cultural Studies in Addiction*, ed. Janet Farrell Brodie and Marc Redfield (Berkeley: University of California Press, 2002), 108.

22. Oxford English Dictionary, Third online edition.

23. See 1 Corinthians 6: 9–13.

24. Levine, "The Discovery of Addiction," 148. For an important corrective to Levine's conflation of "addiction" with "the disease model," see Hickman, *Secret Leprosy*, 7–9. On the history and politics of the term *addiction* and its analogues, see William L. White, "The Lessons of Language: Historical Perspectives on the Rhetoric of Addiction," in Tracy and Acker, *Altering American Consciousness: The History of Alcohol and Drug Use in the United States, 1800–2000*, 33–60.

25. Charles Lamb, "Confessions of a Drunkard," in *Some Enquiries into the Effects of Fermented Liquors. By a Water Drinker* (London: J. Johnson & Co., 1814), 209.

26. William Wordsworth, "Advertisement to *Lyrical Ballads*," *Selected Poems and Prefaces*, ed. Jack Stillinger (Boston: Houghton Mifflin, 1965), 447–48.

27. David Lloyd and Paul Thomas, *Culture and the State* (New York: Routledge, 1998), 7.

28. In his discussion of the "ideo motor," a reverie in which the intellect was heightened and the will dormant, Carpenter contended that "the automatic action follows the same course of the habitual lines of Thought"; far from a mere mental aberration, this process was foundational to the subject's material existence. See See William B. Carpenter, *Principles of Human Physiology* (1839; repr., London: Churchill, 1876), 338–46.

29. William James, *Habit* (New York: Henry Holt, 1890), 51.

30. Athena Vrettos, "Defining Habits: Dickens and the Psychology of Repetition," *Victorian Studies* 42 (Spring 1999/2000), 400.

31. Charles Darwin, *The Descent of Man*, ed. James Moore and Adrian Desmond (1871; London: Penguin, 2004), 119. Darwin also made habit central to the formation of emotions in *The Expression of Emotions in Man and Animals* (1872; Chicago: University of Chicago Press, 1965), ch. 1. For a different analysis associating habit to Lamarckism, see Gillian Beer, *Darwin's Plots: Evolutionary Narrative in Darwin, George Eliot, and Nineteenth-Century Fiction* (1983; repr., Cambridge: Cambridge University Press, 2000), 20.

32. See Walter Pater, *Studies in the History of the Renaissance* (1873; repr., New York: Oxford University Press, 1986), 152.

33. Peters, "British Medical Response," 464.

34. For a discussion of habit in the context of the transformation from acts to identities and sovereignty to normalization, and with respect to pragmatist philosophy, see Valverde, *Diseases of the Will*, 137–42; for habit as an "otherwise" to addiction, see Sedgwick, "Epidemics of the Will," 138–40.

35. Alfred, Lord Tennyson, "The Lotos-Eaters," *Alfred Lord Tennyson: Selected Poems*, ed. Aidan Day (London: Penguin, 1991), 62.

36. Indeed, even that quintessentially American organization, Alcoholics Anonymous, was inspired by an English evangelical organization, The Oxford Group. For more on the history of A.A., see Susan Chever, *My Name Is Bill: Bill Wilson—His Life and the Creation of Alcoholics Anonymous* (New York: Simon and Schuster, 2004).

37. See Claybaugh, *Novel of Purpose*.

38. Paul Gilroy, *The Black Atlantic: Modernity and Double Consciousness* (Cambridge: Harvard University Press, 1993), 49.

39. Gilroy, *Black Atlantic*, 55.

40. For broader discussions of citizenship, embodiment, and the public sphere that have informed this argument, see Warner, *Publics and Counterpublics*; idem, "The Mass Public and the Mass Subject," in *Habermas and the Public Sphere*, ed. Craig Calhoun (Cambridge, MA: MIT Press, 1992), 377–401; Lauren Berlant, *The Queen of America Goes to Washington City: Essays on Sex and Citizenship* (Durham: Duke University Press, 1997); and Russ Castronovo, *Necro-Citizenship: Death, Eroticism, and the Public Sphere in the Nineteenth-Century United States* (Durham: Duke University Press, 2001).

41. Castronovo, *Necro-Citizenship*, 69.

42. For more on the British Pharmacy Act of 1868, which attempted to regulate opium and opiates but amounted to a labeling restriction, see Berridge and Edwards, *Opium and the People*, 120; for the difficulties attending drug and alcohol restrictions in the U.S. before the reform movements of the 1890s, see H. Wayne Morgan, *Drugs in America: A Social History, 1800–1980* (Syracuse: Syracuse University Press, 1981), ch. 6.

43. For more on Ireland as a locus of addiction and countermodernity, see David Lloyd, "Counterparts: *Dubliners*, Masculinity, and Temperance Nationalism," in *Future Crossings: Literature between Philosophy and Cultural Studies*, ed. Ziarek Krzysztof and Seamus Deane (Evanston, IL: Northwestern University Press, 2000), 193–220; for other critically ignored commonwealth texts about addiction, see Marcus Clarke, "Cannabis Indica," in *Michael Wilding*, ed. Marcus Clarke (Queensland: University of Queensland Press, 1976), 541–55; and Maud Diver, *The Great Amulet* (New York: John Lane, 1908).

44. Sedgwick, "Epidemics of the Will," 132.

45. William S. Burroughs, *Naked Lunch: The Restored Text*, ed. James Grauerholz and Barry Miles (New York: Grove, 2001), 214.

46. Edward Levinstein, *Morbid Craving for Morphia* (1878), Addiction in America: Drug Abuse and Alcoholism (New York: Arno Press, 1981), 10.

47. Carsten Holthouse, "Critical Remarks and Suggestions on Inebriety and Its Treatment," *Proceedings of the Society for the Study and Cure of Inebriety* 12 (November 1885): 12.

48. *Hansard's Parliamentary Debates*, 3rd series, vol. 245, "House of Lords–Habitual Drunkards' Bill," 8 May 1879, col. 1947–48.

49. Berridge, "Society," 1017–18.

50. The late nineteenth-century disease model also displaced the older, Brunonian model of stimulation and sedation, and furnished a basis for theorizing habit. See Peters, "British Medical Response," 487.

51. Susan Sontag, *Illness as Metaphor* (New York: Farrar, Straus and Giroux, 1978), 58.

52. Keane, *What's Wrong with Addiction?* 8.

53. On the failure of contemporary discourse on addiction to address underlying political issues, and the withdrawal of self-help groups from the public sphere, see Forbes, *False Fixes*, 20; and Valverde, *Diseases of the Will*, 204.

54. As another example, the largely U.S. metaphor of alcohol as a "King," "Prince," or "tyrant" spoke to a late-eighteenth-century moment of national democratic self-formation that continued to resonate through the nineteenth century, but with decreasing urgency. The renunciation of tea, as T. H. Breen has reminded us, also played a central role in helping Americans imagine democratic nationhood as "private consumer experiences were transformed into public rituals." T. H. Breen, " 'Baubles of Britain': The American and Consumer Revolutions of the Eighteenth Century," *Past and Present* 119 (May 1988): 104.

55. On the reverence for the recovering addict's self-statement, see Keane, *What's Wrong with Addiction?* 67.

56. In Foucault's description of *countermodernity*, "the high value of the present is indissociable from a desperate eagerness to imagine it, to imagine it otherwise

than it is, and to transform it not by destroying it but by grasping it in what it is. . . . It is an exercise in which extreme attention to what is real is confronted with the practice of a liberty that simultaneously respects this reality and violates it." Michel Foucault, "What Is Enlightenment?" *Ethics: Subjectivity and Truth: Essential Works of Foucault, 1954–1984*, vol. 1, ed. Paul Rabinow (New York: New Press, 1997), 311.

57. See David Amigoni, "Introduction: Victorian Life Writing: Genres, Print, Constituencies" in *Life-Writing and Victorian Culture* (Aldershot: Ashgate, 2006), 2.

58. Ian Baucom, "Introduction: Atlantic Genealogies," *South Atlantic Quarterly* 100:1 (Winter 2001): 3.

59. Roland Barthes, "Toward a Psychosociology of Contemporary Food Consumption," in *European Diet from Pre-Industrial to Modern Times*, ed. Elborg Forster and Robert Forster (New York: Harper and Row, 1975), 48.

60. "Sensation Novels," *Quarterly Review* 113 (1863): 483.

61. For a very good account of addiction in terms of Kantian sublimity and French aesthetics, see Richard Klein, *Cigarettes Are Sublime* (Durham: Duke University Press, 1993).

62. The best (and broadest) social history is Morgan, *Drugs in America*. See also Rorabaugh, *Alcoholic Republic*; Eric Burns, *The Spirits of America: A Social History of Alcohol* (Philadelphia: Temple University Press, 2004); Brian Spiller, *Victorian Public Houses* (London: David and Charles, 1972); and John Watney, *Mother's Ruin: A History of Gin* (London: Owen, 1976). Other useful sources of primary material include Morgan, *Yesterday's Addicts: American Society and Drug Abuse, 1865–1920* (Norman: University of Oklahoma Press, 1974); and John Strasbaugh and Donald Blaise, eds., *The Drug User: Documents, 1840–1960* (New York: Blast, 1991).

63. While Marx's discussion of commodity fetishism is certainly relevant to the habitual consumption of drugs, it cannot explain the important differences between addiction and other modes of consumption; Marx merely describes them all as illusions produced by the same false consciousness: "the nature of these needs, whether they arise, for example, from the stomach, or the imagination, makes no difference." See Karl Marx, *Capital: A Critique of Political Economy*, vol. 1, trans. Ben Fowkes (1867; trans. London: Penguin, 1990), 125. For Marx's most famous metaphorical invocation of addiction—that religion is "the opium of the people"—see "Critique of Hegel's Philosophy of Right," www.marxists.org/archive/marx/works/1843/critique-hpr/intro.htm, accessed 16 January 2008. For Freud's view, that addictions substitute for and replace masturbation, see Sigmund Freud, letter to Wilhelm Fleiss, 22 December 1897, in *The Complete Letters of Sigmund Freud to Wilhelm Fliess, 1887–1904*, trans. and ed. Jeffrey Moussaieff Masson (Cambridge: Belknap, 1985), 287. In general, clinical psychoanalysis embeds addiction in a heteronormative framework of psychosexual development divorced from cultural materiality; it tends to reduce addiction to a generalized notion of individualized compulsion in which the underlying disorder could manifest as a variety of symptoms. See Lance Dodes, "Compulsion and Addiction," *Journal of the American Psychoanalytic Association* 44:3 (1994): 821; and Brian Johnson, "Psychoanalysis of a Man with Active Alcoholism," *Journal of Substance Abuse Treatment* 9 (1992): 113.

64. For a survey of recent approaches to these growing fields, see Roddey Reid and Sharon Traweek, eds., *Doing Science + Culture: How Cultural and Interdisciplinary Studies Are Changing the Way We Look at Science and Medicine* (New York: Routledge, 2000).

65. David Lenson, *On Drugs* (Minneapolis: University of Minnesota Press, 1995), xvii. For another polemic against present-day U.S. drug policy and for an embrace of drugs, see Lawrence Driscoll, *Reconsidering Drugs: Mapping Victorian and Modern Drug Discourses* (New York: Palgrave, 2000), 10.

66. Jacques Derrida, "The Rhetoric of Drugs," in Alexander and Roberts, *High Culture*, 19–43.

67. Michel Foucault, "Nietzsche, Genealogy, History," in *Language, Counter-Memory, Practice: Selected Essays and Interviews*, ed. Donald F. Bouchard (Ithaca: Cornell University Press, 1977), 140.

68. Fernand Braudel, *On History* (1969; trans. Chicago: University of Chicago Press, 1980), 4.

69. Richard Spruce, "Some Remarkable Narcotics of the Amazon Valley," *Ocean Highways* 55:1 (August 1873): 184–91. For a somewhat valedictory account of his and others' botanical imperialism, see Peter Raby, *Bright Paradise: Victorian Scientific Travellers* (Princeton: Princeton University Press, 1992), chs. 3, 4. For both the native and imperial discourses on *ayahuasca*, see Luis Eduardo Luna and Steven F. White, eds., *The Ayahuasca Reader: Encounters with the Amazon's Sacred Vine* (Santa Fe: Synergetic Press, 2000).

70. Oxford English Dictionary, Third Online Edition.

71. Neil McKendrick, John Brewer, and J. H. Plumb, *The Birth of a Consumer Society: The Commercialization of Eighteenth-Century England* (London: Europa Publications, 1982), 9; and John Brewer, " 'The Most Polite Age and the Most Vicious': Attitudes toward Culture as a Commodity, 1660–1800," *The Consumption of Culture, 1600–1800: Image, Object, Text*, ed. Ann Bermingham and John Brewer (London: Routledge, 1995), 350.

72. Charlotte Sussman sketches Britain's increasing anxiety about its accumulation and consumption of colonial goods in telling language: "As the century wore on, the riches of the New World were increasingly perceived as less an accessible cornucopia than a dangerous addiction." Sussman, *Consuming Anxieties: Consumer Protest, Gender, and British Slavery, 1713–1833* (Stanford: Stanford University Press, 2000), 13.

73. James Dana, "The African slave trade. A discourse delivered in the city of New-Haven, September 9, 1790, before the Connecticut Society for the Promotion of Freedom," (New Haven: Thomas and Samuel Green, 1791), 7. Available through Early American Imprints, 1st series; accessed 20 December 2006.

74. For a succinct account of alcohol's instrumentality to the slave trade, see Eric Williams, *Capitalism and Slavery* (1944; repr., London: André Deutsch, 1964), 78–81. On the general overlap of temperance and abolition, see Brian Harrison, *Drink and the Victorians*, 94; and Gusfield, *Symbolic Crusade*, 54. On African-American temperance movements, see Donald Yacovone, "The Transformation of the Black Temperance Movement, 1827–1854: An Interpretation," *Journal of the Early Republic* 8:3 (Autumn 1988): 281–97; Benjamin Quarles, *Black Abolitionists*

(New York: Oxford University Press, 1969), ch. 5; Denise Herd, " 'We Cannot Stagger to Freedom': A History of Blacks and Alcohol in American Politics" in *Yearbook of Substance Use and Abuse*, ed. Leon Brill and Charles Winick (New York: Human Sciences Press, 1985), 3:141–86; idem. "The Paradox of Temperance: Blacks and the Alcohol Question in Nineteenth-Century America," in *Drinking: Behavior and Belief in Modern History*, ed. Susanna Barrows and Robin Room (Berkeley: University of California Press, 1991), 354–75; and James Morone, *Hellfire Nation: The Politics of Sin in American History* (New Haven: Yale University Press, 2003), 297.

75. On the temperance plot, see Herbert Ross Brown, *The Sentimental Novel in America, 1789–1860*, vol. 2 (Durham: Duke University Press, 1940), ch. 2; and Parsons, *Manhood Lost*, 26–29. For an accessible collection of rare temperance autobiographical writings, see John W. Crowley's *Drunkard's Progress: Narratives of Addiction, Despair, and Recovery* (Baltimore: Johns Hopkins University Press, 1999). For an amusing diatribe on the temperance plot, see Edmund Pearson, *Queer Books* (New York: Doubleday, 1928). Not much has been written on British temperance fiction.

76. Coke Richardson, "Horace Saltoun," *The Cornhill Magazine* (1861), 233.

77. Quoted in Morgan, *Drugs in America*, 34.

78. Horace B. Day, et al. *The Opium Habit, With Suggestions as to the Remedy* (New York: Harper & Brothers, 1868), 239.

79. William Rosser Cobbe. *Doctor Judas: A Portrayal of the Opium Habit* (Chicago: S. C. Griggs and Company, 1895), 125–26. A contemporary commentator, Gleadell, concurs: "For the Oriental opium-smoker, however, there is always hope of reclamation, but when once the white man is seized with the opium-hunger he is irredeemably lost, and his degradation becomes infinitely more pitiful and complete than that of the most abject 'Celestial.' " W. H. Gleadell, "Night Scenes in Chinatown, San Francisco," *The Gentleman's Magazine* 278 (January–June 1895): 584.

80. Hickman, *Secret Leprosy*, 66–72.

81. A famous similar phenomenon of enthusiastic support followed by repudiation of a drug as habit-forming took place with respect to Freud's early advocacy of cocaine, particularly as a cure for morphine addiction, in the 1880s. See Sigmund Freud, *Cocaine Papers*, ed. Robert Byck (New York: New American Library, 1974).

82. For a fuller description of modern or "Paris" medicine, see Michel Foucault, *The Birth of the Clinic: An Archaeology of Medical Perception*, trans. A. Sheridan Smith (1963; repr., New York: Vintage, 1994), 35. See also Ivan Waddington, "The Role of the Hospital in the Development of Modern Medicine: A Sociological Analysis," *Sociology* 7 (1973): 211–24; Norman Jewson, "The Disappearance of the Sick-Man From Medical Cosmology, 1770–1870," *Sociology* 10 (1974): 369–85; and George Rosen, *From Medical Police to Social Medicine: Essays on the History of Health Care* (New York: Science History Publications, 1974). For an interesting argument on behalf of self-medication and against medical knowledge and its alliance with the modern state, see S. W. F. Holloway, "The Regulation of the Supply of Drugs in Britain before 1868," in *Drugs and Narcotics in History*, ed. Roy Porter and Mikulas Teich (Cambridge: Cambridge University Press, 1995), 77–96.

83. See Nancy Armstrong, *Desire and Domestic Fiction: A Political History of the Novel* (New York: Oxford University Press, 1987).

84. James Eli Adams, *Dandies and Desert Saints: Styles of Victorian Masculinity* (Ithaca: Cornell University Press, 1995), 9.

85. Habermas distinguishes male-dominated coffee houses from salons, which included women; see Jürgen Habermas, *The Structural Transformation of the Public Sphere: An Inquiry into a Cateogry of Bourgeois Society*, trans. Thomas Burger (Cambridge, MA: MIT Press, 1991), 33. See also For a study that asserts women's presence in coffee houses as proprietors, staff, and occasional guests, see Anthony Clayton, *London's Coffee Houses: A Stimulating Story* (London: Historical Publications, 2003), 98–100.

86. See "The Chloroform Habit," in Morgan, *Yesterday's Addicts*, 149.

87. Michel Foucault, *The History of Sexuality*, vol. 1, trans. Robert Hurley (1976; New York: Vintage, 1990), 138.

88. Giorgio Agamben, *Homo Sacer: Sovereign Power and Bare Life*, trans. Daniel Heller-Roazen (1995; Stanford: Stanford University Press, 1998), 8; emphasis in original.

89. See Giorgio Agamben, *State of Exception*, trans. Kevin Attell (Chicago: University of Chicago Press, 1995).

90. Eugenic policy on alcoholics and addicts varies in breadth and degree. In Britain, Caleb Saleeby's *Parenthood and Race Culture* (1909) advocated sterilizing alcoholics and addicts; in Indiana, habitual drunkards, along with the mentally challenged and people infected with sexual diseases, could not marry; and in Iowa in 1911, prison inmates who were addicts, sex offenders, or epileptics could be sterilized. See Daniel Kevles, *In the Name of Eugenics: Genetics and the Uses of Human Heredity* (1985; repr., Cambridge: Harvard University Press, 1998), 100. The most wide-ranging and intensive eugenic policies against addicts and alcoholics were enacted as part of the Third Reich's state management and Final Solution. See Hermann Fahrenkrug, "Alcohol and the State in Nazi Germany, 1933–1945," in Barrows and Room, *Drinking*, 315–34; and Robert Proctor, *Racial Hygiene: Medicine under the Nazis* (1988; Cambridge, MA: Harvard University Press, 2006), 202. For a more recent emergence of eugenics with respect to addiction in public discourse, see Daniel Costello, "Is CRACK Wack?" available at http://dir.salon.com/story/mwt/feature/2003/04/08/crack/index.html, accessed 30 October 2006.

91. Anonymous ("Remorse"), "The Slavery of Drink: To the Editor of the Daily Telegraph," *Daily Telegraph*, 24 August 1891, 3. Ellipses in original.

92. Other confessional texts from the same period commence in a similar fashion. See Anonymous, "Habitual Drunkenness," *The Westminster Review* 129 (May 1888): 600.

93. From "Despair" and "Resolution" (25 August), 3; and A. Brand and "Redeemed" (1 September 1891), 3.

94. "Cyclist," "The Slavery of Drink," (2 September), 3; "Prairie Oyster," "The Slavery of Drink," (4 September), 3; A. Dauglish, "The Slavery of Drink," (5 September), 3.

95. Conan Doyle, "The Slavery of Drink," (3 September). Doyle took a keen interest in the topic and was, along with H. G. Wells and G. R Sims, a member of the Society for the Study of Inebriety. See Berridge, "Society," 1005–6.

1. Pioneers of Inner Space

1. Fitz Hugh Ludlow, *The Hasheesh Eater* (1857), ed. Stephen Rachmann (New Brunswick, NJ: Rutgers University Press, 2006), 15; hereafter cited in the text as *HE*.

2. On De Quincey and the genre of autobiography, see Joshua Wilner, "Addiction and Autobiography: The Case of Thomas De Quincey," *Genre* 14 (1981): 493–503; Canon Schmidt, "Narrating National Addictions: De Quincey, Opium, and Tea," in *High Anxieties: Cultural Studies in Addiction*, ed. Janet Farrell Brodie and Marc Redfield (Berkeley: University of California Press, 2002), 63–84. On the broader context of personal narrative, see Ann Fabian, *The Unvarnished Truth: Personal Narratives in Nineteenth-Century America* (Berkeley: University of California Press, 2000). On twentieth-century autobiographies about drug and alcohol use, see Edmund B. O'Reilly, *Sobering Tales: Narratives of Alcoholism and Recovery* (Amherst: University of Massachusetts Press, 1997).

3. On the development of geography in the service of imperialism in nineteenth-century Britain and the United States, see Helena Michie and Ronald Thomas, "Introduction," *Nineteenth-Century Geographies: The Transformation of Space from the Victorian Age to the American Century* (New Brunswick: Rutgers University Press, 2003), 1–22. Bruno Latour's concept of "metrology" is also helpful; see Bruno Latour, *Science in Action: How to Follow Scientists and Engineers through Society* (Cambridge, MA: Harvard University Press, 1987), 215–57.

4. Myra Jehlen, *American Incarnation: The Individual, the Nation, and the Continent* (Cambridge, MA: Harvard University Press, 1986), 1.

5. Bayard Taylor, "The Vision of Hasheesh," *Putnam's Monthly Magazine*, April 1854, 404.

6. See, for example, Amy Kaplan, *The Anarchy of Empire in the Making of U.S. Culture* (Cambridge, MA: Harvard University Press, 2002); Amy Kaplan and Donald Pease, eds., *Cultures of United States Imperialism* (Durham: Duke University Press, 1993); and Robyn Wiegman and Donald E. Pease, eds., *The Futures of American Studies* (Durham: Duke University Press, 2002).

7. Spivak usefully reworks Martin Heidegger's notion of "worlding"; see Gayatri Chakravorty Spivak, "Three Women's Texts and a Critique of Imperialism," *Critical Inquiry* 12:1 (Autumn 1985): 243; and its update in *A Critique of Postcolonial Reason: Toward a History of the Vanishing Present* (Cambridge, MA: Harvard University Press, 1999), 112–97.

8. Jacques Derrida, "The Rhetoric of Drugs," in *High Culture: Reflections on Addiction and Modernity*, ed. Anna Alexander and Mark S. Roberts (Albany: State University of New York Press, 2003), 26.

9. The standard texts in this critical paradigm are John Barrell, *The Infection of Thomas De Quincey: A Psychopathology of Imperialism* (New Haven: Yale University Press, 1991); Nigel Leask, *British Romantic Writers and the East: Anxieties of Empire* (Cambridge: Cambridge University Press, 1992), pt. 3; Josephine McDonagh, *De Quincey's Disciplines* (Oxford: Clarendon, 1992); idem, "The Imperial Imagination," in *Reviewing Romanticism*, ed. Philip W. Martin and Robin Jarvis (New York: St. Martin's Press, 1992); and Barry Milligan, *Pleasures and Pains: Opium and the Orient*

in Nineteenth-Century British Culture (Charlottesville: University Press of Virgina, 1995).

10. De Quincey constantly refers to himself as eating opium, though he also describes measuring grains and drinking laudanum. For convenience and consistency, I refer to the object of his habituation as opium.

11. See Walter Colton, "Turkish Sketches: Effects of Opium," *The Knickerbocker*, April 1836; Bayard Taylor, "The Vision of Hasheesh," *Putnam's Monthly Magazine*, April 1854, 402–8; John Harrison Hughes, "The Autobiography of a Drug Fiend," *Medical Review of Reviews*, 1916, 27–43, 105–20, 173–90. For other drug autobiographical writing from 1820 to 1920, see Anonymous, *Advice to Opium Eaters* (London: W. R. Goodluck, 1823); Anonymous, *Opium-Eating: An Autobiographical Sketch by an Habituate* (Philadelphia: Claxton, Remsen, and Haffelfinger, 1876); Anonymous ("A Reformed Inebriate"), *Back from the Mouth of Hell; or, The Rescue from Drunkenness* (Hartford: American Publishing Company, 1878); Morris F. Baldwin, "The Panorama of a Life, and Experience in Associating and Battling with Opium and Alcoholic Stimulants" (1878), *American Perceptions of Drug Addiction: Five Studies, 1872–1912*, ed. Gerald N. Grob (New York: Arno, 1981); Anonymous, "The Chloroform Habit as Described by One of Its Victims," in *Yesterday's Addicts: American Society and Drug Abuse, 1865–1920* (1884–85), ed. H. Wayne Morgan (Norman: University of Oklahoma Press, 1974), 147–52; Anonymous ("An Habitual Drunkard"), "Habitual Drunkenness," *The Westminster Review* 129 (May 1888): 600–612; Anonymous, "Confessions of a Young Lady Laudanum Drinker," *Journal of Mental Sciences* (January 1889), 545–550; Henry H. Earle, *Confessions of an American Opium-Eater: From Bondage to Freedom* (Boston: James H. Earle, 1895); the autobiographical excerpts from the "Fuller diary" in Oscar Jennings, *The Morphia Habit and Its Voluntary Renunciation: A Personal Relation of Suppression after a Twenty-Five Years' Addiction* (London; Ballière, Tindall, and Cox, 1909); and Anonymous ("An Ex-Patient"), "The Psycho-Analysis of an Inebriate: A Record of Experiences and Reflections," *British Journal of Inebriety* 12 (1915): 22–27. For the concept of manifest destiny as cultural and literary logic rather than a specific set of events, see Wai Chee Dimock, *Empire for Liberty: Melville and the Poetics of Individualism* (Princeton: Princeton University Press, 1989), 10.

12. Amy Kaplan, *The Anarchy of Empire in the Making of U.S. Culture* (Cambridge, MA: Harvard University Press, 2002), 16.

13. For the concept of the contact zone, see Mary Louise Pratt, *Imperial Eyes: Travel Writing and Transculturation* (London: Routledge, 1992).

14. See Alexander and Roberts, *High Culture*. For addiction in the context of deconstructing class, taste, identity and subjectivity, see Regenia Gagnier, *The Insatiability of Human Wants: Economics and Aesthetics in Market Society* (Chicago: University of Chicago Press, 2000), 240–41.

15. Alina Clej, *A Genealogy of the Modern Self: Thomas De Quincey and the Intoxication of Writing* (Stanford: Stanford University Press, 1995).

16. See, for example, the essays in the Spring 2005 issue of *Studies in Romanticism*.

17. In a characteristic piece, James Bower Harrison, writing in *The Journal of Psychological Medicine* in 1854, attempts to reconcile Coleridge's and De Quincey's

accounts of opium use with more properly medical sources; see James Bower Harrison, "The Psychology of Opium Eating," (1854), reprinted in *Drug Dependence* 3 (March 1970): 27–38. On De Quincey's long relevance to Victorian medicine as both positive and negative example, see Barry Milligan, "Morphine-Addicted Doctors, the English Opium-Eater, and Embattled Medical Authority," *Victorian Literature and Culture* 33:2 (2005): 541–53. On De Quincey's presumed relevance to 1960s drug subcultures, see the 1968 and 1988 forewords to Alethea Hayter, *Opium and the Romantic Imagination: Addiction and Creativity in De Quincey, Coleridge, Baudelaire and Others* (Berkeley: University of California Press, 1968; rev. ed., Wellingborough: Crucible, 1988).

18. Another strand of De Quincey's imitations is formed by the anonymous comic parodies published in *Blackwood's Edinburgh Magazine*, two soon after the original publication of the *Confessions*, the other around the time of its revision. See "The Confessions of An English Glutton," *Blackwood's Edinburgh Magazine*, January 1823, 86–93; "Noctes Ambrosianae," *Blackwood's Edinburgh Magazine*, October 1823, 482–503; and "A Recent Confession of an Opium-Eater," *Blackwood's Edinburgh Magazine*, December 1856, 629–36.

19. Margaret Russett, *De Quincey's Romanticism: Canonical Minority and the Forms of Transmission*, Cambridge Studies in Romanticism, no. 25 (Cambridge: Cambridge University Press, 1997), 151.

20. Russett, *De Quincey's Romanticism*, 18.

21. Neither hashish nor opium is a hallucinogenic drug; whether De Quincey and Ludlow really hallucinated is undecidable. If their mental journeys are fictitious, a cultural explanation becomes even more appropriate.

22. Anonymous, *Opium-Eating*, vii.

23. William Rosser Cobbe, *Doctor Judas: A Portrayal of the Opium Habit* (Chicago: S. C. Griggs and Company, 1895), 108.

24. Twentieth-century British drug autobiographies are, by contrast, far less anxious about invoking De Quincey; some never even mention him. See, for example, James S. Lee, *The Underworld of the East: Being Eighteen Years' Actual Experiences of the Underworlds, Drug Haunts, and Jungles of India, China, and the Malay Archipelago* (1935; repr., London: Green Magic, 2000) and H. H. Robinson, *A Modern De Quincey: Autobiography of an Opium Addict* (1942; repr., Bangkok, Thailand: Orchid Press, 2004), 55.

25. Louis J. Bragman, "A Minor De Quincey." *Medical Journal and Record* 121 (January-June 1925), www.druglibrary.net/schaffer/hemp/history/bragman.htm, accessed 30 January 2006.

26. Thomas De Quincey, *The Confessions of an English Opium-Eater and Other Writings*, ed. Grevel Lindop (London: Oxford World's Classics, 1985), 51; hereafter cited in the text as *CEOE*.

27. On working-class use of opium, see Virginia Berridge and Griffith Edwards, *Opium and the People* (London: St. Martins, 1999), chs. 3, 4. Elizabeth Gaskell gives the working class anti-hero John Barton an opium addiction in *Mary Barton* (1848), perhaps to distinguish him slightly, after the influence of De Quincey.

28. Richard Burton, *The Anatomy of Melancholy*, ed. Holbrook Jackson (New York: New York Review of Books, 2001), II, 90.

29. Alexander Crichton, *An Inquiry into the Nature and Origin of Mental Derangement* (1798; repr., New York: AMS Press, 1976), 29–31.

30. Joseph Sheridan Le Fanu, "Green Tea," in *The Broadview Anthology of Victorian Short Stories*, ed. Dennis Denisoff (Ontario: Broadview, 2004), 249.

31. Le Fanu, "Green Tea," 263.

32. Brenda Mann Hammack, "Phantastica: The Chemically Inspired Intellectual in Occult Fiction," *Mosaic* 37:1 (March 2004): 83–99, available at http://lion.chadwyck.com/searchFulltext.do?id=R01710180&divLevel=0&area=abell&forward=critref_ft, accessed 5 July 2007.

33. On Victorian women's excessive reading see Kelly J. Mays, "The Disease of Reading and Victorian Periodicals," in *Literature in the Marketplace: Nineteenth-Century British Publishing and Reading Practices*, ed. John O. Jordan and Robert L. Patten (Cambridge: Cambridge University Press, 1995), 165–93. Two exceptions to this model replicate De Quinceyan hallucination; see Kate Chopin, "An Egyptian Cigarette" (1901), in *A Vocation and a Voice: Stories* ed. Emily Toth (London: Penguin, 1991), 67–71; and Mary C. Hungerford, "An Overdose of Hashish," in *Sisters of the Extreme: Women Writing on the Drug Experience*, ed. Cynthia Palmer and Michael Horowitz (Rochester, VT: Park Street Press, 2000), 62–65.

34. Russett, *De Quincey's Romanticism*, 18.

35. Louis Figuier, *The Races of Man* (London: Chapman and Hall, 1872), 366–67. For primary accounts of "running amuck" in British imperial documents, see Norman Chevers, *A Manual of Medical Jurisprudence for Bengal and the North-Western Provinces* (Calcutta: F. Carbery, Bengal Military Orphan Press, 1856); for histories contextualizing the topic, see John C. Spores, *Running Amok: An Historical Inquiry* (Athens: Ohio University Press, 1988); James H. Mills, *Madness, Cannabis, and Colonialism: The "Native Only" Lunatic Asylums of British India, 1857–1900* (Basingstoke: Macmillan, 2000); Margaret Shennan, *Out in the Midday Sun: The British in Malaya, 1880–1960* (London: John Murray, 2000); and Waltraud Ernst, *Mad Tales from the Raj: The European Insane in British India, 1800–1858* (New York: Routledge, 1991).

36. De Quincey, "Suspiria de Profundis," in *Confessions of an English Opium-Eater and Other Writings*, 131.

37. Leask, *British Romantic Writers*, 211.

38. D. W. Cheever, "Narcotics," *North American Review* 197 (October 1862): 375.

39. Arthur Conan Doyle, *The Sign of Four* (1890; repr., Letchworth: Broadview Press, 2001), 9. In keeping with his fulfillment of this model, Holmes frequently embodies the exotic, for example, in "The Man with the Twisted Lip." Holmes had a fictional cousin in the Decadent writer M. P. Shiel's Prince Zaleski, an aristocratic detective-Aesthete who smoked cannabis. See M. P. Shiel, *Prince Zaleski and Cummings King Monk* (1895; repr., Sauk City, WI: Arkham House Publishers, 1977), 5.

40. William Blair, "An Opium-Eater in America," *The Knickerbocker*, July 1842, 47–57; hereafter cited in the text as "OEA."

41. Friedrich A. Kittler, *Discourse Networks, 1800/1900*, trans. Michael Metteer with Chris Cullens (Stanford: Stanford University Press, 1990), 7–8.

42. Mark S. Roberts, "Addicts without Drugs: the Media Addiction," in Alexander and Roberts, *High Culture*, 346.

43. Clej, *Genealogy of the Modern Self*, 10.
44. McDonagh, "The Imperial Imagination," 127.
45. Dimock, *Empire for Liberty*, 8–9.
46. Donald P. Dulchinos, *Pioneer of Inner Space: The Life of Fitz Hugh Ludlow, Hasheesh Eater* (Brooklyn: Autonomedia, 1998), 90–96.
47. Charles Baudelaire, *Artificial Paradises* (1860; repr., New York: Citadel, 1996), 70; emphasis in original.
48. Baudelaire, *Artificial Paradises*, 74.
49. Sadie Plant, *Writing on Drugs* (New York: Picador, 1999), 49.
50. Richard Slotkin, *The Fatal Environment: The Myth of the Frontier in the Age of Industrialization, 1800–1890* (Norman: University of Oklahoma Press, 1985), 40.
51. Fitz Hugh Ludlow, *The Heart of the Continent: A Record of Travel across the Plains and in Oregon* (New York: Hurd and Houghton, 1870), 45; hereafter cited in the text as *HC*.
52. Slotkin, *Fatal Environment*, 221.
53. Another example of the related imagery of the American West and the Orient can be found in Whitman's "A Passage to India." Walt Whitman, *Leaves of Grass*, ed. Jerome Loving (Oxford: Oxford World's Classics, 1990), 315–23.
54. Milligan, *Pleasures and Pains*, 48.
55. It is worth noting that both the concept of the continental West as merely empty and Ludlow's model of it as the ruins of Oriental empires reinscribe the genocidal depopulation of the Native Americans who lived there. For the nineteenth-century view of the white dispossession of Native Americans, which was often represented as tragic self-abjection rather than either white commercial violence or military genocide, see Peter C. Mancall, " 'I Was Addicted to Drinking Rum': Four Centuries of Alcohol Consumption in Indian Country," *Altering American Consciousness: The History of Alcohol and Drug Use in the United States, 1800–1900*, ed. Sarah W. Tracy and Caroline Jean Acker (Amherst: University of Massachusetts Press, 2004), 97–98. For the emergence of hallucinogenic rituals in Native American cultures in the 1890s, see Robert C. Fuller, *Stairways to Heaven: Drugs in American Religious History* (Boulder: Westview Press, 2000), 38. For a nineteenth-century ethnographic description, see James Mooney, "The Peyote Plant and Ceremony," repr. in *The Drug User: Documents: 1840–1960*, ed. John Strausbaugh and Donald Blaise (New York: Blast, 1991), 173–77.
56. Ludlow appears not to have considered that readers might grow weary of extended descriptions of someone else's self-expansion. Boon, *The Road of Excess*, 153.
57. Slotkin, *Fatal Environment*, 38.
58. Dulchinos, *Pioneer of Inner Space*, 153.
59. Quoted in Dulchinos, *Pioneer of Inner Space*, 153.
60. Fitz Hugh Ludlow, "The Household Angel," *Harper's Bazaar*, 30 May–22 August 1868, and "What Shall They Do to Be Saved?" in *The Opium Habit, with Suggestions as to the Remedy*, ed. Horace B. Day (New York: Harper & Brothers, 1868).
61. H. H. Kane, "A Hashish House in New York" (1888), in Strausbaugh and Blaise, *The Drug User*, 171.
62. Kane, "A Hashish House," 165.

63. On the gendered, racial, and sexual transformations at the heart of opium den fiction, see Milligan, *Pleasures and Pains*, chs. 5, 6. See also Frank Norris, "The Third Circle" (1897), Blanchard Jerrold and Gustave Doré, *London: A Pilgrimage* (1868), Charles Dickens, *The Mystery of Edwin Drood* (1871), and Arthur Conan Doyle, "The Man with the Twisted Lip" (1891).

64. Anonymous ("No. 6606"), "A Modern Opium Eater: A Newspaper Man's Story of His Own Experiences with the Drug," *American Magazine*, June 1914, 33.

65. Caroline Jean Acker, *Creating the American Junkie: Addiction Research in the Classic Era of Narcotic Control* (Baltimore: Johns Hopkins University Press, 2002), 5–7.

66. Todd DePastino, *Citizen Hobo: How a Century of Homelessness Shaped America* (Chicago: University of Chicago Press, 2003), 128, 126.

67. On the critically renovated term "cosmopolitanism," see Pheng Cheah and Bruce Robbins, eds. *Cosmopolitics: Thinking and Feeling beyond the Nation* (Minneapolis: University of Minnesota Press, 1998).

68. Daniel Frederick MacMartin, *Thirty Years in Hell* (Topeka: Capper, 1921), 20; hereafter cited in the text as *TYH*.

69. Jack Black, *You Can't Win* (1926; repr., Edinburgh: AK Press/Nabat, 2000), 117; and Ben Reitman, *Sister of the Road: The Autobiography of Boxcar Bertha* (1937; repr., Edinburgh: AK Press/Nabat, 2002), 67–71.

70. Roberts Bartholow, *Manual of Hypodermic Medication* (Philadelphia: J. B. Lippincott, 1869), 18.

71. Celeste Langan, *Romantic Vagrancy: Wordsworth and the Simulation of Freedom* (Cambridge: Cambridge University Press, 1995), 12.

72. See, for example, Glenn Shirley, *West of Hell's Fringe: Crime, Criminals, and the Federal Peace Officer in Oklahoma Territory, 1889–1907* (Norman: University of Oklahoma Press, 1978).

73. Eve Kosofsky Sedgwick, "Epidemics of the Will," in *Tendencies* (Durham: Duke University Press, 1993), 133.

74. See John W. Crowley, *The White Logic: Alcoholism and Gender in American Modernist Fiction* (Amherst: University of Massachusetts Press, 1994).

75. William S. Burroughs, *Naked Lunch: The Restored Text*, ed. James Grauerholz and Barry Miles (New York: Grove, 2001), 11; see also Burroughs, *Junky* (1953; repr., New York: Penguin, 1977).

76. See Timothy Melley, *Empire of Conspiracy: The Culture of Paranoia in Postwar America* (Ithaca: Cornell University Press, 1995).

77. Boon, *Road of Excess*, 264–65.

78. Aldous Huxley, *The Doors of Perception and Heaven and Hell* (1954; repr., New York: HarperCollins Perennial Classic, 2004), 84–85.

79. Sidney Cohen, *The Beyond Within: The LSD Story*, 2nd ed. (New York: Atheneaum, 1970), xvii.

80. Alan Liu, "Local Transcendence: Cultural Criticism, Postmodernism, and the Romanticism of Detail," *Representations* 32 (Fall 1990): 76–77.

81. Baudelaire, *Artificial Paradises*, 76.

2. "Mankind Has Been Drunk"

1. For literary and historical analyses of the slavery metaphor of drink, see John W. Crowley, " 'Slaves to the Bottle': Gough's Autobiography and Douglass' Narrative," in *The Serpent in the Cup: Temperance in American Literature*, ed. David S. Reynolds and Debra J. Rosenthal (Amherst: University of Massachusetts Press, 1997): 115–35; Denise Herd, "The Paradox of Temperance: Blacks and the Alcohol Question in Nineteenth-Century America," in *Drinking: Behavior and Belief in Modern History*, ed. Susanna Barrows and Robin Room (Berkeley: University of California Press, 1991), 354–75; Gretchen Murphy, "Enslaved Bodies: Figurative Slavery in the Temperance Fiction of Harriet Beecher Stowe and Walt Whitman," *Genre* 28 (Spring/Summer 1995): 95–118; and Elaine Frantz Parsons, *Manhood Lost: Fallen Drunkards and Redeeming Women in the Nineteenth-Century United States* (Baltimore: Johns Hopkins University Press, 2003), 26–29. On the metaphor of self-enslavement with respect to the anti-masturbation movement, the public sphere, and white masculine embodiment, see Russ Castronovo, *Necro Citizenship: Death, Eroticism, and the Public Sphere in the Nineteenth-Century United States* (Durham: Duke University Press, 2001), ch. 2.

2. Catherine Sinclair, *Cross Purposes: A Novel* (London: Bentley, 1855), 237.

3. Michael Warner, *Publics and Counterpublics* (New York: Zone, 2002), 282. Generally speaking, the temperance movement advocated the moderate use of alcohol, and allowed medical uses of spirits and ecclesiastical uses of wine. The more radical "teetotal" movement prohibited all consumption of alcohol, and required its members to take a pledge. Historical convention typically conflates these movements by referring to them as "the temperance movement." I follow this tradition, marking out teetotalism where necessary.

4. William Cowper, "The Task" (1785), available at www.gutenberg.org/dirs/etext03/ttask10.txt, accessed 5 July 2007.

5. On Britain's moral self-justification of its global financial and military dominance by virtue of its having ended the slave trade, see David Turley, *The Culture of English Antislavery, 1780–1860* (London: Routledge, 1991), 46; and Audrey Fisch, *American Slaves in Victorian England: Abolitionist Politics in Popular Literature and Culture* (Cambridge: Cambridge University Press, 2000), 5.

6. Abraham Lincoln, "Address to the Washington Temperance Society of Springfield, Illinois," 22 February 1842; reprinted in *Abraham Lincoln: Speeches and Writings 1832–1858*, vol. 1 (New York: Library of America, 1989), 89. For the argument that the Temperance Address gave Lincoln the opportunity to venture the prospect of gradual abolition in a displaced context, see John Channing Briggs, *Lincoln's Speeches Reconsidered* (Baltimore: Johns Hopkins University Press, 2005), 59.

7. See Benezet, *The Potent Enemies of America Laid Open; being some account of the baneful effects attending the use of distilled spirituous liquors, and the slavery of the Negroes* (Philadelphia: Joseph Crukshank, 1774), available through Early American Imprints, series 1, no. 42675, accessed 6 July 2007; idem., *The mighty destroyer displayed, in some account of the dreadful havock made by the mistaken use as well as abuse of distilled spirituous liquors. By a lover of mankind* (Philadelphia: Joseph Crukshank, 1774),

Early American Imprints, series 1, no. 42555, accessed 6 July 2007; Benjamin Rush, *An enquiry into the effects of spirituous liquors upon the human body, and their influence upon the happiness of society* (Philadelphia: John McCulloch, 1791), Early American Imprints, series 1, no. 46277, accessed 6 July 2007. For Rush's centrality to temperance in the U.S., see Harry Gene Levine, "The Discovery of Addiction: Changing Conceptions of Habitual Drunkenness in America," *Journal of Studies on Alcohol* 39:1 (1978), 152. For the Quaker antislavery activist Sturge, R. T. Cadbury of the chocolate-making family, and radical temperance activist J. S. Buckingham, see Brian Harrison, *Drink and the Victorians* (London: Faber and Faber, 1971), 94, 110–13.

8. Lyman Beecher, *Six Sermons on the Nature, Occasions, Signs, Evils and Remedy of Intemperance* (New York: American Tract Society, 1827), 63.

9. "C.W." [Christopher Weedon?], "Rumselling and Pro-Slavery," *The Colored American*, 20 March 1841.

10. "Rochester Colored Total Abstinence Association," *The Colored American*, 4 December 1841. On the African(-American) temperance movement, see Benjamin Quarles, *Black Abolitionists* (New York: Oxford University Press, 1969), 92–100; Donald Yacovone, "The Transformation of the Black Temperance Movement, 1827–1854: An Interpretation," *Journal of the Early Republic* 8:3 (Autumn 1988), 281–97; Denise Herd, "We Cannot Stagger to Freedom: A History of Blacks and Alcohol in American Politics," in *Yearbook of Substance Use and Abuse*, ed. L. Brill and C. Winick (New York: Human Sciences Press, 1985), 3:141–86; idem, "The Paradox of Temperance: Blacks and the Alcohol Question in Nineteenth-Century America," in Barrows and Room, *Drinking*, 354–75.

11. Heman Humphrey, *Parallel between Intemperance and the Slave Trade* (Amherst, MA: J.S. & C. Adams, 1828), 20–21; hereafter cited in the text as *PI*.

12. Benjamin Parsons, "The Slavery of Strong Drink," *The Teetotal Times*, no. 3, May 1846, 18.

13. James Fitzjames Stephen, "The Opium 'Resolution,' " *The Nineteenth Century* 29, no. 172 (June 1891): 854–55.

14. W. J. Rorabaugh, *The Alcoholic Republic: An American Tradition* (Oxford: Oxford University Press, 1979), 214.

15. David Brion Davis, "Reflections on Abolitionism and Ideological Hegemony," in *The Antislavery Debate: Capitalism and Abolitionism as a Problem in Historical Interpretation*, ed. Thomas Bender (Berkeley: University of California Press, 1992), 173.

16. Frederick Douglass, *My Bondage and My Freedom* (1855) ed. John David Smith (London: Penguin, 2003), 302.

17. William Whipper, "Speech by William Whipper, Delivered before the Colored Temperance Society of Philadelphia," 8 January 1834, reprinted in *Black Abolitionist Papers*, vol. 3: *The United States, 1830–1846*, ed. Peter C. Ripley (Chapel Hill: University of North Carolina Press, 1991), 120; hereafter cited in the text as "SWW."

18. On the Negro Convention Movement and its transformation into the AMRS, see Howard Holman Bell, *A Survey of the Negro Convention Movement, 1830–1861* (New York: Arno, 1969); Julie Winch, *Philadelphia's Black Elite: Activism,*

Accommodation, and the Struggle for Autonomy, 1787–1848 (Philadelphia: Temple University Press, 1988); and Richard P. McCormick, "William Whipper: Moral Reformer," *Pennsylvania History* 43:1 (January 1976): 23–46.

19. Yacovone, "Transformation of the Black Temperance Movement," 285.

20. Quarles, *Black Abolitionists*, 97; Yacovone, "Transformation of the Black Temperance Movement," 284–85.

21. Associating this kind of argument with Frederick Douglass, Herd offers another perspective: "The values that Douglass and other black leaders promoted, which today seem accommodating and bourgeois, had at the time a concrete meaning that gave them a sense of genuine militancy. The idea that blacks should be educated, own property, run their own churches and institutions, stage protests against the government, and openly defy state laws was a bold affront to the slave system and indeed to the conventional social hierarchy in America." Herd, "Paradox of Temperance," 363.

22. This is not to claim that there are no instances of the metaphor's use among free northern blacks, but they are rare and the irony is obviously different. Whipper, for example, suggests that they must maintain sobriety in order to persuade white powers that African(-Americans) were fit to be emancipated. For accounts of the racial politics of African-American novelists' representation of temperance, see Shelley Block, "A Revolutionary Aim: The Rhetoric of Temperance in the Anglo-African Magazine," *American Periodicals* 12 (2002): 9–24; and Robert S. Levine, "Disturbing Boundaries: Temperance, Black Elevation, and Violence in Frank J. Webb's *The Garies and Their Friends*," *Prospects: An Annual of American Cultural Studies* 19 (1994): 349–74. For an insightful comparison of the slavery metaphor in Gough's and Douglass' autobiographies, see Crowley, "Slaves to the Bottle."

23. John K. Cornyn, *Dick Wilson, The Rum-Seller's Victim; or, Humanity Pleading for the Maine Law* (1853; repr., Ann Arbor: University of Michigan Library, 2005), 361, available at www.hti.umich.edu/cgi/t/text/textidx?c=moa;idno=ABF2585.0001.001, accessed 6 June 2006.

24. For an example of the way in which temperance could appear to elide chattel slavery in the name of moral reform or spiritual salvation, see John B. Gough, *Autobiography and Personal Recollections of John B. Gough* (1845; repr., Springfield, MA: Bill, Nichols & Co., 1870), 219.

25. On *Ten Nights*, see John W. Crowley, ed., *Drunkard's Progress: Narratives of Addiction, Despair, and Recovery* (Baltimore: Johns Hopkins University Press, 1999), 29; Herbert Ross Brown, *The Sentimental Novel in America, 1789–1860* (Durham: Duke University Press, 1940), 204; David S. Reynolds, "Black Cats and Delirium Tremens: Temperance and the American Renaissance," in *The Serpent in the Cup: Temperance in American Literature*, ed. David S. Reynolds and Debra J. Rosenthal (Amherst: University of Massachusetts Press, 1997), 31; and Barbara Cohen-Stratyner, "Platform Pearls: Or, 19th c. American Temperance Performance Texts," *Performing Arts Resources* 16 (1991): 72–73.

26. C. B. Macpherson, *The Political Theory of Possessive Individualism: Hobbes to Locke* (Oxford: Oxford University Press, 1962), 3.

27. Maurice S. Lee, *Slavery, Philosophy, and American Literature, 1830–1860* (Cambridge: Cambridge University Press, 2005), ch. 2.

28. Paul Gilroy, *The Black Atlantic: Modernity and Double Consciousness* (Cambridge: Harvard University Press, 1993), chs. 1, 2.

29. On the "consumer revolution," see Neil McKendrick, John Brewer, and J. H. Plumb, *The Birth of a Consumer Society: The Commercialization of Eighteenth-Century England* (London: Europa Publications, 1982); John Brewer, " 'The Most Polite Age and the Most Vicious': Attitudes toward Culture as a Commodity, 1660–1800," in *The Consumption of Culture, 1600–1800: Image, Object, Text*, ed. Ann Bermingham and John Brewer (London: Routledge, 1995), 341–61; Charlotte Sussman, *Consuming Anxieties: Consumer Protest, Gender, and British Slavery, 1713–1833* (Stanford: Stanford University Press, 2000); and Philip Gould, *Barbaric Traffic: Commerce and Antislavery in the Eighteenth-Century Atlantic World* (Cambridge, MA: Harvard University Press, 2003); hereafter cited in the text as *BT*.

30. On sugar, the consumable central to the Atlantic slave trade that connected the banal, everyday habits of the British laboring classes to the colonial and slave labor feeding them, see Sidney W. Mintz, *Sweetness and Power: The Place of Sugar in Modern History* (London: Penguin, 1985), 180.

31. John Wesley, *Letter to a Friend concerning Tea* (1748; repr., London: A. Macintosh, 1825), 10.

32. Quoted in Sussman, *Consuming Anxieties*, 28. For a creative analysis linking Hanway's essay to the "war on drugs" rhetoric of the 1980s and 1990s, see Marek Kohn, *Narcomania: On Heroin* (London: Faber and Faber, 1987), 16–23.

33. William Wilberforce, *A Letter on the Abolition of the Slave Trade Addressed to the Freeholders and Other Inhabitants of Yorkshire* (London: T. Cadell and W. Davis, 1807), 339.

34. Timothy Morton, "Blood Sugar," in *Romanticism and Colonialism: Writing and Empire, 1780–1830*, ed. Tim Fulford and Peter J. Kitson (Cambridge: Cambridge University Press, 1998), 87–106.

35. Samuel Taylor Coleridge, "A Lecture on the Slave Trade," *Lectures 1795: On Politics and Religion, Collected Works Samuel Taylor Coleridge*, vol. 1, ed. Lewis Patton and Peter Mann (London: Routledge and Kegan Paul, 1971); 247–48.

36. James Dana, *The African slave trade. A discourse delivered in the city of New-Haven, September 9, 1790, before the Connecticut Society for the Promotion of Freedom* (New Haven: Thomas and Samuel Green, 1791), 7. Available through Early American Imprints, 1st series, accessed 20 December 2006.

37. Dwight Theodore Weld, *American Slavery as It Is: Testimony of a Thousand Witnesses* (1839; New York: Arno Press, 1968), 132.

38. Thomas Clarkson, *An Essay on the Slavery and Commerce of the Human Species, Particularly the African* (1786; repr., Miami: Mnemosyne Publishing, 1969), 47.

39. Benezet, *Potent Enemies*, 12.

40. Clarkson, *Essay on the Slavery and Commerce*, 63.

41. John Newton, "Thoughts on the African Slave Trade" (1788), reprinted in *Slavery, Abolition and Emancipation: Writings in the British Romantic Period*, vol. 2: *The Abolition Debate*, ed. Peter J. Kitson (London: Pickering and Chatto, 1999), 86–87.

42. Charles Ambler, "Alcohol and the Slave Trade in West Africa, 1400–1850," in *Drugs, Labor, and Colonial Expansion*, ed. William Jankowiak and Daniel Bradburd (Tucson: University of Arizona Press, 2003), 73–88.

43. Quoted in Ambler, "Alcohol and the Slave Trade," 83.

44. Ignatius Sancho, "Letters of the Late Ignatius Sancho, an African" (1782), reprinted in *Slavery, Abolition and Emancipation: Writings in the British Romantic Period*, vol. 1: *Black Writers*, ed. Sukhdev Sandhu and David Dabydeen (London: Pickering and Chatto, 1999), 104.

45. Eric Williams, *Capitalism and Slavery* (1944; repr., London: André Deutsch, 1964), 78.

46. For an exemplary case analysis, see George Metcalf, "A Microcosm of Why Africans Sold Slaves: Akan Consumption Patterns in the 1770s," *Journal of African History* 28:3 (1987): 377–94.

47. See Anne C. Bailey, *African Voices of the Atlantic Slave Trade: Beyond the Silence and the Shame* (Boston: Beacon, 2005) ch. 3.

48. Quobna Ottobah Cugoano, *Thoughts and Sentiments on the Evil of Slavery* (1787), ed. Vincent Carretta (New York: Penguin, 1999), 26.

49. *Pennsylvania Gazette*, August 2, 1744.

50. Morton, "Blood Sugar," 102.

51. Rush, *Spiritous Liquors*, 3. "Dropsy" would likely be referred to today as edema, a symptom characterized by excessive swelling due to the collection of lymph, rather than its own disease.

52. Lee, *Slavery, Philosophy*, 77.

53. William L. Van Deburg, *Slavery and Race in American Popular Culture* (Madison: University of Wisconsin Press, 1984), 71.

54. Ronald Walters, "The Erotic South: Civilization and Sexuality in American Abolitionism," in *Abolitionism and American Reform Series*, vol. 4: *Abolitionism and Issues of Race and Gender*, ed. John R. McKivigan (New York: Garland, 1999), 360–61.

55. Rorabaugh, *Alcoholic Republic*, 135.

56. Yacovone, "Black Temperance," 290–91.

57. Frederick Douglass, *My Bondage and My Freedom*, 63.

58. C. L. Innes, *A History of Black and Asian Writing in Britain, 1700–2000* (Cambridge: Cambridge University Press, 2002), 95.

59. Francis Fedric, *Slave Life in Virginia and Kentucky; or, Fifty Years of Slave Life in the Southern States of America* (1863; repr., Chapel Hill: University of North Carolina, 1999), 41; electronic edition, "Documenting the American South" series, available at http://docsouth.unc.edu/neh/fedric/fedric.html, accessed 12 July 2007.

60. Fedric, *Slave Life*, 86.

61. William Craft, *Running a Thousand Miles for Freedom* (1860; repr., Baton Rouge: Louisiana State University Press, 1999), 13.

62. Craft, *Running*, 14.

63. Moses Grandy, *Narrative of the Life of Moses Grandy, Late a Slave in the United States of America*, reprinted in *North Carolina Slave Narratives: The Lives of Moses Roper, Lunsford Lane, Moses Grandy, & Thomas H. Jones*, ed. William L. Andrews (1843; Chapel Hill: University of North Carolina Press, 2003), 154–86.

64. Fitz Hugh Ludlow, "If Massa Put Guns into Our Han's," *Atlantic Monthly* 15 (April 1865): 510.

65. Orlando Patterson, *Slavery and Social Death: A Comparative Study* (Cambridge, MA: Harvard University Press, 1982), 336–37.

66. Ludlow, "If Massa Put Guns into Our Han's," 511. *Mania a potu* was a catchall term for apparently insane drunken violence, often referring to the shakings, hallucinations, and psychosis of delirium tremens, the term that superseded it.

67. Douglass, *My Bondage*, 73.

68. For example, Stowe used *tobacco* as a code word for alcohol in letters lamenting her son Frederick's dissipation under the influence of southern friends at Andover. See Joan D. Hedrick, *Harriet Beecher Stowe: A Life* (New York: Oxford University Press, 1994), 140.

69. Historians of slavery have tended not to disrupt the nineteenth-century temperance theory of slave masters' intemperance; for an exception, see Eugene D. Genovese, *Roll, Jordan, Roll: The World the Slaves Made* (1972; repr., New York: Vintage, 1976), 17.

70. Benjamin Franklin, *The Autobiography and Other Writings*, ed. Kenneth Silverman (London: Penguin, 2003), 82.

71. Big planters' attempts to restrict the sale of liquor by poorer whites to slaves may have made slave drunkenness appear to be a problem, but this had more to do with limiting slaves' opportunity for independent behavior than with curtailing actual drunkenness. Genovese, *Roll, Jordan, Roll*, 641–46.

72. Genovese, *Roll, Jordan, Roll*, 641–46; and Herd, "Paradox of Temperance," 355–56.

73. Fedric, for example, notes that in the 1820s and 30s, when many people still regarded alcohol as energy and nutrition, masters gave it to their slaves to enhance their productivity, though with the opposite effect. See Fedric, *Slave Life*, 47.

74. Fredrick Douglass, *Narrative of the Life of Frederick Douglass, an American Slave* (1845), ed. Houston A. Baker Jr. (New York: Penguin, 1982), 114.

75. Harriet Jacobs, *Incidents in the Life of a Slave Girl* (1861), ed. Jean Fagan Yellin (Cambridge, MA: Harvard University Press, 1987), 119.

76. Douglass, *Narrative*, 115–16.

77. Saidiya Hartman, *Scenes of Subjection: Terror, Slavery, and Self-Making in Nineteenth-Century America* (New York: Oxford University Press, 1997), 23.

78. Hartman, *Scenes*, 49.

79. Stowe's short temperance fiction includes "The Drunkard Reclaimed," "Let Every Man Mind His Own Business," "Only a Glass of Wine," and "The Coral Ring." For an analysis of the "slavery of drink" metaphor in Stowe's short temperance fiction, see Murphy, "Enslaved Bodies"; see also Cynthia S. Hamilton, "Dred: Intemperate Slavery," *Journal of American Studies* 34:2 (2000) 264; and Nicholas Warner, *The Spirits of America: Intoxication in Nineteenth-Century American Literature* (Norman: University of Oklahoma Press, 1997), 193–95.

80. See Hedrick, *Harriet Beecher Stowe*, 255, 382–83, 307–8.

81. Karen Halttunen, "Gothic Imagination and Social Reform: The Haunted Houses of Lyman Beecher, Henry Ward Beecher, and Harriet Beecher Stowe," in *New Essays on Uncle Tom's Cabin*, ed. Eric J. Sundquist (Cambridge: Cambridge University Press, 1986), 126.

82. Charles Edward Stowe and Lyman Beecher Stowe, *Harriet Beecher Stowe: The Story of Her Life* (Boston: Houghton Mifflin, 1911), 61–62.

83. Warner, *Spirits of America*, 191.

84. Halttunen, "Gothic Imagination"; Hortense J. Spillers, "Changing the – Letter: The Yokes, the Jokes of Discourse, or, Mrs. Stowe, Mr. Reed," in *Slavery and the Literary Imagination: Selected Papers from the English Institute, 1987*, new series 13, ed. Deborah McDowell and Arnold Rampersad (Baltimore: Johns Hopkins University Press, 1989), 25–61; Robyn Wiegman, *American Anatomies: Theorizing Race and Gender* (Durham: Duke University Press, 1995); Karen Sanchez-Eppler, *Touching Liberty: Abolition, Feminism, and the Politics of the Body* (Berkeley: University of California Press, 1993); Lauren Berlant, "Poor Eliza," *American Literature* 70:3 (September 1998): 635–68; Christina Zwarg, "Fathering and Blackface in *Uncle Tom's Cabin*," *Novel: A Forum on Fiction* 22:3 (Spring 1989): 274–87.

85. Harriet Beecher Stowe, *Uncle Tom's Cabin* (1852), ed. Elizabeth Ammons (New York: W. W. Norton, 1994), 297–98; hereafter cited in the text as *UTC*.

86. Harriet Beecher Stowe, *A Key to Uncle Tom's Cabin: Presenting the Original Facts and Documents upon which the Story is Founded Together with Corroborative Statements Verifying the Truth of the Work* (Boston: John P. Jewett & Co., 1853), 39, col. 2.

87. Charles Dickens, *Great Expectations* (1860), ed. David Trotter (London: Penguin, 2003), 348.

88. Warner, *Spirits of America*, 191–92; and Carol Mattingly, *Well-Tempered Women: Nineteenth-Century Temperance Rhetoric* (Carbondale: Southern Illinois University Press, 1998), 145.

89. Spillers, "Changing the Letter," 32.

90. The passage from Proverbs makes it clear that Tom is referring to St. Clare's habits of solitary drinking: "Look not thou upon the wine when it is red, when it giveth his colour in the cup, when it moveth itself aright. At the last it biteth like a serpent, and stingeth like an adder." Proverbs 23:31–32. Lyman Beecher had used the same Biblical reference to open the first two of his *Six Sermons on Intemperance* (1827).

91. Achille Mbembe, "Necropolitics," *Public Culture* 15:1 (Winter 2003): 21.

92. The cases *Harrison v. Berkeley* (1847) and *Skinner v. Hughes* (1850) are described in Parsons, *Manhood Lost*, 27; her source is Helen Tunnicliff Catterall, ed., *Judicial Cases Concerning American Slavery and the Negro*, 5 vols. (Washington, D.C.: Carnegie Institution, 1926–1937).

93. Parsons, *Manhood Lost*, 28.

94. Thurlow Weed Brown, *Minnie Hermon; or, The Curse of Rum* (1857; repr., New York: Henry S. Goodspeed, 1878), 105. See also Cornyn, *Dick Wilson*, 82.

95. Philip Fisher, *Hard Facts: Setting and Form in the American Novel* (New York: Oxford University Press, 1985), 120.

96. For a summary of the critical focus on Tom, see Samuel Otter, "Stowe and Race," in *The Cambridge Companion to Harriet Beecher Stowe*, ed. Cindy Weinstein (Cambridge: Cambridge University Press, 2004), 19; for a reading of his simultane-

ous deracialization and ascension to moral superiority, see Wiegman, *American Anatomies*, 198.

97. Harriet Beecher Stowe, *Dred: A Tale of the Great Dismal Swamp* (1856), ed. Robert S. Levine (Chapel Hill: University of North Carolina Press, 2000), 472.

98. Stowe, *Dred*, 195.

99. Harriet Beecher Stowe, *My Wife and I; or, Harry Henderson's Story* (New York: J. B. Ford, 1871), 314.

100. Frederick Douglass, *The Frederick Douglass Papers. Series One: Speeches, Debates, and Interviews*, vol. 1: *1841–46*, ed. John W. Blassingame (New Haven: Yale University Press, 1979), 58.

101. Lincoln, "Temperance Address," 89–90. For a nuanced reading of this speech, see Briggs, *Lincoln's Speeches Reconsidered*, 75.

102. Timothy Hickman, *The Secret Leprosy of Modern Days: Narcotic Addiction and Cultural Crisis in the United States, 1870–1940* (Amherst: University of Massachusetts Press, 2007), 23.

103. Walt Whitman, *Franklin Evans; or, The Inebriate: A Tale of the Times* (1842; repr., New York: Random House, 1929), 170.

104. On Douglass's travels to Ireland and Britain, see *Liberating Sojourn: Frederick Douglass and Transatlantic Reform*, ed. Alan J. Rice and Martin Crawford (Athens: University of Georgia Press, 1999). On Woodhouse and Benson, see Elizabeth Malcolm, *Ireland Sober, Ireland Free: Drink and Temperance in Nineteenth-Century Ireland* (Dublin: Gill and Macmillan, 1986), 162–63.

105. See Malcolm, *Ireland Sober, Ireland Free*, and Paul A. Townend, *Father Mathew, Temperance, and Irish Identity* (Dublin: Irish Academic Press, 2002).

106. George Bretherton, "Against the Flowing Tide: Whiskey and Temperance in the Making of Modern Ireland," in Barrows and Room, *Drinking*, 155.

107. David Lloyd, "*Dubliners*, Masculinity, and Temperance Nationalism," in *Future Crossings: Literature between Philosophy and Cultural Studies*, ed. Krysztof Ziarek and Seamus Deane (Evanston: Northwestern University Press, 2000), 200.

108. Lloyd, "*Dubliners*," 209.

3. Impostors of Freedom

1. Henry G. Cole, *Confessions of an American Opium Eater: From Bondage to Freedom* (Boston: James H. Earle, 1895), 136.

2. W. Xavier Sudduth, "The Psychology of Narcotism," *Journal of the American Medical Association*, 10 October 1896, 797. For other instances of the "slavery" metaphor in medical and psychological writings, see H. Gibbons, "Letheomania," *Pacific Medical and Surgical Journal* 3 (April 1870): 481–95; S. W. Caldwell, "Hypodermatic Medication," *Mississippi Valley Medical Monthly* 5 (February 1885): 60–63; and Leslie E. Keeley, *The Morphine Eater: From Bondage to Freedom* (Dwight, IL: C. L. Palmer & Co., 1881), 26.

3. Edward Payson Roe, *Without a Home* (1881; repr., New York: Dodd, Mead and Co., n.d.); hereafter cited in the text as *WH*.

4. Cole, *Confessions of an American Opium Eater*, 2.

5. Russ Castronovo, *Necro Citizenship: Death, Eroticism, and the Public Sphere in the Nineteenth-Century United States* (Durham: Duke University Press, 2001), 63.

6. David S. Reynolds, *Beneath the American Renaissance: The Subversive Imagination in the Age of Emerson and Melville* (New York: Knopf, 1988), 66–68.

7. I discuss MacMartin at length in chapter 1. See Daniel Frederick MacMartin, *Thirty Years in Hell* (Topeka, KS: Capper, 1921). See also "O.W.," *No Bed of Roses: The Diary of a Lost Soul* (New York: Gold Label Books, 1930).

8. See Fred V. Williams, *The Hop-Heads: Personal Experiences Among the Users of "Dope" in the San Francisco Underworld* (San Francisco: Walter N. Brunt, 1920); and Winifred Black, *Dope: The Story of the Living Dead* (New York: Star Company, 1928).

9. Karen Sánchez-Eppler, "Temperance in the Bed of a Child: Incest and Social Order in Nineteenth-Century America," in *The Serpent in the Cup: Temperance in American Literature*, ed. David S. Reynolds and Debra J. Rosenthal (Amherst: University of Massachusetts Press, 1997): 74.

10. On Roe's tenement visits, see Mary Roe, *E. P. Roe: Reminiscences of His Life*, vol. 18 of *The Works of E. P. Roe* (New York: P. F. Collier and Son, 1902), 465.

11. On Roe's life and career, see James D. Hart, *The Popular Book: A History of America's Literary Taste* (Berkeley: University of California Press, 1961), 121; Fred Lewis Pattee, *A History of American Literature since 1870* (New York: Cooper Square Publishers, 1968), 387–88; and Luther Mott, *Golden Multitudes: The Story of Best Sellers in the United States* (New York: Macmillan, 1947), 147–48.

12. Pattee, *History of American Literature*, 387.

13. Mott, *Golden Multitudes*, 148; Pattee, *History of American Literature*, 387–88.

14. The morphine addict Mrs. Henry Lafayette Dubose in Harper Lee's *To Kill a Mockingbird* (1960) is another late example.

15. Castronovo makes a similar point regarding what he sees as the nation's hyper-embodiment in white masculinity: "Somatic notions of power and its abuse offer substantial political dividends: the white body that is simultaneously enslaving and enslaved recasts the relation of master and slave so that it is neither a relation nor a dialectic. Slavery instead is an insular, privatized system based neither on 'consent' nor on national policy." Castronovo, *Necro Citizenship*, 96.

16. On the history of hypodermic medication, see Virginia Berridge and Griffith Edwards, *Opium and the People* (1981; repr., London: St. Martin's, 1999), 139–41; for a fuller account, see Norman Howard-Jones, "A Critical Study of the Origins and Early Development of Hypodermic Medication," *Journal of the History of Medicine* 2 (Spring 1947): 201–49. The most useful American primary sources are Roberts Bartholow, *Manual of Hypodermic Medication* (Philadelphia: J. B. Lippincott & Co., 1869); and Harry Hubbell Kane, *The Hypodermic Injection of Morphia: Its History, Advantages, and Dangers* (New York: Chas. L. Bermingham and Co., 1880).

17. Silas Weir Mitchell, *Wear and Tear; or, Hints for the Overworked* (1887; repr., New York: Arno, 1973), 28, 9.

18. George Beard, *American Nervousness: Its Causes and Consequences* (1881; repr., New York: Arno, 1972), vii.

19. Mitchell, *Wear and Tear*, 30.

20. Anonymous ("A Reformed Inebriate"), *Back From the Mouth of Hell; or, The Rescue from Drunkenness* (Hartford: American Publishing Company, 1878), 28–29.

21. Sudduth, "Psychology of Narcotism," 798.

22. T. D. Crothers, *The Disease of Inebriety from Alcohol, Opium, and Other Narcotic Drugs* (New York: E. B. Treat, 1893), 317.

23. D. M. Barr, "The Hypodermic Use of Morphia," *Medical and Surgical Reporter* 41 (15 November 1879): 426.

24. See Gibbons, "Letheomania," 481.

25. Gibbons, "Letheomania," 492–93.

26. Caldwell, "Hypodermatic Medication," 60–63.

27. For a systematic inventory and analysis of pathological lying in U.S. medical literature, see William H. Swatos Jr., "Opiate Addiction in the Late Nineteenth Century: A Study of the Social Problem, Using Medical Journals of the Period," *International Journal of the Addictions* 7:4 (1972): 746–47.

28. William Rosser Cobbe, *Doctor Judas* (Chicago: S. C. Griggs and Company, 1895), 48.

29. Keeley, *Morphine Eater*, 23.

30. Anonymous, *Opium-Eating*, 58–59.

31. Maria Weed, *A Voice in the Wilderness* (Chicago: Laird and Lee, 1895).

32. See Roy Porter, *The Greatest Benefit to Mankind: A Medical History of Humanity* (New York: W. W. Norton, 1999), 675.

33. In liberal-democratic society, "the individual is essentially the proprietor of his own person and capacities, for which he owes nothing to society." See C. B. Macpherson, *The Political Theory of Possessive Individualism: Hobbes to Locke* (Oxford: Oxford University Press, 1962), 263.

34. C. H. Hughes, "The Opium Psycho-Neurosis: Chronic Meconism or Papaverism," *Alienist and Neurologist*, January 1884, 123.

35. William T. Alexander, *History of the Colored Race in America* (1887; repr., New York: Negro Universities Press, 1968), 144.

36. Ronald G. Walters, "The Erotic South: Civilization and Sexuality in American Abolitionism," in *Abolitionism and Issues of Race and Gender*, vol. 4 of *Abolitionism and American Reform*, ed. John R. McKivigan (New York: Garland, 1999), 368.

37. The anonymous Union veteran also uses the term in conjunction with an inability to work: "I could do, and did, nothing but stand and gaze vacantly; too nerveless and shattered to attempt any mental labor." Anonymous, *Opium-Eating*, 65.

38. Jacques Derrida, "The Rhetoric of Drugs," in *High Culture: Reflections on Addiction and Modernity*, ed. Anna Alexander and Mark S. Roberts (Albany: State University of New York Press, 2003), 32.

39. Keeley, *Morphine Eater*, 17. Capitalizing on the demand for a morphine cure, Keeley developed a very profitable "bichloride of gold" cure in 1879. For more on Keeley, see Timothy Hickman, *The Secret Leprosy of Modern Days: Narcotic Addiction and Cultural Crisis in the United States, 1870–1940* (Amherst: University of Massachusetts Press, 2007), 51–58; for an account of an experience with the Keeley Cure, see John Harrison Hughes, "The Autobiography of a Drug Fiend," *Medical*

Review of Reviews (1916): 27–43, 105–20, 173–90; for a comic song parodying the cure, see James Thornton, *The Famous Keeley Cure* (London: Frank Harding, n.d.).

40. In actuality, the influence of the war on the emergence of addiction in the period between 1865 and 1900 has been overstated. Even so, the large quantities of opium issued to troops on both sides, the efforts of veterans to conceal addictions for fear of losing their pensions, and the decline in opium imports around 1900, when many veterans passed away, cannot be ignored. See David Courtwright, *Dark Paradise: Opiate Addiction in America before 1940* (Cambridge, MA: Harvard University Press, 1982), 54–56; and Mark A. Quinones, "Drug Abuse during the Civil War (1861–1865)," *International Journal of the Addictions* 10:6 (1975): 1007–20.

41. David Musto, *The American Disease: Origins of Narcotic Control*, 3rd ed. (New York: Oxford University Press, 1999), 2.

42. This pessimism reflected the friction between the medical establishment, which remained optimistic, and the public it served, which, especially in the United States, felt itself victimized by the iatrogenic scandals. In the European context, Bynum points out that the enthusiasm for inebriate homes coincided with disenchantment with psychiatric asylums. W. F. Bynum, "Alcoholism and Degeneration in 19th Century European Medicine and Psychiatry," *British Journal of Addiction* 79 (1984): 63.

43. John W. Crowley and William L. White, *Drunkard's Refuge: The Lessons of the New York State Inebriate Asylum* (Amherst: University of Massachusetts Press, 2004), 10.

44. Quoted in Mary Roe, *E. P. Roe*, 466.

45. Donald A. Ringe, *American Gothic: Imagination and Reason in Nineteenth-Century Fiction* (Lexington: University Press of Kentucky, 1982), 177, 180.

46. Gretchen Murphy, "Enslaved Bodies: Figurative Slavery in the Temperance Fiction of Harriet Beecher Stowe and Walt Whitman," *Genre* 28 (Spring/Summer 1995): 110.

47. Robyn Wiegman, *American Anatomies: Theorizing Race and Gender* (Durham: Duke University Press, 1995), 40.

48. Elaine K. Ginsburg, introduction to *Passing and the Fictions of Identity*, ed. Elaine K. Ginsburg (Durham: Duke University Press, 1995), 3.

49. Jocelyn's putative Irishness provides a hint of a more traditionally racialized identity and also supports a racial logic of passing within whiteness. On Irish blackness and its relation to alcohol, see David Roediger, *The Wages of Whiteness: Race and the Making of the American Working Class*, rev. ed. (London: Verso, 1999), 133–63. On the figure of the Irish drunkard, see Richard Stivers, *A Hair of the Dog: Irish Drinking and American Stereotype* (University Park: Pennsylvania State University Press, 1976), 136–53.

50. See H. Wayne Morgan, *Drugs in America: A Social History, 1800–1980* (Syracuse: Syracuse University Press, 1981), 34.

51. Eve Kosofsky Sedgwick, *Epistemology of the Closet* (Berkeley: University of California Press, 1990), 172.

52. I discuss shame in the context of queerness at greater length in chapter 5. Recently, theorists have begun to consider shame as a productive locus of queer affect; see Eve Kosofsky Sedgwick, *Touching Feeling: Affect, Pedagogy, Performativity* (Dur-

ham: Duke University Press, 2003), 35–65; and Heather Love, *Feeling Backward: Loss and the Politics of Queer History* (Cambridge: Harvard University Press, 2007).

53. Courtwright, *Dark Paradise*, 110.

54. David Brion Davis, "Reflections on Abolitionism and Ideological Hegemony," in *The Antislavery Debate: Capitalism and Abolitionism as a Problem in Historical Interpretation*, ed. Thomas Bender (Berkeley: University of California Press, 1992), 175–76.

55. On the stereotype of the white southern woman's incapacity for labor, see Catherine Clinton, *Plantation Mistress: Woman's World in the Old South* (New York: Pantheon, 1982); and Anne Firor Scott, *The Southern Lady: From Pedestal to Politics, 1830–1930* (Charlottesville: University Press of Virginia, 1970).

56. William L. Van Deburg, *Slavery and Race in American Popular Culture* (Madison: University of Wisconsin Press, 1984), 37.

57. Roy Rosenzweig, *Eight Hours for What We Will: Workers and Leisure in an Industrial City, 1870–1920* (Cambridge: Cambridge University Press, 1983), 61.

58. See Catherine Gallagher, *The Industrial Reformation of English Fiction: Social Discourse and Narrative Form, 1832–1867* (Chicago: University of Chicago Press, 1985), ch. 1.

59. G. W. M. Reynolds ["Gracchus"], "Letters to the Working Classes. No. 1." *The Teetotaler*, 24 October 1840, 141.

60. For an analysis of George Eliot's *Felix Holt* (1866) that demonstrates the addictive body as unfit for citizenship, see Pamela K. Gilbert, *The Citizen's Body: Desire, Health, and the Social in Victorian England* (Columbus: Ohio State University Press, 2007), ch. 9.

61. Brian Harrison distinguishes between the "rough" and the "respectable" within the working class: roughness connoted any of the behaviors attending the leisure of casual laborers, including public drunkenness, carousing, profanity, and noisiness; respectability marked the working- or middle-class man who dressed neatly, drank rarely or moderately, and in other ways appeared to respect himself. Harrison, *Drink and the Victorians* (London: Faber and Faber, 1971), 24–25. See also Peter Bailey, *Leisure and Class in Victorian England: Rational Recreation and the Contest for Control, 1815–1885* (London: Methuen, 1978), 48; Joseph Livesey, "To the Young Men Who Are Not Teetotalers," *The Staunch Teetotaler*, no. 4, April 1867, 49–51; and Henry Mayhew, *London Labour and the London Poor*, vol. 1, Electronic Text Center, University of Virginia Library, available at http://etext.virginia.edu/etcbin/toccernew2?id=MayLond.sgm&images=images/modeng&data=/texts/english/modeng/parsed&tag=public&part=all, accessed 8 July 2007.

62. Radicals William Lovett and John Collins attacked the widespread practice whereby Tory campaigns would buy votes with drinks. William Lovett and John Collins, *Chartism: A New Organization of the People* (1840; repr., Leicester: Leicester University Press, 1969), 59.

63. See Amanda Claybaugh, *The Novel of Purpose: Literature and Social Reform in the Anglo-American World* (Ithaca: Cornell University Press, 2007), ch. 3.

64. To be sure, Dickens represented opium smoking in *The Mystery of Edwin Drood* (1871), but this unfinished novel remains best understood in the context of briefer opium den sketches, since it does not develop a full psychological depiction

of opium addiction. See Barry Milligan, *Pleasures and Pains: Opium and the Orient in Nineteenth-Century British Culture* (Charlottesville: University Press of Virginia, 1995), chs. 5 and 6.

65. Charlotte Brontë, *Jane Eyre* (1847) ed. Stevie Davies (London: Penguin, 2006), 492.

66. E. P. Thompson, *The Making of the English Working Class* (1963; repr., New York: Vintage, 1966), 411. Jane Lilienfeld develops a reading of the novel in the context of addiction, using the *Diagnostic and Statistical Manual of Mental Disorders*, 4th ed. (DSM-IV) to diagnose Henchard retrospectively. Lilienfeld, " 'I Could Drink a Quarter-Barrel to the Pitching': The Mayor of Casterbridge Viewed as an Alcoholic," in *The Languages of Addiction*, ed. Jane Lilienfeld and Jeffrey Oxford (New York: St. Martin's Press, 1999), 225–44.

67. Thompson, *Making of the English Working Class*, 12.

68. Jane S. Collins, *Free At Last* (Pittsburgh: Murdoch, Kerr & Co., 1896), 155–56.

69. Paul Gilroy, *The Black Atlantic: Modernity and Double Consciousness* (Cambridge: Harvard University Press, 1993), 39.

70. *Free at Last* belongs in Lauren Berlant's archive of narratives of "infantile citizenship," in which political innocence or illiteracy represents "an ambivalent encounter between America as a theoretical ideality and American as a site of practical politics." See Lauren Berlant, *The Queen of America Goes to Washington City: Essays on Sex and Citizenship* (Durham: Duke University Press, 1997), 28.

71. See Denise Herd, " 'We Cannot Stagger to Freedom': A History of Blacks and Alcohol in American Politics," in *Yearbook of Substance Use and Abuse*, ed. Leon Brill and Charles Winick (New York: Human Sciences Press, 1985), 3:141–86.

4. Needling Desires

1. Terry Parssinen, *Secret Passions, Secret Remedies: Narcotic Drugs in British Society, 1820–1930* (Manchester: Manchester University Press, 1983), 102.

2. Virginia Berridge and Griffith Edwards, *Opium and the People: Opiate Use and Drug Control Policy in Nineteenth and Early Twentieth Century England*, rev. ed. (London: Free Association Books, 1999), 145.

3. *The Report from the Select Committee on Habitual Drunkards; Together with the Proceedings of the Committee, Minutes of Evidence, and Appendix*, Parliamentary Papers, vol. 9, House of Commons, 13 June 1872, 49.

4. W. A. F. Browne, "Opiophagism," *Journal of Psychological Medicine*, n.s., 1 (1875): 49.

5. Seymour Sharkey, "Morphinomania," *The Nineteenth Century*, September 1887, 339.

6. Earlier writings about opium had desultorily identified such key features as the body's tolerance to substances and withdrawal from them, yet there was no consensus that addiction was a disease until this period. See Parssinen, *Secret Passions*, 85–86.

7. Physicians, inevitably male, were also among the first morphine addicts; but their deceptions were represented differently. Two British novels about male ad-

dicts are Katherine Cecil Thurston, *The Masquerader* (1896; London: Harper and Brothers, 1904; later editions titled *John Chilcote, M.P.*), whose male protagonist takes morphia "tabloids," or pills; and Mary Lake, *The Drug Slave* (London: Cassell and Company, Ltd., 1913), whose addict is a conventional domestic villain. I discuss the doctor-addict at greater length in chapter 5.

8. Pryce's now exceedingly rare novel is in the Sadleir Collection at the University of California, Los Angeles. For more on Pryce, see John Sutherland, *The Stanford Companion to Victorian Fiction* (Stanford: Stanford University Press, 1989), 513.

9. Morphinomania discourse resembles the contemporaneous emergence of anorexia and hysteria but differs significantly in the widespread assumption that women's self-pleasuring constitutes a disease disqualifying them from political freedom. The foundational Victorian text that shifted the spectacle of "fasting girls" from religious miracle to pathology was William Hammond, *Fasting Girls: Their Physiology and Pathology* (New York: G.P. Putnam, 1879); on the history of anorexia, see Joan Jacobs Brumberg, *Fasting Girls: A History of Anorexia Nervosa*, 2nd ed. (Cambridge, MA: Harvard University Press, 2000); on hysteria, see Elaine Showalter, *The Female Malady: Women, Madness, and English Culture, 1830–1980* (New York: Pantheon Books, 1985).

10. Wilkie Collins, *Armadale* (1866), ed. John Sutherland (London: Penguin, 1995), 426–27.

11. Wilkie Collins, *The Moonstone* (1868), ed. John Sutherland (Oxford: Oxford University Press, 1999). Although Blake experiences withdrawal pains from quitting smoking cigars, nicotine—generally speaking—was not considered an addictive substance in the nineteenth century. For the first novel about "nicotomania," see Guy Thorne [Cyril Arthur Ranger Gull], *The Cigarette Smoker: Being the Terrible Case of Uther Kennedy* (London: Greening and Company, 1902). For an interpretation of *The Moonstone* that views addiction broadly, see Hema Chari, "Imperial Dependency: Addiction, and the Decadent Body," in *Perennial Decay: On the Aesthetics and Politics of Decadence*, ed. Liz Constable, Dennis Denisoff, and Matthew Potolsky (Philadelphia: University of Pennsylvania Press, 1999), 215–32.

12. For a different model relating literature to medicine in the early nineteenth century, see Peter Logan, *Nerves and Narratives: A Cultural History of Hysteria in Nineteenth-Century Prose* (Berkeley: University of California Press, 1997).

13. The following discussion of Hunter and Wood is indebted to a quite old but still useful essay, Norman Howard-Jones, "A Critical Study of the Origins and Early Development of Hypodermic Medication," *Journal of the History of Medicine* 2 (Spring 1947): 201–49; as well as Berridge and Edwards, *Opium and the People*, 139–41.

14. Quoted in Francis E. Anstie, "Preface," *The Practitioner* 1:1 (1868): i–ii.

15. Anstie, "Preface," i.

16. Wilkie Collins, letter to Mrs. Elizabeth Benzon, 26 February 1869. *The Letters of Wilkie Collins*, vol. 2: *1866–1889*, ed. William Baker and William M. Clarke (Basingstoke: Macmillan, 1999), 319.

17. Francis E. Anstie, "The Hypodermic Injection of Remedies," *The Practitioner* 1 (1868): 38.

18. T. Clifford Allbutt, "The Use of the Subcutaneous Injection of Morphia in Dyspepsia," *The Practitioner* 2 (1869): 341.

19. T. Clifford Allbutt, "On the Hypodermic Use of Morphia in Diseases of the Heart and Great Vessels," *The Practitioner* 3 (1869): 343.

20. Berridge and Edwards, *Opium and the People*, 141.

21. Whereas the hypodermic injection of opiates dominated the emergent medical discourse of addiction, opium-smoking, always seen as a custom or habit, did not. For extensive interpretations of opium-smoking, see Barry Milligan, *Pleasures and Pains: Opium and the Orient in Nineteenth-Century British Culture* (Charlottesville: University Press of Virgina, 1995).

22. T. Clifford Allbutt, "On the Abuse of Hypodermic Injections of Morphia," *The Practitioner* 5 (1870): 327.

23. Allbutt, "On the Abuse of Hypodermic Injections," 329.

24. Allbutt, "Use of the Subcutaneous Injection," 343.

25. Allbutt, "On the Abuse of Hypodermic Injections," 328.

26. On the medical administration of stimulants, see Brian Harrison, *Drink and the Victorians* (London: Faber and Faber, 1972), 306. The quantity of alco-hol prescribed by Victorian doctors for all manner of ailments was frequently quite staggering; as the tide began to turn in the 1870s, such cases fell under increasing scrutiny. One doctor was scandalized to report his predecessor's treatment of a pneumonia patient with "one ordinary bottle of brandy, one bottle of champagne, and one bottle of old port wine daily for nine months." See Hugh Norris, "Therapeutic Alcoholism," *The Lancet*, 2 February 1878, 186.

27. "Drawing Room Alcoholism," *The Saturday Review*, 21 January 1871, 75.

28. On medical carelessness and attempts to reform the administration of alcohol and morphine, especially to female patients, see "The Peril and Plague of Narcotics," *The Lancet*, 1 May 1886, 846; and "Domestic Hypodermic Injections," *The Lancet*, 9 February 1878, 215.

29. Francis E. Anstie, "On the Use and Abuse of Alcohol By Women," *The Practitioner* 6 (1871): 88.

30. "Doctors and Alcohol," in *The Doctor* 2 (1 January 1872): 21.

31. Lionel Smith Beale, "Alcohol Indiscriminately Prescribed," *The Medical Times and Gazette*, 9 December 1871, 721.

32. Lilian Lewis Shiman, *Crusade against Drink in Victorian England* (New York: St. Martin's Press, 1988), 35–36. George Eliot's *Middlemarch* included a subplot about the lethal administration of alcohol and opiates to the self-induced alcoholic Raffles.

33. Kathy Alexis Psomiades, *Beauty's Body: Femininity and Representation in British Aestheticism* (Stanford: Stanford University Press, 1997), 5.

34. Davenport-Hines, *Pursuit of Oblivion*, 114.

35. Maria Weed, *A Voice in the Wilderness* (Chicago: Laird and Lee, 1895); hereafter cited in the text as *VW*.

36. For novelistic representations of the sea voyage cure, see William Dean Howells, *The Lady of the Aroostook* (Boston: Houghton, Osgood, 1879) and Walter Besant, *The Demoniac* (1890; repr., Bristol: J. W. Arrowsmith, n.d.).

37. For an interesting discussion of the medical politics of women's masturba-

tion, sexual stimulation by husbands and doctors, and hysteria, as well as, not coincidentally, alcohol, coffee, and tea, see Rachel Maines, *The Technology of Orgasm: "Hysteria," the Vibrator, and Women's Sexual Satisfaction* (Baltimore: Johns Hopkins University Press, 1999).

38. On this point, see Ros Ballaster, "Addicted to Love? Woman and/as Mass Culture" in *Beyond the Pleasure Dome: Writing and Addiction From the Romantics*, ed. Sue Vice, Matthew Campbell, and Tim Armstrong (Sheffield: Sheffield Academic Press, 1994), 143–48.

39. H. Gibbons, "Letheomania," *Pacific Medical and Surgical Journal* 3 (April 1870): 487.

40. Edward Levinstein, *Morbid Craving for Morphia*, trans. Charles Harrer (1878; repr., New York: Arno Press, 1981), 6.

41. Levinstein, *Morbid Craving*, 112.

42. Levinstein, *Morbid Craving*, 45.

43. Démétrius Alexandre Zambaco, quoted in Sharkey, "Morphinomania," 337. Zambaco was fascinated and repulsed by women's penetrative self-pleasuring, as his case study, "Masturbation and Psychological Problems in Two Little Girls" demonstrates; see Jeffrey Moussaieff Masson, ed., *A Dark Science: Women, Sexuality, and Psychiatry in the Nineteenth Century* (New York: Farrar, Straus and Giroux, 1986), 61–89.

44. "The Fashionable Woman," *The Saturday Review*, 8 August 1868, 185.

45. Arnould de Liedekerke, *La belle époque de l'opium* (Paris: Le Sphinx, 1984), 99; my translation. For a discussion of French fiction about women morphine addicts, see Marcus Boon, *The Road of Excess: A History of Writers on Drugs* (Cambridge, MA: Harvard University Press, 2002), 46–53; for a more generalized and speculative configuration of women, fiction making, and addiction, see Avital Ronnell, *Crack Wars: Literature, Addiction, Mania* (Lincoln: University of Nebraska Press, 1992).

46. Arthur Machen, *The Anatomy of Tobacco* (1884; repr., New York: Knopf, 1926), 176–77.

47. Richard Pryce, *An Evil Spirit*, 2 vols. (London: T. Fisher Unwin, 1887), 2:73–74; hereafter cited in the text as *ES*.

48. "New Novels," *The Saturday Review*, 25 June 1887, 916.

49. D. A. Miller, *The Novel and the Police* (Berkeley: University of California Press, 1988), 146–47.

50. "New Novels," 916.

51. A. Innes Shand, "Contemporary Literature: Readers," *Blackwood's Edinburgh Magazine* 126 (August 1879): 237. For the earlier complaint, see "Sensation Novels," *Quarterly Review* 113 (1863): 481–514.

52. Oscar Wilde, *Collins Complete Works: Centenary Edition* (Glasgow: HarperCollins, 1999), 1074.

53. At a meeting of the Society for the Study of Inebriety in 1886, President Norman Kerr recommended F. Mabel Robinson's novel *Disenchantment: An Everyday Story* as a sympathetic and clinically accurate representation of inebriety. Norman Kerr, "Welcome to Mr. Axel Gustafson," *Proceedings of the Society for the Study*

of Inebriety 10 (October 1886): 3–6 The novel, about a habitually drunken Irish M.P. and his disappointed wife, exchanges temperance propaganda for domestic melodrama. See F[rances] Mabel Robinson, *Disenchantment: An Everyday Story* (London: Viztelly, 1886). For further commentary on clinical realism in novels, see Nestor Tirard, "Disease in Fiction," *The Nineteenth Century* 20 (July–December 1886), 579–91.

54. Francis E. Anstie, "On the Effects of the Prolonged Use of Morphia by Subcutaneous Injection," *The Practitioner* 6 (1871): 156.

55. Anstie, "On the Effects of the Prolonged Use," 150.

56. Allbutt, "On the Abuse of Hypodermic Injections," 329.

57. Francis E. Anstie, "Health," *The Cornhill Magazine* 3(March 1861): 332. For Anstie's further dissemination of modernizing Victorian ideas of health, nutrition, and stimulation, see also "Corpulence," *The Cornhill Magazine* 7, no. 40 (April 1863): 457–68; "Does Alcohol Act as Food?" *The Cornhill Magazine* 6, no. 33 (September 1862): 319–29; "Food: How to Take It," *The Cornhill Magazine* 4 (July–December 1861): 281–94; and "Food: What It Is," *The Cornhill Magazine* 3 (January–June 1861): 460–72.

58. Christina Rossetti, "Goblin Market" in *Christina Rossetti: The Complete Poems*, ed. R. W. Crump (London: Penguin, 2001), 5–20.

59. "Abuse of Hypodermic Injections," *The Medical Press and Circular*, 19 June 1878, 514.

60. "Abuse of Morphia Injections," *The Doctor*, 1 March 1874, 42.

61. H. H. Kane, *The Hypodermic Injection of Morphia: Its History, Advantages, and Dangers* (New York: Chas L. Bermingham & Co., 1880), 285.

62. "Domestic Hypodermic Injections," 215. See also "Morphinomania," *The Lancet*, 10 September 1887, 532–33; and J. St. T. Clarke, "The Sudden Discontinuance of Hypodermic Injections of Morphia after Protracted Use," *The Lancet*, 11 January 1879, 70.

63. Robert Hichens, *Felix: Three Years in a Life* (London: Methuen, 1902), 207; hereafter cited in the text as *F*.

64. "Rita" [Eliza Margaret Jane Humphreys], *Queer Lady Judas* (London: Hutchinson & Co., 1905), 173; hereafter cited in the text as *QLJ*.

65. "Abuse of Morphia," 42.

66. David Trotter, *Paranoid Modernism: Literary Experiment, Psychosis, and the Professionalization of English Society* (Oxford: Oxford University Press, 2001), 275.

67. Lawrence Rothfield, *Vital Signs: Medical Realism in Nineteenth-Century Fiction* (Princeton: Princeton University Press, 1992), 135.

68. Rothfield, *Vital Signs*, 139.

69. Clouston refers throughout to lying as a physiological symptom of various disorders, which include behaviors such as talking to oneself, associating with the lower classes, and worshipping eccentrically; these examples show that Clouston is medicalizing social deviance and non-conformity. See T. S. Clouston, "Diseased Cravings and Paralysed Control: Dipsomania; Morphinomania; Chloralism; Cocainism," *Edinburgh Medical Journal* 35, no. 6 (December 1889): 508–21, 689–705, 793–809, 985–90.

70. Judith R. Walkowitz, *City of Dreadful Delight: Narratives of Sexual Danger in Late-Victorian London* (Chicago: University of Chicago Press, 1992), 46.

71. "Drawing Room Alcoholism," 76.

72. "Drawing Room Alcoholism," 76.

73. A companion piece decried habitual drunkenness among overworked, inevitably male merchants; it obviously lacked an argument about suffrage. "Counting-House Alcoholism," *The Saturday Review*, 15 April 1871, 462–63.

74. Quoted in de Liedekerke, *La belle époque*, 97; my translation.

75. The habitual drunkenness of Annie Chapman, one of Jack the Ripper's victims, was often mentioned; one letter-writer to *The Daily Telegraph* cited her demise as a reason for total abstention from alcohol. See C. F. Aldridge, "The Slavery of Drink," *The Times*, 2 September 1891, 3.

76. See Alice Ilgenfritz Jones and Ella Merchant, *Unveiling a Parallel: A Romance* (1893), ed. Carol A. Kolmerten (Syracuse: Syracuse University Press, 1991).

77. See Michel Foucault, *The History of Sexuality*, vol. 1, trans. Robert Hurley (1976; New York: Vintage, 1990), part 5.

78. *Felix* expands on the plot of an earlier short story by Hichens, "The Collaborators," which was published in the *Pall Mall Magazine* in 1893 and collected in *The Folly of Eustace* in 1896. In it, the decadent young writer Andrew Trenchard falls in love with an older, married morphia habitué in an attempt to save her from her habit, but he becomes enthralled by the drug himself. See Robert S. Hichens, *The Folly of Eustace and Other Stories* (New York: D. Appleton and Co., 1896). For a discussion of "The Collaborators" in the context of popular literary representations of decadence, see Kristen MacLeod, *Fictions of British Decadence: High Art, Popular Writing, and the Fin-de-Siècle* (Basingstoke, U.K.: Palgrave MacMillan, 2006), 102–3.

79. Rita (1856–1938) was a successful writer of satirical novels aimed at female library subscribers, including *Souls* (1903), which secured her fame. See *The Oxford Companion to Edwardian Fiction*, ed. Sandra Kemp, Charlotte Mitchell, and David Trotter (Oxford: Oxford University Press, 1997), 343.

80. For an excellent discussion of the cultural discourse surrounding morphine and other drug use among women entertainers of the demimonde during this period, see Marek Kohn, *Dope Girls: The Birth of the British Drug Underground* (London: Granta, 1992).

81. Rita Felski, *The Gender of Modernity* (Cambridge, MA: Harvard University Press, 1995), 65.

82. Mary Cholmondeley, *The Lowest Rung* (Leipzig: Tauchnitz, 1908). Cholmondeley (1859–1925), was best known for the satirical New Woman novel *Red Pottage* (1899). See Kemp Mitchell, and Trotter, *Oxford Companion to Edwardian Fiction*, 64–65.

83. Cholmondeley, *Lowest Rung*, 82–86.

84. For a comprehensive recovery of women's writing about drug experiences, see Cynthia Palmer and Michael Horowitz, eds., *Sisters of the Extreme: Women Writing on the Drug Experience* (Rochester, VT: Park Street Press, 2000).

85. Michelle McClellan, " 'Lady Tipplers': Gendering the Modern Alcoholism

Paradigm, 1933–1960," in *Altering American Consciousness: The History of Alcohol and Drug Use in the United States, 1800–2000*, ed. Sarah W. Tracy and Caroline Jean Acker (Amherst: University of Massachusetts Press, 2004), 267–97.

5. "Afflictions à la Oscar Wilde"

1. Ed Cohen, *Talk on the Wilde Side: Toward a Genealogy of a Discourse on Male Sexualities* (New York: Routledge, 1993), 101.

2. John Harrison Hughes, "The Autobiography of a Drug Fiend," *Medical Review of Reviews* (1916): 35.

3. Hughes, "Autobiography of a Drug Fiend," 37.

4. Critical texts that observe the parallel construction of homosexual and addicted identities include Virginia Berridge and Griffith Edwards, *Opium and the People: Opiate Use and Drug Control Policy in Nineteenth and Early Twentieth Century England*, rev. ed. (London: Free Association Books, 1999), xxxi; Sadie Plant, *Writing on Drugs* (London: Picador, 1999), 162–67; Eve Sedgwick, "Epidemics of the Will," in *Tendencies* (Durham: Duke University Press, 1993), 130–31; Richard Davenport-Hines, *The Pursuit of Oblivion: A Global History of Narcotics* (New York: W. W. Norton, 2002), 222–23; Caroline Jean Acker, *Creating the American Junkie: Addiction Research in the Classic Era of Narcotic Control* (Baltimore: Johns Hopkins University Press, 2002), 185–86; and Jennifer Terry, *An American Obsession: Science, Medicine, and Homosexuality in Modern Society* (Chicago: University of Chicago Press, 1999), in passing.

5. See Jonathan Ned Katz, *The Invention of Heterosexuality* (New York: Penguin, 1995), esp. ch. 3. On the various addicted manias, see Norman Kerr, *The Lancet*, 9 July 1887, 70; idem, "Second Presidential Address," *Proceedings of the Society for the Study and Cure of Inebriety* 4 (April 1885): 1–5; Axel Gustafson, "Inebriety and Volition," *Proceedings of the Society for the Study and Cure of Inebriety* 1 (April 1884): 28–32; and J. Muir Howie, "The Treatment of Inebriety," *Proceedings of the Society for the Study and Cure of Inebriety* 5 (June 1885): 1–14.

6. Weeks and Cohen, for example, each discuss the Criminal Law Amendment Act in the context of the broader regulation of men's sexuality. Cohen, *Talk on the Wilde Side*; and Jeffrey Weeks, *Sex, Politics, and Society: The Regulation of Sexuality since 1800* (London: Longman, 1989). See also Cocks, *Nameless Offences*.

7. John D'Emilio and Estelle B. Freedman, *Intimate Matters: A History of Sexuality in America*, 2nd ed. (Chicago: University of Chicago Press, 1997), 123.

8. See George Blackwell, *The Inebriates Acts, 1879–1898, Together with the General Regulations for the Management and Discipline of Certified Inebriate Reformatories and Inebriate Retreats* (London: Butterworth & Co., 1899); and Roy M. MacLeod, "The Edge of Hope: Social Policy and Chronic Alcoholism, 1870–1900," *Journal of the History of Medicine and Allied Sciences* 22 (1967): 215–45.

9. Davenport-Hines, *Pursuit of Oblivion*, 222–23.

10. Karl Abraham, "The Psychological Relations Between Sexuality and Alcoholism" (1908), reprinted in *Selected Papers of Karl Abraham* (London: Hogarth Press, 1954), 83.

11. Wilhelm Stekel, *Peculiarities of Behaviour: Wandering Mania, Dipsomania, Cleptomania, Pyromania and Allied Impulsive Acts*, vol. 1, trans. James S. Van Teslaar (London: Williams Norgate, Ltd., 1925), 228, 202.

12. Plant, *Writing on Drugs*, 164–65.

13. Studies of gay urban subcultures tend to focus on London and New York. See George Chauncey, *Gay New York: Gender, Urban Culture, and the Making of the Gay World, 1890–1940* (New York: Basic Books, 1994); Matt Cook, *London and the Culture of Homosexuality, 1885–1914* (Cambridge: Cambridge University Press, 2003); and Seth Koven, *Slumming: Sexual and Social Politics in Victorian London* (Princeton: Princeton University Press, 2004). On the phenomenon of blackmail in bridging public and private cultures, see Cocks, *Nameless Offences*, ch. 4; on the sexualization of urban life in ways that intersect with queer meanings and experiences, see Judith Walkowitz, *City of Dreadful Delight: Narratives of Sexual Danger in Late-Victorian London* (Chicago: University of Chicago Press, 1992); and Lynda Nead, *Victorian Babylon: People, Streets, and Images* (New Haven: Yale University Press, 2000).

14. George R. Sims, *The Devil in London* (New York: Dodge Company, 1909), 144. From the early 1850s, "Bloomerites" referred to women who wore "rational dress," or knee-length trousers for physical exercise.

15. Robert Hichens, *Felix: Three Years in a Life* (London: Methuen, 1902), 289.

16. Oxford English Dictionary, Third Online Edition.

17. Thomas Hardy, *The Mayor of Casterbridge* (1886), ed. Keith Wilson (London: Penguin, 2003), 17.

18. Émile Zola, *L'Assommoir*, trans. Arthur Symons (1894; repr., London: T. Werner Laurie, 1928), 359.

19. See, for example, Heather Love, *Feeling Backward: Loss and the Politics of Queer History* (Cambridge, MA: Harvard University Press, 2007).

20. Judith Halbertam, *In a Queer Time and Place: Transgender Bodies, Subcultural Lives* (New York: New York University Press, 2005), 4.

21. Elizabeth Freeman, "Time Binds, or, Erotohistoriography," *Social Text* 23 (Fall–Winter 2005): 57.

22. Jennifer Terry, "Theorizing Deviant Historiography," *differences* 3:2 (1991), 70.

23. Eve Kosofsky Sedgwick, *Epistemology of the Closet* (Berkeley: University of California Press, 1990), 25.

24. See Sharon Marcus, *Between Women: Friendship, Desire, and Marriage in Victorian England* (Princeton: Princeton University Press, 2007); Holly Furneaux, "Charles Dickens' Families of Choice: Elective Affinities, Sibling Substitution, and Homoerotic Desire," *Nineteenth-Century Literature* 62:2 (September 2007): 153–92; James Eli Adams, *Dandies and Desert Saints: Styles of Victorian Manhood* (Ithaca: Cornell University Press, 1995); and H. G. Cocks, *Nameless Offences: Homosexual Desire in the Nineteenth Century* (London: I. B. Tauris, 2003).

25. *Alcoholics Anonymous: The Story of How Many Thousands of Men and Women Have Recovered from Alcoholism*, 4th ed. (New York: Alcoholics Anonymous World Services, 2001), 18.

26. Sigmund Freud, Letter to Wilhelm Fliess, 22 December 1897, *The Complete*

Letters of Sigmund Freud to Wilhelm Fliess, 1887–1904, ed. Jeffrey Moussaieff Masson (Cambridge: Belknap, 1985), 287.

27. Quoted in Russ Castronovo, *Necro Citizenship: Death, Eroticism, and the Public Sphere in the Nineteenth-Century United States* (Durham: Duke University Press, 2001), 67. Temperance and anti-masturbation had various figures in common, including Sylvester Graham. See Robert Mighall, " 'A Pestilence which Walketh in Darkness: Diagnosing the Victorian Vampire," in *Spectral Readings: Towards a Gothic Geography*, ed. Glennis Byron and David Punter (New York: St. Martin's Press, 1999), 108–24.

28. Laqueur develops the analogy between masturbation and addiction in part by noting the similar language and conceptualizations used in Samuel August David Tissot's *Onania* (1712), Thomas Trotter's *Essay on Drunkenness* (1804), and Freud's letter to Fleiss (1897), quoted below. Thomas Laqueur, *Solitary Sex: A Cultural History of Masturbation* (New York: Zone, 2003), 238–45. Sedgwick, interestingly, finds in Jane Austen's *Sense and Sensibility* (1811) the emergence of addiction coded as masturbation. See Sedgwick, "Jane Austen and the Masturbating Girl," *Critical Inquiry* 17:4 (Summer 1991): 818–37.

29. See Sedgwick, *Epistemology*, 9.

30. This dimension also links to the history of masturbation, particularly the anxieties about women's solitary reading central to anti-masturbation discourse. See Laqueur, *Solitary Sex*, 302–27. In the nineteenth century, women's reading of sensation fiction was repeatedly likened to "dram drinking," "diseased craving," and "overfeeding." I mention this as a non-gendered phenomenon in the introduction. See also "Sensation Novels," *Quarterly Review* 113 (1863): 483; Herbert Maxwell, "The Craving For Fiction," *The Nineteenth Century*, June 1893, 1046–61; and Alfred Austin, "The Vice of Reading," *Temple Bar Magazine* 42 (September 1874): 251–57. For secondary analysis, see Kelly J. Mays, "The Disease of Reading and Victorian Periodicals," in *Literature in the Marketplace: Nineteenth-Century British Publishing and Reading Practices*, ed. John O. Jordan and Robert L. Patten (Cambridge: Cambridge University Press, 1995), 165–93; and Pamela J. Gilbert, *Disease, Desire, and the Body in Victorian Women's Popular Novels* (Cambridge: Cambridge University Press, 1997). On the discourse of women's excessive, addictive consumption of romance novels, see Janice Radway, *Reading the Romance: Women, Patriarchy, and Popular Literature* (Chapel Hill: University of North Carolina Press, 1984) and Ros Ballaster, "Addicted to Love? Woman and/as Mass Culture," in *Beyond the Pleasure Dome: Writing and Addiction from the Romantics*, ed. Sue Vice, Matthew Campbell, and Tim Armstrong (Sheffield: Sheffield Academic Press, 1994), 143–48.

31. C. R. Francis, "On the Value and Use of Opium," *Medical Times and Gazette*, 28 January 1882, 88.

32. See Sax Rohmer, *Dope* (New York: A. L. Burt, 1919) and Thomas Burke, *Limehouse Nights* (1916; New York: McBride & Co., 1919), 159.

33. Helen Keane's devastating critique of the discourse of sex addiction points out numerous internal incoherences, biases, and elisions. See Keane, *What's Wrong with Addiction?* (New York: New York University Press, 2002), 147–48.

34. See Janice Irvine, "Regulated Passions: The Invention of Inhibited Sexual Desire and Sexual Addiction" in *Deviant Bodies: Critical Perspectives on Difference in*

Science and Popular Culture, eds. Jennifer Terry and Jacqueline Urla (Bloomington: Indiana University Press, 1995), 314–37.

35. See Stephen Heath, "Psychopathia Sexualis: Stevenson's Strange Case," *Critical Quarterly* 28:1–2 (Spring 1986): 93–108; Wayne Koestenbaum, *Double Talk: The Erotics of Male Literary Collaboration* (New York: Routledge, 1989), 145–51; Showalter, *Sexual Anarchy*, ch. 6; and George Haggerty, *Queer Gothic* (Champaign: University of Illinois Press, 2006), ch. 6.

36. Showalter, *Sexual Anarchy*, 112.

37. R. L. Stevenson, *The Strange Case of Dr. Jekyll and Mr. Hyde* (1886), ed. Jenni Calder (London: Penguin, 1979), 84; hereafter cited in the text as *JH*.

38. Some critics have noticed the story's amenability to addiction or alcoholism but have used models of addiction from other time periods to explicate it. Daniel Wright, for example, uses Patrick Carnes's theory of sex addiction from the early 1990s to diagnose Jekyll; and Thomas Reed inconsistently historicizes the story's representation of addiction, at times referring to E. M. Jellinek's 1950s model of the "gamma alcoholic" to describe Jekyll. By contrast, Lisa Butler does a better job of late nineteenth-century contextualization, broadening the discussion to include evolutionary biology and the social purity movement. See Daniel L. Wright, "The Prisonhouse of My Disposition: A Study of the Psychology of Addiction in *Dr. Jekyll and Mr. Hyde*," *Studies in the Novel* 26:3 (Fall 1994): 254–67; Thomas L. Reed Jr., *The Transforming Draught: Jekyll and Hyde, Robert Louis Stevenson, and the Victorian Alcohol Debate* (Jefferson, NC: McFarland, 2007), 58; Lisa Butler, " 'That Damned Old Business of the War in the Members': The Discourse of (In)temperance in Robert Louis Stevenson's *The Strange Case of Dr. Jekyll and Mr. Hyde*," *Romanticism on the Net* 44 (November 2006), available at www.erudit.org/revue/ron/2006/v/n44/014000ar.html, accessed 9 July 2007; and Plant, *Writing on Drugs*, 66–71.

39. Adams, *Dandies and Desert Saints*, 13.

40. Sedgwick, *Epistemology of the Closet*, 172.

41. See Eve Kosofsky Sedgwick, *Touching Feeling: Affect, Pedagogy, Performativity* (Durham: Duke University Press, 2003), ch. 4.

42. "Rita" [Eliza Margaret Jane Humphreys], *Queer Lady Judas* (London: Hutchinson & Co., 1905), 158.

43. Guy Thorne [Cyril Arthur Ranger Gull], *The Cigarette Smoker: Being the Terrible Case of Uther Kennedy* (London: Greening and Company, 1902), 5.

44. M. Kellen Williams, " 'Down with the Door, Poole': Designating Deviance in Stevenson's *Strange Case of Dr Jekyll and Mr Hyde*," *English Literature in Transition, 1880–1920* 39:4 (1996): 426.

45. This argument incorporates the idea of the "lesbian phallus" through a historicized rather than a psychoanalytic framework, although Rita's story certainly offers a rich field for the latter. For the lesbian phallus as a reworking of Freudian and Lacanian phalli, see Judith Butler, *Bodies That Matter: On the Discursive Limits of "Sex"* (New York: Routledge, 1993), ch. 2.

46. Michel Foucault, *The History of Sexuality*, vol. 1, trans. Robert Hurley (1976; New York: Vintage, 1990), 105.

47. Samuel Guy, *The Doctor's Notebook; or, Tales of My Patients* (London: Ward and Lock, 1864), iv.

48. Coke Richardson, "Horace Saltoun," *The Cornhill Magazine*, 1861, 229–49, 299–317, 433–47.

49. John Saunders, *The Tempter Behind* (1919; repr., Boston: D. Lothrop Company, n.d.).

50. Kate Jordan, "The Grey Land of Drugs: Arranged from the Confessions of a Sojourner," *Pearson's Magazine* 42 (October 1916): 302–3; hereafter cited in the text as "GLD."

51. Sedgwick, *Epistemology of the Closet*, 172.

52. Thorne, *Cigarette Smoker*, 62–67.

53. Francis E. Anstie, *Stimulants and Narcotics: Their Mutual Relations* (Philadelphia: Lindsay and Blakiston, 1865), 332.

54. Daniel Frederick MacMartin, *Thirty Years in Hell* (Topeka, KS: Capper, 1921), 33.

55. MacMartin, *Thirty Years in Hell*, 146, 162. For a discussion of queerness and alcoholism in Jack London's *John Barleycorn* (1913), see Mark Seltzer, *Serial Killers: Death and Life in America's Wound Culture* (London: Routledge, 1998), 94–96.

56. Anne Brontë, *The Tenant of Wildfell Hall* (1848; repr., New York: Penguin, 1996), 33; hereafter cited in the text as *TWH*.

57. Adams, *Dandies and Desert Saints*, 7.

58. As is well known, Anne Brontë insisted on fictionalizing her brother Patrick Branwell Brontë's struggles with alcohol and opium, incurring sister Charlotte's disapproval. On Branwell's addictions and descent into delirium tremens, see Juliet Barker, *The Brontës* (New York: St. Martin's Press, 1994), 516, 564. See also Jill Matus, "Strong Family Likeness: *Jane Eyre* and the *Tenant of Wildfell Hall*," in *The Cambridge Companion to the Brontës*, ed. Heather Glen (Cambridge: Cambridge University Press, 2002), 102.

59. Ellen Wood, *Danesbury House* (1860; repr., London: Ward, Lock & Co., n.d.), 300.

60. Andrew Barr identifies this as a British custom, followed in the United States in the eighteenth and early nineteenth centuries; whereas British men drank port after dinner, their U.S. counterparts drank madeira. Barr also notes that the British, unlike Americans, did not characteristically drink before dinner until after World War I. See Andrew Barr, *Drink: A Social History of America* (New York: Carroll and Graf, 1999), 131, 51.

61. W. M. Thackeray, *Vanity Fair* (1848), ed. John Cary (London: Penguin, 2001), 38.

62. Walter Besant, *The Demoniac* (1890; repr., Bristol: J. W. Arrowsmith, n.d.).

63. Coulson Kernahan, *A Literary Gent: A Study in Vanity and Dipsomania* (London: Ward, Lock, and Company, 1895).

64. F. Mabel Robinson, *Disenchantment: An Everyday Story* (London: Viztelly, 1886).

65. Mary Lake, *The Drug Slave* (London: Cassell and Company, 1913), 2.

66. Leda Burke [David Garnett], *Dope-Darling: A Story of Cocaine* (1919; repr., London: T. Werner Laurie, n.d.), 117. For a discussion of habitual drunkenness interfering with marriage in temperance narratives, see Elaine Frantz Parsons, *Manhood Lost: Fallen Drunkards and Redeeming Women in the Nineteenth-Century United*

States (Baltimore: Johns Hopkins University Press, 2003); for an analysis of the dynamics of alcoholism and marriage in the postwar United States, see Lori Rotskoff, *Love on the Rocks: Men, Women, and Alcohol in Post–World War II America* (Chapel Hill: University of North Carolina Press, 2002). On Garnett and *Dope-Darling* in the cultural and literary context of the Great War, see Marek Kohn, *Dope Girls: The Birth of the British Drug Underground* (London: Granta, 1992), 23–24.

67. Lee Edelman, *No Future: Queer Theory and the Death Drive* (Durham: Duke University Press, 2004), 9.

68. Jeff Nunokawa, "All the Sad Young Men: AIDS and the Work of Mourning," in *Inside/Out: Lesbian Theories, Gay Theories*, ed. Diana Fuss (New York: Routledge, 1991), 312.

69. Radclyffe Hall, *The Well of Loneliness* (1928; repr., New York: Anchor, 1990), 387.

70. Ibid., 388.

71. Ibid., 375, 397.

72. Saunders, *Tempter Behind*, 302.

73. Burke, *Dope-Darling*, 48.

74. *The Doctor*, 1 January 1872, 21–22.

75. Oscar Wilde, *The Picture of Dorian Gray* (1891), ed. Robert Mighall (London: Penguin, 2003), 123; hereafter cited in the text as *DG*.

76. Curtis Marez, *Drug Wars: The Political Economy of Narcotics* (Minneapolis: University Press of Minnesota, 2004), 89.

77. Readers may be wondering about another potential example of addiction in *The Picture of Dorian Gray*, Lord Harry's quip that "a cigarette is the perfect type of a perfect pleasure. It is exquisite, and it leaves one unsatisfied" (77). While the point that smoking leaves one in a state of continued desire speaks to an aspect of addiction, the statement also clearly leaves space for aesthetic pleasure, a compensation that is beside the point of addiction. As Richard Klein puts it, "Smoking is such a worthless, unproductive activity that it lends itself to becoming the whole purpose of life—if life is to be justified aesthetically, and not according to some utilitarian principle." Richard Klein, *Cigarettes are Sublime* (Durham: Duke University Press, 1993), 43. See also Jeff Nunokawa, *Tame Passions of Wilde: Styles of Manageable Desire* (Princeton: Princeton University Press, 2003), 116.

78. Louis Menand, *Discovering Modernism: T. S. Eliot and His Context* (New York: Oxford University Press, 1987), 84.

79. See Adams, *Dandies and Desert Saints*, 221.

80. Wilde appropriated a Nordauvian discourse of degeneration, morbidity, and hereditary determination, remotivating it in the services of art, in order to subvert its taxonomic power. See William Greenslade, *Degeneration, Culture and the Novel, 1880–1940* (Cambridge: Cambridge University Press, 1994), 123.

81. Linda Dowling, *Hellenism and Homosexuality in Victorian Oxford* (Ithaca: Cornell University Press, 1995), 134.

82. John Addington Symonds, *Memoirs*, ed. Phyllis Grosskurth (Chicago: University of Chicago Press, 1986), 278.

83. Walter Pater, *Studies in the History of the Renaissance* (1873; New York: Oxford University Press, 1986), 152.

84. Ellen F. Pinsent, *No Place for Repentance* (London: T. Fisher Unwin, 1896), 65.

85. Symonds, *Memoirs*, 182.

86. John Addington Symonds to Robert Louis Stevenson, 3 March 1886, *The Letters of John Addington Symonds*, vol. 3, ed. Herbert M. Schueller and Robert L. Peters (Detroit: Wayne State University Press, 1969), 120–21.

87. Roger Smith, *Trial by Medicine: Insanity and Responsibility in Victorian Trials* (Edinburgh: Edinburgh University Press, 1981), 48.

88. Anstie, *Stimulants and Narcotics*, 174.

89. On the atavist and the professional, see Stephen D. Arata,"The Sedulous Ape: Atavism, Professionalism, and Stevenson's Jekyll and Hyde" *Criticism* 37:2 (Spring 1995), 233–59; see also Judith Halberstam, *Skin Shows: Gothic Horror and the Technology of Monsters* (Durham: Duke University Press, 1995), 69.

90. Haggerty, *Queer Gothic*, 126.

91. Myron Schultz, "The 'Strange Case' of Robert Louis Stevenson," *Journal of the American Medical Association* 216:1 (5 April 1971): 93.

92. This plot point is identical to one in another famous text of addiction and queerness, Christina Rossetti's "Goblin Market" (1862). There, the goblin fruit that first makes Laura pine and draw near death, on second eating revives her. This makes sense only in the context of habituation, as an analogue of withdrawal. Christina Rossetti, "Goblin Market" in *Christina Rossetti: The Complete Poems*, ed. R. W. Crump (London: Penguin, 2001), 5–20.

93. Allbutt, "On the Abuse of Hypodermic Injections of Morphia," *The Practitioner* 5 (1870): 329.

94. Norman Kerr, "Recent Civil and Criminal Trials Complicated with Inebriety: The Need for a Reformed Jurisprudence and Amended Legislation," *Proceedings of the Society for the Study of Inebriety* 28 (April 1891): 6.

95. Norman Kerr, "President's Inaugural Address," *Proceedings of the Society for the Study and Cure of Inebriety* 1 (April 1884): 3; and idem, *Inebriety: Its Etiology, Pathology, Treatment, and Jurisprudence* (Philadelphia: Blakiston, 1888), 208.

96. Hughes, "Autobiography of a Drug Fiend," 118.

97. MacMartin, *Thirty Years in Hell*, 134.

98. Norman Kerr, "Recent Civil and Criminal Trials," 14.

99. Butler, *Bodies That Matter*, 225.

100. Peter K. Garrett, "Cries and Voices: Reading *Jekyll and Hyde*," in *Dr. Jekyll and Mr. Hyde after One Hundred Years*, ed. William Veeder and Gordon Hirsch (Chicago: University of Chicago Press, 1986), 63–64.

101. Richardson, "Horace Saltoun," 446.

102. The phenomenon of the doctor-addict is well documented in histories of addiction. See Berridge and Edwards, *Opium and the People*, 145; Davenport-Hines, *Oblivion*, 116; H. Wayne Morgan, *Drugs in America: A Social History, 1800–1980* (Syracuse: Syracuse University Press, 1981), 41–43; and David Courtwright, *Dark Paradise: A History of Opiate Addiction in America* (Cambridge, MA: Harvard University Press, 1982), 41.

103. Berridge and Edwards, *Opium and the People*, 145.

104. "Fatal Result of Morphia Taking," *The Lancet*, 31 March 1888, 638.

105. Henry Obersteiner, "Chronic Morphinism," *Brain* 2 (January 1880): 451.

106. "Fatal Result of Morphia Taking," 638.

107. Morris F. Baldwin, "The Panorama of a Life, and Experiencing Associating and Battling with Opium and Alcoholic Stimulants" (1878), reprinted in *American Perceptions of Drug Addiction: Five Studies, 1872–1912*, ed. Gerald N. Grob (New York: Arno, 1981), 79.

108. Showalter, *Sexual Anarchy*, 113.

109. Simon Petch, "The Sovereign Self: Identity and Responsibility in Victorian England," in *Law and Literature: Current Legal Issues 1999*, vol. 2, ed. Michael Freeman and Andrew D. E. Lewis (Oxford: Oxford University Press, 1999), 405.

110. Haggerty, *Queer Gothic*, 127–28.

111. Cocks, *Nameless Offences*, 7.

112. Robert Louis Stevenson, "A Note on Realism" (1883), in *The Art of Writing and Other Essays*, available at www.gutenberg.org/dirs/etext96/artow10h.htm, accessed 26 July 2007.

6. Un-Death and Bare Life

1. The temperance novel *The Vampyre* builds extensively on this analogy. See *The Vampyre*, By the Wife of a Medical Man (London: A. W. Bennett, 1858). Abraham Lincoln, "Address to the Washington Temperance Society of Springfield, Illinois," 22 February 1842; reprinted in *Abraham Lincoln: Speeches and Writings 1832–1858*, ed. Don E. Fehrenbacher, vol. 1 (New York: Library of America, 1989), 88.

2. Christopher Craft, " 'Kiss Me with Those Red Lips': Gender and Inversion in Bram Stoker's *Dracula*," *Representations* 8 (Fall 1984): 117.

3. Robert T. Eldridge, "The Other Vampire Novel of 1897: *The Blood of the Vampire* by Florence Marryat," *New York Review of Science Fiction* 10:6 (February 1998): 10–12.

4. Nina Auerbach, *Our Vampires, Ourselves* (Chicago: University of Chicago Press, 1997), 83.

5. For interpretations that read Transylvania as a coded version of Ireland and Dracula and the other vampires as Irish, see Michael Valdez Moses, "The Irish Vampire: Dracula, Parnell, and the Troubled Dreams of Nationhood," *Journal X* 2:1 (Autumn 1997): 66–111; Canon Schmidt, "Mother Dracula: Orientalism, Degeneration, and Anglo-Irish Subjectivity at the Fin de Siècle," *Bucknell Review* 38:1 (1994): 25–43; and Stephen D. Arata, "The Occidental Tourist: *Dracula* and the Anxiety of Reverse Colonization," *Victorian Studies* 33 (Summer 1990): 633–34.

6. Arata, "Occidental Tourist," 623.

7. Hesketh Bell, *Obeah: Witchcraft in the West Indies* (London: Sampson, Low, Marston & Co., 1893), 190.

8. Marlene Tromp, *Altered States: Sex, Nation, Drugs, and Self-Transformation in Victorian Spiritualism*, Studies in the Long Nineteenth Century Series (Albany: State University of New York Press, 2006), 141. For a novel about a colonial soldier

attempting to break his addiction to opium smoking, see Maud Diver, *The Great Amulet* (1908; repr., London: William Blackwood and Sons, 1911).

9. Walter Besant, *The Demoniac* (1890; Bristol, J. W. Arrowsmith, n.d.). On the iconography of the temperance ship earlier in the century, see Lilian Lewis Shiman, *Crusade against Drink in Victorian England* (New York: St. Martin's Press, 1988), ch. 2; and Virginia Berridge, "The Society for the Study of Addiction, 1884–1988," Special Issue, *British Journal of Addiction* 85 (1990): 1000. For a temperance novel that demonstrated the fallacy of the drink-free colony by sending its protagonist on a mistaken trip to Australia for a cure, see T. P. Wilson, *Frank Oldfield; or, Lost and Found* (1855; London: T. Nelson and Sons and the United Kingdom Band of Hope, n.d.).

10. In *Darkest England*, William Booth outlined a similar plan to export the lumpenproletariat to distant colonies. See Laura Sagolla Croley, "The Rhetoric of Reform in Stoker's *Dracula*: Depravity, Decline, and the Fin-de-Siécle 'Residuum,' " *Criticism* 37, no. 1 (Winter 1995): 85–108.

11. Orlando Patterson, *Slavery and Social Death: A Comparative Study* (Cambridge, MA: Harvard University Press, 1982), 336.

12. For interpretations that make use of degeneration and degenerative paradigms, see Arata, "Occidental Tourist"; Croley, "Rhetoric of Reform"; Ernest Fontana, "Lombroso's Criminal Man and Stoker's Dracula," *Victorian Newsletter* 66 (Fall 1984): 25–27; Judith Halberstam, "Technologies of Monstrosity: Bram Stoker's Dracula," *Victorian Studies* 36:3 (Spring 1993): 333–52; Robert Mighall, " 'A Pestilence which Walketh in Darkness': Diagnosing the Victorian Vampire," in *Spectral Readings: Towards a Gothic Geography*, ed. Glennis Byron and David Punter (New York: St. Martin's Press, 1999), 108–24; and Rosemary Jann, "Saved by Science? The Mixed Messages of Stoker's *Dracula*," *Texas Studies in Literature and Language* 31:2 (Summer 1989): 273–87.

13. Max Horkheimer and Theodor W. Adorno, *Dialectic of Enlightenment: Philosophical Fragments*, (1947) trans. Edmund Jephcott, ed. Gunzelin Schmid Noerr (Stanford: Stanford University Press, 2002), 26.

14. Heman Humphrey, *Parallel between Intemperance and the Slave Trade* (Amherst, MA: J. S & C. Adams, 1828), 16; Charles Dickens, *Sketches by Boz* (1839; repr., New York: Penguin, 1995), 566; William Rosser Cobbe, *Doctor Judas: A Portrayal of the Opium Habit* (Chicago: S.C. Griggs and Company, 1895), 131.

15. Franz Hartmann, "Vampires," *Borderland* 3 (1896): 355.

16. Edith Blinn, *The Ashes of My Heart* (New York: Mark-Well, 1916), 270.

17. Winifred C. Black, *Dope: The Story of the Living Dead* (New York: Star Company, 1928).

18. Upton Sinclair, *The Wet Parade* (New York: Farrar and Rinehart, 1931), 245.

19. Mark Seltzer, *Serial Killers: Death and Life in America's Wound Culture* (New York: Routledge, 1998), 90.

20. Other eugenic fiction of the period about inebriates and addicts includes Ellen F. Pinsent, *No Place for Repentance* (London: T. Fisher Unwin, 1896); and Guy Thorne [Cyril Arthur Ranger Gull], *The Cigarette Smoker: Being the Terrible Case of*

Uther Kennedy (London: Greening and Co., 1902), and *The Vintage of Vice* (London: Greening and Co., 1913; originally published in 1912 under the title *The Drunkard*).

21. Susan Sontag, *Illness as Metaphor* (New York: Farrar, Straus and Giroux, 1978), 3.

22. Michel Foucault, *The History of Sexuality*, vol. 1, trans. Robert Hurley (1976; New York: Vintage, 1990), 142.

23. On the notion of "molecular" approaches to "emergent life," see Nikolas Rose, *The Politics of Life Itself: Biomedicine, Power, and Subjectivity in the Twenty-First Century* (Princeton: Princeton University Press, 2007), 57–58, 80–82; on death as a metaphor for U.S. political subjectivity, see Russ Castronovo, *Necro Citizenship: Death, Eroticism, and the Public Sphere in the Nineteenth-Century United States* (Durham: Duke University Press, 2001); on "necropolitics" as the subjugation of modern populations within "deathworlds," see Achille Mbembe, "Necropolitics," *Public Culture* 15:1 (2003): 39–40. Many contemporary theorists route their arguments through Hannah Arendt's *Origins of Totalitarianism* (1966), in order to link the racism of nineteenth-century imperialism to that of twentieth-century instances of genocide, most obviously the Holocaust.

24. Berridge, "Society for the Study of Addiction," 999.

25. T. S. Clouston, "Diseased Cravings and Paralysed Control: Dipsomania; Morphinomania; Chloralism; Cocainism," *Edinburgh Medical Journal* 35:6 (December 1889): 509.

26. Norman Kerr, "Inebriate Criminal Responsibility," *Proceedings of the Society for the Study and Cure of Inebriety* 16 (April 1888): 12.

27. On Morel, see W. F. Bynum, "Alcoholism and Degeneration in 19th Century European Medicine and Psychiatry," *British Journal of Addiction* 79 (1984): 61–62; and William Greenslade, *Degeneration, Culture and the Novel, 1880–1940* (Cambridge: Cambridge University Press, 1994),16–17.

28. W. F. Bynum, "Alcoholism and Degeneration," 62.

29. For Maudsley, see esp. *Responsibility in Mental Disease* (London: Henry S. King, 1874), 283; for his connection to Morel, see Daniel Pick, *Faces of Degeneration* (Cambridge: Cambridge University Press, 1993), 203–16; on Maudsley and degeneration more generally, see Elaine Showalter, *The Female Malady: Women, Madness, and English Culture, 1830–1980* (New York: Pantheon, 1985); on Skae, see *The Report from the Select Committee on Habitual Drunkards; Together with the Proceedings of the Committee, Minutes of Evidence, and Appendix*, Parliamentary Papers, vol. 9, House of Commons, 13 June 1872, 31–33; for Sankey's early work, see "Will and Volition," *Journal of Psychological Medicine*, n.s., 1 (April 1875): 56–66; on Clouston, see "Diseased Cravings."

30. Norman Kerr, *Inebriety: Its Etiology, Pathology, Treatment, and Jurisprudence* (Philadelphia: Blakiston, 1888), 33–34.

31. Marie Corelli, *Wormwood: A Drama of Paris* (1890), ed. Kristin MacLeod (Ontario: Broadview, 2004), 255. For a brief discussion of Wormwood in the context of Corelli's literary career, see Annette R. Federico, *Idol of Suburbia: Marie Corelli and Late-Victorian Literary Culture* (Charlottesville: University Press of Virginia, 2000), 71–75.

32. Other narratives of addiction that enlist degeneration include Coke Richardson, "Horace Saltoun," *The Cornhill Magazine*, 1861, 229–49, 299–317, 433–47; Émile Zola, *L'Assommoir*, trans. Arthur Symons (1894; repr., London: T. Werner Laurie, 1928), 356; and, of course, Stevenson's *The Strange Case of Dr. Jekyll and Mr. Hyde* (see chapter 5).

33. Patrick Brantlinger, *Dark Vanishings: Discourse on the Extinction of Primitive Races, 1800–1930* (Ithaca: Cornell University Press, 2003), 191.

34. August Weismann, *The Germ-Plasm: A Theory of Heredity*, trans. W. Newton Parker and Harriet Rönnfeldt (London: Walter Scott, 1893).

35. Francis Galton, "On the Causes Which Operate to Create Scientific Men," *The Fortnightly Review* 13 (1873): 351, available at http://galton.org, accessed 30 May 2007.

36. Galton, "On the Causes," 351. Galton also advanced this specific argument in "A Theory of Heredity," *Contemporary Review* 27 (1875): 80–95, available at http://galton.org, accessed 30 May 2007.

37. Berridge, "Society for the Study of Addiction," 1011.

38. In addition to the following quoted SSI papers, see, for example, Thomas E. Morton, "The Problem of Heredity in Reference to Inebriety," *Proceedings of the Society for the Study of Inebriety* 42 (8 November 1894): 2–14; Mansfield A. Holmes, "The Hereditary Effects of Habitual versus Periodical Inebriety," *Proceedings of the Society for the Study of Inebriety* 45 (July 1895): 1–5; and Rev. A. K. Cherrill, "Can Acquired Characteristics Be Inherited?" *Proceedings of the Society for the Study of Inebriety* 52 (May 1897): 14–16.

39. See the "discussion" section following Norman Kerr, "A Reply to Archdall Reid," *Proceedings of the Society for the Study of Inebriety* 58 (November 1898): 15.

40. William Booth, *In Darkest England, and the Way Out* (1890), available at www.gutenberg.org/dirs/etext96/detwo10.txt, accessed 8 July 2007. On Victorian reformers, see Judith Walkowitz, *City of Dreadful Delight: Narratives of Sexual Danger in Late-Victorian London* (Chicago: University of Chicago Press, 1992), 31.

41. Mearns also documented children "taken by the hand or carried in the arms to the gin-palace, and not seldom may you see mothers urging and compelling their tender infants to drink the fiery liquid." Andrew Mearns, *The Bitter Cry of Outcast London* (1883), ed. Anthony Wohl (Leicester, U.K.: Leicester University Press, 1970), 67, 62.

42. David Gutzke, " 'The Cry of the Children': The Edwardian Medical Campaign against Maternal Drinking," *British Journal of Addiction* 79 (1984): 71–84. On the centrality of maternity to eugenics in the United States, see Wendy Kline, *Building a Better Race: Gender, Sexuality, and Eugenics from the Turn of the Century to the Baby Boom* (Berkeley: University of California Press, 2001).

43. See Angelique Richardson, *Love and Eugenics in the Late Nineteenth Century: Rational Reproduction and the New Woman* (Oxford: Oxford University Press, 2003).

44. Virginia Berridge and Griffith Edwards associate the fear of racial degeneracy with the opium den fascination. See Berridge and Edwards, *Opium and the People: Opiate Use and Drug Control Policy in Nineteenth and Early Twentieth Century England*, rev. ed. (London: Free Association Books, 1999), 199; Davenport-Hines

discusses it quite broadly, at times making degeneration synonymous with decadence. Richard Davenport-Hines, *The Pursuit of Oblivion: A Global History of Narcotics* (New York: W. W. Norton, 2002), ch. 6.

45. "Gin Lane" and "Beer Street" were engravings by William Hogarth depicting the drunken degradation of the poor during the height of gin's popularity in the 1750s. Dickens also wrote about gin, and emphasized its relationship to poverty, in an 1835 sketch, "Gin-shops": "Gin-drinking is a great vice in England, but poverty is a greater; and until you can cure it, or persuade a half-famished wretch not to seek relief in the temporary oblivion of his own misery, with the pittance which, divided among his family, would just furnish a morsel of bread for each, gin-shops will increase in number and splendour." Dickens, *Sketches by Boz*, 220. The most interesting and comprehensive cultural history of gin in Britain remains John Watney, *Mother's Ruin: A History of Gin* (London: Owen, 1976).

46. See Henry Mayhew, *London Labour and the London Poor* (1851; repr., London: Penguin, 1985); James Greenwood, *The Seven Curses of London* (1869; repr., Oxford: Basil Blackwell, 1981), sec. 5; Booth, *In Darkest England*, esp. ch. 5, sec. 4; G. R. Sims, *The Devil in London* (New York: Dodge Company, 1909); and Lady Eastlake, "Drink: the Vice and the Disease," *Quarterly Review* 139: 278 (July–October 1875): 396–434.

47. The Habitual Drunkards' Act of 1879, renamed the Inebriates Act in 1888, and renewed again in 1898, are together referred to as the Inebriates Acts. See George Blackwell, *The Inebriates Acts, 1879–1898* (London: Butterworth & Co., 1899); and Roy M. MacLeod, "The Edge of Hope: Social Policy and Chronic Alcoholism, 1870–1900," *Journal of the History of Medicine and Allied Sciences* 22 (1967): 215–45.

48. On Tottie Fay and Jane Cakebread, see Thomas Holmes, "Habitual Inebriates," *Contemporary Review* 75 (May 1899): 740–46.

49. D. A. Miller, *The Novel and the Police* (Berkeley: University of California Press, 1988).

50. Alexander Peddie, "The Habitual Drunkards Act, 1879: Inefficient, and Not Adequate to Accomplish the Important Objects Desirable," *Proceedings of the Society for the Study and Cure of Inebriety* 7 (January 1886): 10.

51. Arnold White, *Efficiency and Empire* (1901), ed. G. R. Searle (Brighton: Harvester Press, 1973), 104.

52. Caleb Saleeby, *Parenthood and Race-Culture: An Outline of Eugenics* (London: Cassell and Company, Ltd. 1909), 245. Saleeby is quoting Kipling's "Letters of Travel," which appeared in newspapers in 1908. See G. R. Searle, *Eugenics and Politics in Britain, 1900–1914* (Leyden: Noordhoff, 1976), 19; for another eugenic analysis of drug addiction from the same period, see Harrington Sainsbury, *Drugs and the Drug Habit* (London: Methuen, 1909).

53. Daniel Pick, " 'Terrors of the Night': *Dracula* and 'Degeneration' in the Late Nineteenth Century," *Critical Quarterly* 30:4 (1988): 71–87. See also Kathleen Spencer, "Purity and Danger: Dracula, the Urban Gothic, and the Late Victorian Degeneracy Crisis." *ELH* 59 (1992): 213; Franco Moretti, "The Dialectic of Fear," *New Left Review* (November–December 1982): 67–85; Ernest Fontana, "Lombro-

so's Criminal Man"; Croley, "Rhetoric of Reform"; and Jann, "Saved by Science?" 283.

54. Croley, "Rhetoric of Reform," 85.

55. Bram Stoker, *Dracula* (1897), ed. Glennis Byron (Ontario: Broadview, 1998), 383; hereafter cited in the text as *D*.

56. On the rise of the concept of recidivism within criminality, see Leon Radzinowicz and Roger Hood, *The Emergence of Penal Policy in Victorian and Edwardian England*, vol. 5 (Oxford: Clarendon, 1990), 120–21.

57. Greenslade, *Degeneration, Culture and the Novel*, 120.

58. Berridge and Edwards, *Opium and the People*, 70.

59. H. Wayne Morgan, *Drugs in America: A Social History, 1800–1980* (Syracuse: Syracuse University Press, 1981), 14–15.

60. Gordon Stables, "The Confessions of an English Chloral-Eater," *The Pall Mall Magazine* 6:26 (April 1875): 181.

61. Stables, "Confessions," 181.

62. Henry Lyman, *Artificial Anaesthesia and Anaesthetics* (New York: W. Wood and Co., 1881), 276.

63. Leonard Wolf names Hughes' Blood Pills, Glennis Byron opts for Clarke's World-Famed Blood Mixture. Leonard Wolf, ed., *The Annotated Dracula by Bram Stoker* (New York: Clarkson N. Potter, 1975), 209; and Stoker, *Dracula*, ed. Byron, 273.

64. W. A. F. Browne, "Morbid Appetites of the Insane," *Journal of Psychological Medicine*, n.s., 1 (April 1875): 242.

65. John L. Greenway, "Seward's Folly: *Dracula* as a Critique of 'Normal Science' " *Stanford Literature Review* 3 (1986), 217.

66. *The Spectator*, 31 July 1897, 150–51; and Stoker, *Dracula*, 483.

67. Charles Egerton Jennings, *Transfusion: Its History, Indications, and Modes of Application* (New York: C. H. Goodwin, 1884), 1.

68. On metrology as the creation of a center of calculation, where distant objects are measured, recorded, and rendered knowable through imperial technoscience, see Bruno Latour, *Science in Action: How to Follow Scientists and Engineers Through Society* (Cambridge, MA.: Harvard University Press, 1987), 215–57.

69. Friedrich A. Kittler, *Discourse Networks, 1800/1900*, trans. Michael Metteer with Chris Cullens (Stanford: Stanford University Press, 1990), 354.

70. Kittler, *Discourse Networks*, 355.

71. Oxford English Dictionary, Third Online Edition.

72. E. P. Thompson, "Time, Work-Discipline, and Industrial Capitalism," *Past and Present* 38 (December 1967): 69.

73. *The Athenaeum*, 26 June 1897, 835; and Stoker, *Dracula*, 481.

74. Craft, "Kiss Me," 125.

75. Halberstam, "Technologies of Monstrosity," 345.

76. Garrett Stewart, "Count Me In: *Dracula*, Hypnotic Participation, and the Late-Victorian Gothic of Reading," *LIT: Literature Interpretation Theory* 5 (1994): 10.

77. Thomas Carlyle, *Rescued Essays of Thomas Carlyle*, ed. Percy Newberry (London: The Leadenhall Press, 1909), 28.

78. Marryat's work is beginning to garner interest after critical neglect. See Sian Macfie, " 'They Suck Us Dry': A Study of Late Nineteenth-Century Projections of Vampiric Women," in *Subjectivity and Literature from the Romantics to the Present Day*, ed. Philip Shaw and Peter Stockwell (London: Pinter, 1991), 58–67; Alexandra Warwick, "Vampires and the Empire: Fears and Fictions of the 1890s," in *Cultural Politics at the Fin-de-siècle*, ed. Sally Ledger and Scott McCracken (Cambridge: Cambridge University Press, 1995), 202–20; Eldridge, "Other Vampire Novel"; K. Octavia Davis, "Geographies of the (M)other: Narratives of Geography and Eugenics in Turn-of-the-Century British Culture," Ph.D. diss., University of California, San Diego, 1998; Lillian E. Craton, "Odd Bodied: Physical Difference and Ideology in Nineteenth-Century Fiction," Ph.D. diss., Emory University, 2006; and Brenda Mann Hammack, "Scientizing Hybridity: The Case of Florence Marryat's Vampire," *SEL: Studies in English Literature 1500–1900* 48:4 (Autumn 2008; forthcoming). Because it relates the novel to eugenics, Davis's dissertation chapter is closest to my own analysis, though it departs from my concerns to focus on the colonial geography of Jamaica and its relationship to Harriet's mother.

79. On the degenerative aspect of this subplot, see Andrew Maunder, introduction to *Love's Conflict* in *Varieties of Women's Sensation Fiction 1855–1890*, vol. 2: *Domestic Sensationalism* (London: Pickering & Chatto, 2004), xxiv.

80. Florence Marryat, *The Blood of the Vampire* (London: Hutchinson & Co., 1897), 28; hereafter cited in the text as *BV*.

81. Francis Galton, *Inquiries into Human Faculty and its Development* (1883; repr., London: J. M. Dent, 1907), 17–18.

82. James Eli Adams, *Dandies and Desert Saints: Styles of Victorian Masculinity* (Ithaca: Cornell University Press, 1995), 218.

83. Hartmann, "Vampires," 355. On *Borderland*, see Alex Owen, *The Place of Enchantment: British Occultism and the Culture of the Modern* (Chicago: Chicago University Press, 2004), 28.

84. See Marryat, *There Is No Death* (New York: National Book Company, 1891), 174–76. For a novel that more directly associates addiction with Spiritualism, see Timothy Wilfred Coakley, *Keef: A Life-Story in Nine Phases* (Boston: Charles E. Brown & Co., 1897).

85. Marryat's father, the naval novelist Frederick Marryat, was himself stationed in the West Indies and may have served as a model for Phillips. See Davis, "Geographies," 190n9.

86. Charlotte Brontë, *Jane Eyre* (1847), ed. Stevie Davies (London: Penguin, 2006), 337.

87. Brontë, *Jane Eyre*, 327.

88. Davis, "Geographies," 206–7.

89. On the New Woman writers of the fin-de-siècle who reinvented the standard Victorian novelistic plot of love and marriage along eugenic lines, see Richardson, *Love and Eugenics*.

90. Katie Trumpener, *Bardic Nationalism: The Romantic Novel and the British Empire* (Princeton: Princeton University Press, 1997), 169.

91. Kenealy, "Beautiful Vampire," 45.

92. Patterson, *Slavery and Social Death*, 338.

93. Giorgio Agamben, *Homo Sacer: Sovereign Power and Bare Life*, trans. Daniel Heller-Roazen (1995; Stanford: Stanford University Press, 1998), 8.

94. Craft, "Kiss Me," 117.

95. Zygmunt Bauman, *Mortality, Immortality, and Other Life Strategies* (Stanford: Stanford University Press, 1992), 156.

96. Bauman, *Mortality, Immortality, and Other Life Strategies*, 24. See Jean Baudrillard, *Symbolic Exchange and Death*, trans. Iain Hamilton Grant (London: Sage, 1993), 126.

97. For Bauman's more specific analysis of racism in relation to the Holocaust and scientific modernity, see his *Modernity and the Holocaust* (1989; rev. ed., Ithaca: Cornell University Press, 2000).

98. Bauman, *Mortality, Immortality, and Other Life Strategies*, 110.

99. Ibid.

100. Agamben, *Homo Sacer*, 126.

101. Arata, "Occidental Tourist," 640. On Stoker's interest in eugenics, as expressed in his 1905 novel *The Man*, see Pick, "Terrors of the Night," 84.

102. Daly similarly characterizes the text's instrumentality as "an allegory that helped to construct the future that its own narrative could then be seen to reflect." Nicholas Daly, *Modernism, Romance, and the Fin de siècle: Popular Fiction and British Culture, 1880–1914* (Cambridge: Cambridge University Press, 1999), 35. Reversing historical causality, Sue-Ellen Case makes a similar claim for *Dracula*'s relevance to twentieth-century genocidal discourse when she claims that the rhetoric of Hitler's *Mein Kampf* (1926) "invented the vampiric position: the one who waits, strikes, and soils the living, pure blood." Sue-Ellen Case, "Tracking the Vampire," *differences* 3:2 (1991): 6.

Afterword: The Biopolitics of Drug Control

1. See Marek Kohn, *Dope Girls: The Birth of the British Drug Underground* (London: Granta, 1992).

2. See Edith Blinn, *The Ashes of My Heart* (New York: Mark-Well, 1916); Thomas Burke, *Limehouse Nights* (1916; New York: McBride & Co., 1919); idem, *More Limehouse Nights* (New York, George H. Doran, 1921); *Broken Blossoms*, dir. D. W. Griffith, 1919; Sax Rohmer, *Dope* (New York, A. L. Burt, 1919); and Lady Dorothy Mills, *The Laughter of Fools* (London: Duckworth, 1920).

3. Blinn, *Ashes*, 283.

4. On the association of African Americans with cocaine around 1900, see David Musto, *The American Disease: Origins of Narcotic Control*, 3rd ed. (New York: Oxford University Press, 1999), 6n15; see also Richard Davenport-Hines, *The Pursuit of Oblivion: A Global History of Narcotics* (New York: W. W. Norton, 2002), 200; and Timothy Hickman, *The Secret Leprosy of Modern Days: Narcotic Addiction and Cultural Crisis in the United States, 1870–1940* (Amherst: University of Massachusetts Press, 2007), 80.

5. Quoetd in Musto, *American Disease*, 305n15.

6. H. Wayne Morgan, *Drugs in America: A Social History, 1800–1980* (Syracuse: Syracuse University Press, 1981), 93.

7. Quoted in James Morone, *Hellfire Nation: The Politics of Sin in American History* (New Haven: Yale University Press, 2003), 304.

8. Virginia Berridge, "The Origins of the English Drug 'Scene,' 1890–1930," *Medical History* 32 (1988): 53–56.

9. Caroline Jean Acker, *Creating the American Junkie: Addiction Research in the Classic Era of Narcotic Control* (Baltimore: Johns Hopkins University Press, 2002), 2.

10. Bram Stoker, *Dracula* (1897), ed. Glennis Byron (Ontario: Broadview, 1998), 49.

11. Ibid., 233.

12. Lee Edelman, *No Future: Queer Theory and the Death Drive* (Durham: Duke University Press, 2004), 3. On frenzied anxiety about children's contamination by drugs in the early decades of this century, see Davenport-Hines, *Pursuit of Oblivion*, 195–97; for vivid descriptions of cocaine causing boys to become supernaturally monstrous beings, see Fred V. Williams, *The Hop-Heads: Personal Experiences among the Users of 'Dope' in the San Francisco Underworld* (San Francisco: Walter N. Brunt, 1920), 70.

13. My account of U.S. involvement in managing the opium supply to the Philippines draws on Davenport-Hines, *Pursuit of Oblivion*, 202–8; and Musto, *American Disease*, 25–28.

14. "Anti-Opium Prayer Union," *The Friend of China* 6:1 (January 1883): 8. On the anti-opium movement, see Virginia Berridge and Griffith Edwards, *Opium and the People: Opiate Use and Drug Control Policy in Nineteenth and Early Twentieth Century England*, rev. ed. (London: Free Association Books, 1999), ch. 14; and Geoffrey Harding, *Opiate Addiction, Morality and Medicine: From Moral Illness to Pathological Disease* (New York: St. Martin's Press, 1988), 23–47. See also Marek Kohn, *Narcomania: On Heroin* (London: Faber and Faber, 1987), 28.

15. See Zhen Yangwen, *The Social Life of Opium in China* (Cambridge: Cambridge University Press, 2005), 88, 98; Frank Dikötter, Lars Laamann, and Zhou Xun, *Narcotic Culture: A History of Drugs in China* (London: Hurst and Company, 2004), 54–55, 62; and Berridge and Edwards, *Opium and the People*, 193.

16. "The White Man's Burden" was originally titled "An Address to America." "The White Man's Burden," in *Rudyard Kipling: Selected Poems*, ed. Peter Keating (London: Penguin, 2000), 82–84, 207.

17. Quoted in Davenport-Hines, *Pursuit of Oblivion*, 209.

18. Musto, *American Disease*, 26, 27.

19. Ibid., 51.

20. Davenport-Hines, *Pursuit of Oblivion*, 211.

21. Ibid., 132–34.

22. This discussion is drawn from Virginia Berridge, "War Conditions and Narcotics Control: The Passing of Defence of the Realm Act Regulation 40B," *Journal of Social Policy* 7:3 (July 1978): 285–304; and Davenport-Hines, *Pursuit of Oblivion*.

23. Quoted in Virginia Berridge, "Drugs and Social Policy: The Establishment of Drug Control in Britain, 1900–30," *British Journal of Addiction* 79 (1984): 21.

24. "Report on the Royal Commission on Opium," *The Lancet*, 27 April 1895, 1078. My account of the Royal Commission is also drawn from Davenport-Hines,

who mounts an argument for the validity of the Anglo-Indian physicians' testimony; as well as Berridge and Edwards's account, which suggests that the commission's inquiry was both comprehensive and stage-managed, and that the anti-opium movement was both "out-maneuvered" and its propaganda "exaggerated." Davenport-Hines, *Pursuit of Oblivion*, 181–94; and Berridge and Edwards, *Opium and the People*, 185–88. See also Terry Parssinen, *Secret Passions, Secret Remedies: Narcotic Drugs in British Society, 1820–1930* (Manchester: Manchester University Press, 1983), 144–63. For medical arguments comparing Indian opium-smoking favorably to British gin-drinking, see James Fitzjames Stephen, "The Opium 'Resolution,' " *The Nineteenth Century* 29, no. 172 (June 1891): 851–56; and "Adjourned Discussion on Opium, led by Sir William Moore," *Proceedings of the Society for the Study of Inebriety* 40 (May 1894): 1–11.

25. On the Rolleston Report, see Kohn, *Narcomania*, 85–86; Berridge and Edwards, *Opium and the People*, 271–79; and Berridge, "Drugs and Social Policy," 25–28.

26. Historians who take this stance include Davenport-Hines, Kohn, Marez, and Musto; Berridge leans in that direction as well. For a succinct explanation of this position vis-à-vis criminalization in the United States and medicalization in Britain, see Parssinen, *Secret Remedies*, 201–20. Jonnes stands out as an exception to this rule; see Jill Jonnes, *Hep-Cats, Narcs, and Pipe Dreams: A History of America's Romance with Illegal Drugs* (New York: Scribner, 1996). For an iteration of this position on the recent U.S. history of addiction, particularly its relationship to underworlds, see Eric Schlosser, *Reefer Madness: Sex, Drugs, and Cheap Labor in the American Black Market* (Boston: Houghton Mifflin, 2003), ch. 1.

27. Berridge, "Drugs and Social Policy," 28.

28. Quoted in Berridge, "War Conditions," 300.

29. I deliberately avoid what David Forbes refers to as "a simple, all-encompassing conspiracy theory that claims that the capitalist class or white ruling elite encourages drugs in poor neighborhoods as a deliberate way to sedate the residents or even as a form of genocide." David Forbes, *False Fixes: The Cultural Politics of Drugs, Alcohol, and Addictive Relations* (Albany: State University of New York Press, 1994), 33. Rather, I claim that the purposeful devaluation of addicted life, combined with institutional neglect of the poor and people of color, amounts to bureaucratic and systematic killing akin to genocide normally conducted by military means.

30. William Whipper, "Speech by William Whipper, Delivered before the Colored Temperance Society of Philadelphia," Philadelphia, 8 January 1834, reprinted in *Black Abolitionist Papers*, vol. 3: *The United States, 1830–1846*, ed. Peter C. Ripley (Chapel Hill: University of North Carolina Press, 1991), 120.

31. Helen Keane, *What's Wrong with Addiction?* (New York: New York University Press, 2002), 164.

INDEX

Susan Zieger was born in Staten Island, New York, and attended Stuyvesant High School. She received her BA degree from Dartmouth College; MSc from the London Centre for the History of Science, Medicine, and Technology; and PhD in English literature from the University of California, Berkeley. In 2006–7 she was awarded a fellowship from the American Council of Learned Societies for the completion of this book. Her work has appeared in *Victorian Studies*, *American Literature*, *PMLA*, and *Genre*, among other journals. She is presently assistant professor of English at the University of California, Riverside, and lives in Pasadena with her partner, Nathan Boyd, and their two cats, Oscar and Jones.